THE SUICIDAL EMBRACE

THE SUICIDAL EMBRACE

Hitler, the Allies, and the Origins of the Second World War

David R. Beisel

Circumstantial Productions

First edition

Circumstantial Productions Publishing
Six South Broadway
Nyack, New York 10960

Book design by Charlton Burch

ISBN: 1891592149
Library of Congress Control Number: 2003108425

Thanks to Atlantic Syndication, 17/18 Haywards Place, Clerkenwell, London EC1R 0E, England, for permission to use David Low's cartoons and to the Centre for the Study of Cartoons and Caricature, University of Kent, Canterbury, for providing copies of Low's cartoons for use in this book.

CONTENTS

ALL CENTRAL EUROPE
SEEMS TO ME TO BE ENACTING
A FANTASY WHICH I CANNOT INTERPRET.

—*Rebecca West*, 1940

For Sheila and Jordan

PREFACE

The title of this study is taken from a statement made by Neville Chamberlain in 1931, six years before he became Great Britain's Prime Minister. His sense then that the powers were already locked in a drama of mutually willed catastrophe was eclipsed after 1939 by the standard explanation of World War II as solely "Hitler's War."

Historical research since 1939 has quite consistently confirmed the standard conclusions, proving beyond all doubt Hitler's central role in the conflict. Still, the findings of such historians as A.J.P. Taylor, and scores of others since 1960, must also be taken seriously. These scholars have found that the Allies wittingly and unwittingly gave Hitler opportunities. Although in the 1960s that observation produced a fierce controversy among historians and the public, for most people today World War II remains Hitler's War. Yet reputable scholars continue to recognize that the standard, popular view needs to be modified. James Stokesbury's widely read *Short History of World War II* (1980) notes without stirring any controversy that: "one can still assert that Hitler did cause the war, but no longer so dogmatically or so unqualifiedly. He has become *a* cause rather than *the* cause." Other prominent historians agree. D. C. Watt writes in *How War Came* (1989) that the causes of the war should be extended to include "a multitude of accomplices." Overy and Wheatcroft state in their *Road to War* (1990): "the documents of the time make clear beyond ambiguity there was a much larger cast of actors." In *Hitler, 1936-1945: Nemesis* (2000), Ian Kershaw concludes that the road to war was in part prompted by the "sins of omission and commission by others—including the British government and its French allies—which had assisted in enabling Hitler."[1]

The standard way of explaining this involvement of others is to enumerate all the reasons why the Allies adopted the policy of appeasing Hitler. But standard explanations usually ignore a number of contradictions. As the documents make clear, many people, including the architect of appeasement Neville Chamberlain himself, knew what Hitler was going to do and predicted it. As the following pages show, they saw him as a bully and said so, concluding that the only way to stop him was by force. Yet when it came to stopping him, everyone, including Chamberlain, ignored this conclusion.

The usual explanations for appeasement—guilt over the Versailles Treaty, fears for the fate of civilization, and, in the Great Depression, not enough money for rearmament—all seem right, at least in part. Taken as a whole, however, they are unable to explain the several contradictions in the historical record. To help clarify some of these issues, the current study looks to answers from a neglected area of historical causation, feelings and fantasies, and finds that some of those feelings and fantasies—largely unacknowledged at the time and since—may have played some role in preventing the Allies from acting to stop Hitler.

It is necessary to be completely clear about this. I believe that the critics of appeasement, then and now, were and are correct. While there can be no guarantees for any of the "Ifs" of history, Churchill, at least, claimed at the time and later that a Grand Alliance would have made World War II an "unnecessary war," a view shared today by many historians. They believe that Germany's aggression could have been stopped early on—in 1935 or 1936, even in 1938. Because it wasn't, Hitler's evil was tragically unleashed upon the world.

This study presents in outline some of the barely acknowledged emotional reasons for this complex, elusive process. Essentially a long interpretive essay, it is based on archival materials published independently, and on archival materials quoted by historians. A careful examination of the secondary literature has also revealed that many historians have at various times caught hold of different bits and pieces of this hidden story, and because some of the interpretations which appear in the following pages are non-traditional, those traditional historians are quoted at length.

Careful attention to these documents, to the words, images, and behaviors of the leaders, diplomats, and media at the time, has shown what looks like a number of powerful fantasies. At the beginning of his 1938 novel *Nausea*, Jean-Paul Sartre wrote: "I do not think the historian's craft is much given to psychological analysis."[2] His observation is still largely true today and is one reason why Rebecca West could not make much sense of the fantasy she found unfolding in Central Europe in the late 1930s. The current study finds that the metaphor of "the family of nations" was one of the elusive fantasies that played a central role in this emerging tragedy. At war's outbreak, a number of Europeans thought so too, sensing and saying that the conflict was somehow a civil war within the European "family."

While the notion of the family of nations is not new, this study explores the possibility that, even as metaphor, it may have been of greater significance for interwar diplomacy than is usually acknowledged. Since the following book is written for a general audience as well as for scholars, it includes brief discussions of several theories, methods, and findings which have moved us, over the last thirty years, towards a better understanding of the role of fantasies and emotions in history. This includes the influence of stress on emotions and on conscious and unconscious decision-making, the possible influence of trauma, traumatic reliving, and childhood history, the ideas of projection, projective "containers," and group delegation. Efforts have been made to integrate these ideas and findings in order to better understand how real the notion of the family of nations was to people in the 1930s and how significant it was in the coming of the Second World War.

More than ever it is essential to clarify some of these issues, especially the idea of a civil war within the European "family," since the rise of neo-conservatism and neo-Nazism world-wide has led some, from Holocaust deniers to openly racist white supremacists, to a false questioning of the historical record for political reasons. Part of this political effort has been the distortion and misuse of the notion of a European civil war. In West Germany, the late-1980s public debate known as the *Historikerstreit* turned on a neo-conservative effort to modify history. The controversy began with the German historian Ernst Nolte, who called his book on World War II "The European Civil War."[3] The following study explicitly rejects any connection with Nolte's neo-conservative apologia while recognizing that the notion of a bloody "fratricide" is indeed part of the historical record.

And that record is clear. Hitler did all the things we always thought he did. But the evidence is also clear that others, German and non-German alike, helped and encouraged him—some intentionally, some unintentionally, perhaps some even unconsciously.

I FEELINGS AND FOREIGN AFFAIRS

THE WHOLE OF EUROPE {IS} IN A STATE OF NERVOUS ANXIETY...
THEREBY PRECIPITATING THE ADVENT OF HITLER...
WE ARE ALL LOCKED IN A SUICIDAL EMBRACE
WHICH WILL PROBABLY DROWN THE LOT OF US![1]
—*Neville Chamberlain*, 1931

Diplomats in the interwar years were as emotional as anyone else. Jan Masaryk, Czech Ambassador to Britain, took to his bed with grief during the Czech crisis. Vojtech Mastny, Czech ambassador to Berlin, broke into tears when he heard how his country had been cut apart by the four-power agreement at Munich.[2] The historical record is filled with things like British foreign ministers wanting to tell the Russians to go "jump in the Baltic sea," British prime ministers smiling at French premiers while mumbling through closed train windows that the French "could go to hell," and ambassadors reading replies with red faces and trembling hands, or dashing off to their embassies after first bursting out in sobbing laughs. Sometimes there was no love lost even among allies, a high British official saying of the French statesman Poincaré that "he was not our idea of a Frog," or the French Premier Daladier calling Prime Minister Chamberlain "a desiccated stick" and the King of England "a moron," or another high British official saying of Daladier that he "evidently drinks and it has rotted him," which, accurate descriptions or not, surely contain emotions usually thought to be under the control of rational diplomats. Mussolini's foreign minister, Count Galeazzo Ciano, demanded that Italian diplomats adopt the *tono fascisto*, a tough, expressionless exterior, a tip off that they too, no less than others, were prone to emotional outbursts.[3]

Yet with few exceptions, emotions seem to play hardly any role in the diplomatic histories written by historians.

Perhaps this omission is with good reason, for over the centuries historians have worked hard to keep feelings out of their accounts. In the name of objectivity they have evolved a rational model of how the world works. It has served them well, revealing much about human affairs by showing how historical actors can sometimes control impulses and passions while operating with Machiavellian calculation and reasoned self-interest. Nowhere is this more evident than in the study of international affairs.

Diplomats are usually perceived as moving with computer-like logic from coolly reasoned policies. They do make mistakes, and errors occur, since no one can foresee every eventuality. Yet in general, leaders are portrayed as coldly rational. A recent statement by historian Gaines Post Jr. on the appeasement policy is typical: "Reason guided Chamberlain's conception of decision making," he says. "Logic prescribed his scheme for deterrence." Even Hitler's outbursts have been explained away. A leading historian of Nazi foreign policy claims that Hitler "was quite capable of getting himself into a rage (which became genuine) whenever it suited his purposes."[4]

Hitler certainly did this. But there is ample evidence that there were other times—perhaps many times—when his feelings got the better of him, when he was engulfed by emotions having little or nothing to do with conscious, calculated political manipulation. This too must be taken into account, for otherwise there is always the danger that history, at least diplomatic history, will be peopled with two-dimensional figures.

Of course, historians do not avoid emotions entirely. Excluding them from their accounts would be irrational. Love of country, fear of strangers, and various hatreds have always been part of their standard repertoire. German anger at the Treaty of Versailles, Western fears of the Soviet Union, and British terror of air attack have all been invoked to help explain the origins of the Second World War. Once in a while, scholars sense that the interwar years seem more emotional. Historian Gordon Craig and political psychologist Alexander George have said: "There is no doubt that the emergence of public sentiment...in the 1930s... worked...to jeopardize national interest." German propaganda in the period was more often able to influence governments everywhere by stirring up popular opinion, because "people felt more than they thought and had strong hostilities and fears that could be easily mobilized." Among diplomatic historians, this is a rare enough admission, and reminds us that in the 1930s, at least, popular emotions were a factor historians need to consider. In fairness, there have been a few systematic efforts at assessing the psychology of conscious and unconscious emotions in diplomacy and statecraft in general, but when it comes to the Second World War, on those rare occasions when feelings are recognized at all they are either not analyzed, or are not analyzed deeply, or are deemed wholly appropriate and self-evident.[5] The possibility of other, deeper feelings is rarely considered.

This has been the case for a long time. In his 1958 study of the origins of the Second World War, French diplomatic historian Pierre Renouvin felt that standard historical approaches were too limiting: "Diplomatic history alone cannot provide the answers," he wrote: "One must also bear in mind the underlying economic and psychological forces." Yet ten years later, Gordon Wright's history of the Second World War began by asserting that the assessment of motives is "a realm in which even the resources of depth psychology do not suffice to guide the historian's hand."[6] Things are somewhat different today. Resources now exist which can help move historians, including diplomatic historians, toward a better understanding of the complexities of human motivation.[7]

Much of the new research over the last thirty years has focused on the neglected area of unconscious process, especially on repressed feelings embedded in fantasies.

Common sense and personal experience as well as psychological studies tell us that human beings are fantasy makers. That fantasies should sometimes be acted out is not at all surprising since it is a familiar notion that people often act according to their beliefs, even if those beliefs are not fully rational or fully conscious.

And it is also understood, by psychology, common sense, and everyday experience, that people tend to be more emotional when they undergo stress.[8] When stress levels rise, people over the long run characteristically experience extreme emotional reactions. It is well known that stressors have physiological consequences; they have significant psychological consequences as well. It is not unusual for someone at some point in the course of a lifetime to feel that they are on an emotional roller coaster, or that they are temporarily going "crazy." All this means is that the person's normal intra-psychic defenses are not working as well as they had been before and are failing to keep repressed feelings fully in check. Under stress people sometimes act not just more emotionally but sometimes more irrationally. Diplomats, and their bosses, often reported experiencing such stresses in the interwar years.

When Hitler violated the Treaty of Versailles in March 1936 by sending troops into the Rhineland, the question was: Would there be war? "The forty-eight hours after the March into the Rhineland," Hitler later said, "were the most nerve-racking of my life." His nervousness was intensified by anxiety-filled reports from a crew of worried German diplomats in London. Later, as war approached over Poland, accounts agreed on "the strain which Hitler showed and which found expression in his haggard appearance and temperamental outbursts."[9]

At the time of the Czech Crisis in the summer of 1938, British Ambassador Sir Nevile Henderson, who was suffering from cancer, returned to London from Berlin to see his doctor. But the stress of the diplomatic crisis was also working on him. "He does not look at all fit and is obviously in a very nervous and overwrought state," judged one observer, "quite unfit to be in such a post at such a time." The same crisis, said another participant, "put a heavy strain on the staff of the Embassy; most of us worked a twelve-hour day during the summer months," working on Saturdays and Sundays, and sometimes long into the night. From the first until the 21st of September 1938, said First Secretary of the Berlin Embassy Sir Ivone Kirkpatrick, "I do not think I put my foot outside the building." The embassy became, "the gloomiest house I have ever inhabited." The new physical and emotional stresses were being experienced by everyone in Europe, and particular crises were all the more stressful because they came on top of a period of already intense, prolonged tension, especially for diplomats: "In 1938," Kirkpatrick added, "the pace {had} quickened. Our lives, which had hitherto been intolerably active, began in retrospect to seem almost leisurely."[10]

At the time of the Czech Crisis, French Ambassador to Berlin François-Poncet "lapsed into despondent inactivity," was "exhausted" and unable to visit the German Foreign Office for two weeks. Lord Runciman, who had worked hard to help resolve the crisis in Czechoslovakia but returned to London a failure, was also in quite a state. "I saw Runciman this evening," wrote Oliver Harvey in his diary: "I was horrified at his appearance. He looks ten years older and ashen and very anxious." The crisis left President Beneš of Czechoslovakia looking drawn, exhausted, and beaten while the seventy-year-old British Prime Minister Sir Neville Chamberlain, who had never been in an airplane before, flew back and forth to Germany three times in September 1938, trips which, in addition to the seriousness of the war crisis, impacted on his physical and emotional condition. A letter to his sisters summarized his emotional state: "Events…entailed terrific physical and mental exertions," he wrote: it was "one prolonged nightmare." He admitted, "I came nearer...to a nervous breakdown than I have ever been in my life." Chamberlain's predecessor Stanley Baldwin had, indeed, suffered a nervous breakdown. A few years later, Hitler's invasion of Russia in June 1941 left the steely Stalin too shaken to continue, the evidence, while disputed, convincingly showing that Stalin took to his bed—or at least uncharacteristically disappeared—for several days before returning to direct the war. Churchill, a lifelong depressive, feared the times when the "Black Dog" would be upon him.[11] It was a condition he sought to escape, but only exacerbated, by his self-medicating bouts of heavy drinking.

The increased levels of stress brought on by specific diplomatic crises were all the more intense because they came on top of a prolonged period of general tension which had prevailed, and continued to prevail, throughout the interwar years.

There was the ongoing massive disorientation caused by The Great War of 1914-1918 and its immediate aftermath. Old kingdoms and ancient empires had collapsed. Kings had fled or been deposed; new governments had replaced them. New countries had been formed. Families that had lived in one country for generations suddenly found themselves living in another. There was starvation, deprivation, disease, and death. New fears built upon old ones. Propaganda had inflamed hatreds on all Home Fronts, hatreds that did not die easily. Millions had suffered in countless ways, millions had been killed, millions more had been maimed, millions were now orphans. Others had been kept behind barbed wire as prisoners of war. Everyone seemed victimized by a number of revolutions, some of which were still going on, while fears of new ones filled the future with dread. A generation was awash with grief. Parenting had been disrupted. Pain had engulfed humanity. Trauma—collective and massive—was everywhere. It was recognized, then and now, as a major turning point in human history.

The war was immediately followed by the great influenza pandemic of 1919, which killed an additional 20,000,000 worldwide. Then the interwar years brought additional stressors of their own, as suggested by phrases like political and economic "search for stability" or the military "search for security." Feminists, not to mention women in general, were breaking sexual and other kinds of rules in the Jazz Age. Everywhere "The Modern" was breaking out. And Russian and other communists threatened to overthrow capitalism. As partial escape from the tension, economic life sometimes exploded into manic activity, until the Great Depression reminded everyone after 1929 of the deprivations of 1914-1918. The new totalitarian states seemed to press human cruelty to new heights, while wars and threats of war engendered perpetual tension.

American journalist Louis Fischer, who reported from Europe during the period, felt that the interwar years were more stressful than at any other time. French historian Pierre Renouvin who had lost an arm in World War I felt the same way, writing of the Great Depression: "the shock was so great, so prolonged, that the very foundations of the economic and social order seemed to be threatened....It was not only an economic and social crisis, or even a moral crisis. It was a crisis of the psychology of the public." Nor did things improve over time, for "when the crisis eased," said Renouvin, "feelings of instability and insecurity remained." Broadcast journalist William L. Shirer who covered Europe from Berlin, called his memoirs of the 1930s *The Nightmare Years*, and confessed that he and fellow journalist Edward R. Murrow had become so depressed by the Czech Crisis that they met in Paris to drown their sorrows following the Munich Agreement. Other journalists, and some diplomats and statesmen, also regularly tried to escape through alcohol. Such self-medicating efforts offered only temporary relief, however, and even trips abroad offered no vacation from perpetual stress. Austrian author Stefan Zweig knew first hand how "Europe and anxiety about Europe were not to be eluded by travel, not even by journeys to far-off places." He explained how "landing one night in Pernambuco under the Southern Cross...I read on a news placard of the bombing of Barcelona and of the execution of a Spanish friend....There was no escape, not by day, not by night; always I was in a torment of anxiety about Europe." Modern radio and newsreels had produced a condition which afflicted his entire generation: "it was reserved for us to have to know and co-sense whatever evil happened on our globe at the moment of its occurrence."[12]

Despite observations like these, most standard studies of the origins of World War II have paid scant attention to stressors as psychological phenomena, still less to the emotions and irrational fantasies that can be documented to have emerged out of them. In the orthodox explanation for its outbreak, World War II is Hitler's war, understood as his rational, long-term plan. In this traditional rendering, he brilliantly manipulated the powers. Britain and France, riddled with guilt over the harsh Treaty of Versailles they had imposed on a defeated Germany in 1919, now felt that Germany was entitled to compensations and capitulated to Hitler's demands. Undermined by the Great Depression, France and Britain neglected their own rearmament, and lived in fear that another Great War would destroy civilization. They offered Hitler a series of well intentioned, if misguided, concessions known as "appeasement." He exploited these peace offerings, gobbling up one country after another. Too late the Allies came to their senses and scrambled to contain Germany by a series of last-minute diplomatic and military moves. Hitler then cynically completed a pact dividing Poland with Stalin, the other brutal dictator of the time. War was the result, of civilization and justice against barbarism and evil, maybe the last in which the forces of good and evil were so clearly drawn.

This summary is somewhat oversimplified, for there is

certainly more to traditional explanations of appeasement than one short paragraph can suggest. And it is necessary to add the fact that Hitler *was* responsible. Still, one wonders if there isn't something more—something emotional—that needs to be added to the traditional story.

In 1961, a popular British historian stunned scholars and readers of history by proposing a different scenario. A.J.P. Taylor noted how Hitler had been blamed for everything by the documents introduced at the Nuremberg Trials. While the Nazis were certainly guilty of genocide and other atrocities, Nuremberg, said Taylor, had worked in part to absolve the Allies from any responsibility for World War II. In a curious way, the Nuremberg Trials also allowed the Germans to do the same by blaming Hitler for everything. The documents were therefore "suspect." They had been compiled by lawyers to build a case, said Taylor, and were now "dangerous" for historians to use. Hitler's *Mein Kampf* was not a design for the future, but was mere political rhetoric written to win domestic votes. Hitler's words to his generals, like the secret, top-level meeting of November 1937 on contingency plans for German expansion, could not be taken seriously. According to the minutes of the meeting, Hitler spoke of war by 1943, not 1939, when war actually broke out: how, then, could he have "planned" it? Taylor concluded that Hitler was a traditional German statesman, merely trying to unite all Germans. The Allies gave him opportunities and he took them. Hitler did not act, but was acted upon. When war came, everyone had blundered into it. [13]

Not surprisingly, both the standard story *and* Taylor's revisionist explanation pay little attention to feelings. Yet when Taylor's book was published, historians, by the thousands, were outraged. "I tried to write history in detachment," he later said, "my critics were concerned to express their emotions."[14] They did so without noticing the difference between their own outrage and the so-called "rational motives" they invariably invoked to describe the diplomats they wrote about.

In retrospect, the critical reactions to Taylor's book came as something of a surprise. Some of what he said was indeed startling, but some of what he said was not really all that new. Men of impeccable political credentials had already argued that the actions of the Allies had boosted Hitler's ambitions. World War II, said Churchill, was an "unnecessary war,"[15] and could have been prevented if only the Allies had banned together.

It is a tribute to the force of tradition that many in the world today can at least say that Hitler started World War II, but forty years after the uproar over the *Origins of the Second World War* few people, outside of historians, have ever heard of A.J.P. Taylor. This is doubtless because some of what he said was simply wrong, but it must also be considered that the world has a strong emotional investment in keeping Hitler solely responsible. Again, Hitler was responsible. But some of Taylor's insights clearly have merit since it is now widely recognized by historians that allied actions often paved Hitler's way.[16]

Why did the Allies do this? An answer begins to emerge from looking at the diplomatic origins of the Second World War through a psychological microscope. Psychological historians—but many narrative historians as well—have sensed that behind many behaviors in the past there lies a shadowy underworld of motives hidden from the unaided eye. But not everyone feels this way. The wish not to know is a central part of what it means to be human, especially when knowing a denied or disguised thing makes one feel especially uncomfortable. Some critics have felt compelled to deny not only the existence of this emotional underworld, but also the validity of the instruments used to uncover it. But one cannot see the amoeba unless one looks through the microscope. The critics' refusal to look is regrettable, since (to change metaphors for a moment) there is no way to picture a jigsaw puzzle whole if every time a piece of the puzzle is brought forward it is declared to be impertinent, impossible, or irrelevant.

There were clear political processes at work in the origins of the Second World War, and economic and ideological processes as well. Perhaps many, or even all, were partly, or fully, psychological too. All intertwined and moved together. But the existence of several independent but interrelated processes does not mean that they stand as better alternatives to psychological explanations, only that simultaneous processes were at work.

Did feelings matter in the diplomatic decisions of the 1930s? Were they embedded in fantasies? What fantasies did people share? How were they circulated within countries and across borders? It is already clear that under stress, leaders and diplomats could not help but allow feelings into their words and behaviors. This does not mean that they were necessarily irrational, only that they could be.

II FANTASIES AND FOREIGN AFFAIRS

THE UNITY OF EUROPE IS NOT A FANTASY, BUT REALITY ITSELF; WHAT IS FANTASTIC IS THE BELIEF IN FRANCE, GERMANY, ITALY OR SPAIN AS SUBSTANTIVE AND INDEPENDENT UNITS.[1]
—*Ortega y Gasset*, 1941

While living in Wales in World War II, psychologist Melanie Klein began treating a ten-year-old boy named Richard whom she described in her *Narrative of a Child Analysis*.[2] Richard was a bright boy whose anxieties had naturally increased with the outbreak of war ("he was particularly frightened of air raids, and bombs"). He was preoccupied, almost obsessed, with the war, and was unusually well informed, reading three newspapers a day and listening to all the news on the radio. In treatment, he became fascinated with a map of Europe hanging on the wall behind Klein's desk. Richard began projecting into this map his own inner conflicts and some of the dynamics then taking place in his family. He sometimes saw the contours of Europe's countries as people, or as parts of his own body. Klein used the map as a therapeutic device to capture Richard's attention and tap the unconscious fantasies he was projecting into it.

Such projections are not only the product of neurotic ten-year-old boys distressed by the terrors of war. They are, apparently, the common practice of humankind, and are found in many places and times. The late William Niederland, a professor of clinical psychiatry, has shown how maps and geographical configurations served as containers into which people have continually projected primitive body fantasies from antiquity to the present.[3] Psychological anthropologist Howard Stein and other scholars have elaborated on and expanded these findings.[4] After a lifetime of experience, psychoanalyst Alex Strachey long ago came to understand that people experience a large group, such as a nation, as an enlarged person: "the idea of dividing it up means to them carving up a living body."[5] An early German nationalist, speaking of Prussia's defeat by Napoleon in 1807, had said: "By the Peace of Tilsit Prussia lost some of her limbs."[6] Historians have been talking that way for years.

It is a familiar theme in the history of ideas that groups sometimes see themselves and others as "living bodies." A famous example of this way of thinking can be found in the medieval era. The twelfth-century monk and political thinker John of Salisbury wrote:

> A commonwealth...is a certain body which is endowed with life....Those things which establish and implant within us the practice of religion...fill the place of the soul in the body of the commonwealth....The place of the head in the body of the commonwealth is filled by the prince....The place of the heart is filled by the senate....The duties of eyes, ears, and tongue are claimed by the judges and governors of provinces. Officials and soldiers correspond to the hands. Those who always attend upon the prince are likened to the sides. Financial officers and keepers...may be compared with the stomach and intestines.... The husband men correspond to the feet...it is they who raise, sustain, and move forward the weight of the entire body.[7]

Millions of like-minded Europeans thought this way in the literal-minded Middle Ages. Political thinkers like Hobbes and Rousseau continued to think this way into early modern and modern times, and intellectual historians have made careers tracing such ideas down to the present. Several scholars have shown how organic notions like these crop up even today.

Democratic thinkers too can see political societies as "bodies politic." To Winston Churchill, a problem of Europe after the First World War, as he said at the time, was "a poisoned Russia, an infected Russia, a plague-bearing Russia." The new states in Eastern Europe, created out of the Versailles Treaty would keep it in check: "the 'Sanitary Cordon' which protected Europe from the Bolshevik infection," said Churchill, "was formed by living national organisms vigorous in themselves, hostile to the disease and immune through experience to its ravages."[8] These "living national organisms" were essential to the "health" of Europe. Czech Ambassador Jan Masaryk said he "felt that Chamberlain spent most of his official life explaining that Czechoslovakia was a country and not a contagious disease." Franklin Roosevelt was using the same kind of thinking when he denounced the "epidemic of lawlessness" in an October 1937 Chicago speech where he called for a "quarantine" of the "infected states."[9]

These metaphorical images, of course, are among the ways normal people speak to themselves and each other every day, and as such may contain more emotional power than they are usually given credit for.

American diplomat George F. Kennan used this kind of familiar organic thinking in order to help him better understand the events he was witnessing first hand as a diplomat in Czechoslovakia, recalling in his memoirs how the Hungarian and Polish governments after the Munich Crisis of 1938 helped themselves to the spoils by beginning to "rend…bits…from the flesh of the stricken country."[10] Kennan was only expressing the same type of imagery as many of his contemporaries. Speaking of the British naval blockade of Germany during the First World War, military writer B. H. Liddel Hart said in his 1930 book *The Real War* that "Germany's arteries were subjected to an invisible pressure which never relaxed." In the summer of 1930 the Polish press and Polish leaders had told the world they would fight for Danzig because Danzig made up the "lungs" of the Polish economy. Historian Richard Overy finds that the "biological metaphor was widespread. It can even be found in the official manual of the RAF, *War Manual*: Part I, Operations, May 1935, p. 57 'nerve centers, main arteries, heart and brain'." He notes that—in England —"lungs remained a curiously neglected metaphor."[11]

In Britain, wrote one diplomatic observer at the time, Hitler's demands on Czechoslovakia were seen as a "beautiful plan of bringing about a peaceful amputation," although other people felt that "German opinion did not favor a surgical operation for the amputation of the Sudeten."[12] They were wrong—at least in Göring's mind—when he said that Czechoslovakia was "the vermiform appendix of Europe! We shall have to operate." When the immediate war crisis was temporarily ended by the Munich accord, Chamberlain told the House of Commons that it had been "a painful and difficult operation," a "difficult and delicate operation," but that "the operation was a success."[13]

In events like these, countries, or parts of them, are familiarly seen as being seized, annexed, or even "absorbed." Historians speak this way of these military and administrative processes all the time. They also speak of "amputation," and the like. Nearly every book or article on the Czech Crisis sooner or later gets around to speaking of the "dismemberment" of Czechoslovakia almost (and sometimes) as if it were a literal fact. It is worth considering that when historians do this, they may be capturing not just metaphors but also the actual fantasies of the people they write about. The *Manchester Guardian*, on 20 September 1938, wondered what would happen should the Sudeten regions of Czechoslovakia be "torn from her." Four days later General Ironside began his diary: "To dismember Czechoslovakia." Sometimes all of Europe, not just a single country was imagined as a person, Stefan Zweig saying of Europe after World War I that "bitterness and distrust...remained like an insidious poison in its maimed body," while in 1940 César Saerchinger wrote that "unless it functions as a healthy living body, without gangrene in its limbs, Europe cannot live."[14]

The best historians, even those who have little use for psychology, sometimes acknowledge the explanatory value of such language. Gordon Craig's presidential address to the

American Historical Association in 1983 stated that things "like alliances should be regarded metaphorically as organisms."[15] Yet, we are not talking only of metaphors, but of real fantasies.

Literary and film critics have had no problem in recognizing the symbolic meaning of metaphors, and such analyses are part of their stock in trade. Nevertheless, it is important to make distinctions here, for it is one thing to say that society is like a human body, quite another to say that it *is* a human body. Sometimes, when individuals and groups say society is like a human body they unconsciously mean (or come to believe) that it is a human body. (Of course, by conscious and unconscious tricks and deceptions they can hide this shift in thinking even from themselves.) It is generally acknowledged that such unconscious, partly conscious, and conscious organic thinking can create potentially dangerous conditions in which dehumanized enemies become "microbes," "plague-bearing vermin," or "cancers" preliminary to persecutions, expulsions, mass murders, even wars.

At the same time, one must be clear that not all metaphors are fantasies. Poets, writers, and historians, in charge of their craft, manipulate language in conscious, constructive, and creative ways. Everyday language is also enlivened by the customary use of metaphor and simile. But it is well known that crowds can be manipulated by the use of images to provoke powerful emotional responses. It is a central feature of political propaganda and advertising. And in cases where metaphors are not fantasies, if they are colorful enough and repeated often enough they can contribute to the creation of a certain tone, a certain collective mood.

In any case, many of the things that people say, and how they say them, are already taken seriously by historians. Why can't the images people use, their metaphors and similes, also reveal something of their fantasies? The question of when metaphors are fantasies, or merely ways of speaking, has to be decided in each specific instance. Did Hitler mean it when he said "We have lanced the Jewish abscess," or was he only ranting? Are not metaphors used to color, to enliven language? Precisely: they work because the fantasy-image of the metaphor causes an emotional stir in the audience. And are not metaphors "culture-bound?" Yes: they are habitual ways of speaking, and work so well because people in the group customarily using them share not only the same language, but sometimes the same fantasies. Much scholarly work is needed in this area before these issues can be fully clarified, but the rule of thumb used in this study is to look carefully and seriously at those frequently expressed powerful emotional images which clustered again and again in the language of diplomats, leaders, and the media in the 1930s. If they were widely used, and used often enough, it suggests not only a European-wide culture of shared metaphor, but—as shared symbolic images—a European-wide culture of unconscious fantasy.

This view may not be as unorthodox as it sounds. The technique of content analysis is familiar enough to students of linguistics and of the social sciences, and the conscious manipulation and integration of Nazi ways of thinking and speaking into standard German—the emergence of *Nazi-Deutsch*—has been studied and is well known to students of the German language.

The German geopolitical theorist Karl Haushofer, for example, whose ideas influenced Hitler, spoke in his writings of such things as "traffic arteries in the Rhein choking under the grip of foreigners," and of "raising a border's blood pressure." According to historian Dan Diner, Haushofer's thinking wasn't just metaphorical: for him, "the state {was} a real 'organism'." And Haushofer was not alone, the notion of the state as a real organism was a commonplace throughout Germany and Europe. It coincided with and reinforced Hitler's own ideas. Almost all scholars have concluded that Hitler's language reveals his fantasy that Germany was an organism. *Mein Kampf* is filled with statements like: "from a dead mechanism…must be formed a living organism;" "Could anyone believe that Germany alone was not subject to exactly the same laws as all other human organisms?" "Our movement alone was capable of creating… a national organism." In his speeches Hitler repeated the same themes saying: "In place of…the State—must be set the living organism—the people;" "The German people…had become a body corporate, pulsing through and through with vital inner life;" "The Polish Corridor...is like a strip of flesh cut from our body…a national wound that bleeds continuously, and will continue to bleed till the land is returned to us."[16]

Historians who have noted these themes (Hitler scholars know he repeated them hundreds and hundreds of times) consider them central to Hitler's ideology, and have shown how his ideas were not unique, but resonated with the organic thinking developed by, and rampant among, a good number of earlier nineteenth-century German and European intellectuals. Yet some traditional historians may feel that Hitler's words do not reveal fantasies because they derive *only* from his ideology. That is possible, except that ideologies are not always things in themselves. Feelings and fantasies are already "there." They come first and attract ideas, which are then attached and fitted to them. Ideologies serve several functions, are part justification, allowing people to remain "sane" by projecting inner emotional realities onto the outer world, and part rationalization, sometimes justifying and allowing people to act out their own and other's unconscious fantasies and impulses. In Hitler's case, the psychological origins and meaning of his ideology have been recently explored in Jay Gonen's *The Roots of Nazi Psychology*, which finds, among other things, a twisted mechanico-organic fantasy at its core. Even before Gonen's in depth study, however, numbers of narrative historians, not just psychologically oriented ones, intuited what careful content analysis of Hitler's speeches has since gone on to prove: that he understood Germany in fantasy to be not only a body, but a feminine body, a discovery first identified and detailed by historian Rudolph Binion, later corroborated by other scholars.[17]

Studies confirm Hitler's language was filled with fantasies of Germany not merely as a feminine body, but specifically as a maternal one. (It is worth remembering that these images are not just cultural conventions, but work so well precisely because they *are* cultural conventions.) In regard to Austria, he said in *Mein Kampf*, the aim was "union with the German mother country." "German-Austria must return to the great German mother country"; and "The German nation {must} embrace its own sons within a single state." Moreover, "only he who has felt in his own skin what it means to a German…can measure the deep longing which burns at all times in the heart of children separated from their mother-country."[18] Hitler's words, repeated in the 1920s and 30s, seem to have echoed the fantasies of the early German nationalists who had created the notion of a German nation as a maternal ideal over a hundred years before. Even scholars who have little use for psychology in history sometimes sense the fantasy meaning in Hitler's words. On the use of the word "fatherland" in Hitler's youthful patriotic poems, historian John Lukacs observes: "In spite of the masculine gender of that word, it is as if the fatherland were a feminine entity; these are expressions of devotion to a great, adored, and now endangered mother." The work of psychoanalyst Janine Chasseguet-Smirgel on pre-Nazi and Nazi Germany confirms Lukacs's intuition, showing that it was not just Hitler who longed for "the fantasy fusion with Mother Nature and the maternal soil," but also "the People" who longed to "merge into a single body… unite{d}with the mother's body as constituted by the nation."[19] If Germany was indeed the "fatherland" for millions of his countrymen, it was also their "motherland," and although Hitler frequently used the word "fatherland," it was "motherland" to which they also responded when he used it thousands of times in hundreds of speeches.

This simply confirms what many small-group researchers in psychology and sociology have been finding for nearly thirty years: that people in small groups unconsciously, sometimes consciously, imagine their groups to be feminine, often a "mother."[20] The same holds for members of large groups such as nations. Such notions seem right to us. One has no trouble with the statement: "Britain established her colonies so that she would be assured of her economic prosperity," whereas "Britain established his colonies so that he would be assured of his economic prosperity" just doesn't ring true. There is, of course, a "masculine" side to all of this, when countries are personified as "the fatherland," or as Uncle Sam, or as John Bull. The full relationship between masculine and feminine personifications is presently unclear, but there is nothing inherently contradictory in it. Fantasies are rich and multi-layered. Dualities and magical thinking exist without contradiction in the unconscious; side-by-side fantasies can, and apparently do, co-exist without difficulty.

The "land-as-mother" is even a half-truth, since "Mother Earth's" food and water sustain "her children," a "reality" which serves as a screen onto which the fantasy can be projected. The roots of the notion run deep into the German and European past. The nineteenth-century German nationalist and poet Heinrich Heine, as quoted by Gordon Craig, wrote of "the marriage that I have had with our dear Frau Germania," of how "she pressed me tenderly to her great bosom with {her} virtuous nipples," and, since Heine was a Jew sensitive to the anti-Semitism of the time, how "in the end we lived separated in bed and board," although "it never came to a real divorce."[21]

Groups and countries are obviously neither feminine nor maternal, even though people speak that way all the time, and the metaphor remains a colorful and valuable part of today's public discourse.[22] Nor, of course, was it just Hitler and Germans who thought and spoke this way: virtually all the peoples, diplomats, and decision makers of the 1930s shared the same metaphorical usages and hence, to some extent, the same fantasies. In general, countries were everywhere imagined as feminine. Britain's ambassador to Berlin spoke continuously of Germany as "she," Germany appears as "she" in the British diplomatic correspondence, and in the British press.[23] Britain appears as "she" in the German diplomatic documents, as well as in the rhetoric of Hitler and other Nazi leaders. Stalin's socialist regime shared one thing with the tsars who had gone before; all ruled over "Mother Russia." People outside the Soviet Union saw it the same way. "Russia has been thoroughly beaten by the Germans," said Churchill on 11 December 1917: "Her great heart has been broken." France, too, was imagined as feminine. When Socialist Léon Blum formed his Popular Front government in the mid-1930s a bourgeois friend told him: "France is ready for you. She awaits you like a nervous bride." Later, a member of the conservative group Action Française wrote of Marshal Pétain, that he had "saved France at the very moment of her distress." Pétain later muttered in his sleep: "la France, I have loved only her." That these usages are intrinsic to the grammars of their languages only shows how deeply such fantasies are embedded. Neville Chamberlain's Francophile-brother Austen, British Foreign Secretary in the 1920s, stated that he had always "loved France like a woman," and the image of "Marianne" has been a traditional way of personifying the French republic for years. Mussolini and other Italians could have only one real mistress, "Italia." The Polish constitution of March 17, 1921, declared that "the self-sacrificing struggles of generations" had created a "united and independent mother-country." In the nineteenth century, Czech nationalist poet Viktor Dyk had the Czech motherland utter to her son, the Bohemian nation: "If you leave me, I shall not perish. If you...leave me, you will perish,"[24] thus summarizing the fantasy that, for Czechs at least—and not only for Czechs—

those who inhabit nations are infants who sometimes feel they will actually "die" if they are not in the embrace of their nurturing motherland.

Since they are feminine, when countries are attacked it may seem to some that, in fantasy, they are being sexually molested. British politicians spoke of "the rape of China by Japan" (1933) and on the day following the German takeover of Austria, headlines in the London *Times* famously declared the *Anschluss* to be "The Rape of Austria." Hitler's Minister of Propaganda, Joseph Goebbels, acknowledged that the image was, at least to him, more than mere metaphor when, writing of the *Anschluss* in his diary, he said: "The world press rages. Speaks of rape. Not entirely without justification." European diplomats at the time used the same image, with hundreds of historians repeating it ever since.[25]

Obviously, Austria was not being raped, except in fantasy, but that is precisely why the word stirs our feelings.

It may appear that what is being advanced here is placing too heavy a burden on metaphors, that they are being made to carry more meaning than they can possibly bear. Are a few unrelated metaphors, sprinkled over a vast documentary landscape, being seized whenever and wherever they pop up, then arbitrarily strung together to artificially support a dubious theory? If indeed such fantasies exist, would they not differ from country to country, the fantasy life of Nazi Germany differing from the fantasy life of Great Britain? And if the current study is about diplomacy, why are images from the popular press, from journalists, and from a few novelists being (or about to be) offered in evidence? These are good questions.

Fantasies do differ from county to country, as the following chapters will show. What is at issue here is in part an issue of good faith, as well as of good evidence. The metaphorical images and statements thus far used to illustrate the fantasies of the 1930s are representative, and could be enriched by hundreds of additional examples. They are taken from a variety of documents, including the occasional novel, because the evidence shows them to be pervasive: they existed across Europe, or at least the Europe that is being studied; they are found in the media as well as in the words of diplomats and statesmen; they ranged from top to bottom across the social spectrum in every European country and demonstrate the existence of a European community bound together not only by ideology, economics, conflict, and a shared past, but also by a rich unconscious fantasy life.

In that fantasy life, the expression of a particular cluster of metaphors may reveal how far the person or group expressing that fantasy has regressed under stress. The principle is: the greater the stress, the more the regression to earlier developmental stages, perhaps all the way back to images prevalent in early childhood. The historical documents of the 1930s reveal that under the stresses of diplomatic and domestic crises, some people were sometimes regressed to very early, very primitive, very infantile states.

That is the case when groups and individuals began speaking of countries as if they were rabid, devouring monsters. "German expansionists...have shown themselves resolute and ruthless in devouring Poland," wrote a Canadian scholar in 1940; "and France and Britain, with whom Canada is now associated, are engaged in a grim struggle to defeat the carnivorous nationalism of the Third Reich." When French historian Maurice Baumont wrote that World War II had its origins in the "insatiable appetites of Adolf Hitler," he was accurately capturing the cannibalistic fantasies of oral incorporation expressed by people in the 1930s. Novelist Eric Ambler's pre-war thriller *Cause for Alarm* (1938) speaks of the Rome-Berlin axis as a "strategic unit from the Frisian Islands in the North to the toe of Italy in the South. The toe is waiting to kick Great Britain in the pants. The head is there to gobble up what's left."[26]

French Premier Daladier responded to news of the Nazi-Soviet Pact by telling American ambassador William Bullitt that he feared it "would result in Germany swallowing one {country} after another." Russian Foreign Minister Litvinov told American ambassador Joseph E. Davies that he "could not understand why Great Britain could not see that once Hitler dominated Europe he would swallow the British Isles also." After the *Anschluss*, the *Daily Express* of London believed Germany's aggressive policies would be moderated because "Hitler has enough on his plate with his Vienna schnitzel." In published British documents on the outbreak of the war one finds many statements like that of mid-1938, when Polish and Western diplomats were feeling Poland's relations with Germany were "degenerating into an undignified imitation of the small fish that seek their meat in the wake of the shark." On 27 February 1939 a British diplomat believed "the German mouth is wide open for concessions."[27] On 1 February 1939 George Kennan's dispatch from Czechoslovakia on Czech-German relations spoke of Germany's "digestion" of the Sudeten regions as incomplete. If Germany could include "Bohemia among its undigested acquisitions," he said, he felt that the rest of Czechoslovakia would "almost surely be swallowed up by Hungary and Poland." After the *Anschluss*, Hitler told his military entourage that Czechoslovakia would be next, but "Austria had to be digested first."[28]

British Chargé d'Affaires in Berlin, Sir George Ogilvie-Forbes, wrote to Foreign Minister Halifax in early 1939 that Hitler was "drunk with his resounding successes in Austria and Sudetenland and thirsting still more for political adventure." Earlier, when the German-Polish Non-Aggression Declaration was signed on 26 January 1934, Poland's leader Marshal Pilsudski had remarked in relief how the pact had suddenly changed Poland from being "Germany's hors d'oeuvre to her dessert." Equally prophetic were the words of those opposed to Chamberlain's appeasement policy who feared Hitler would get "Czechoslovakia on a platter served up by the Prime Minister himself," which proved to be the case. In 1930, Mussolini had told Prince Starhemberg that when Austria was swallowed by Germany, European chaos would begin. After Polish troops occupied Teschen, Paul Reynaud told the Polish Ambassador in Paris: "You are satisfied because Hitler has put you in the refrigerator for his next meal." A month before the *Anschluss* showed everyone that Czechoslovakia would be Hitler's next move, Chamberlain was writing in his diary how he feared "Czechoslovakia would be swallowed." All the while, the world press was filled with cartoon images showing Germany as a devouring fish, Nazis as devouring tigers, Hitler as a devouring dog, and Czechoslovakia as having been eaten, being eaten, or about to be eaten.[29]

Primitive fantasies like these can be very frightening when flooding consciousness, or threatening to flood it. When people talk and think these ways it shows that regression under stress has touched, and is stirring up, deep feelings and fantasies, some buried since childhood. Like Melanie Klein's ten-year-old patient, people's unwanted fears, as well as their unwanted wishes, can be partly "escaped" for a time by dumping feelings and fantasies onto others. Countries become containers for people's own projections, including bad feelings about themselves. This seems to have been going on when Churchill wrote of Russia in the *Sunday Express* in 1920 that: "We see the Bolshevik cancer eating into the flesh of the wretched being; we see the monstrous growth swelling and thriving upon the emaciated body of its victim." Hitler was doing much the same when he got rid of the bad feelings he was feeling about himself—experienced as a diseased part—by projecting them into Czechoslovakia as "a tumor...poisoning the whole European organism."[30] Those words, quoting the *New York Times* quoting the *Daily Mail* quoting Hitler, suggest how quickly fantasies can move across borders to touch the minds of millions of people.

This does not mean, of course, that leaders and peoples were experiencing such regressive fantasies all the time. Many thoughts were "conscious," many decisions were "rational." But neither does it mean that all thoughts and decisions were rational. The evidence shows that thoughts and actions were sometimes laced with underlying unconscious fantasies (or at least powerful metaphors), and it seems clear enough from the sources—or at least possible—that leaders and peoples moved into and out of irrational thinking when they saw countries, as they sometimes did, as bodies being cut up or raped, or else as primitive monsters devouring each other.

The documents also reveal at least one other fantasy, which seems to have been continually at work, one less threatening and scary than the others because it was developmentally less regressed: the notion of the European family. This served as a defense to keep especially regressed, re-emerging terrors at bay while helping to organize and thus make sense of other fantasies.

Images in the diplomatic and other documents show that people during the period regularly saw foreign affairs as having something to do with families, an idea which in itself is not surprising. The phrase "family of nations" is familiar enough in international discourse and everyday life, and historians have been talking that way for years.

Reviewing a study of German-U.S. diplomacy for the period 1933-1939, historian Joachim Remak has written: "A vast and complex amount of detail is supplied for the various phases of German-American relations, from honeymoon to divorce." One of Mussolini's motives for the Pact of Steel between Italy and Germany, according to Pierre Renouvin, was that Mussolini wanted "to show Britain and France that the 'courtship' was over." Historian Carl Schorske says that when Russia's behavior toward Germany and the West changed in late July 1939: "The Russian game of pitting its suitors against each other began to be played in earnest." At one point in Italian-German relations, writes another historian, Hitler's aim was to "turn the marriage of convenience into one of inclination. To conduct the courtship Hitler...stepped out of regular diplomatic channels."[31]

It is worth repeating that these familiar ways of speaking and thinking may be more than just metaphors. Phrases like these mean that historians are accurately, and directly, capturing the unconscious, sometimes conscious, fantasies in the ways diplomats and statesmen sometimes speak and think. At times alliances were seen not simply as marriages, but also as the children of marriages—even both at once. "Lord D'Abernon has long been recognized as the god-parent of the 1925 reciprocal security pact," writes historian F. G. Stambrook. "He and Carl von Schubert, the State Secretary of the German Foreign Ministry, were in the habit of referring to it in its initial stages as '*das Kind*'."[32] Oliver Harvey's diary reveals that the temporary alliance between Mussolini and the West, called the Stresa Front, was believed by British diplomat Sir Robert Vansittart to be "his special child," and Harvey's diary itself repeatedly speaks of alliances as "weddings." In his conversations with Emil Ludwig, Mussolini spoke of France and Italy as family members when he referred to "the brotherhood of Latin nations."[33] Family images remain a common usage in today's public discourse[34] confirming the validity of earlier statements like that of historian Henry L. Roberts that in the mid-1930s, "Russia was returning to the family of nations."[35]

The family-of-nations fantasy, it seems likely, is constructed from the customary ways people learn to speak and think. It is also likely that it comes in part from memories all individuals have of the families of their own childhoods. What makes it seem especially real as fantasies go is that it resonates with and is reinforced by historical reality. In premodern Europe, even down to World War I, international politics were largely a family affair, as kings and queens and their kin married for political advantage, before, during, and after which they played out family scenarios with subjects, rivals, and allies alike. Historian Lynn Hunt has found family images to be important in understanding the French Revolution, although she sees them as less of a "cause" than an influence. "I do not mean to reduce politics to fantasies," she has written in her *Family Romance of the French Revolution*. "Yet politics do depend on imagination and hence to some extent fantasy, and family experience is the source of much of that fantasy." She concludes that for the French Revolution at least: "Family issues divided political groups on a conscious and unconscious level." The period after the Revolution is beyond Hunt's study; that was the period when nineteenth-century nationalism began to compete with and supplant dynastic loyalties by emphasizing peoples rather than sovereigns, and the family origins of modern international affairs were gradually driven underground. The dominant metaphor became "the Concert of Europe," but the sense of kinship remained, so that Balzac could still speak of "the great continental family."[36]

An important but neglected study by historian Robert Kann has found that during this period, "the German stud," as he put it, most often served Europe's ruling families, with the "politically most important marriage alignments... between Great Britain and Prussia."[37] Near the century's end, most of Europe's ruling families were still intimately connected by blood ties, what Queen Victoria called "the Royal Mob." Indeed, Victoria—with direct descendants on ten European thrones—had become the "Grandmama of Europe."[38] This familial heritage belongs to the prehistory of the First World War even though historians tend to overlook it, so preoccupied are they with political, economic, strategic, social, and ideological realities, and it has been left to an American film critic and novelist to catch this sense of things, writing some time ago that World War I was "essentially a family squabble, except that the squabbling family happened to be royal, and when kings who are cousins argue, privates die, in the millions."[39]

The family fantasies of the 1920s and 30s, then, while originating in personal family memories, also matched up with and were reinforced by previous historical realities. To be sure, at the end of World War I, monarchies disappeared in several countries, but the habit of thinking in older, traditional ways continued. In the mid-1930s the Spanish philosopher Ortega y Gasset said that: "Inter-European wars have almost always been marked by a curious style that gives them a certain resemblance to family squabbles." The English implied as much when they referred to international disputes as "quarrels," which they did continually in the 1930s.[40] French Foreign Minister Bonnet spoke of the "house of Europe," Beneš spoke of France being "divorced…from its alliances in Central Europe," and Göring, Ribbentrop, and Hitler spoke of the annexation of Austria as "a family affair."[41] So did the London *Observer*.[42]

D. C. Watt asks us to beware not to discard any relevant part of the past and notes that "historians ignore at their peril the beliefs and attitudes of contemporary witnesses to the events they are studying."[43] That means taking seriously such fantasy images as the political cartoon of the Nazi-Soviet Non-Aggression Treaty showing Stalin as Hitler's bride, or another cartoon from the *Sunday Graphic* showing Hitler as Stalin's bride.[44] While the West might be confused over who was "bride" and who "groom," everyone knew a diplomatic "marriage" had taken place. (One cartoon wondered: "How long will the honeymoon last?")

This confirms what Watt pointed out a quarter century ago: "To many people who lived through the years of the 1930s, what seemed to be in train was not the approach of another war between states, but the preliminary stages of a civil war which was taking place throughout Europe." According to Watt, "the civil war theory has been lost sight of in the ensuing flood of detailed monographs."[45] By way of exception, Arno J. Mayer has seen the international politics in the first half of the twentieth century as an "internal and international civil war." [46] His view matches that of people such as Ortega y Gasset, Emil Ludwig, and Adam von Trott zu Solz, a member of the German Resistance, who believed, at least as early as December 1937, that a modern European war would be, like those of the ancient Greeks, a "calamitous fratricide." [47]

Views like these and the evidence presented above confirm the fantasy that foreign affairs are sometimes seen and experienced as a family system. Conversely, when family therapists first started making sense out of family systems they thought in terms of international politics, with its dynamics of "alliance" and "coalition." They have stuck by the analogy without giving it so much as a second thought, just like statesmen who, when they don't use family imagery in their rhetoric, don't have to, so basic, ingrained, and widely understood is the notion.

Of course, international affairs are *not* a family system. It is just that when people think that way, they may act accordingly. Thus, statesmen may be inclined to project experiences from their own families into international affairs.

Historians tend to reject this idea, as do people in the early stages of psychotherapy. R. D. Laing says:

> A young man feels his life has come to a stop. He is preoccupied by the conflict between East and West, the cold war, the balance of terror, techniques of deterrence, one world, the impossibility of divorce, the need for coexistence, the apparent impossibility of coexistence. He has a mission to find a solution, but he feels hopeless, and paralyzed. He does nothing, but feels crushed by his responsibility for the destruction he feels is inevitable.
>
> The structural elements of his preoccupation—conflict, the cold war, emotional divorce, balance of terror, the need for coexistence—resemble those in the relationship between his parents.
>
> But he does not see these resemblances. He insists that his pre-

> occupation with the world situation is not only entirely justified by objective facts but entirely based on them. The world situation is a fact and thousands of people come from families like his, *therefore*, there is no connection.[48]

It may be that the world situation is like that precisely because people come from families like his. That may be in part why some historians tend to deny it; to accept the possibility is to come face to face with our own families, past or present, and the powerful emotions that thoughts of them engender. That may be part of why international affairs are almost always studied as economics, power, or strategic necessity, hardly ever as family relations. To study them impersonally allows us to deny the possible pains, sorrows, and conflicts within our own families.

If diplomacy recapitulates, or may recapitulate, family systems, it seems necessary to go beyond common sense and personal experience. It is important to know something about the psychological studies of how families actually function. Observation and personal experience tell us that some families handle conflicts well, others are able to resolve them peacefully or somehow manage to live with them "diplomatically." Europe, instead, was moving in the 1930s into an episode of collective violence. To learn if the family fantasies of Europeans played any part in that event, one would want to know not more about normal, or even dysfunctional, families, but about pathological ones.

One way to understand the dynamics of pathological families is to look at the work of Martin Grotjahn, one of the first to systematically examine dysfunctional and pathological family processes.[49] Other psychologists have since elaborated and refined his findings, but Grotjahn's studies still stand as exemplary models and can provide a satisfactory way of helping us begin to look at diplomacy.

Every person, says Grotjahn "transfers unconscious images of his inner childhood family to the outer realistic family," like the patient who "re-experienced his mother-son conflict within himself, and projected it onto his family." Many people are like the patient who worked hard to "re-enact in the marriage the nightmare of his childhood." Indeed, "through life we interject into us part of the people of our environment; and simultaneously we project part of our unconscious into the people around us," sometimes enacting an unconscious drama with other family members.

Looked at closely, any neurosis is a "complementary neurosis," involving a whole host of family members who help feed it; one depends upon the other. A marriage can become "a mutual defense pact."

René Laforgue had already shown in 1937 how "two partners in a marriage unconsciously communicate and how they support their complementary neurosis." Often "the symptoms of one member in the family"—the designated patient—"may be the result of a neurotic communication in which one person's clues and orders are followed by the other." The stakes in maintaining the system might be very high:

> Many a man saves his sanity be marrying an insane woman. Unconsciously, he may even recognize his guilt for her psychosis, and understand that her craziness keeps him healthy. Such a man would be highly disturbed if his wife's psychiatric treatment were successful. He then would suffer the temptation of developing his own psychosis, instead of assigning this task to his wife.

This is one reason why these realities are ignored and denied, and why the family tries to sabotage the efforts of any family member seeking to break free of the system.

In such systems, all family members are delegates. In a marriage: "Roles are often assigned by the two partners in silent agreement after an inner struggle; he behaves pleasantly enough only because she has taken over the role of the watchful, punitive superego." Children are delegated too:

> Parents often find vicarious gratification of their own poorly integrated forbidden impulses in the children's acting out. Through their unconscious and ambivalent seductiveness, per-

> missiveness, and inconsistency toward the child, the parents guide it into delinquency—only to punish it severely after the deed. The punishment is vicious and cruel because the parents are crusading against their own sins, which are being lived out by their children.

Psychoanalyst Adelaide Johnson has shown how superego lacunae, or gaps in the conscience, play a role in this process, and family therapist and Hitler biographer Helm Stierlin is only one among many who have corroborated these findings and proven how juvenile delinquents enact the unconscious commands of their parents, even to the point of suicide.[50]

Family therapists do not know at the outset what unconscious scenarios they will find unfolding in any particular family, or how family members will separate out roles, or what emotional issues they will express in their daily routines. But they do know that unconscious scenarios can be acted out.

It is possible that similar processes—and the delegated roles learned by statesmen in the families of their childhood—were re-enacted under stress when statesmen started dealing with other members of the family of nations. And what of the possibility that additional adult traumas, both individual and collective, overlay, intertwined with, or reinforced those earlier family experiences? It seems clear that the fantasies circulating within countries and across borders in the 1930s helped form the general emotional tone in which decisions were made, but did they have anything to do with specific behaviors?

III GREAT BRITAIN

HISTORY WILL WONDER HOW IT CAME ABOUT THAT ANY GOVERNMENT SHOULD HAVE DELIBERATELY CLOSED ITS EYES AND THOSE OF THE NATION TO SO CLEAR AND IMMINENT A PERIL.[1]
—*Sir Ivone Kirkpatrick*, 1957

The course of British policy is well known. In the 1930s appeasement granted concessions to the dictators. It was meant to keep peace; it brought war.

Did British decision-makers act rationally? What were their fantasies? Were they sometimes acting out unconscious personal agendas? The postwar words of career diplomat Ivone Kirkpatrick quoted above clue us to the possibility that something deeply irrational may have been at work in Great Britain.

Sir Ivone's words are somewhat misleading, however, since the Hitler-threat had indeed been noticed—and well understood. Many had sounded alarms, among them Sir Ivone himself. In retrospect, he felt that Britain had "had ample warning, from *Mein Kampf* as well as from every manifestation of German policy, which proclaimed Hitler's intentions from the housetops....The magnitude of German preparations for war, the ruthless speed with which they were pushed ahead and the vast scope of German ambitions were all known."[2]

The documentary evidence confirms Kirkpatrick's conclusions. *Mein Kampf* appeared in an abridged English translation in 1933 to vigorous sales and was widely reviewed. Although it is not known if Baldwin or Chamberlain later read it, people in the Foreign Office knew the book well and produced a summary for Chamberlain. Later, a detailed review of the unexpurgated English edition appeared in a London *Times* Literary Supplement in late-March 1939.[3] In addition, the views of the critics of appeasement were well known since they had kept up steady public and private pressure against appeasement on the grounds that Germany's rearmament meant war, and their statements were widely covered in the press. Already in 1934 John Wheeler-Bennett had warned: "faced with the dread of encirclement...the same leaders of Germany who shot down the 'conspirators' of 30 June without trial might...indulge in some international excess, and thus, Samson-like, precipitate disaster." In June 1935 journalist John Garvin had written in *The Observer* of "the plain undoubted probability that Europe within the next two or three years will be brought to the brink of war." Permanent Under Secretary of the Foreign Office Sir Robert Vansittart continuously pointed out the Nazi menace throughout the 1930s, saying on 7 April 1934: "If we have taken Germany to be a potential enemy we are in the company of most of the political minds in Europe. Everywhere in fact, is to be found the anticipation that within a strictly measurable time Germany will be practicing a policy of blackmail or force."[4]

In 1936, Eden told the Cabinet that the German troops which had just broken the Versailles Treaty by marching into the demilitarized Rhineland were a threat because now Germany could "invade France through Belgium as in 1914;" they would not have to provide large forces for the defense of the Rhine, but could fortify it instead. Churchill told the House of Commons that those fortifications could now constitute a "barrier across Germany's front door, which will leave her free to sally out eastwards and southwards by the back door."[5]

When Hitler announced the annexation of Austria in March 1938, General Ironside wrote in his diary: "We have had ample warning." Six months later, Churchill's press statement during the Munich Crisis hoped to stir the public by noting how the "complete surrender" of Britain and France to the Nazi "threat" was a "collapse" which had placed them in a "weaker" and more "dangerous" situation that would "threaten" the "Western front." Churchill went on after Munich to warn the House of Commons that Munich was "only the first sip, the first foretaste of a bitter cup." He was not the only observer employing oral imagery. Harold Nicolson said: "The tiger is showing his teeth; the cage door is open; the keeper is gone." And a well-known scholar wrote in the *Manchester Guardian* how Britain's "ambition to be eaten last, which inspires our present policy, is intelligible but futile. We shall (if we remain edible) be eaten all the same, nor shall we be consulted as to the date of the ceremony." In March 1939, David Grenfell observed in the House of Commons that: "All that we witness day after day is a steady and violent disintegration of the European system," while appeasement, "instead of modifying or retarding that disintegration, only gives an added impetus to it." By mid-July Chamberlain was writing to his sister how "I am continually getting reports that 'Hitler is still anxious for friendship with England' but how can you reconcile that with the daily poisoning of the wells by Hitler's propaganda department?"[6]

At least as early as February 1934, the government had foreseen Germany as Britain's long-term threat. "Almost every year thereafter the Joint Planning Committee of the Committee of Imperial Defense produced a new edition of their *magnum opus* 'Planning for War with Germany'."[7] British journalists had predicted in private correspondence exactly when Hitler would re-militarize the Rhineland: they said January or February 1936, it happened on 6-7 March.[8] After the *Anschluss*, the young journalist Elizabeth Wiskeman was one of many who predicted (she in *The New Statesman and Nation*) that Czechoslovakia seemed "the obvious victim for Hitler's next Saturday coup."[9] In mid-September 1938, before the Munich Agreement gave part of Czechoslovakia to Hitler, Chamberlain predicted all of Czechoslovakia's eventual fate: "supposing that part of Czechoslovakia were given to Germany," he said to his Cabinet, "what would happen to the rest of the country? It might be said that there would be a helpless strip of territory liable at any moment to be gobbled up by Germany."[10] It happened, as predicted, in March 1939.

All the while, steady streams of reports came in from "British diplomats in Germany that before long—1938-40 are the years most commonly mentioned—Germany would launch the first aggression in an attempt to dominate Europe." In many books and articles journalists issued warnings aplenty, all of which supports A.J.P. Taylor's conclusion that "Allied statesmen were under no illusions as to Hitler's intentions."[11]

What did the British, then, think should be done? A surprising number of journalists, politicians, and diplomats argued that only one thing could stop Hitler: firmness. An astute journalist, in private correspondence sixteen months before Hitler came to power, had written: "Hitlerism seems in one sense to be a sort of national neurosis, and the best way of treating it may be to let it come to the surface and then treat the patient gently but firmly." Shortly after Hitler came to power, the British military representative to the League of Nations, Brigadier Arthur Temperley, wrote Vansittart in early May 1933: "There is a mad dog abroad once more, and we must resolutely combine either to ensure its destruction or at least its confinement until the disease has run its course."[12] After a lack of firmness and many concessions had indeed let the "mad dog" run wild, the *News Chronicle* concluded in late-March 1938: "even a novice must by now have begun to realize that the more you concede to the bullies of Europe the more they demand."[13] In late-spring 1939, Adrian Holman, First Secretary to the Berlin embassy, who dined with Oliver Harvey in mid-June, was convinced that "nothing less than firmness may stop war." Even one of the most prominent proponents of appeasement, Foreign Secretary Halifax, as early as the beginning of March 1938, had said: "The only thing they understand is force...a warning will be useless unless accompanied by a threat to use force."[14]

Perhaps most revealing were the views of the chief architect of appeasement, Neville Chamberlain, who regularly expressed the idea that firmness was the best policy. Chamberlain consistently saw Hitler as a bully who had to be stopped.

When Austrian Chancellor Dollfuss was murdered in 1934, Chamberlain wrote to his sister: "That those beasts should have got him at last and that they should have treated him with such callous brutality makes me hate Nazi-ism and all its works with a greater loathing than ever....I was glad to hear of Mussolini's movements of troops. It's the only thing Germans understand."

In March 1934 he wrote: "For the old aphorism 'Force is no remedy' I would substitute 'The Fear of Force is the only remedy;'" and in July: "we shall be more likely to deter Germany...if we have an air force."[15] One year later, as Mussolini invaded Abyssinia, he said: "If we and France together determined that we could stop him, we could do so, and quite easily." He wrote to sister Ida: "What I shall work for is a Britain strong enough to make it impossible for her wishes to be flouted as Mussolini's had flouted them now." He later confided to his diary that oil sanctions against Mussolini were needed, and told Hoare, "if necessary we ought to give the lead ourselves." Prophetically, he stated what would occur if Britain weakened: "It was inevitable that in such circumstances U.S.A. should decline in future to help us in any way, sanctions crumble, the League would lose its coherence, and our whole policy would be destroyed."[16]

Chamberlain's call for firmness was not merely rhetorical, but was followed by actions:

> He became the chief architect of the Defense White Papers of 1936 and 1937. This was a strange role for a Chancellor of the

> Exchequer to fill, but in fact he was acting more as Prime Minister designate. Taken together, these two White Papers envisaged for the Navy, the laying down of five new capital ships, an increase of twenty cruisers and four aircraft carriers and a steady replacement programme for destroyers and submarines; for the Army the raising of four new battalions of infantry, the modernization of equipment and the expansion of the T.A. for anti-aircraft defenses; and for the Air Force, a front line strength of 1,750 aircraft, exclusive of the Fleet Air Arm. In addition, the 1937 White Paper told of the steps being taken to build up war potential by the construction of 'shadow' aircraft factories and the extension of munitions plants, and also of the first local schemes of air raid precautions.[17]

After reading journalist Stephen Roberts's anti-Nazi book *The House that Hitler Built*, Chamberlain, despite his own conscious efforts to deny its somber message ("if I accepted the author's conclusions I should despair, but I don't and won't"), clearly understood the meaning of the book well enough to tell Eden: "If we couldn't reach agreement, we should have to go in for encirclement and perhaps have an arrangement with Russia."[18] Since at least March 1935 he had believed "Hitler's Germany is the bully of Europe."[19] Three years later he reiterated his conviction: "force is the only argument Germany understands," and believed "we must show our determination not to be bullied." When Austrian Chancellor Schuschnigg went to Germany to negotiate with Hitler over the fate of Austria, Chamberlain said, in late-February 1938, that "he was outrageously bullied by Hitler," and had to capitulate because "Mussolini gave him no support." After the seizure of Czechoslovakia in March 1939, Chamberlain told his cabinet: "if Germany showed signs that she intended to proceed with her march for world domination, we must take steps to stop her by attacking her on two fronts. We should attack Germany not in order to save a particular state, but in order to bring down the bully."[20]

Chamberlain's views were not only consistent, but he believed them to have been proven by experience. Unfounded rumors of German troop movements in May 1938 during the Czech Crisis had led to stern notes to Berlin from London and Paris. Hitler denied there had been any troop movements and in fact there had been none, but the world believed that Allied warnings had stopped him, a belief widely held by the British press and private individuals,[21] a view shared by Chamberlain: "I cannot doubt in my own mind," he wrote, "(1) that the German government made all preparations for a coup; (2) that in the end they decided, after getting our warnings, that the risks were too great."[22]

The British then, including the appeasers, understood Hitler's intentions. They saw him as a bully, often calling him that, and believed that he could be stopped by shows of force. Yet, they did not follow this path.

At the very moment the British were offering Hitler concessions, many people in Britain were proposing alternatives. There were calls for disarmament, but there were also repeated calls for collective security, either through the League of Nations or in a "Grand Alliance."[23] But at every turn, several British governments, sometimes not fully consciously, undermined disarmament,[24] sabotaged the League,[25] or acted in ways which made the other powers feel that Britain couldn't be trusted.[26] Chamberlain (and his Foreign Secretary Lord Halifax) defended themselves against their own conscious awareness of these things by projecting onto others the mistrust that British policy was itself creating—and that they were feeling in themselves—stating as "objective realities" that France, Russia, Germany, and the United States couldn't be trusted.[27]

Taken individually, each of these events can be rationalized away. Looked at collectively, they suggest a pattern of eroding options that were *made* to disappear. The British and French governments' persistent tendencies to overestimate German military strength reinforced the illusion that there was only one option—to cave in.[28] It was not the result of blunder, circumstance, miscalculation, or stupidity, but fit perfectly into the unconscious goals the British and French had set themselves. Could Hitler, in Harvey's words, have been "reigned in"? No one knows for certain because it was never tried.

As the "objective" reasons offered by historians to explain appeasement begin to look more like rationalizations, the evidence suggests that part of the policy of appeasement originated elsewhere, perhaps from hidden psychological needs, three in particular: first, the British need to re-experience early traumas of humiliation; second, the British need to experience aggressive impulses vicariously, by not owning up to their own sadism and identifying with Nazi sadism instead; and third, the need to construct scenarios which would allow them to eventually discharge pent-up aggression by going to war guilt free.

It needs to be remembered that the policy of appeasement had its rational side too. Consciously, the goal was to allow Hitler's demands to be fulfilled in Austria and Czechoslovakia but no farther, and by negotiation, not war. It made sense in a rational world of reasonable statesmen. But in a world of unacknowledged irrational fantasies, the extra stressors of the 1930s meant that these repressed motives—the needs to be humiliated, to vicariously experience their own aggression, and to create a clear conscience—were more compelling, and were acted out within the framework of that conscious, rational policy.

First there is the issue of humiliation.

Deep, massive, and widespread feelings of national humiliation clustered about the Czech Crisis and flooded Britain after Munich, but had been felt intensely by many before. In 1936, Harold Nicholson, particularly sensitive to feelings of humiliation, believed that the failure to stop the remilitarization of the Rhineland meant that the British would have to "swallow this humiliation as best we may, and be prepared to become the laughing stock of Europe."[29] A David Low cartoon from January 1938, before the

Anschluss, shows Britain, France, and the U.S. seated at a table at "Nemesis Restaurant" where a menacing figure, his face cloaked from view but with a nose like Hitler's, presents them with a Bill for not collectively facing up "to aggression when you had the chance." The "Bill" begins with Manchuria and Abyssinia, prophetically including Austria and Czechoslovakia. On the wall is framed "Today's Special: Humble Pie."[30]

When Eden, who opposed appeasement, resigned from Chamberlain's cabinet in February 1938, a member of parliament told the House that there was "joy all over the dictator countries," which made for a "terribly humiliating situation." After the *Anschluss* came the prediction that "Britain would soon find herself left to face the bully alone and to take the thrashing that our own cowardice will have well merited." When an Anglo-French proposal was later made to partition Czechoslovakia, three executive bodies of the Labor movement issued a joint statement calling it a "shameful surrender."[31]

During the Czech Crisis Chamberlain seemed almost driven to humiliate Britain and shame himself. By late August he had concocted on his own an unorthodox strategy: he would fly to Germany to meet Hitler face to face without first telling him he was coming. Called "Plan Z," it shocked even Halifax.[32] When Chamberlain later arranged a meeting through appropriate diplomatic channels and did fly to meet Hitler, a British journalist confided to his diary: "We have chosen a shameful peace and shall have a terrible war. If only we would have learned the lesson and pull ourselves together, put our industries on a war-basis and conscribe men and money. All would not be lost then. But we won't do it, we won't! Disaster is coming, hastened on by ourselves."[33]

Others felt equally humiliated. On 19 September Nicolson found Eden "in the depths of despair" and later in the day found James Pope-Hennessy at the Café Royal "almost in tears over England's shame." One day later General Ironside wrote in his diary: "To dismember Czechoslovakia can only be called 'Peace Without Honor.'" On 30 September Eleanor Rathbone wrote of the "agony and shame over the way in which the Czechs have been let down." Vansittart said that the Nazis "are criminals whose hands are still dripping with blood and who have just slapped our embarrassed face before the world." One English wit said that Chamberlain had "turned all four cheeks" to Hitler. On 3 October, as he defended his Munich Agreement in the House of Commons, Chamberlain's words were interrupted by cries of "Shame" from the floor. "I have nothing to be ashamed of," he said. "Let those who have, hang their heads." It failed to quiet Churchill, who found "the sense of our country falling into the power, into the orbit" of Hitler "unendurable." Clement Atlee's comment was equally pointed: "We have felt humiliation." This sense of dishonor caused some people to experience psychosomatic reactions such as insomnia, nausea, and vomiting. And the feelings persisted, Churchill saying in a speech late in 1938 that it "has been a year of disaster and humiliation the likes of which Great Britain has not known for many generations." Even when the war had come to a close some seven years later, Sir Orme Sargent still suffered from disquieting feelings when he thought of these earlier humiliations.[34]

Shame and humiliation can be followed in Harvey's diary. Some days after the Munich Agreement: "Miss Maxse dined here....She is horrified at the loss of prestige of Great Britain and the potential consequences of this surrender." Lord Tyrrell felt "the shame of Munich was due to past policy over years; at the time itself there was no alternative." For Harvey himself, "my first reaction is one of relief....But many feel it to be a great humiliation." Even Halifax told him "it was a horrid business and humiliating." As with Churchill, feelings did not pass with time. In November 1938 Harvey wrote: "Every scrap of information, secret and public, we get from Germany now shows that the German

Government are laughing at us, despising us and intending to dispossess us morally and materially from our world position."[35]

Understanding what the British were feeling (while hinting at what might lie behind it), was a syndicated cartoon by Cargill seen by Americans in their local newspapers on 23 September 1938. Labeled "Bull's Eye," it shows Hitler and Mussolini throwing balls at a face of John Bull in the middle of a map of Europe. Wearing a hat called "British Prestige," with stars shooting from his head, John Bull has apparently been hit by many balls. As Mussolini prepares to throw another, he turns to Hitler and says: "Hit 'im again! He loves it!"[36]

So the British and Chamberlain, who had experienced the dictators as bullies and predicted what they would do and what to do to stop them, nevertheless helped arrange an international environment which brought about their own humiliation. Leaving aside political, economic, and strategic factors for the moment, it can be argued that this was not "accidental," not an unforeseen consequence of the appeasement policy, which the British felt they had to endure in the name of peace, but, like events in a pathological family system, was an unconsciously arranged event.

It is a familiar notion in psychological history that groups as well as individuals may at times feel compelled to relive original traumas. Why this is so is somewhat obscure. That it takes place has been frequently observed in clinical settings over the last thirty years, reconfirming the findings of many earlier clinicians. Research into trauma has been extensive, has been encouraged by groups such as the Society for the Study of Traumatic Stress, and has been publicized by books such as Judith Herman's *Trauma and Recovery*, and the writings of psychologist Bessel van der Kolk. This research confirms that traumas are profound; that they happen to many people; that they can be produced by a variety of searing events; that people don't always get over them easily; and that for some individuals and groups there is a tendency, even a compulsion, to arrange events so that the original trauma can be relived. It has been discovered that traumas are re-enacted in one of three ways: by exactly re-creating the original trauma; by turning it about 180 degrees, victim becoming victimizer; and, lastly, by re-experiencing it in disguised and symbolic ways. It is clear that the traumatic victim arranges, or seeks out, settings and circumstances that allow or might allow the trauma to be re-enacted. The importance of trauma and the compulsion to relive are not always appreciated by non-psychological historians, but they are recognized by scholars like historian and psychoanalyst Peter Loewenberg who has said: "The evidence is clear: Given a large enough social or collective traumatic event, no one escapes a post-traumatic stress disorder....The symptoms are life-long. No one is immune. Massive trauma is a crucial bridge to history...the theoretical link from individual to group, cohort, population, nation, the world." Among historians, the pioneering scholar on trauma and traumatic reliving is Rudolph Binion, who has shown since the late-1960s how the unconscious inner compulsions of individuals and groups have recreated individual and collective traumas with dramatic and sometimes far-reaching historical consequences.[37]

Because of these observable behaviors among large numbers of Britons in the 1930s, it is possible to argue that the need to re-experience humiliation was an essential emotional goal of appeasement. Whenever they capitulated, they felt humiliated. The process possibly—perhaps very probably—was rooted in their childhood experiences. Studies have shown that despite many cases of devoted, loving parents, there are enough examples of spankings and whippings, cruelties and punishments, distancing and emotional snubbing, sexual assaults, denials of feelings, and the instilling of terrors to provide an ample basis for the storing of repressed traumas which could be stirred up later and acted out under the stresses of adult life. In the first instance, nearly every upper class and upper-middle class Briton experienced a particular very early, very deep narcissistic wounding: abandonment to a nanny.

"For surely it had been an army, a great host of Nannies," writes their historian Gathorne-Hardy, "that had swept Britain sometime in the nineteenth and early twentieth centuries engulfing not just the aristocracy and upper ranks of society, but reaching far down into the middle classes as well." "How was it," he wonders, "that hundreds of thousands of mothers, apparently normal, could simply abandon all loving and disciplining and company of their little children, sometimes almost from birth, to this absolute care of other women, total strangers, nearly always uneducated, about whose characters they must usually have had no real idea at all?"[38] Gathorne-Hardy leaves open the question, but further evidence clarifies the issue of what this did to their children.

Churchill, it is well known, consciously loved his nanny. "It was with his nanny," says biographer Martin Gilbert, "that he found the affection which his parents did not provide." Chamberlain consciously loved his nanny too,[39] a sentiment which must have reverberated through the hearts and minds of thousands upon thousands of leaders of opinion and education, in industry, politics, and the Foreign Office who likewise had been given over to hundreds of thousands of nursemaids, nannies, and governesses. Yet along with love came a host of other feelings, towards nannies and mommies, including rage at being abandoned, which, in the proscribed environment of the Victorian era, had to be repressed and was turned against the self. It is often the case that abandoned children (or children who feel emotionally abandoned) blame their fate on their own "badness" and tend to feel that they deserve to be punished in some way.

When many are traumatized, society may institutionalize that trauma by creating ritual structures allowing it to be passed on and re-experienced. For humiliation, that ritual was the British public school, itself a second abandonment and a place where the repressed rage was both turned against the self and sadistically acted out against others.

These schools, attended by Britain's future decision and opinion makers, were characterized by violence. Until near the end of the nineteenth century, when reform began softening practices, "there was a terrible amount of flogging," a fact confirmed by many testimonials and the research of John Chandos.[40] Boys were regularly beaten for the slightest infractions: two to fifty lashes on the back or buttocks, and whippings which left their backs raw and bloody were considered "normal." Parents were "remarkably indifferent," or "resigned to their son's sufferings at school." Some boys came to "enjoy" the floggings, which were sometimes sexualized by Headmasters and students. The sado-masochism built into floggings was reinforced by the perpetual violence inflicted by boys on boys. There was the "initiation ceremonies of boys running the gauntlet between rows of executioners armed with knotted handkerchiefs, or of having to endure being stoned with rolls packed as hard as pebbles." There was the "tin glove" ritual in which boys' hands were seared with "hot ends" or burning wood, to which "every junior was submitted." One former student remembered: "I kicked and struggled....But I was captured and my hand held fast and I can still recall the grinding thrill of pain as the glowing wood was pressed upon it by the ministering fiend. It was the prologue to the continuous barbarity which was to walk up and down with me."[41] The "tin glove" barbarity was common, boys sometimes having to wear kid gloves long after it had been administered. It existed on top of the ritual kicking and pinching and being forced to drink muddy water, outgrowths of the regular daily bullying. Boys were also exposed to homosexuality, forced on them by Masters and Tutors, and by the older boys who gave the younger ones feminine names and used them as their "bitches."[42] Especially, there was the system of "fagging" in which the younger boys became the older boys' "slaves:" they were ordered about and waited on their masters hand and foot. According to one authority on the practice, "the big boys had a subject race in the persons of the small boys. It was a self-propagating license to bully; the young boys when they got into the sixth form (the fifth form at Eton) revenged themselves on the quivering newcomers."[43] One early critic, whose school-day memories were "hateful" and "agonizing" and had driven him to " bad dreams," said that boys who began as slaves likely ended up as tyrants. Nor were all of these experiences confined to elite institutions. "The minor public schools did their best to emulate the Etons and the Harrows, and at the schools for the poor the boys were starved and bullied into subjection."[44] Out of these experiences came the repressed need to re-experience traumas of humiliation, which came to permeate British society from top to bottom.

The impulse to encourage Hitler's aggression was stimulated by a second psychological need. Anger, one of the "negative" emotions not so easily expressed in Victorian England, had to be repressed. Maintaining a positive self-image decreed that aggressive impulses had to be denied; yet the damage experienced in childhood was so great that turning anger against the self in masochistic ways channeled only part of it. Through Hitler's aggression, Britons could encounter the repressed, split-off, and projected aggression in themselves, using Nazi Germany and Hitler as projective containers. The British could thus vicariously experience their own aggression while denying it.

Nazi sadism was real, was really "out there," and was well understood, the *Liverpool Daily Post*, for example, calling the threat to Czechoslovakia "repellently mean and sadistic."[45] Apparently, what consciously repelled could also for some secretly attract, and while consciously denied, it was their own sadism in Hitler that helped many Britons, whose patriotism was beyond reproach, hold him in high esteem in the 1930s. Recalling in a private letter in December 1937 his visit to Hitler in 1936, Lloyd George thought of him as "the great Leader of a great people," saying, "I only wish we had a man of his supreme quality at the head of affairs in our country today." Prominent pacifist George Lansbury believed in 1937 that Hitler had "saved Germany." G. Ward Price's 1937 book *I Know These Dictators* stated how Hitler's "fondness for children and dogs" was "evidence of {his} good nature;" Price called attention to Hitler's bringing "public order, political peace, more work, better living conditions, and the promise, since fulfilled, to make Germany once more a great nation." For Lord Londonderry in 1938, Hitler had "restored national pride and self-respect;" he was both "example" and "inspiration." Admiration came even from Hitler's critics: he had "performed...superb toils," ruled a Germany he had "raised from the dust," was a "highly competent, cool, well-informed" person, one "with an agreeable manner, a disarming smile, and...a subtle personal magnetism"—words Winston Churchill wrote in 1935 which he must have later come to regret.[46]

Among these judgments were some "rational" or "understandable" reasons why Britons came to admire Hitler and Nazism. There was Nazism's authoritarianism, its "law and order" message, its presumed "efficiency," and other "escape-from-freedom" characteristics.[47] Hitler, it was believed, had "revitalized" Germany. Then, too, Russian espionage had been hard at work in the interwar years, and Nazi Germany seemed to stand as a bulwark against Bolshevism. But there was more to it, something "psychological."

Hitler was imagined as a man possessed of enormous power and strength, things the British consciously and unconsciously wanted to feel for themselves, which, given the economic "impotence" of the Great Depression and the feelings of powerlessness produced by their own policies, was more of an imperative than ever. To Wyndam Lewis in 1931, Hitler was "the expression of current German manhood—resolved with...hardihood...to seize the big bull...by the horns." Power ran from Hitler through the whole Nazi state. Sir Arnold Wilson told the nation over the BBC on 8 May 1934 how "German youth," had been filled with "energy and...enthusiasm," how they had unleashed "great dynamic forces." "The German nation," said Lord Winterton to the House of Commons a year later, "possesses...a mental and physical...virility and determination... seldom exceeded in the world's history." How far the British had come to idealize Hitler, even among those who opposed him, is suggested by Eden's shock upon meeting him for the first time: he was "smaller and slighter than I had expected from his photographs,"[48] so large had Hitler loomed in fantasy.

There could be vicarious thrills for Britons even in voicing denials: "such phrases as 'the Germans are so like us'...is untrue," wrote Sir Horace Rumbold in 1936. "Germans have a streak of brutality...quite absent in the ordinary Englishman"[49] (surely debatable from the standpoint of Irish history or the histories of any of the colonial peoples). In reality, Nazism attracted sadistic, murdering thugs, and it was the responsibility of the British press to alert their readers to this danger. That is perhaps why it is so shocking to read the words of Geoffrey Dawson, the editor of the London *Times*, who could not understand why the Germans were so angry with his newspaper. As he wrote in a private letter in 1937: "I spend my nights taking out anything which I think will hurt their susceptibilities and in dropping in little things which are intended to sooth them." It was up to other newspapers, such as the *Manchester Guardian*, to responsibly run stories containing graphic descriptions of Gestapo tortures. Those stories and descriptions doubtless shocked and repelled many good Britons, even though some other readers who consciously and unconsciously identified with the Nazis (or their victims) must have been secretly thrilled. Germany was a real threat; British policy helped make it a greater one. As historian A.L. Rowse later said: "We were doing Hitler's work for him."[50] Millions liked what they saw, and could participate in Nazi militarism and Hitler's arrogance by proxy while denying (if they had to) the imperial contempt they felt for the "inferior races" of their own far-flung empire.

Yet the British were not merely sadists, or masochists occasionally compelled to act out a humiliation or two. They had "good enough" parenting, and could be, and were, honorable, hardworking, kindly, just, caring and charitable people, empathic enough to root for the underdog. But "good enough" parenting also meant that they would be people of conscience in whom aggressive impulses—even experiencing them second hand through the Nazis—could stir uncomfortable feelings of guilt. The British could identify with Hitler but still be ambivalent about both their impulses and their government's policies.

That the British had a collective conscience, that is, were not mere sadists, helps account for what some historians have found to be a prominent theme during the period—that the "British soul" was at war with itself. They have used words on the order of "schizophrenic" or "ambivalent" to describe it.[51] People like Lord Rothermere, for example, owner of the *Daily Mail*, symbolized this generalized ambivalence. He was: "an erratic amateur politician who was both pro-and anti-German at once, a vocal apologist for Nazism, and a strident alarmist in the campaign for rearmament."[52] Such ambivalence was projected into journalistic accounts of the Nazi state, which tended to "range between a gruesome picture of butterless woe and non-stop jamboree" and could be symbolically enacted by whole families when they split over British policy, Duff Cooper mentioning that among his own circle of acquaintances alone, twelve couples were at odds over the Munich Agreement.[53]

It is not surprising that without resolution—as the stresses of normal, everyday life mingled with the stresses of international crises and the repressed feelings trying to push their way into consciousness—everything for the British was beginning to seem intolerable. Vicarious enjoyment wasn't enough. Their need to discharge aggression, and associated feelings, became ever more imperative and manifested itself in a disguised "wish" for war.

Few openly said that war was wanted, and although many people did not want war, even for many of the ambivalent, the growing sense that war was inevitable was in part an open expression of an unconscious desire. The psychological principle here is: "the fear is the wish." That is, the repressed and denied desire is turned around and defensively experienced as a fear. This is not the case for everybody at all times, but for some people some of the time. And, of course, feeling that war is inevitable does not mean that it *is* inevitable. Yet such feelings not only reflect sentiment but, as would be the case with fear, help create the tone, the mood in which people live, work, and think.

The sense of inevitability appeared in the British press, circulated in government memos, showed up in private thoughts confided to diaries, and, even as he tried to deny the possibility, in the phrase "inevitability of war" so often used by Chamberlain in his public addresses. One time at least he seems to have come close to disclosing the hidden connection, the "suicidal embrace," between Britain and Nazi Germany when he wrote in November 1938 to his sister Ida "there really did seem to be a kind of predestined course to Anglo-German relations."[54] The British sense of inevitability was noticed by German diplomats, obliged like all diplomats on station to gauge the climate of opinion, who then wrote home about it. Foreign journalists sensed it was a general feeling throughout the country.[55] The British Foreign Office seems to have become resigned to the idea. Halifax, as revealed by minutes from his Foreign Policy

Committee meetings, made the notion of inevitability part of his either/or thinking.[56] Novelists naturally picked up, reinforced, and circulated the idea. "War is coming. 1941, they say," Orwell wrote in his 1939 novel *Coming Up for Air*, both the inevitability of war and the likelihood of air attack appearing obsessively throughout his story. Meanwhile, the hero of Eric Ambler's 1938 thriller *Epitaph for a Spy* mused: "It would be good now, I thought, to be in Paris. There you could listen to the rustle of leaves unconscious of the pains of humanity in labor, of a civilization hastening to destruction. There, away from this brassy sea and blood-red earth, you could contemplate the twentieth-century tragedy unmoved: unmoved except by pity for mankind fighting to save itself from the primeval ooze that welled from its own unconscious being."[57] Popular 1939 films such as *Gunga Din* and *The Four Feathers* captured and reinforced the war mood by glorifying sacrifice, Empire, and the British military past, while H.G. Wells's novel *The Shape of Things to Come* (1933) and its film version *Things to Come* (1936) predicted a civilization-ending war by 1940.

The inevitability of war, identification with Nazi strength and sadism, and the need to re-experience childhood traumas of humiliation were all driving forces, which contributed to the ill-advised appeasement policy, indeed, giving it its compelling emotional energy. If only the British (like the suicidal patient in or out of treatment) could have consciously felt and recognized these things for what they were rather than denying and repressing them, they would have been far better off, more rational, and less likely to act them out. It seems that humiliation especially maintained its hold over them in the 1930s. For those who find this unconvincing, it is well to remember the consensus among historians on the role that humiliation played for the Germans—their 1918 defeat, the dictated Treaty of Versailles, and the French occupation of the Ruhr which are normally seen as major reasons for Hitler's rise to power and Germany's later aggression. If humiliation was an important motivator for Germans, why couldn't it be for Britons as well? Hitler, Nazis, and Germans served to contain and reflect Britain's feelings of aggression, while the British served reciprocally as container and mirror for the German's own partly projected feelings of humiliation. British rage, stirred by childhood victimizations and the humiliations of their own current making, pressed for release. The difference was Germany's conscious intent versus Britain's unconscious intent, but that is another matter.

The pressing need to discharge repressed aggression led the British in 1938 and 1939 to project their feelings onto the world, which led them to believe in several utterly groundless rumors of war.[58] Historian T. Desmond Williams proposed that even as early as 1938 the attitude of the Foreign Office was a kind of self-fulfilling prophecy, since "the Foreign Office had proved itself right in so far as its own policy was partly responsible for Hitler's decision to go to war after Poland in 1939."[59] Exactly how deep and sweeping these unconscious wishes were is suggested by voting patterns in Parliament where, even though the opposition nearly always outnumbered the government (due to the disaffection of dissident conservatives), and where vocal opposition to appeasement had been frequent and articulate, nearly every time votes in favor of appeasement were called, the government won by large majorities despite its numerical disadvantage.[60]

These unconscious wishes for war could be felt and acted out most comfortably only if the British conscience was assuaged. This meant arranging sufficiently convincing scenarios to assure themselves and the world that they, in fact, were blameless. And the British were quite open about how important this was.

As early as 16 September 1936 a *Manchester Guardian* leader called for a diplomatic offer to Germany which, even if it "failed to avert a war...would at least free many men and women in England from the feeling that when war comes, they may be as guilty as those whom they are sent to kill." As Henderson put it privately to Halifax: "our moral case must be copper-bottomed."[61] Harvey said: "We shall only get the British public to give their best and to fight on a moral issue." Lord Tyrrell spoke of "the vital importance of keeping our issue with the Nazis on a moral plane."[62] At another time Henderson said to Halifax that the government must keep up illusions: "HMG cannot go so far as to wash their hands of Austrians and Sudetendeutschen; that would look too cynical and immoral." Cadogan wrote in his diary, "we must have a moral position," and confided that: "We must go on being cowards up to our limit, but *not beyond*." Duff Cooper wrote to Halifax that the U.S. could be brought in to fight for Britain only "<u>on one condition</u>: It must be an ideological war—a war based on moral principle."[63] Halifax agreed. But some of this was a bit of self-deception on his part, for it was not only the United States that needed to be calmed by moral principle, his biographer noting that his "nature and experience were such that the only war supportable to him was a Holy War." Apparently, by 1 September 1939 he had convinced himself: Britain's conscience was clear, he told the House of Lords.[64]

Chamberlain too, was convinced—and convincing. In an 11:15 A.M., 3 September 1939, radio broadcast, he told his country: "We have a clear conscience, we have done all that any country could do to establish peace." Two days before the radio address he had told the House of Commons: "We shall stand at the bar of history knowing that the responsibility of this terrible catastrophy lies on the shoulders of one man, the German Chancellor." On 10 September he wrote to his sisters: "My persistent efforts have convinced the world that no part of the blame can lie here."[65] By 2 September, all the British papers were agreed: it was Hitler's war. As Churchill said to the House of Commons the next day: "Our hands may be active, but our consciences are at rest."[66] Appeasement had seen to it.

In that process, Hitler had been used, psychologically, in another way.

With long term stressors pushing repressed material into consciousness, many Britons sensed that their own intra-psychic defenses were crumbling. "I can see the war that's coming," wrote Orwell in *Coming Up for Air*. "There are millions of others like me....They can feel things cracking and collapsing under their feet." The frequent use of images like these is an important indicator of stress, some psychological historians have argued, since cracking and collapsing images, along with metaphors of tidal waves, earthquakes and volcanic eruptions, signify in symbolic form the actual partial collapse (or fear of collapse) of intra-psychic defenses. When these images appear with frequency, or begin to cluster at certain times, they show (or may show) that repressed feelings are flooding (or are threatening to flood) consciousness. While the sources contain many more regressed images of devouring monsters than volcanic eruptions, there may be something to this. A Chamberlain biographer notes in passing how his references to volcanoes began to increase in 1939, and Chamberlain may not have been the only Briton—or European—feeling this way. The possible eruption of a war could surely feel like a seismic disturbance, and that is precisely why people were projecting a sense of their own disintegrating defenses into it. With disintegrating defenses—symbolized by such things as the title of journalist G.R.E. Gedye's popular 1939 book *Fallen Bastions*—Britons began experiencing strange, frightening, and uncomfortable new feelings.They thought they were going "crazy." "England is a lunatic asylum," said journalist Douglas Reed in his 1939 best seller *Disgrace Abounding*. Reed had already declared all of Europe *Insanity Fair* in an earlier book, the title of which struck such a responsive symbolic chord with the public that it helped catapult the book through thirty-six impressions between April and December 1938. The London

Times chimed in by saying that humanity was "heading for the madhouse," the *Daily Herald* spoke of "the crazy state of the World," and Churchill thought "the whole equilibrium of Europe has been deranged."[67]

The British sought ways to escape these feelings by projecting them not only onto the world in general, but into Hitler, a convenient container for Europe's own feelings of "craziness." In late-January 1939, H.G. Wells wrote in the *News Chronicle* that "Hitler is a certifiable lunatic who should be put away." Harvey had heard that Hitler had "spoken like a madman," a judgment shared by Chamberlain's Cabinet, many members of which had often spoken of Hitler as "the mad Chancellor." Chamberlain used the out-of-control Hitler in the same way, speaking of him as early as 1938 as "half mad' and a "lunatic."[68] Hitler could certainly act irrationally, and often appeared to be out of control, which made it all the easier for people to use him in these ways. Like the pathological couple described by Grotjahn, with Hitler certifiably crazy, the British could feel sane.

In mid-July 1939 the Cardiff *Western Mail* perfectly summed up several of the unconscious processes and fantasies which had been at work in British minds in the late-1930s: "We shall be forced...to arrest this madness sooner or later," it said, "and having tried all methods of appeasement in vain, we had better arrest it now before we lose our allies and are weakened by further humiliating concessions to a ravenous and insatiable Power." Madness, humiliation, powerlessness, capitulation, guilt-free resistance, and devouring monsters were all there, wrapped up in one neat package. Just a year earlier, when it seemed as if the Czech Crisis could not be solved by peaceful means, Ivone Kirkpatrick left Hitler expecting war: "I felt an overwhelming sense of relief that war would come," he said. "In the Embassy the feeling was the same."[69]

The Munich capitulation meant no relief that year, but the British promise to protect Poland's frontiers made in late-March 1939 promised relief by a guilt-free war sometime in the near future. The decision to guarantee Poland's frontiers, writes its historian, had itself been "made in an atmosphere of panic, humiliation, and moral hysteria. A frantic urgency to do something—anything—replaced a calm consideration of alternatives." When the guarantee was announced it was "received almost joyfully by much of the British press."[70] When German troops marched into Poland, relief was in sight.

But Chamberlain still prevaricated, and when it appeared on 1 September that he would capitulate once more, his Cabinet and Parliament were flooded with emotions. They were "aghast." They were filled with "bewildered rage." When his temporizing at last came to an end, but before the ultimatum he eventually agreed to was finally sent, an illuminating exchange took place between a member of Parliament and Halifax. Asked, "Foreign Secretary, can you give me any hope?" Halifax replied: "If you mean hope of a war, I think I can promise you a certainty for tomorrow." His interrogator answered: "Thank God." Halifax later revealed his own relief that Hitler had not come up with any last minute "terms."[71]

It must be remembered that these emotional strivings took place in the context of an external world where economic factors, strategic realities, and political considerations mattered very much. The British, and all the powers, were not operating on unconscious and irrational levels at all times, but only some of the time, and it needs to be said that the appeasement policy was not infinitely open-ended. The conscious, rationalized goal was to allow Hitler to take Austria and the German-speaking part of Czechoslovakia, but no more, and by negotiation, never war. This may have made sense if Hitler was a responsible, rational statesman. It is just that for his own intra-psychic reasons, and for Germany's emotional needs, he was bent on territorial expansion, and worked toward the goal of an eventual war no matter what the Allies gave him. It is easy to lose sight of these external facts when the focus, as in this study, is on inner feelings and fantasies. Yet it must also be remembered that the British well knew what Hitler was planning and knew exactly what would stop him, imagining all the while that he would respond rationally to reasonable offers while calling him "insane," "a lunatic," and "the mad chancellor."

Hitler was the central cause; he had gotten the war he consciously wanted. But the British too were satisfied; they had gotten a war they unconsciously wanted. It would allow them to discharge their own aggressive feelings after a series of humiliating capitulations, which had been driven by an unconscious need to relive earlier childhood humiliations. This aggression could be unleashed with a certainty now that right and justice were on their side. On the conscious level, there was fear, anger, and resignation. There was also a sense of relief. The British adopted a business-like tone of "let's get this over with." When the killing finally began, with bad, aggressive, and crazy feelings safely harnessed in the sadistic and violent Hitler, Churchill could tell the House of Commons: "Outside, the storms of war may blow and the lands may be lashed with the fury of its gales, but in our own hearts this Sunday morning there is peace."[72] Neville Chamberlain, the architect of appeasement, had seen to it.

IV CHAMBERLAIN AND BRITAIN

WE...HAD COME TO A STAGE WHEN...
FANTASY BECOMES A COMPULSION TO SUICIDE....
OUR SUICIDAL IMPETUS {WAS} NEVILLE CHAMBERLAIN.[1]
—*Rebecca West*, 1940

Neville Chamberlain said, "half a dozen people could take my place while war was in progress," and was being perhaps more accurate than he knew when he said that it had been different before the war, for then "I was indispensable, for no one else could carry out my policy."[2]

This may reveal a certain arrogance, a trait in Chamberlain's character remarked upon by many observers, but by temperament, inclination, and personal unconscious agenda, Chamberlain possessed to an uncanny degree the necessary prerequisites to fulfill Britain's collective, unconscious wishes. This was sensed by the Soviet ambassador who believed Chamberlain saw himself as a man called "to fulfill a sacred mission."[3] Anyone could run a war; he was one of the few who could serve one up guilt-free.

In this activity, Chamberlain served Britain as its group-fantasy delegate, a concept familiar to psychological historians. The notion of leader-as-delegate comes from family therapy and has been applied to the U.S. presidency.[4] Leaders, like members of a family, can be assigned unconscious tasks as their group's delegate, which can then be acted out. How groups call forth the particular leaders they unconsciously need at particular moments remains unclear—indeed, may never be fully understood—but it seems to have something to do with the leader's adult personality and unconscious agendas, both formed, in part, during childhood.

Little is known about the first six years of Chamberlain's life. His first official biographer, Keith Feiling, gives hints of closeness with Mother, of "dim memories of a sea holiday" he shared with her in Wales, of "a locket she wore," and of "a few of her books" he later inherited.[5] There was a nanny, and, apparently, later "governesses...shared" with other family members.[6]

His childhood included two siblings from his father's first marriage—Beatrice and Austen, seven and six years his senior—and, eventually, three younger sisters—Ida, Hilda, and Ethel, one, three, and four-and-a-half years his junior. It is difficult to judge how much nurture he got from his mother. He did have to "share" her with the other children; and, of course, there was the nanny. He was, on the other hand, his mother's first born and only son, and indirect evidence suggests he was able to bond and love: he later married, had two children, was photographed smiling in 1937 holding his grandson, and once dismissed a candidate to be his child's governess on the grounds that she "lacked tenderness."[7] At the same time, failure to bond sufficiently is suggested by his living with his father and stepmother until he was forty-two. One historian notes that a recent biographer's "idyllic descriptions of Chamberlain's close-knit family life do not fully harmonize with Mrs. Chamberlain's depressions and nervous breakdown, nor with the fact that...{the} children often never saw their parents from one week's end to another."[8]

Early care was compromised by the birth of three siblings in succession, which, along with the general emotional distancing of nineteenth-century British child rearing, suggest deeper wounds than the typical narcissistic damage accompanying normal growing up. The "loss" of maternal love was painfully reinforced by a major trauma at age six: the death of his mother in childbirth. His earliest reported memory was of an aunt "coming to tell him he would never see his mother again."[9]

Mother's death was augmented by his grandmother's death in the same year, and by his father's emotional distancing.

"Twice widowed within twelve years before he was forty," writes Feiling, Joseph "encased himself in outward armor, grimly finished off his mayoralty, in 1876 entered Parliament {and} buried himself under tides of work." Joseph was unable to handle his own grief, and couldn't help his children with theirs: he never mentioned the death of his first wife until Neville's half-brother Austen was twenty-five years old "and even now I can't do it without the tears coming into my eyes," he said. After the death of Neville's mother, he told a friend: "no one has a right to be happy in this brutal world," saying to another, there was only one way to handle it, "to work constantly and not to think." One of Joseph's biographers adds that by distancing himself he "retarded the emotional growth of the children."[10]

Abandoned by mother and father in a little over a year and a half the not yet eight-year-old Neville was abandoned again to boarding school, which he came to hate. Children in such circumstances not only repress rage, but can turn it against themselves, blaming their own "badness" for what has happened to them.

It was his father's youngest sisters Caroline and Clara who were chosen by Joseph to care for his children. Both were ill-suited maternal surrogates. Neville "always remembered" his aunt's welcoming words on his first homecoming from boarding school. Throwing himself ecstatically into her arms, he heard her say: "Neville, your cap's crooked," and resolved never to kiss her again.[11]

Except for the admiring younger sisters with whom he maintained a life-long correspondence—and to whom he poured out his soul in later letters—it seems unlikely that he could have found as much love as he needed in his family. How Joseph treated him before his second wife's death is not known, but his son's adult recollection focused on his father's "piercing eye" which, he judged, "few could face... with comfort." Summarizing their relationship, he recalled how "for a good many years I respected and feared him more than I loved him."[12]

Death, distancing, abandonment, love enjoyed then lost, the inability to express feelings, powerful repression, and anger directed against the self were all parts of Chamberlain's personality, complicated and reinforced by the brutalities and humiliations—like those of other Britons—accompanying his years at public school, where, his biographers note, he was "badly bullied as a boy."[13] These were some of the reasons why he was compelled to arrange for Britons to be humiliated, and put himself in a position to be badly bullied by the Germans "who are," he said, "bullies by nature."[14]

His deference and self-deprecation—he never felt worthy of office and always had to be "called"[15]—reflect poor self-esteem and suggest displaced and repressed rage. This intensified with his father's distancing and clear preference for older son Austen—Neville's half-brother and major sibling rival[16]—who was being groomed for a political career in England while Neville was forced to spend his early twenties in heroic efforts to save a failing sisal plantation in the Bahamas. Joseph took responsibility for having sent Neville into that impossible situation; but, in typical masochistic fashion, Neville blamed himself.[17]

As an adult he remained emotionally withdrawn. When his father remarried, his new stepmother reproached him for being too unsociable. In letters he often reproached himself for his "accursed shyness" as a boy, and it is startling to hear those who knew him as an adult say he was even more reserved than his repressed contemporaries.[18] He loathed displays of emotion in public, frequently denounced British sentimentality and could not allow private feeling even into his diary. He "could not commit introspection to paper, and when he did so during an unhappy time, he later cut out the page." He was rarely able to establish affectionate bonds, but "was capable of intensive and malicious hatred of despised enemies." He used his wife as a target of anger, letters to her being filled with bitter criticisms.[19]

While some anger could be displaced and sometimes expressed, other feelings were deeply repressed and would have to be acted out. In domestic politics, Chamberlain savaged his opponents, the masochistic side of his sadism driving him to willfully seek their bitter retorts. Unlike his predecessor Stanley Baldwin, whose toned down style was the result of his willingness to respect the feelings and dignity of the opposition, Chamberlain employed "a fierce parliamentary debating style" in which "the logic, responsibility and intelligence of opposing members was mercilessly attacked." Baldwin had told him as early as 1932—Chamberlain himself later revealed—that whenever "I spoke in the House of Commons…I looked upon the Labour party as dirt." In his diary he wrote: "They are dirt." As early as 5 March 1937 Anthony Eden regretted Chamberlain's tactics, fearing that when he "became Prime Minister affairs would go less smoothly in the country than with Baldwin" because he "would not be able to resist scoring off the opposition."[20]

Historians have judged that Chamberlain had "an extremely obstinate nature which refused to change." Throughout the period of appeasement, as criticisms against his policies increased, he clung "even more tenaciously and stubbornly to his original course."[21] Summing up several studies, historian Alan Beattie concluded:

> Unlike Baldwin, Chamberlain as Prime Minister was unshielded from his critics. His willingness to commit himself personally and unreservedly to the policy of appeasement inevitably gave rise to an over-simplified identification of the Prime Minister with the major issues of the day. In Cabinet and in Parliament he constantly rejected the arbitrational role, which had been an important source of Baldwin's relative anonymity and immunity from attack. The replacement of Eden by Halifax as Foreign Secretary in February 1938 meant that…Chamberlain was thus obliged (and was the reverse of unwilling) to bear the major burden of parliamentary defense.[22]

After that, when diplomacy was moved from the Foreign Policy Committee of his cabinet into his own hands, he became even more vulnerable to attack. It is hard to avoid the judgment that "Chamberlain's political isolation was a problem of his own making."[23]

His isolation from parliament, cabinet, and Foreign Office meant he could be easily blamed for anything and everything that went awry, a role his masochism welcomed. Yet serving as eventual group-scapegoat was only one reason for his isolation: acting alone allowed people to imagine him as a kind of dictator, the British Adolf Hitler.

The words "dictator" and "dictatorship" were applied to Chamberlain several times in Harvey's diary, as in October 1938 when he predicted that Chamberlain "will resist widening the Government to the uttermost, as it will spell the end of his own dictatorship." Speaking of Chamberlain, Lord Londondery wrote to Halifax in August 1939 that: "From 1931 he has always made mistakes, and as the 'Dictator' of our Administration from that time he is responsible for all our troubles." His half-brother Austen had identified with dictators while Foreign Minister in the 1920s praising Mussolini, which led Harvey and Eden to believe that admiration for dictators ran in the family.[24]

The identification with Nazi Germany went public, only sometimes disapprovingly, as when Douglas Reed wrote: "The *Times* said that at Munich, 'Mr. Chamberlain had given the first example of the Führerprinzip…as applied to British policy.'"[25] The notion was reinforced with the publication in February 1939 of J.R.E. Gedye's *Fallen Bastions*, "probably the most influential journalist's book of the 1930s," which meant to be critical when it called him "Gauleiter Chamberlain" and "Führer Chamberlain."[26] That he might have secretly enjoyed these fantasies himself is hard to believe, although he did write to his sister that on his way to meeting Hitler at Berchtesgaden "I felt quite fresh and was delighted with the enthusiastic welcome of the crowds who were waiting in the rain, and who gave me the Nazi salute and shouted 'heil' at the top of their voices."[27]

It seems likely that Chamberlain's appeasement policy was driven by another half-conscious personal motive as well: his wish to be like his father, and, in his own mind, win his father's love by being like and maybe outdoing the favored sibling-rival, half-brother Austen. Both Joseph and Austen had earlier worked to reach accommodations with Germany, the father as Colonial Secretary in the 1890s, Austen as Foreign Secretary in the 1920s. Indeed, it had been Austen who frequently applied the word "appeasement" to diplomacy. And to make competitive matters worse, Austen had won the Nobel Prize. Through appeasement with Germany, Neville could imaginatively become both his father and his brother, and could out-Austen Austen.

It seems that at least one more personal motive may have played some part in forming his championing of appeasement and appeasement's eventual "inevitable" outcome in war. There is evidence to suggest that he likely harbored an unconscious wish for Germans to die in order to avenge the death of his cousin Norman.

Both Neville and Norman had served together on the Birmingham City Council during World War I, the younger man looking up to Neville as guide and mentor, saying that Neville "roused in me all the sensations of a willing and enthusiastic follower." He, in turn, described Norman as "the most intimate friend I had."[28] Both were separated when Norman entered the army and Neville was called to national government as Minister of National Service, which meant that Neville was responsible for seeing to it that conscription moved along smoothly. They were separated again when Norman went off to fight on the continent. They were separated forever when he was killed on the Western Front.

Chamberlain was devastated. His cousin's death affected him "even more deeply than his own father's death had done." It compromised his immune system. He fell ill with "chicken-pox, gout, sciatica, and then gout again." He wrote in his diary: "Somehow I had always associated Norman with anything I might do in the future. He was like a brother to me." One wonders if he was suffering from survival guilt when he wrote: "His life was devoted to others, and I feel a despicable thing beside him." Deeply depressed, he visited France in order to stand beside his cousin's grave. Later, trying to work through his loss, he produced a privately published laudatory biography, *Norman Chamberlain: a Memoir*, the only book he ever wrote, which, he said, "eased my conscience."[29] Why did his conscience need easing?

As Minister of National Service he had been "partly responsible for sending the flower of British youth to their death."[30] Did Norman's death now make the fate of the hundreds of thousands of otherwise faceless dead suddenly very real to him? Was he feeling more guilt, and an especial hatred for Germans? Wasn't Norman's death alone enough to make him feel murderous rage toward them? Chamberlain's biographer Iain Macleod has written: "Neville's abiding hatred of war was born of the death in action of Norman Chamberlain." Macleod may be right in reverse. Chamberlain's conscious hatred of war helped him cover an unconscious hatred of Germans, a toned down version of which had been available at least once to his conscious mind. On his visit to Norman's grave in France, he also visited P.O.W. camps, where, his diary records, he saw German prisoners "herded into their barbed wire cages in the evening... a humiliating spectacle for humanity, they looked like slaves, but," he added, "I felt no sympathy for them."[31] How could he? They had killed Norman.

Chamberlain's experiences were matched by millions of other Britons. In his book *Britain Between the Wars*, historian C.L. Mowat writes that in the 1930s "the sense of loss and waste was still strong. Hardly a family had not lost one or more of its sons, often in the first promise of youth.

Widows struggling to bring up fatherless children, women in there twenties, their sweethearts killed, facing long years of spinsterhood."[32] Other scholars have noted: "Roughly three-quarters of a million British men died in the First World War, out of a total population of 38 million, and these deaths were concentrated in a single age cohort of young men....About a third of the dead were married, leaving about 248,000 widows and 381,000 children....The others left parents, grandparents and siblings." It was in this context —the 1920s—that psychoanalyst John Bowlby, reflecting the tone of the times, first recognized the importance of separation in children's lives.[33]

Had British society come fully to grips with these massive casualties? Had anyone in Europe? Had sufficient mourning, individual and collective, taken place? Acceptance of loss, such as it was, did not run deep. How deep, how rage filled, how revengeful were their buried unspoken resentments? As much as others in Europe, it seems Britons had not "gotten over" the war.

Humiliations at the hands of the Germans in the 1930s, then, could provoke and justify a murderous rage, which could eventually be channeled into a new, guilt-free war to avenge those earlier hurts. Did Chamberlain's personal agenda match Britain's collective wish? It is hard, even impossible, to prove.

Still, to do the work of delegate, Chamberlain would have had to be cued from time to time by group commands, and to stay in favor—in a compensatory quest to win the love he had missed as a child—he would have been obliged to act out the group's unconscious agenda. Evidence shows that he was quite sensitive to public opinion and responded to group cues, even though it is a talent denied him by some historians. Alan Beattie, for one, argues that Chamberlain "had none of Baldwin's almost reverential attitude toward 'public opinion,' and laid no claim to have inherited his predecessor's alleged 'feel' for the workings of the English mind...elections and public opinion did not play the important part in his political life they had assumed in Baldwin's."[34]

It was just the opposite. Private Secretary to the Prime Minister John Colville felt at the time that Chamberlain "likes to be set on a pedestal and adored, with suitable humility, by unquestioning admirers." Far from being indifferent, Chamberlain listened carefully to what the British and other publics had to say so he could win their admiration. Indeed, he had earlier regretted that "I should never be a favourite with the press, like Father or Winston," so that when he did become a favorite he could enjoy the attention. Likewise, whatever was given could be taken away. On a state visit to France in the fall of 1938 Harvey recorded how "at Paris we were met by Daladier and Bonnet plus a guard of honor. Crowds in the streets—very drastic *service d'ordre*— cheers, but some boos near the Gare du Nord. '*Vive Eden*!' and '*A bas Munich*.'" On the next day: "P.M. annoyed with the papers this morning—all of which speak of boos in the streets yesterday."[35]

Another indicator of Chamberlain's sensitivity to public opinion is that he tended to put more stock in newspapers than he did in Foreign Office memoranda: "as a rule his letters referred to a particular press account rather than Foreign Office information," a practice which "carried over into the period when he was prime minister." To him: "press reports seemed to be a more first-hand source of information. Chamberlain invariably preferred his own perceptions to information gathered by others." After Munich he was convinced that the press was to blame for the belief advanced by critics that Munich had only averted war for the time being. He expressed the wish that the "British newspapers could be barred from printing material from the continental press except for accounts supportive of his position." The growing resistance to appeasement caused him to become so upset that "he attempted to take his mind off the critics by reading his fan mail."[36] He was particularly sensitive because he was trying through the public as parental substitute (as was the practice with so many other leaders) to obtain the approval that had eluded him in childhood.

Chamberlain's popularity was at its height immediately after Munich, a mission of peace the London *Times* saw in military terms: "No conqueror returning from a victory on the battlefield has come home adorned with nobler laurels." Sir Orme Sargent, standing behind Chamberlain while the crowds outside 10 Downing Street cheered him, said: "You'd think we'd won a major war instead of selling out a minor country." The *Sunday Dispatch* forecast that positive sentiments would sweep him "to a high pinnacle in history," and a request came in from Greece "for a piece of his umbrella to be used as a relic in an icon."[37]

If these things produced good feelings in him, the words of critics could hurt, and Chamberlain could be cued by both kinds of messages. This helps answer an important question raised some forty years ago by William Rock: "The historian is left frankly puzzled about the extent to which Chamberlain had a *carte blanche* to do essentially anything he liked."[38] That was because Chamberlain could not be used as a scapegoat if it was acknowledged that the public was unconsciously helping him create "his" policies. And he was given *carte blanche* precisely because he didn't have to be formally "told" what to do: cued by covert commands, he could then be blamed for acting out what some Britons wanted.

Many of these commands took the form of ongoing criticisms, continuing after Munich, which, after years of encouraging humiliating behavior, now demanded a firmer stance, including the frequent chant "We want Churchill." Harvey's diary in late-fall 1938 reveals the feeling that Chamberlain was weak and that his government was "tumbling."[39]

The decisive moment came in mid-March 1939 when Hitler seized the rest of Czecho-Slovakia. When by the end of the month the government gave a guarantee to defend the frontiers of Poland Chamberlain was reacting to a group wish. The "stiffening of Britain's attitude...did not originate with the government. It originated with Parliament, with the press, and with the now very politically-conscious public."[40] Public opinion polls confirm the move from ambivalence to firmness and a more open, if still partly hidden wish for war. The year before, in April 1938, a Gallup poll had found that only 33 percent of the British public favored assistance to Czechoslovakia. In March 1939, 87 per cent favored a military alliance between Britain, France, and Russia, and in April 1939, 72 per cent favored guarantees to Poland. Three months later, in July 1939, 76 per cent said they were ready to fight for Danzig.[41] Churchill, astonished by the shift, sensed its irrationality: "History...can be scoured and ransacked to find a parallel to this sudden and complete reversal of five or six years' policy of easy-going, placatory appeasement, and its transformation overnight into a readiness to accept an obviously imminent war on far worse conditions and on the greatest scale."[42] It just didn't make sense. A.J.P. Taylor also found it difficult to explain this "underground explosion of public opinion such as the historian cannot trace in precise terms," noting that "British opinion was stirred as it had not been by the absorption of Austria or the capitulation at Munich."[43] The difference was that by now appeasement had done its psychological work. Capitulation after capitulation, humiliation after humiliation meant the British could finally go to war with a clear conscience.

The reality was that the bully Hitler could have and should have been stopped years before, but the need in Britain to stop him now was suddenly felt to be especially urgent. "Just as they had been doing since the announcement of the guarantee to Poland, the *Manchester Guardian*, the *Daily Herald*, and the *News Chronicle* pressed daily, and with increasing vigor, for an extension of Britain's anti-aggression commitments." All the Liberal, independent, and Labor newspapers "were practically unanimous in their urgent demand for further action, and quickly." On 8 April, the *News Chronicle* "decried Britain's 'dilatoriness'," and like the *Manchester Guardian*, found the Government's slowness "incredible….Something further must be done speedily." So desperate were they that: "Weeks, days, even hours, are precious." The need for urgency was apparent in the assault on Chamberlain in Parliament: "In the Commons, Chamberlain was subjected to incisive questioning almost daily, frequently in none too genial terms. 'Does the Prime Minister not realize,' Hugh Dalton asked on 12 July, 'that these very long delays…are causing disquiet in the country…?'"[44] Chamberlain's wish to please this newly aggressive public opinion mixed with his personal need to discharge repressed rage and avenge Norman's death in a guilt-free war as he moved away from appeasement to contemplate a firmer stand against Hitler.

Public pressure came on top of other pressures, which joined with the heavy strain he had been under for a long time. In the early days of the Czech Crisis, his repressed rage, and other repressed feelings which had been threatening to burst into consciousness, found their way, symbolically, into his words: "We are like people living at the foot of a volcano, and we remember it blew up once before and we begin to wonder whether it is to be our fate to be smothered in ashes or see our homes destroyed and devoured in burning lava," he said on 12 May 1938. Low reinforced the image by depicting Chamberlain in a 1938 cartoon atop a volcano rejecting the aide of Soviet-fireman Foreign Minister Litvinov. With continuing domestic criticisms and the stress of one diplomatic crisis after another, his speeches came more and more to reflect his own inner turmoil. Historian Larry Fuchser notes that his "speeches were remarkably consistent in their major themes. Always, there was the image of a world poised on the brink of disaster, falling avalanches, teetering on the edge of the abyss, the eruption of volcanoes."[45]

Chamberlain was not alone, and the people around him were undergoing similar stresses, which intensified and reinforced his own. From early 1938 until the outbreak of war, Cadogan's diary reveals an endless stream of one "awful day" after another "awful day" after another. Cadogan felt overworked, putting in "about 16 hours a day." He was: "Back at F.O. after dinner as usual—I never get away before midnight." During the Czech Crisis he noted: "Record of 3 Cabinets in one day!" and whenever one immediate crisis was at the forefront of his mind, there was always the dim consciousness of an ever-growing backlog of untouched work waiting when the crisis came to an end. At times he felt "too overwhelmed with work;" he felt, "I must get away." Weather conditions contributed to his moods. One day was "beastly dark and depressing," another day he "went home —at 11—depressed," only to have another "shattering day" leave him "depressed and dispirited." Deep physical and emotional fatigue set in among those around him: "Henderson said he was exhausted," in fact, "everyone— including P.M. exhausted!" During the Czech Crisis, Chamberlain confessed to him just before his radio address to the nation, "I'm wobbling all over the place!"—a feeling corroborated by Chamberlain's later revelation that he had felt closer to a nervous breakdown than he had ever felt in his life. When the stresses became even greater, Chamberlain began thinking more irrationally, coming up with Plan Z, it will be remembered, an unprecedented, unannounced, and uninvited flight to see Hitler, which shocked his advisers. His language continued to suggest how deeply he was affected: "In these strenuous days," he wrote to his sister, "I have lost all sense of time and recollection of days, and I hardly know, and certainly have now no wish to recall, where I was a week ago. I only know that, as the hours went by, events seemed to be closing in, and driving us to the edge of the abyss with a horrifying certainty and rapidity.... I daresay Annie has told you or will tell you, of the birth of the last desperate snatch at the last tuft of grass on the very edge of the precipice."[46]

He sometimes felt, he said, "as though he were two Neville Chamberlains. There was {the} one whom the mass of the people still flocked after and greeted wherever he went," after which, he said, 'I go back to the House of Commons, and listen to the unending stream of abuse of the Prime Minister." By early 1939, the British press seems to have tried using him, as it used Hitler and Mussolini, as a container for the public's projected out-of-control feelings, suggesting, by innuendo, that he was crazy. During his January 1939 trip to Italy, the British press reported that the police of Taranto had discovered a naked man walking down the street with nothing but an umbrella. "I'm Mr. Chamberlain," he explained, and was sent to a hospital for observation.[47]

As 1939 unfolded, the long, increasing, and bitter criticisms he had been sensitively receiving were filling him to the brim with a sense of his own personal badness; for the first time he began using the word "poison" to describe the international situation. He began projecting those feeling onto Europe and Hitler when he said that Hitler was daily poisoning the wells, which, of course, Hitler was. But projecting these feelings into Europe and Hitler wasn't enough to escape them.

As early as 1935 he had expressed his willingness in political campaigns to use the classic device of diverting a divided electorate from domestic issues by uniting it through fears of a foreign threat.[48] To do so now—not that it was anything but an unconscious intention—would serve to bring an end to his personal crisis and the intolerable criticisms of press, public, and Parliament. On the eve of war, he told his sisters, "life had become nothing short of an interminable ordeal." His mind had been working "at three times its ordinary pace." His images again reveal a sense of dangerous, out-of-control irrational forces when he said he felt "like a coachman negotiating a carriage down a difficult path on the edge of a very steep cliff." He captured the process whole when he said: "the final long-drawn-out agonies that preceded the actual declaration of war were as nearly unendurable as could be. We were anxious to bring things to a head."[49]

Although these pressures were great, even as Germany invaded Poland, yet another, ambivalent, competing impulse continued to restrain him. This other unconscious factor seems to have contributed to his appeasement policy too, especially once he became Prime Minister. It has to do with guilt, and the need to deny his own ambition, that is, his own aggression. His guilt (and the wish for masochistic punishment) intensified when he became Prime Minister because he had actually attained what had eluded both his father and his brother. Going beyond them was fraught with danger—and a thrilling excitement—understood, as it must have been, on unconscious levels as a kind of symbolic murder. Then the actual death of Austen about the same time that he *did* become Prime Minister could not help but stir memories of his own repressed anger stored against his major sibling rival since childhood. And it was not only Austen whom he had bested, but also Father, that is, the father *in* Austen, for Austen's own desperate need for approval had consciously made him try to become Joseph, "by identifying himself fanatically with his father's opinions, and by turning himself physically into the mirror image of his father, complete with monocle and severe countenance."[50]

This helps explain why, when the time came for war, Chamberlain's personal agenda—his need to deny his own aggression and be humiliated for it, his very powerful need to be punished—momentarily overwhelmed his and the nation's other need, to discharge aggression, and he wavered once more. There was a day-and-a-half's delay after Germany's invasion of Poland before Chamberlain entered the House of Commons in the early evening of 2 September 1939 with most of his cabinet and all the M.P.s expecting an announcement that an ultimatum had been delivered to Hitler. What Chamberlain said instead was: "If the German Government should agree to withdraw their forces, then His Majesty's Government would be willing to regard the position as being the same as it was before the German forces crossed the Polish frontier. That is to say, the way would be open to discussion between the German and Polish Government on the matters at issue between them." It meant that after a day-and-a-half's delay, no ultimatum had been sent.

"The House was aghast," wrote Leo Amery. "For two whole days the wretched Poles had been bombed and massacred and we were still considering within what time-limit Hitler should be invited to tell us whether he felt like relinquishing his prey!...Was all this...the prelude to another Munich?....This time any similar announcement would have been met by a universal howl of execration."[51]

Chamberlain's need for masochistic surrender, which had so ably served the unconscious needs of many Britons for two years, was now at odds with the new agenda. Finally, he decided: "If the French Government were to insist on a time-limit of forty-eight hours," he telephoned Paris, "it would be impossible for the Government to hold the situation here."[52] To the end, he felt the need to shift responsibility elsewhere.

Chamberlain had found his excuse, but he did not "cause" the war. That was Hitler's doing. Chamberlain was guilty only of unconscious complicity. Hitler was the aggressor. Again, many Britons wanted to stop him, but for reasons rooted in their own childhoods and adult traumas—including the deaths of their sons and husbands, brothers and fathers in 1914-1918—it appears they unconsciously sought revenge, needing several humiliations to convince themselves that acting out their own anger was now morally justified. Chamberlain's own unconscious agenda had made him the perfect candidate for the job. In this sense, his policy of appeasement was reinforced by the countless positive and negative cues he had received from supporters and detractors alike. Every charge that he was weak was countered and shown to be wrong, at least in his own mind, by even firmer commitments to appeasement. In this sense Chamberlain was, at least in part, Britain's delegate. Nor, as it turns out, was serving as a group-delegate that unusual a role. Other leaders, including Hitler, were cued in various ways to fulfill their share of Europe's unconscious family agenda.

V HITLER AND GERMANY

SHE IS THE PROBLEM CHILD OF THE EUROPEAN FAMILY;
AND PROBLEM CHILDREN ARE DANGEROUS
WHEN THEY ARE OUT TO "GET THEIRS."
GERMANY IS A PROBLEM CHILD
WITH A LOADED PISTOL IN HER HAND.[1]
—*César Saerchinger,* 1940

Before returning to the details of the diplomatic story, it is necessary to determine the influences that played upon Hitler and the roles he played for the German people so as to better understand the roles he played for the family of Europe.

It is clear that Hitler was his own man, had his own agenda, embraced his own ideology, and was self-motivated. The evidence also shows that, like Chamberlain, he was cued by others, such as Ribbentrop, the Nazi Party, or even, at times, by the broader German public. There is no question that he was exquisitely attuned to the wishes of the German people. Many, in and out of the Nazi party, confirmed it, from peasants to intellectuals. "I read and heard Adolf Hitler," reported one German farmer, "and his words went right to my marrow." Said one early Nazi: "Hitler responds to the vibrations of the human heart with the delicacy of a seismograph." Psychologist Carl Jung believed: "He is the loudspeaker which magnifies the inaudible whispers of the German soul until they can be heard by the German's conscious ear." This aspect of Hitler's personality is nowhere better documented than in Rudolph Binion's *Hitler Among the Germans.*[2]

What accounted for this remarkable "inner accord" between the leader and the led, which allowed him to be inspired, even cued, by his audiences? Binion explains it on the basis of the collective trauma shared by Hitler and experienced by all Germans in the loss of the First World War. They were certainly bonded by this common traumatic event. Yet part of the answer also seems to come from the "fit" between Hitler's childhood and the childhoods of other Germans.

In psychological history, childhood is recognized as of general and often specific importance because it *is* important. Common sense, personal experience, observation, and the scientific evidence of the last hundred years confirm it. It is not that a particular childhood causes adult behavior so much as it is that childhood *influences* adult behavior. How important childhood is in any given instance depends on many things, but in general, good childhoods help people do certain things, bad childhoods move people in other ways.

The evidence suggests that Hitler's childhood was not particularly good, and may have been particularly bad. Adolf's father, Alois, like nearly every other German and Austrian father of the late-nineteenth century, beat his son. Does this mean that Hitler was an "abused child?" Erich Fromm did not think so. Of Hitler's father he has written: "He was not a tyrant, but an authoritarian...he never beat his son."[3]

Fromm was an eminent psychoanalyst, keen social observer, and pioneer in applied psychoanalysis; he was not an historian. The historical evidence contradicts Fromm, pointing to the clear likelihood of Hitler as an abused child. In an interview in 1946, Hitler's younger sister Paula stated: "It was especially my brother Adolf, who challenged my father to extreme harshness and who got his sound thrashings every day."[4] Virtually all the scholars who have studied German childrearing concur that this was the common practice of the time.[5]

Historian Robert Waite quotes Bridget Hitler, the Irish wife of Adolf's half-brother Alois Jr., as saying that her husband had spoken often of his childhood and revealed that his father had "a very violent temper....{He} often beat the dog until it...wet the floor. He often beat the children, and on occasion...would beat his wife Klara."[6] According to the reconstruction of the popular writer John Toland: "Alois Jr. complained bitterly that his father frequently beat him 'unmercifully with a hippopotamus whip,' but in the Austria of those days," says Toland, "severe beatings of children were not uncommon, being considered good for the soul. Once the boy skipped school for three days to finish building a toy boat. The father, who had encouraged such hobbies, whipped young Alois, then held him 'against a tree by the back of his neck' until he lost consciousness."[7]

While Toland's invocation of a "hippopotamus whip" cannot be corroborated and sounds apocryphal, other evidence confirms the overall picture. Historian Robert Waite cites Franz Jetzinger's interview with "Joseph Mayrhofer, a farmer who was for many years mayor of Leonding, had been a close friend of Alois and, after his death was appointed Adolf's guardian. In 1948, when he was 80 but still alert and clear-minded, he admitted that Alois Hitler had been something of a tyrant: 'The boy stood in awe of him...he was strict with his family. No kid gloves as far as they were concerned; his wife had nothing to smile about.'"[8] Seen in the light of Toland's observation that "in the Austria of those days severe beatings of children were not uncommon," Mayrhofer's approving words suggest that Alois's treatment of his family was severe even by the standards of contemporaries.

Although he denied that any physical abuse had taken place, Mayrhofer went on to contradict himself when he quoted Alois as saying about Adolf: "That miserable urchin! I'll bash him yet!"[9] Mayrhofer's last words are consistent not only with the findings of several researchers on childhood history in nineteenth-century central Europe but with what Hitler said about himself. Speaking of being beaten, Hitler said that he "resolved never again to cry when my father whipped me. A few days later I had the opportunity of putting my will to the test. My mother, frightened, took refuge in front of the door. As for me, I counted silently the blows of the stick which lashed my rear end."[10] This, Toland's version, is not the only one. Citing Hitler's secretary as having heard him say, "I never loved my father. I therefore feared him all the more. He had a terrible temper and often whipped me," Waite reports Hitler's boast as: "My father gave me 230 blows!"[11]

Some writers have denied Alois's abusive behavior; others have tried to explain it away; Jetzinger is typical of both efforts:

> It is also said that Adolf used to get merciless beatings from his father. This is based on an alleged remark of Angela's to her half-brother, 'Adolf, do you remember how mother and I used to hang on to father's uniform coat tails when he was trying to hit you?' But Alois Hitler ceased to wear a uniform when he retired in June 1895, and during the year preceding his retirement he had been living away from his family. 'The beatings' must have taken place when Adolf was only five, or even younger— in other words, they never took place at all.
>
> It is true that the Führer himself once told his secrtaries that his father had given him thirty stripes in the small of the back, but that, like a Red Indian under torture, he had never made the smallest sound. Apart from the fact that Hitler related this in the same breath as other fabulous Red Indian stories, we know that he was addicted to acting the hero before the young ladies of his entourage and there is no reason whatever to believe this improbable story. For one thing, his father was far too responsible a man to have administered so savage a punishment, and moreover in the Leonding period, to which the tale refers, he was in his sixties and past caring much about young Adolf's misdemeanours.[12]

Most historians have adopted similar denials, some going as far as to assert that Hitler's evil was so great, so perverse, so beyond the pale that it can never be understood, that even *trying* to do so is an obscene act. (His evil, they believe, could not have resulted from repressed murderous rage derived from childhood beatings, which, according to Jetzinger, "never took place at all.") Others scholars argue that the evidence for Hitler's childhood trauma is merely an "abuse excuse," a notion recently re-circulated in the United States in the public outrage over a proposed four-part television mini-series on Hitler's youth. As *The New York Times* put it: "A program that shows Hitler becoming a demonical dictator because his father beat him would either have to trivialize history or be a satire worthy of Mel Brooks," a judgment rendered before anyone had even seen the program, or knew if childhood beatings were part of it. As for historians, most don't mention the possibility of child abuse, and the few who allow that Alois's beatings are part of the historical record say they don't amount to much. It is surprising in this respect for historian John Lukacs, no friend to psychological analysis, to acknowledge that Hitler's "father was domineering and crude: he drank; he mistreated his wife; he beat his young son." Even more surprisingly, Lukacs admits that these things may have had an effect: "to a few insightful observers throughout his adult life {Hitler} gave the impression that he had been a deeply humiliated child." More typical, though, is historian Ian Kershaw whose recent biography of Hitler has been widely praised. Kershaw accepts the evidence for Alois as a distant and abusive father who beat his son, then adds: "What the legacy for all this was for the way Adolf's character developed must remain a matter for speculation."[13]

It may be a matter for speculation only to those who have had limited experience with child abuse. Social workers, psychologists, and those who work with abusing parents and abused children will be tempted to see the words of Jetzinger and Kershaw, as well as the attitudes of other scholars and historians who think and speak this way, as defensive. Some psychological historians will also argue that the history of childhood in Germany confirms the pattern of physical abuse described by Hitler and others. Many historians will not be convinced. One cannot prove conclusively that Hitler was abused by saying, or even by proving, that other Germans, or even many other Germans, were abused. Nor are many historians likely to be convinced by an often-quoted passage from *Mein Kampf*:

> Imagine, for instance, the following scene: In a basement apartment, consisting of two stuffy rooms, dwells a worker's family of seven. Among the five children there is a boy of, let us assume, three years. This is the age in which the first impressions are made on the consciousness of the child....The very narrowness and overcrowding of the room does not lead to favorable conditions. Quarreling and wrangling will very frequently arise as a result. In these circumstances, people do not live with one another, they press against one another. Every argument, even the most trifling...leads to loathsome wrangling without end. Among the children, of course, this is still bearable; they always fight under such circumstances....But if this battle is carried on between the parents themselves, and almost every day in forms which for vulgarity often leave nothing to be desired, then, if only gradually, the results of such visual instruction must ultimately become apparent in the children. The character they will inevitably assume if this mutual quarrel takes the form of brutal attacks of the father against the mother, of drunken beatings, is hard for anyone who does not know this milieu to imagine. At the age of six the pitiable little boy suspects the existence of things that can inspire even an adult with nothing but horror. Morally poisoned, physically undernourished, his poor little head full of lice, the young 'citizen' goes off to public school.[14]

Social workers, psychologists, and those who work with abused children will be tempted to view this passage as a statement of Hitler's own childhood, although, on the surface, he is talking about "someone else's" experiences. Memories of such abuse can remain repressed well into adulthood, even forever. Historians might acknowledge the fact but still insist the passage cannot be used to represent Hitler's childhood since it is not specifically about that childhood, nor does it reflect Hitler's comparatively roomy, middle class home, and, in addition, says nothing about a father abusing a child—only a wife. It cannot be used to suggest even the *tone* of Hitler's childhood since there are no social worker's case studies nor any documentary evidence in Hitler's own hand from that time detailing that abuse. For historians who want such proofs, and who find it difficult to think in terms of displacement and symbolic meanings, the "abused-child" hypothesis will forever remain inconclusive.

What of Hitler's mother, Klara? Here biographers and psychologists are more in accord. Virtually all have seen her as a devoted and loving mother and as a counterpoise to the punitive Alois. Historian Bradley F. Smith says: "The only serious charge ever raised against her is that because of this love and devotion she was over-indulgent and thus encouraged a sense of uniqueness in her son—a somewhat strange charge to be brought against a mother. The children did not share this view. Her stepchildren and her own offspring who survived infancy loved and respected their mother."[15]

The central event in Klara's life and subsequent relationship with Adolf was the sudden death of her first three children within six weeks from diphtheria in 1887-88. This trauma meant that when her next child, Adolf, was born in 1889 she poured into him all her love and affection. He became the apple of her eye, the substitute for her lost children, the spoiled child who was able to later act the part of spoiled child as an adult. Despite his special treatment, he nevertheless must have developed mixed feelings toward her. "The beatings he had suffered from his father," writes Waite, "must have increased his ambivalence toward his mother, who was either unable or unwilling to protect him from his father's attacks." But, on the whole, the consensus is that he loved her intensely: the two clung together "out of psychic need."[16]

Alice Miller, a Swiss psychotherapist well known in the United States for her book *The Drama of the Gifted Child* (originally titled *Prisoners of Childhood*), and for her pioneering advocacy of abused children, has studied the history of German child rearing, including Hitler's childhood.

"It is probably no accident," she writes, " that all the biographers who paint this lovely Madonna-like portrait are men." Even if Klara did "spoil" Adolf, Miller asks, is that love? It is "a contradiction in terms if we take love to mean that the mother is open and sensitive to her child's true needs. This is precisely what is lacking if a child is spoiled, i.e. if his every wish is granted and he is showered with things he does not need—all this simply as ersatz for that which parents are unable to give the child because of their own problems." What of the symbiotic union idealized by male biographers?

> It is scarcely conceivable that her son, in his early period of symbiosis with his mother, imbibed feelings of peace, contentment, and security along with her milk. It is more likely that his mother's anxiety, the fresh memories of her three dead children reactivated by Adolf's birth, and the conscious or unconscious fear that this child would die too were all communicated directly to her baby as if mother and child were one body. It was also of course impossible for Klara to experience her anger toward her self-centered husband, who left her to her anguish. All the more, then, did her baby—who, after all, did not have to be feared like her domineering husband—come to feel the force of those negative emotions.[17]

Some historians may find this argument too speculative, or inconclusive at best since it is not based on any direct documentary evidence. Klara, they would assert, must be found to have uttered actual words that would reveal these unconscious processes. And, in their way, historians would be right. Others might feel that Miller's explanation is convincing circumstantially since it is not "speculation," but a reasoned judgment rooted in the findings of psychology and a lifetime of experience in clinical practice. In their way, they too would be right.

Dr. Eduard Bloch, the Hitler family physician who had treated Klara's breast cancer and, after escaping Hitler's Europe, published a two-part reminiscence in *Collier's*

Magazine in March 1941 ("My Patient, Hitler"), confirmed in the article the extraordinary ties he had noticed between son and mother: "I have never witnessed a closer attachment," he said. A hitherto unpublished 60-page memoir written by Dr. Bloch between 1941 and 1946, recently published by the Leo Baeck Institute, reconfirms Dr. Bloch's earlier observation. He says again of Hitler: "He was his mother's darling and idolized her." That the symbiosis, or at least a very strong attachment, went on into adulthood is suggested by Hitler's carrying Klara's picture with him throughout his life; she even accompanied him into death, her picture looking down on him from the wall of the Berlin bunker in April 1945 as he committed suicide. Their deep involvement, symbiotic or not, was, as Miller suggests, not just a curious thing in itself, or tied only to Hitler's personality, but was deeply connected to Klara's own psychology. Although Miller doesn't mention it, contemporary accounts suggest that Klara was especially sad. Kershaw's reading of the sources and sensible judgments about the circumstances of her life (three dead children, a domineering husband who occasionally lashed out physically and emotionally) lead him to conclude that Klara "made the impression of a saddened careworn woman."[18] That sadness in turn suggests an ongoing depression that would have made it hard for her to give "sufficient" love to her son and points to something else at work in their symbiotic union.

Rather than love given, Klara was seeking love in return. She desperately needed to cling to Adolf, the substitute for the children who had been lost earlier, and for her unfulfilling and oppressive marriage to Alois. It seems probable that Adolf was overindulged at the breast, and, as the documents do show, was infantilized, made into a rage-filled child who, ambivalently wanted to remain infantilized while needing at the same time to desperately escape the symbiosis. Klara could not let go. Psychologists know that such early closeness can interfere with the drive for separation and individuation, carefully delineated by Margret Mahler and others. Those mothers who cannot "let go" are not promoting love, for in the words of family psychologist and Hitler psychobiographer Helm Stierlin: "Instead of experiencing conflicts he can manage, the child suffers an archaic, terrifying ambivalence. Caged into a closeness from which there is no escape, he loses all sense of autonomy...this triggers murderous wishes...to bite, mutilate, and destroy the mother."[19]

This may not fully explain Hitler's later policies but cannot be entirely dismissed. Beatings by Alois, along with Klara's inability to free Adolf from herself (and herself from Adolf) help account for the pent-up fury at Hitler's core. Why murderous rage was later channeled against Jews is another question, but its origins in abusive child rearing seem to have been echoed in the childhood experiences of many other Germans. There it lay repressed, a reservoir waiting to be tapped, in the Nazi case as a flood of rage against the hated Jew and other enemies. The final word isn't in, but evidence from the history of childhood indicates that, from the standpoint of abuse, millions of Germans who didn't have Klara as a mother seem to have had similar painful experiences.[20]

That most Germans in the nineteenth and early-twentieth century suffered various kinds of arbitrary physical and emotional punishment is important since it connects to some related if circumstantial evidence from the research of Stanford University psychologist Ernest R. Hilgard and his wife Josephine Hilgard.[21] They have shown that hypnotizability correlates with physical and emotional child abuse: that is, abused children can be more easily hypnotized as adults. That would mean that abused children are more susceptible to group-trance states as adults. Hitler's audiences responded to what he actually said, of course, but his hypnotic abilities—or, as it is often called, his ability to "mesmerize audiences"—is frequently invoked as an example of his indefinable "charisma." One thinks of the cheering thousands at the semi-staged Nuremberg rallies, and the cheering thousands who spontaneously lined the way of Hitler's motorcades, as well as the transfixed millions who heard Hitler's hypnotic voice on their inexpensive radio sets or over loud speakers in their town squares.

And it has been conclusively proven (in studies confirmed in the every day work of psychologists and social workers) that abusing parents were themselves abused children. This does not mean that abused children will automatically grow up to become child abusers, but it does mean that in the large majority of cases only those who have been abused will become abusers. These people are compelled to recreate with their own children (and the children of others) what has been done to them.

It has been argued above that societies can institutionalize and ritualize traumas in order to symbolically relive them, and the Nazis seem a special case in point. They established institutions that seem in some ways to have recapitulated their own childhood experiences. The Hitler Youth, for example, was meant for control, to keep an eye on adults, to provide a pool of soldiers who would later willingly die in Hitler's armies, and, at least for the enthusiastic former Hitler Youth Alfons Heck, also constituted "a massive case of child abuse." As much as displaced hatreds and the permission given by Hitler to act out murderous rage, punitive German childhoods help account for the tendency of some Germans to act out their early abuses on others, perhaps even to recapitulate them exactly, or symbolically, in the concentration camps of Germany and the death camps of the east.[22]

Hitler, nevertheless, seems somehow different from other Germans; there seems "more" to him. He was Germany's leader, and one can reasonably ask: if so many millions were physically and emotionally abused, why didn't *they* become Hitlers? But, of course, they did—by encouraging "his" sadism and acting out "his" wishes they vicariously experienced their own impulses while masking them through rationalizations like the familiar "We were only following orders." Yet, while Germans could hide these sadistic impulses from themselves, as Führer of the Nazi Party, and well before he became Germany's leader, Hitler's rhetoric could be sadistic in the extreme. (It is likely one of the reasons people voted for him.) But what made him uniquely able to express these sadistic impulses? Alice Miller offers a partial answer: "Hitler never had a single other human being in whom he could confide his true feelings; he was not only mistreated but also prevented from experiencing and expressing his pain; he didn't have any children who could have served as objects for abreacting his hatred; and, finally, his lack of education did not allow him to ward off his hatred by intellectualizing it."[23] Miller forgets that Hitler was self-taught and was therefore able to sublimate some of his rage through intellectualizations, however distorted his thinking. But Miller's words do seem to account for something, and help round out the psychological picture. Yet at least one additional major piece of the puzzle is missing: the historical link between leader and led, or, Hitler's group-fantasy function.

This subject is complicated by the fact that Hitler played numerous, sometimes contradictory roles for Germans, as he did for the rest of the world.

There is Hitler's role before, during, and especially after the Second World War as the twentieth century's personification of evil. There is no getting around the fact that he was evil, and the judgment is well deserved. But because of the idea that he alone caused World War II and was responsible for the murder of European Jews, blaming him as the only criminal allowed his contemporaries, including Germans, to feel better about themselves, "the Führer takes responsibility" being a theme which could be played out even by the most sadistic S.S. thug.

Hitler embraced several other social and political roles as well. The authors of *The Authoritarian Personality* (1950) showed how, as the dictatorial Führer, he recapitulated the role of father in Nazi Germany. The paternal authoritarian family structure of pre-Nazi Germany, they argued, had created authoritarian personality types who embraced Hitler's tyranny without so much as a second thought. This famous book followed an earlier, important, and neglected psychological study, *Fatherland. A Study of Authoritarianism in the German Family* (1948), which was based on immediate post-war testing and interviews with Nazi sympathizers, as well as with non-Nazis. The idea of Hitler as a kind of "surrogate-father" has become a standard way of thinking and speaking about Nazi Germany ever since. Extreme authoritarian parenting is, of course, a kind of child abuse in itself and is emotionally damaging even without physical punishment because it impairs the development of an independent self. Although evidence shows that the regressive appeal of merging with larger groups—kingdoms, religions, ideologies, nations, or tribes—is universal, and is part of what it means to be human, such mergers seem more likely sought by those whose self has been stolen by abusing and authoritarian parents. In a recent article, "Surrendering Identity," psychoanalyst Arno Gruen delineates the childhood origins and psychodynamics of this process and offers case studies of two of Hitler's henchmen, Hermann Göring and Rudolf Hess. In addition, the words of a recent interview with one of Hitler's secretaries, the late Traudl Junge, link back, circumstantially and suggestively, to the abusive German childrearing mentioned above. After a half-century of reflection, Junge concluded that Hitler was ruled "not by knowledge but by emotion." The "effect he had on us was more than just charisma, you know. When he went off somewhere without us, the moment he was gone, it was almost as if the air around us had become deficient. Some essential element was missing: electricity, even oxygen, an awareness of being alive. There was a vacuum." Existence itself depended on him. This helps us better understand why someone like Göring could say: "It is not I who live, but the Führer who lives in me." Similar feelings tied average Germans, besides the inner circle and an awe-struck, impressionable twenty-three year old secretary, to the authoritarian father they saw, needed to see, and believed they had in the Führer.[24]

A variant on the authoritarian theme, and a rich elaboration of the historical data, appears in Peter Loewenberg's early psychohistorical investigation of the Nazi youth cohort[25] wherein he argues that the traumatic childhood memories of many Germans—absent and defeated fathers, nutritional as well as emotional deprivations during World War I—were reawakened by economic depression and political uncertainty in the years 1930-1932. These new stressors set off regressions to earlier experiences, with many young Germans voting for Hitler as surrogate-father. Of course, many older Germans also voted for Hitler, some in part because they too were stressed, regressed, and recalled the physical and emotional distresses of World War I and wanted a father too.

Hitler's role as father figure is corroborated by many sources, including the oral testimonies in the documentary film *Hitler's Fatal Attraction* where Traudl Junge remembers him "as a kind and fatherly chief." One contemporary present as a Hitler Youth at the Nuremberg rallies felt as if Hitler "spoke directly to me, father to son." A third explained, "I loved him like a father, I would have died for him." Junge, one of the few who shared his last days in the Berlin bunker, said: "When he died I felt so lonely, as if my father had died."[26]

According to Kershaw, Hitler served Goebbels as a father figure, a role the evidence shows he clearly played for many others as well. But there are clues that something more was at work, an additional fantasy that appears to contradict (or maybe even compliment) the fatherly role. Hitler also existed in part as a maternal figure; he was for many

Germans both father *and* mother. These combined roles are implicit in the thinking of adults who imposed on German children poems such as the one read regularly in kindergartens across the Reich, which reveals something about their own adult longings: "Dear Führer/ We love you like/ our fathers and mothers./ Just as we belong to them,/ we belong to you." This matched, reinforced, and was reinforced by the same kind of longing expressed in a children's coloring book: "My Führer!/ I know you well and love you/ like father and mother. I will always obey you/ like father and mother. And when I grow up I will help you/ like father and mother. And you will be proud of me/ like father and mother."[27]

These paternal, at times maternal images, sometimes both together, were joined by other fantasies. Because he was a veteran, Hitler's overt connection to the Great War allowed him to become something deeply significant to Germans as a veteran. Historian Omer Bartov has made a convincing case for Hitler as the German Army's symbolic, imaginary "unknown soldier" where he became, in fantasy, both a father and a son. During the Second World War he "represented to the troops both their fathers, mythologized as the heroic and tragic warriors of World War I, and themselves," who were, Bartov writes, "the hopeless, desperate, and tough *Landser* (simple soldiers), wreaking revenge on a 'world of enemies.'" Even before that, his simple corporal's uniform and firery rhetoric "resurrected Germany's fields of glory by personifying the forgotten soldier and acting out his rage and frustration."[28] Thus, during the interwar peace Hitler stood as a symbolic link between the unresolved emotional issues of Germany's present and its recent traumatic past.

It may seem that Hitler's group fantasy roles are beginning to get out of hand. How can he be all of these things at once, father, mother, "unknown soldier," son? It is worth remembering that multiple images can and do exist in the "logic" of the unconscious without contradiction, an important point to keep in mind when looking at Hitler's additional fantasy roles.

There is, surprisingly, Hitler as "love object." Some Germans, unable to face the painful truths about the Nazi era, have confessed in their post-war interviews to the deep affection they had and many still harbor for their Führer. Alison Owings's study of women's memories of the Third Reich contains one chapter titled "We Did Love Our Führer, Really!" a sentiment corroborated, for example, by the ecstatic cheering millions, men and women, who, welcomed him back from Paris as a conquering hero in 1940. For others, the flames of that open affection have not died, as journalist Gitta Sereny reminds us in the title of her 1996 essay on Hitler-enthusiast François Genoud, quoting him as saying: "The Truth is, I loved Hitler." The connection between affectionate feelings and erotic arousal is usually not explored by historians, and while for many people today the thought is repugnant, some hints from other sources suggest that Hitler existed as a fantasy sex object for many Germans, both men and women. (It is well known that he did not marry, he said, because he wanted all German women to imagine themselves as his bride.) How important male, as well as female, sexual fantasies were in accounting for his popularity is still an elusive unknown, but needs to be acknowledged as a hidden and perhaps not so hidden part of Hitler's group appeal. As psychotherapist George Victor has written: "millions adored Hitler, killed for him, and died for him. Without taking the love he aroused into account, explanations of Hitler's influence are incomplete." Victor's book offers a few tantalizing and illuminating examples of Hitler's erotic appeal, a subject which needs closer study. [29]

Then there is the messianic, even apocalyptic Hitler, the charismatic outsider "chosen" by Providence to purify and renew Germany, Europe, and the world, who, like the returned Jesus (or the semi-"divine being" descending from the skies at the beginning of the Nazi propaganda film *Triumph of the Will*) was "destined" to establish a thousand-year reign.

Authoritarian, maternal nurturer, father substitute, warrior, unknown soldier, apocalyptic savior, and sometime fantasy sex object. Again, on the level of conscious logic these fantasy roles may sometimes clash and contradict one another. Yet he was able to be all these things to people because contradictory images (along with magical thinking) exist side by side in the unconscious, and there is no inherent reason why they cannot all be held in a person's psyche simultaneously.

What else by way of roles? Most argue: nothing. The crucial one seems paternal. Quoting psychoanalyst Erik Erikson (but implying agreement with Adorno's earlier authoritarian personality study) political psychologist John Stoessinger is "convinced that the secret of Hitler's charismatic grip on Germany had its roots in the authoritarian structure of the German family."[30] But Erikson himself offered another explanation, one deserving at least passing mention: Hitler's role as fantasy adolescent. "He was the Führer: a glorified older brother, who took over prerogatives of the fathers without over identifying with them," wrote Erikson. "He was the unbroken adolescent...a gang leader who kept the boys together by demanding their admiration." He was "the tough adolescent," who gave what "the smoldering rebellion in German youth had been waiting" for, permitting each youth, in the throes of a renewed Oedipal conflict and identity crisis, to know that no one "need stand in the way of his love for his mother Germany."[31] It worked, in part, though Erikson doesn't say it here, because Germany was a feminized "maternal" object not only to Hitler, but for other Germans as well.

Emphasizing the regressive nature of Nazism seems right, and it can be persuasively argued that Hitler did embody an adolescent fantasy for other Germans. But this, too, does not seem to go far enough. Nazism was a collective regression under stress, but beyond unconscious fantasies of adolescent rebellion, even past childhood: it was, it seems, a deep regression to "infantile rebellion." Hitler was surrogate-father, surrogate mother, imagined sex object, savior, older sibling, and rebellious adolescent in multi-layered, interpenetrating fantasies. He was also Germany's raging child.

Over and again, in Germany and throughout Europe, Hitler was imagined and encouraged to be that child. The images are so frequent they go beyond political rhetoric. Joseph Goebbel's Foreword to the book, *Adolf Hitler: Pictures from the Life of the Führer 1931-1935*, published in Germany in 1936, declared that Hitler "understood how to speak to the people, whose child he always was and always will be."[32] During the Beer Hall Putsch, Karl-Alexander von Müller had said that Hitler reminded him of a child "beaming with joy...he had a childlike, frank expression I shall never forget."[33] Martha Dodd, daughter of the American Ambassador to Berlin, noted during the 1936 Olympics, "if a German would win...he would spring to his feet with wild and childish joy,"[34] and British diplomat Sir Ivone Kirkpatrick observed Hitler behaving "like a spoiled, sulky child."[35] Hitler also provoked impulses in older women to mother him. "Motherly types such as Frau Bruckmann, wife of the publisher, and Frau Bechstein, widow of the piano manufacturer, and another woman in her 60s, a retired schoolteacher named Carola Hoffman, would feed him his favorite tortes, cluck approval, stroke his head, and call him 'My little wolf' as he sat at their knee."[36]

But it was not Hitler as a cute, cuddly child who attracted, but rather Hitler as the raging child. His image today comes largely from the films of the period which almost always get around to showing a ranting Führer addressing large audiences, an image which is accurate, at least in part.[37] But rage-filled rhetoric was a Nazi staple for other Nazi speakers as well as for Hitler, and it may be that part of their emotional appeal came from the hidden need for German audiences to hear and see again the raging authoritarian fathers of their childhoods now seemingly reincarnated in Hitler and other Nazis. In this way Germans, and Europeans too, could artfully combine the past raging child of their angry authoritarian fathers with the angry child embedded in themselves.

The Hitler as child fantasy was reinforced by many messages from abroad. Dorothy Thompson's 1932 book *I Saw Hitler* refers to him several times as a "little man," and left no doubt what she meant when she wrote: the "Little Man… has no weapons to speak of: a few pistols, some of them charged with water or caps."[38] The "little man" image was favored by the Western press and repeated countless times. Germany itself was shown in a David Low cartoon as a fat baby (1924), and in other Low cartoons Hitler was shown as a child trying to grow up (1930), as a child blowing up a giant balloon of himself (1933), as an angry cupid (1933), with other statesmen in a nursery as babies playing blocks with countries (1934), as a cupid shooting arrows from a machine-gun into Britain (1936), and with Mussolini, as kids, playing with blocks.[39]

Before coming to power he was sometimes portrayed as "a little fellow" in the German press; after coming to power, the image continued with a book in Germany containing anti-Nazi cartoons from abroad which showed him that way.[40] In America, the fantasy of Hitler as a child was spontaneously expressed as readers "adorned *Life's* second anniversary baby cover {Jan. 1938} with Hitlerian mustaches," and sent them back to *Life* "by the dozens."[41]

One American psychiatrist once "wondered why Germans followed this particular leader who was essentially so childish; what was it in them…that responded to this immature person?"[42] One conclusion is that it was precisely the abused and raging child in Hitler who reminded Germans of the abused and raging child within themselves. *Kleiner Mann—Was Nun?* {*Little Man—What Now*} was the title of Hans Fallada's 1932 runaway bestseller, a popular film version of the same name recapturing and reinforcing the feeling when it was released the following year. It was in part the title which gave both novel and film their popularity, capturing the regressed emotional state of Germans in a time of acute political and economic stress.[43] As we shall see, the same was true abroad, where Hitler was imagined as an out-of-control raging child and was encouraged to keep playing that role. In these ways, the fantasy at the head of this chapter—that "Germany is a problem child with a loaded pistol in her hand"—could be made "real" in the fantasy European family.

As for the Führer himself, the way Germans and the rest of the world thought about him was the way he sometimes thought about himself. Many times he spoke of himself as a child. If Hitler's World War II table talk is to be believed, he spoke of himself in the period 1920-1923 as naïve, saying: "I was intellectually a child at the bottle."[44] Elsewhere he said: "We regulate living relations between the sexes. We form the child!" In 1927 he remarked how "the best and greatest are more than all others rooted in their people—are not children of the state, but exclusively children of the all-mother: their own nation."[45] The fantasy persisted in his April 1939 Reichstag reply to Roosevelt where he again used the phrase "only a child in politics," asserting, "I myself am a child."[46]

Hitler was capable of acting that way. Waite notes how "one of the striking personal characteristics of this political giant...was his infantilism," and stresses Hitler's childishness as the first of his personal qualities. Even without Waite's reminder, one is struck at once by Hitler's temper tantrums, his tendency to run away, sulk or rage when frustrated, his fondness for sweets, his passion for the adolescent "Western" novels of Karl May (often read as an adult), his excessive orality expressed in his aggressive oratorical style and in his hunger for Lebensraum to "feed the starving German masses" who were not starving, his fondness for his favorite films *Snow White and the Seven Dwarfs* and *King Kong*, his interest in child star Shirley Temple, his absentmindedly whistling "Who's Afraid of the Big Bad Wolf," and making competitive games with his entourage out of counting the number of men seen wearing beards—not to mention his childish glee when he was given eighteen new Mickey Mouse cartoons as a Christmas present in 1937. He often dressed like a "child," preferring to wear lederhosen, and not just to make a cultural point: "Having to change into long trousers," he said, "was always a misery to me."[47] In moments of stress Hitler compulsively sucked his little finger. And there was his passion for toys. "In the basement of the Reich's Chancellery, there was a miniature cannon with a barrel about 30 inches long and a special silencer built into the chamber. Hitler delighted in loading, aiming, and firing the little piece himself. His targets were wooden buildings and figures of 'enemy' soldiers: Polish, English, French, and Russian—the Russians were painted with ugly, leering faces. As a very special favor to his friend Mussolini, Hitler let him play with his toy, loading and shooting it himself."[48] Mussolini's own childishness was doubtless stirred as he enjoyed playing at phallic potency with Hitler.

The United States Office of Strategic Services, America's World War II intelligence agency and the forerunner of the CIA, compiled a Source Book on Hitler. It contains an account of a former cabinet minister's visit to Hitler's office. The Source Book must be used with caution since much of the evidence in it is hearsay and has not been, nor can ever be, fully authenticated. It nevertheless remains a valuable resource since it deals not only with Hitler's putative behavior, but with the perceptions and fantasies of others about him. The minister's visit reported here was intended to discuss financing for yet another Hitler-project, but took an unexpected turn. "When the door was opened, there was Hitler lying on the floor with a number of toy buildings carefully arranged in front of him....His first remark was 'Isn't this beautiful? We must make Berlin the most beautiful city in the world.' The official agreed that it was, but maintained that its realization at the moment was impossible.... Suddenly he turned to his visitor and said like a little child with tears in his voice: 'But you can't take this away from me. I will be so unhappy. You must let me have it!'"[49] Nor was this unique: as reported by his architect Albert Speer, he frequently played at rebuilding Berlin with architectural models.

The childish Hitler is well known to historians. Hitler's recent biographer Ian Kershaw, who has little use for a hyphenated "psycho-history" set off in quotes, nevertheless turns to psychology and uses psychological words and concepts when pressed to explain some of Hitler's character traits, noting that he "was redolent of the spoilt child turned into the would-be macho-man. His inability to comprehend the unwillingness of the British government to yield to his threats produced tantrums of frustrated rage. The certainty that he would get his way through bullying turned into blind fury whenever his bluff was called,"[50] in other words, a perfect fit for Britain as well as for Germany's unconscious needs.

That leaders often act in childish ways says as much about their fantasy role in groups as it does about their upbringing. There were political, economic, social, and historical reasons why so many people responded to what Hitler said and what the Nazis promised, then seem to have delivered. But to have chosen and followed Hitler as a leader suggests that many Germans were also regressed to early levels of thought and feeling. They identified with him. They chose an abused child to lead them in part because he was capable of acting out—and promised to let them act out—their most primitive and violent infantile fantasies.

These ideas are somewhat akin to the familiar, and now somewhat unfashionable, notion of "national character" which sociologists and historians have used frequently in the past and have seen as growing out of a complex mix of customs, mores, and rituals, what people remember and don't remember about their shared past, and other factors, such as language, ideas, and ideologies. National character—different ways of thinking and being—is transmitted and reinforced by the process historians and sociologists call "socialization," and childhood experience is part of this. All of these forces may be important, but in psychological history childhood experiences tend to play the more prominent role.

This may shed some light on an issue yet to be addressed: Germans, like the British, had humiliation issues too. Their defeat in World War I, the Versailles Treaty, and the Ruhr occupation came on top of the humiliations suffered in their brutalized childhoods. Why wasn't it they, instead of the British, who got to play out humiliations on the public stage? Part of the answer lies in the family roles assigned to each nation by the European fantasy system, and part lies in the role that each country's "national character" inclined it to take.

Both partners in any sado-masochistic relationship know how to play both roles, and people can easily act the masochist in one relationship while being a sadist in another. This was certainly the case for the British who, humiliated by Germany in the 1930s, could be masochistic in Europe and (for example, through their Empire) sadistic abroad. Psychotherapists know that the masochist has a slightly healthier make up, since it is the masochistic partner who is more likely to seek help (if they do seek help) because they have experienced slightly better parenting. When applied to Britain and Germany, this suggests that "good enough" parenting in Britain had produced something of an individual and public conscience (Gandhi exploited it through passive resistance to build sufficient guilt in the British, despite their sadism, to help achieve the independence of India). There was a more marked tendency in Britain to turn anger against the self, while for Germans humiliations ignited a rage more likely to be directed at the world. Harsher, more punitive authoritarian childhoods made them more likely, when under prolonged heavy stress, to act out their repressed rage rather than, as with the British, to work toward a more polite, "gentlemanly" conscience-relieving later discharge of the same aggression.

If Germans were under such heavy stress, it follows that their regressive fantasies would include the longing to escape to a simpler, problem-free time, one connected to thoughts of very early childhood moments, remembered as blissful and stress free, when they merged with *Mutter*. Anyone who reads *Mein Kampf* cannot fail to be struck by the theme of intense longing for such a return. "A longing rose stronger and stronger in me," wrote Hitler, "to go at last whither since my childhood secret desires and secret love had drawn me." It was "my most ardent and heartfelt wish: the union of my beloved homeland with the common fatherland, the German Reich. Even today many would be unable to comprehend the greatness of such longing, but... I address myself to all those who, detached from their mother country, have to fight even for the holy treasure of their language, who are persecuted and tortured for their loyalty to the fatherland, and who now, with poignant emotion, long for the hour which will permit them to return to the heart of their faithful mother....Only he who has felt in his own skin what it means to be a German, deprived of the right to belong to his cherished fatherland, can measure the deep longing which burns in the hearts of children separated from their mother country."[51]

Hitler's images, merging maternal and paternal themes, were repeated almost hypnotically in *Mein Kampf* and in countless speeches which resonated in the longing hearts of millions of Germans. Regressed under stress, they longed for something they had experienced as infants—blissful early symbiosis with a maternal object. Hitler's rhetoric, in this case as in others, was a shrewd intuitive device, both a personal wish and part of Germany's agenda.

German Motherland as fantasy stand-in for Klara has long been recognized. Hitler understood "Germany as a symbolic representation of the mother figure," wrote Erich Fromm. Hitler's words reveal how "little Adolf" longed to "return to the arms of the beloved mother—Germany," said Erik Erikson.[52] The studies of Binion, Waite, Koenigsberg, and Stierlin agree. So does John Lukacs. The power of his mother and his mother in Germany is symbolic in Hitler's plans for his intended monumental new capital of the Nazi Empire, to be called Germania.

Binion argues that the crucial link between Hitler's mother and German motherland was first forged at Klara's death in 1907: "The surrogate he chose for his missing mother was Germany—not the German state or territory, but the German Volk, the nation, the imperishable 'people itself as substance of flesh and blood.'" After recovering from his gassing on the Western front in 1918, the mother-mother county link was re-forged during Hitler's psychosomatic relapse at Pasewalk Hospital with the traumatic news that Germany had lost the war and his hallucination of being called upon to restore what had been lost. As Binion says: "To his unconscious mind the summons to revive and avenge Germany came as a summons to revive and avenge his dying mother. More, it came as a summons from her: this is graphic in the authorized version of the hallucination, with the words from on high mediated by a motherly nurse 'who holds the twitching, feverish soldier...in her arms.'"[53]

Waite reconfirms Germany as Hitler's fantasy mother: "Passion for the Motherland pulsates through his prose," he said, adding that, "it is worth emphasizing that Hitler used this term rather than the more usual Fatherland."

Klara was "identified...with the German Motherland it was his mission in life to save." And Waite notes that "Hitler's unusual metaphors and turns of phrase indicate something very personal: that he transferred his love for his own mother to Germany and saw himself as the savior of the Motherland menaced by the 'Jewish peril.'" He quotes Koenigsberg for good measure that Hitler "relocated his mother in Germany."[54]

Helm Stierlin comes to the same conclusion. Hitler emerged from his various experiences the "delegate of his new 'mother' Germany." In Stierlin's work there is a new twist central to a fuller understanding of Hitler's leadership role, the notion that he became "the bound delegate" of his mother.

One of the pioneers of family therapy, Stierlin confirmed how children can be delegated by their parents to act out parental wishes. This goes beyond consciously delegated tasks, like wanting a son to become an athlete, or a daughter to become a doctor or to marry one, and extends to unconscious delegations. All children, even in normal families, learn to be their parents' delegates, and even in "healthy" families can be empowered to enact pathological wishes, including desires to express repressed impulses the parents cannot permit themselves. "Here the child stimulates the parents' imagination with hints or vivid descriptions of his exploits, allowing his parent to experience vicarious thrills." Such thrills are then conveniently disowned by the parent who scolds and punishes the child "for the very things he (more or less covertly) has asked him to do."[55]

Children, says Stierlin, can also be "sent out into life to realize unfulfilled parental aspirations." They can affirm a parent's sense of "goodness" by providing a "living contrast by being bad," and can be made into the family's chief "mischief-maker, troubled, crazy, or delinquent. Parents can covertly encourage children to commit, and seek punishment for, delinquent acts about which they themselves still harbor (mostly unconscious) guilt." Most difficult of all is that children sometimes have to "embody and externalize the badness and craziness that a parent, in his innermost self, feels and fears to be his personal fate because such madness looms as part of the family's endowment. Living under the (disavowed) threat and spell of madness, such a parent often seems impelled to search for—and in the process, induce—madness in the child. Thus the child becomes the external caretaker of the parent's extended madness." Dependent, susceptible to suggestion, conditioned to act in certain ways and punished if he does not, the child is also driven by another motive: to try to "sustain or recoup his parents'...approbation and love, a love now made contingent on how he executes his mission(s)."[56] After careful study of Hitler's childhood family dynamics, Stierlin concludes that Klara unconsciously and perhaps semi-consciously, recruited Adolf to "fulfill four major missions: First, the mission to 'give by receiving,' i.e., to absorb his mother's regressive gratification and in so doing, to nurture her—a mission he could execute only by remaining deeply dependent on, and close to, her; second, the mission to be the living proof of her worthiness as mother; third, the mission to furnish Klara's life, through his exploits, with importance, excitement, and power by proxy; and, finally, the mission to serve as ally, avenger, and redeemer in her underhanded struggles with her oppressive and disloyal husband."[57]

Every biographer confirms that Hitler felt a deep sense of mission. He often spoke of the hand of Providence calling upon him or saving him from danger so he could carry out his world-historic tasks. He felt "the goddess of history" was watching.[58] Was it Klara? He had been sensitized as a child to act out parental—especially maternal—delegations as if they were his own. Was it a role he replayed as "son" to the German motherland?

This sounds like a startling suggestion, for certainly

Hitler had a mind of his own, an ideology of his own, and could be incredibly stubborn. On the other hand, it is clear that he loved the adulation of crowds and was quite capable of playing to an audience, and probably developed his role as delegate very early in his political career. After a lecture in 1919, Professor Karl-Alexander von Müller noted how Hitler interacted with a group of men who "seemed spell-bound by one of their number who was haranguing them with mounting passion in a strangely guttural voice. I had the peculiar feeling that their excitement derived from him and at the same time they, in turn, were inspiring him."[59] But in a totalitarian state, it has been argued, all communication moves from the top down. How could an oppressed group "cue" Hitler?

There were the mass rallies during which he responded to group "suggestions" in the same way that the group responded to him. He loved the feeling. These interactions predate the years of power, and it is possible that bargains of delegation were struck then.[60] But it must first be determined if Hitler could be "cued" and was not just enjoying the adulation of the crowds.

The major biographers agree—although they may not put it in such terms—that something like cueing was happening around the time of the Beer Hall Putsch in 1923 and seems all the more plausible because of Hitler's well known hypersensitivity to criticism. His prestige had been badly damaged by a failed demonstration against the Socialists on 1 May. There was growing sentiment from party cadres that he was weakening, that he was a man who "made revolution only with his mouth." "Even an 'assassination plot'… could do little to revive Hitler's popularity," writes Fest. "Another shrewd observer noted early in May that Hitler's star seemed 'to be waning.'" The Nazis were a "leaderless party." Several "long-term followers attempted to rouse him, above all urging him to break with 'Putzi' Hanfstaengl, who had introduced the virtuous Hitler to 'lovely ladies'...calling for more and more 'champagne parties.'" According to Fest, "Hitler no longer had a choice on the evening of November 6. Since the defeat of May 1...the call to act was almost unavoidable...the storm troopers themselves were impatiently pressing for action." Kershaw agrees: "Hitler was under pressure to act."[61]

Bullock concurs: "failure to act now must mean the collapse of the Nazi Party and the total discredit of its leader. Lieutenant Wilhelm Bruckner later gave evidence that he had begged Hitler to strike soon, since 'the day is coming when I won't be able to hold the men back. If nothing happens now, they'll run away from us,'"[62] he said. Toland adds: "Early that September Hitler attempted to bolster his slipping prestige," quoting two Nazi leaders to the effect that something had to be done "to keep the men together." "These were the urgings Hitler needed."[63]

This does not prove that Hitler was always prompted by group commands—in actuality he often ignored or defied Party pressures on him—but it does show that at times he could be. A full-scale study is needed, but a few additional tentative suggestions can be made.

For a regime that ruled in part by terror, it is remarkable that it paid so much attention to forming consensus—Goebbels's propaganda machine, for example. It is also remarkable that a terror state should make such strenuous efforts to keep track of public opinion. That is in part because Nazi Germany wasn't so much of a terror state in its beginnings, and it appears that Hitler wanted to be loved, not feared—or at all odds much less feared. "Curiously enough," writes William Carr, "in some respects dictatorships seem more responsive to public feeling than other forms of government. From Gestapo reports Göring was keenly aware of the unresolved tensions lying beneath the surface conformity of the masses." One historian has even argued, somewhat convincingly, that Hitler was more concerned with and sensitive to popular opinion than some democratic leaders.[64] At times Hitler was deeply interested in public feelings, commenting disdainfully during the Czech Crisis, for example, on the silent crowds in Berlin when war seemed near.

Several studies of public opinion, along with histories of everyday life in Nazi Germany, collected oral histories, several memoirs, and other testimonials, have shown that the Nazi propaganda machine could not manipulate people as completely as today's popular imagination has come to believe. One historian has argued that the whole notion of a terror state is overdrawn and that Hitler relied more on consensus than fear. Another scholar has suggested that even in oppressive regimes several subtle ways exist for people to express displeasure, even resistance, through society's "hidden transcripts." He writes: "At its most elementary level the hidden transcript represents an acting out in fantasy—and occasionally in secretive practice—of the anger and reciprocal aggression denied by the presence of domination."[65] For any regime, no matter how repressive, there is always the possibility of open but symbolic and disguised expressions of hostility, as in various passive aggressive behaviors, absenteeism, and work slowdowns.

Popular films may constitute one of these hidden transcripts. Certainly, it is possible for them to communicate group feelings. For example, the number of new war films (and war novels) produced in Germany in the late 1920s went up steadily before 1933, then increased dramatically in the early years of the Nazi era, with "peace" novels (and "peace" films) showing a steep decline. German historian Wolfram Wette has seen this as a striking confirmation that in the German public at large a "militant and anti-pacifist trend began some years before Hitler's accession to power." The notion reinforces the argument that Germany's recent troubled past had joined with the stressors of the Great Depression, high unemployment, and political turmoil to regress Germans to levels of repressed childish rage which they could then experience and re-experience in aggressive war movies. Moreover, their rage was mirrored by Hitler's rage, then (as later) exemplified as Germany's raging-child delegate. But rather than the thematic focus of films (and novels) communicating merely a general tone, it is just possible that sometimes specific films could cue leaders into feeling certain ways or doing specific things. (President Nixon's viewing of *Patton* comes to mind.) One example for Nazi Germany—a possible hidden transcript—is the film *Der Herrscher* (*The Ruler*), which has been called by historian David Stuart Hull "the most important political film of the year," (1937). It starred the most famous German film actor Emil Jannings, who "was awarded the National Film Prize at the annual May Day celebrations, and...was given a special award for 'superlative human character impersonation.'" In the film Jannings plays a steel magnate who falls in love with his secretary after his wife dies. When he plans to marry her, his grown-up children attempt to have him certified insane. According to the British critic who saw the film at its July release in England, it presented the magnate "very much in the light of a dictator (his workers actually call him their Führer). There is also one stretch of rhetoric at a board meeting where he tells his co-directors that it is their duty to obey him even though it might mean ruin," and when he hears of an attempt to certify him insane, "he does in fact behave exactly like a dangerous lunatic."[66]

The film, consciously meant as entertainment, seems to have offered, unconsciously, a way for some Germans to experience, express, and circulate some of their hidden true feelings. They could relate to *Der Herrscher* because the real Führer was behaving exactly like a dangerous lunatic, although publicly and privately they couldn't say so. Was the film meant in part as a prediction, or a wish for the future? When shown abroad, did its transparent symbolism reinforce the notion that Hitler, represented by the Hitler-symbol, *der Herrscher*, was crazy and should continue to be used as a container for Europe's out-of-control feelings, or was Hitler's own raging behavior enough? Could Hitler have understood the film's theme as a cue or a criticism? Did he see it, hear about it, or discuss it? If so, is there anyway to assess its impact on him? Would he have identified with the main character? How would he have felt about a rebellion against "the film's" Führer, or about "his" children declaring him insane? These questions, probably far too speculative for most historians, would need to be explored before any conclusions could be reached, but it seems clear enough at least that this film shows how subversive fantasies, as well as aggressive ones, can circulate freely even in dictatorships. That suggests that on unconscious levels Hitler, like any leader—like Chamberlain—could be at least temporarily cued by displays of public displeasure, expressed in the symbolic forms explicit and implicit in society's several hidden transcripts. It seems to be especially true for a hypersensitive leader who, like Hitler, had been exquisitely attuned to carry out delegated tasks since childhood.

One of Hitler's emotional tasks was to transform group depression, to make Germans feel better. He could do this by making them feel strong, and because of the emotional damage sustained in his own childhood it remained a perpetual quest of his own. It follows that anything that made Hitler feel weak (including things that made him feel he was losing control) would prompt him to act in ways to prove that he was strong and in control. One of the ways he, and Germans, could feel strong was by rearming, by breaking the Versailles Treaty, by threatening war, and thereby winning foreign policy successes. Every time the generals cautioned him against war because Germany (read "Hitler") was weak, their cautions had the opposite effect, moving him on to newer, riskier foreign policy gambles, despite, and because of, his generals conscious efforts to restrain him. Until 1941, each success had the effect of undercutting their opposition.[67]

This is not to say that Hitler's foreign policy goals were driven by domestic emotional issues alone: there was his own conscious agenda as he strove to fulfill the foreign policy goals he had set out in *Mein Kampf* and in his speeches, as well as all that was to be emotionally (and strategically) gained from his successes abroad. Yet domestic factors were also understood by several observers to be motivating him at the time. "It looks like Hitler—who they say spoke like a madman—felt he must bring off some 'coup' to reassure himself after his recent and damaging internal crisis," observed Harvey from London, "and he has chosen Austria."[68] Hitler's first Foreign Minister, Neurath, commented on how Hitler hoped to whip up popular support for his regime by foreign policy successes, a classic technique Hitler knew well since he had described it to Sir Eric Phipps as early as December 1933.[69]

There is solid evidence that Hitler felt under increasingly heavy stress from late-1937 into 1938. There was troubling evidence of labor unrest in the Third Reich to add to his other stressors,[70] and he complained about several physical ailments which, if not entirely psychosomatic in origin, were exacerbated by the pressures he felt at home, from abroad, and from the feelings welling up inside himself. There is a tendency to overlook these stressors, especially among those who downplay psychology and seek to explain behavior by physiology alone.

The quest for the physiological causes of Hitler's behavior can be largely defensive, allowing scholars to proceed as if emotions don't matter. On the other hand, it is equally true that psychological historians have largely ignored organic issues. Bert Edward Park, who has studied the role of illness among several world leaders, remarks that: "organic disease states may prompt the appearance of psychiatric disturbance, an important point that the psychohistorians have not dealt with successfully in Hitler's case." In reality, efforts to explain Hitler by organic causes have turned up some important medical facts. Syphilis as a cause has resurfaced and is compellingly argued in Deborah Hayden's new book *Pox*, which seems to have convinced the reviewer in *The New York Times*. In any case, the question of syphilis needs to be seriously reexamined. There is also compelling evidence, and more agreement, that Hitler suffered from Parkinson's disease, the symptoms of which became more acute in the latter stages of the war. Dr. Morell's mildly toxic injections and Hitler's poor lifelong nutritional practices played their parts too, but again, more acutely in the latter stages of the war. While psychiatrists have diagnosed him as "psychopathic," "abnormal," "sociopathic," and "a narcissistic personality with paranoid trends," they are generally agreed that these were not the result of organic causes. The consensus, in addition, is that he was not clinically insane, a view confirmed by at least one of his doctors and generally accepted by historians. The answer to the Hitler enigma then lies not in physiology but in psychology. Clearly, the two are linked, scientific studies showing that child abuse and other repeated traumas can, and do, have neurological consequences. But while most historians are reluctant to connect child abuse to electrochemical processes in the brain, still less to later behavior, they do sometimes recognize personality factors, from whatever their origins, in explaining Hitler's irrationality. Take, for example, the influence of the Hitler cult, which he first helped create, then later re-absorbed. "Hitler swallowed the Führer cult itself, hook, line, and sinker," writes Kershaw. "He was the most ardent believer in his own infallibility and destiny," concluding: "It was not a good premise for rational decision making."[71]

That Hitler's decision-making, certainly his thinking, was becoming increasing irrational in the late 1930s is recognized by virtually everyone, and not only because of organic causes. This, more than any specific illness, is what counts. Nor is his irrationality entirely the result of the arrogance of power, or Hitler's fantasies of his own infallibility, as Kershaw would have it, all of which surely played a part. What goes missing from the usual historical, even medical, analysis is the influence of stress on Hitler's physical and mental states, and how the two interacted.

It is well known that he complained to Speer of stomach disorders, as he did in 1936, and spoke of shattered nerves and insomnia in late-1937 and early 1938.[72] His thoughts began to turn "morbid." He began to speak often of his own death. He declared in his secret talk to his generals as early as 5 November 1937 (the Hossbach Memorandum which recorded his contingency planning for war in central Europe) that this talk should be considered his "testamentary bequest in case of my decease."[73] In early May 1938, in one of the last documents written by his hand before the war, he prepared his Will and Testament.[74] Hitler was filling up with "bad feelings." "These morbid thoughts," one historian has said, "probably strengthened his conviction that he 'could wait no longer' as he told the German Foreign Minister Neurath when the latter tried to dissuade him from war."[75]

Unleashing war meant unleashing the repressed rage within him. Bad feelings of being "poisoned" were made "real" through the organic metaphor and projected into an external container: Czechoslovakia—which he spoke of as a "tumor"—became the target. Already on 7 December 1937 a secret update of his Operation Green called for an offensive war, but Hitler had still been unable to bring himself to act by 20 May 1938.[76] Cues from the German and world press changed that.

Unfounded rumors of German troop movements on 20 May circulated through Europe provoking stern warnings to Berlin from London and Paris. Chamberlain believed those warnings had worked to restrain Hitler, while Hitler's denials were interpreted in the Western press as humiliations.[77] That he "backed down" was a theme repeated by the

German press. The hypersensitive Hitler reacted by regressing even more, by plunging into an infantile "black rage" for eight days at the Berghof. When he returned to Berlin still angry, Operation Green was changed: "It is my unalterable decision to smash Czechoslovakia by military action in the near future," he said. The date chosen was 1 October.[78]

One student of the Czech Crisis believes that without the intervention of the press Czechoslovakia could easily have remained on the diplomatic back burner for many months,[79] but perhaps not. Another historian believes that the change to the 1 October invasion date for Operation Green indicates "the seriousness with which Hitler took his own press campaign,"[80] and this does seem to be the case. His rage at being humiliated had been provoked. Germany manipulated him through the German press, as it had several times through various hidden and not so hidden transcripts, just as Klara had manipulated him before. German "Motherland" cued "her child" Adolf, while a host of other signals arrived from abroad.

VI BRITAIN AND GERMANY

WE CANNOT ANY LONGER TOLERATE
THE TUTELAGE OF BRITISH GOVERNESSES.[1]
—*Adolf Hitler*, 1938

If Hitler was tuned to and responded to the wishes of the German people, he was at least theoretically capable of hearing conscious and unconscious cues from abroad. What is the evidence? Who might have cued him and how?

Hitler's connection with the world began every day in late-morning as his manservant laid out newspapers for him to read while his bath was being drawn. This does not prove much beyond the fact that Hitler read, or sometimes read, his morning papers, nor does it prove that he was ever motivated to do anything specific by what he read. Still, D.C. Watt argues for the powerful influence of the press on a fundamentally reactive Hitler when he writes that he "sat back and waited for events to light up in him that spark of intuition as to where and when to make his next move which made him so quickly the dominant figure in Europe. His almost instinctive sense of timing was based on the same source as that from which he originally formed his views of politics, from his reading in the press." Nor was it only the domestic press: "his Reichspresschef, Otto Dietrich reported directly on the tone of comment in the leading newspapers of Europe." Kershaw confirms these influences.[2] Although Watt doesn't mention it, in addition to the domestic and international press, Hitler could be cued by direct diplomatic exchanges, not only by those he personally experienced but by those directly reported to him or by those he in some way heard about. The evidence shows that at times "passive" Hitler's "intuitions" were being regularly fed by messages from abroad.

Of all the countries in the European family, the one he

heeded most was Great Britain. The British knew that cueing Hitler was at least possible since Ambassador Rumbold had reported to London early in the game that "Hitler is...alive to every popular instinct." And the sources corroborate A.J.P. Taylor's intuitive judgment of some forty years ago that much of interwar diplomacy was an "Anglo-German duologue."[3]

The answer to why Hitler's attentions were so intently focused on Britain lies not just in Britain's great power status, but also in Hitler's perceptions which, like the rest of Europe, he drew in part from the European family fantasy, a fantasy the British had themselves helped perpetuate by their own conscious, semi-conscious, and unconscious self-perception.

When classical scholar Gilbert Murray spoke to a large audience at London's Queens Hall in late-1938, he wondered how it was that Spain could have been written off by, "the land that once held the Mother of Parliaments."[4] Britain not only held the "Mother of Parliaments" but was the imperial "Mother Country" which had "spawned" a "brood" of "offspring" and ruled over numerous "childlike" colonial peoples. One "offspring," the United States, had, in "adolescent" rebellion, won its independence, or, in a slightly different but related organic metaphor, had been "born" of revolution. Other "offspring" eventually "grew up" and, after reaching "maturity," were granted autonomous status as Dominions. The maternal image easily found its way into literature, Orwell writing of the two major characters in his *Burmese Days*, that it was their habit to "pretend the British Empire was an aged female patient."[5] "Mother Britain" still retained its place at the center of the Commonwealth, and Britannia, not John Bull, ruled the waves.

To be sure, John Bull had been around in British political cartoons for a long time, frequently cavorting with Britannia, Europa, or both for most of the nineteenth century. The same cartoon images continued into the twentieth century, and in the 1930s the British satirical humor magazine *Punch* regularly featured John Bull, but, as one historian points out, always alongside "his battle-axe wife Britannia." The world press naturally caught hold of and repeated these images. Political cartoonists could and did merge male and female, portraying John Bull "in a family way" without anyone giving it so much as a second thought. "I've got a pain round my belt line," says John Bull to "Doctor" Chamberlain in a 1938 cartoon, because, having eaten the world, his enormous "pregnant" belly seems ready to explode. Many political cartoons regularly portrayed Britain in maternal roles built around nursery-rhyme themes. In 1938, the humiliated British "Lioness" lies in a sickbed called "Czech Crisis" with Little Red Riding Hood, a basket of "Assorted War Scares" in hand, saying ironically: "What Terrible Teeth You Have Grandma." Also in 1938, a black, "Old-Mother-Hubbard" Britain discovers a dachshund-Germany ready to devour African colonies after consuming Austria and Czechoslovakia. Books of political cartoons reproducing these maternal images were printed in Germany in the 1930s.[6]

There are indications that many Germans thought about Britain in these ways without cartoon reinforcement from abroad. It does not diminish the courage of the heroes of the German Resistance, for example, to observe that several resistance leaders demonstrated what looks like dependent thinking about Britain, before and during the war, by imagining they could move against Hitler only with British aide.[7]

Royal marriages in the latter nineteenth century helped reinforce the fantasy of Britain's maternal image by flooding Europe with a "flock of English and half-English princesses," who, says one historian, "introduced more than just chintzes and nannies and rice puddings into the royal households of the Continent." They also introduced English, which soon superseded French as the language of most Continental courts. "Royal children were being educated in English, and in England, by the score."[8] With English and half-English princesses as the consorts of kings and nobles before and after 1914, it was natural for Europeans at large to think more and more in terms of the formula: "princesses" equal "mothers," connecting backward to "Mother Britain."

It was the same for Germany, where Kaiser Wilhelm II's British mother made him the grandson of Queen Victoria. Did Hitler associate England and Victoria, by positive or negative identifications, with the Kaiser? It is still unclear. Robert Waite made a beginning in understanding both Wilhelm and Hitler psychologically, but his book *Kaiser and Führer* is more a "parallel lives" than a comparative study, and although he observes that "Hitler and Wilhelm II despised each other" and that "each sought to use the other for his own political purposes," his book unfortunately leaves us pretty much in the dark about what Hitler knew and fantasized about Wilhelm. Of course, Wilhelm's "new course" of *Weltpolitik*, his support for the Boers in the Boer War, his naval building, threats, provocations and bluster made him look a little like the bad boy bully of Europe before 1914. Insofar as one can tell, Hitler didn't think of him along these lines, however, at least consciously. A few hints as to his views come from Hitler's meandering World War II table talks where he mentions Wilhelm only rarely, saying that his "behavior was unworthy of a monarch," that he was "tactless," "vain," and "stupid," that he had "bad taste," was "Jewish," and a "strutting puppet,"[9] words sounding more like an angry son directed at a father figure (and hence connected to displaced memories of Alois) than to Wilhelm as the grandson of Victoria. The full details of Hitler's fantasies, how much they allowed him to identify with the Kaiser, or, as Wilhelm's "successor," how strongly they may have reinforced his fantasies about the maternal governess Britannia, needs more, and careful, study. Could the Führer in his imaginings, like the Kaiser, be in "reality" not only the "son," but also the "grandson" of Mother Britain? Whatever further research reveals, it seems clear from Hitler's own words that he experienced Britain, as did others, as a maternal object, seeing himself in unconscious fantasy as its out-of-control child, particularly since the British sent him that message.

There is no inherent contradiction in Hitler thinking this way, since he and others could think simultaneously of Germania as their "mother" and Britannia as their "mother," the logic of the unconscious—or better, the psycho-logic of the unconscious, as has been mentioned several times—allowing for multiple and contradictory fantasies to exist side by side, or even, from time to time, to merge with one another. This is clear in Hitler's maternal-like fantasies about Great Britain.

He often spoke of the British "governess," including his 9 October 1938 speech quoted at the beginning of this chapter. He spoke of the "British Motherland" and "her colonies" in the Hossbach Memorandum. He spoke repeatedly of Britain as one of the "midwives of Versailles." His sense of almost childlike dependency is revealed by his continual, insistent protests that Germany was *not* inferior to Britain which he made in his 28 April 1939 speech to the Reichstag, where, to flaunt his independence, he unilaterally denounced the Anglo-German Naval Agreement of 1936.[10]

In the beginning of that 28 April speech, Hitler had spoken of how "I have always expounded the idea of a close friendship and collaboration between Germany and England." He declared it was not only his, but Germany's wish. "In my Movement I found innumerable others of like mind. Perhaps they joined me because of my attitude in the matter." Hitler's personal wish for formal collaboration with Britain went back to the early days of the Nazi movement and had been expressed in *Mein Kampf* where he said that the "new Reich must again set itself on the march along the road of the Teutonic Knights of old, to obtain by the

German sword sod for the German plow....For such a policy there was but one ally in Europe: England."[11] Geopolitical theorist Karl Haushofer was one of the many who sided with him in believing that Germany and Britain should join together. This was, in part, a traditional idea, a continuity mentioned by historian Andreas Hillgruber, among others, who has noted the "common desire of all statesmen in Berlin from 1890 to 1945 to forge some sort of link with London."[12] But part of the impulse was personal, Hitler's effort to recapture in fantasy his childhood "secret alliances" with Klara against Alois. "With England alone was it possible," *Mein Kampf* said, "our rear protected, to begin the new Germanic march."[13] The need to protect his rear was geographic and strategic, of course—the need to protect Germany from the danger of a two-front war—but part was also personal, springing, one can guess, from memories and fears of childhood beatings, the wish for Klara's protection against Alois's assaults, and the desire to turn against his tormenter. It could only have produced anger, or at least ambivalence, at "England." Had not Klara at those times stood by and waited, much as Mother Britain would do again in the 1930s?

Hitler is purported to have said "England needs a sword on the continent," and in his authenticated public statements one can hear the reality beneath the ambivalence of denial: "if England may look upon Germany as a vassal State," he said in his 28 April 1939 speech, "then our love and friendly feelings have indeed been wasted on her." The overt alliance he longed for never had to materialize so long as the hidden, unconscious one worked so well. Yet, the admired Britain of *Mein Kampf* became, by late-1937, the "hate-inspired" antagonist of the Hossbach Memorandum. Overy and Wheatcroft have called this "a profound historical irony...{for} this was just the stage at which efforts to give Germany what she wanted were at their height; yet in Germany it was exactly the point at which anti-British hostility became a significant factor, the point where Hitler began to perceive Britain as an enemy, not a friend."[14] They observe but don't explain. Why did the change occur?

The answer is psychological, the transformation resulting from the European family system, namely, the increased cueing coming from Britain in the fall of 1937 and after. Hitler's desire to no longer tolerate the "tutelage of the British governesses," to no longer serve as "England's... vassal state," stemmed from his anger at Mother Britain's increased "commands," even as he felt driven to pick up on her cues. He had been ambivalent toward Klara too, performing as her delegate and longing for symbiosis while at the same time striving for separation and individuation, even as he repressed his fear of engulfment and the urge to "bite, mutilate, and destroy," intolerable urges he felt toward the "Mother" Britain he now wanted to destroy as much as for the German "Motherland" he eventually did destroy.

What commands did Mother Britain send? Since it was necessary for Hitler to be the fantasy container as Britain's and Europe's out-of-control, raging child, Germany was often told it was lawless, which Hitler took as a command and which did little to curb German lawlessness. The Nazis were "gangsters," wrote British ambassador Sir Horace Rumbold in his dispatches back home. Harvey's diary speaks of "the Nazi gangsters" and "highwaymen's methods." Frank Ashton-Gwatkin saw Hitler as "something of a cross between a Salvationist and a gunman." Lord Lothian's efforts to exonerate Hitler simply served to reinforce the same image when he wrote that he was "a visionary rather than a gangster." General Ironside had no doubt that "force is the only thing which tells with these...gangsters." Halifax compared Göring to a "modern Robin Hood" who produced "on me a composite impression of film star {and} gangster." Others in the European family reinforced the image: Göring, said Ciano, gave "a slight suggestion of Al Capone."[15]

Private sentiments were reinforced by public discourse, John Wheeler-Bennett's 1934 book *The Disarmament Deadlock* declaring that hopes for disarmament and security were "vain until the gangster element has been eliminated from international politics." The theme reappeared over and again in the British press, the *News Chronicle* criticizing the *Daily Mail* because: "It blesses and encourages every swashbuckler who threatens the peace of Europe." The Cardiff *Western Mail* said Britain should not trust Hitler because: "He is a gangster who must be arrested at the first opportunity, unless the German People are capable of removing him." Of course, it was an accurate description: Hitler and the Nazis were gangsters, and worse. The theme appropriately continued into the war and after with Elizabeth Wiskeman writing of Nazi "criminals" and "gangsters" and A.L. Rouse using the term several times in his book *Appeasement*,[16] all of which was reinforced by the horrific revelations of Nazi crimes at the Nuremberg trials.

Did these images of gangsterism count for Germans? If measured by efforts to deny the charge, they mattered very much. In justifying the events of *Kristallnacht*, Joseph Goebbels wrote in the *Völkischer Beobachter* that "the Jewish press of North America stirred up hatred" by describing "the people who rose up against Jews as...bands of gangsters...it is all a medley of lies." Gangster films were banned in the Third Reich, and the Nazis boasted that they had eliminated crime. In further efforts to deny the realities of their bad behavior and bad intentions, the Germans sought international confirmation for what they wanted themselves and the world to believe, that they were mature adults with a respect for the law, which were the psychological and propagandistic motives driving their diplomatic need to consummate what they insisted on calling "Gentlemen's Agreements" with other countries—an "absurd phrase," says A.J.P. Taylor, which was an "invention of Papen's."[17]

German efforts to break free of the gangster image did not work because the charge of lawlessness was reinforced by Germany's actual lawless behavior. In the same way that some parents encourage juveniles to be delinquent, Britain encouraged Germany, thus allowing all of Europe, like the parents of juvenile delinquents, to experience Europe's repressed sadism vicariously. But as important as were general commands to be lawless, more important were the specific messages Britain sent to Germany.

Three events should be enough to illustrate how the British government and press "clued" Hitler at critical junctures: first, Hitler's 1937 decision to move against Austria and Czechoslovakia; second, his 1938 decision to annex the Czech Sudetenland; third, his reaction to Britain's formal warning on 23 August 1939 not to attack Poland.

It is worth remembering the words of London *Times* editor Geoffrey Dawson in his 23 May 1937 letter to Lord Lothian, cited above in Chapter III, in which he wondered why the Germans were so angry at the *Times*, admitting, "I spend my nights taking out anything which I think will hurt their susceptibilities and in dropping in little things which are intended to soothe them." It was certainly one of the ways the British helped create a general climate encouraging Hitler. In any case, Hitler's intentions to move against Austria and Czechoslovakia were clear as of 5 November 1937, if not before. The Hossbach Memorandum reported him to have spoken then of Britain and France—in part projectively—as Germany's "hate-inspired" antagonists. He envisioned several contingencies, but "our first objective must be to overthrow Czechoslovakia and Austria." In this famous document, Hitler repeatedly used such words as "weakness" and "disintegration." He believed "sterility was setting in," and felt "disorders" were immanent, preoccupations which suggest he was reacting to feelings that his own intra-psychic defenses were disintegrating, which he then projected onto Europe. The discharge of his own aggression was rationalized by his conclusion that "Germany's problems could be solved only by the use of force." Germany at this moment was not only the symbiotic Klara, but, as he merged in fantasy with "her," Germany became himself. He believed that war was now possible because "almost certainly Britain, and probably France as well, had already tacitly written off the Czechs and were reconciled to the fact that this question would be cleared up in due course by Germany."[18] Was this merely guesswork, or was Hitler's intuition based on some real cues coming from abroad?

For several weeks in the fall of 1937, long before Hitler's secret November meeting, the British press had been discussing central Europe, Austria and Czechoslovakia in particular. The press had speculated on how Hitler might be given a free hand in central Europe in exchange for German guarantees accepting British control of Germany's former colonies. In this environment, two weeks before the conference in the Reich Chancellery and the words recorded by Hossbach, Clement Attlee criticized his own government by telling the House of Commons: "The policy of this Government throughout, right on from 1931, has always been to try and appease the aggressor by the sacrifice of weaker states." In retrospect, Atlee's words sound like a prediction of things to come. Even though historian Neville Thompson counts this as the first formal anti-appeasement statement in parliament, anti-appeasement statements could themselves contain hidden cues. Although Atlee was speaking of Britain's policies regarding Manchuria and Abyssinia, such statements could be understood as a general confirmation of Britain's continuing policy toward Germany, and in any case there were other, more direct, clues. Before Hitler's secret 5 November meeting, the Duke and Duchess of Windsor, through cheering German crowds, had come to visit Hitler at Berchtesgaden, and, while published sources are ambiguous about what passed between Duke and Führer in their twenty-minute private meeting, the mere presence of the Duke and Duchess as Hitler's guests worked, at least in Hitler's mind, to symbolize British friendship and encourage his ambitions.[19]

At the time of the Hossbach Memorandum, the British government, not just the press, was actually talking about how he could be given a free hand in central Europe: "we all favored approach to Hitler and offer of a bilateral declaration of our policy," reads Harvey's diary on 7 November 1937. "Then approach regarding Czechoslovakia could also be made" which "gave autonomy to Sudeten."[20] Chamberlain planned to use Halifax's upcoming visit to Germany as a way of opening new negotiations.

Halifax met Hitler at Berchtesgaden on 19 November. Three days before the official announcement of what had been discussed was made public to the House of Commons, the *Evening Standard* scooped the story with Vladimir Poliakoff reporting in the paper on 20 November that: "in return for the agreement {on colonies} Hitler would expect the British Government to leave him a free hand in Central Europe,"[21] exactly what Hitler was led to believe by Halifax's visit.

A.J.P. Taylor, citing several primary sources, sums up what Halifax communicated at the meeting—and what it meant. "Halifax said all that Hitler expected to hear. He praised Nazi Germany 'as the bulwark of Europe against Bolshevism'; he sympathized with past German grievances. In particular he pointed to certain questions where 'possible alterations might be destined to come about with the "passage of Time."' They were Danzig, Austria, and Czechoslovakia. Taylor judged that "Halifax's remarks, if they had any practical sense, were an invitation to Hitler to promote German nationalist agitation in Danzig, Czechoslovakia, and Austria; an assurance also that this agitation would not be opposed from without." Halifax said these things while Eden, whose memoirs later blamed Halifax for not being firm, actually reinforced them in London by telling Ribbentrop: "'People in England recognised that a closer connection between Germany and Austria would have to come about sometime.'" The message was further reinforced by news from France. "Papen, on a visit to Paris, 'was amazed to note' that Chautemps, the premier, and Bonnet, then finance minister, 'considered a reorientation of French policy in Central Europe as entirely open to discussion,'" and had "'no objection to a marked extension of German influence in Austria.'"[22]

The Halifax visit was used, according to historian Gerhard Weinberg, "to further the interpretation that Britain would acquiesce in German designs." Even Weinberg, whose study of German foreign policy has little use for either psychology or the complicity of the Allies, admits: "The soundings from London were taken in Germany...as confirmation of Hitler's views that Britain would not fight for Austria or Czechoslovakia, and that it was safe for him to move."[23] On 29 November, as one observer said at the time, "The *Times* published a leading article which, in reference to the relationship between Germany and Austria, then looming up as the next crisis point in European affairs, carefully launched the suggestion that Austria's destiny lay with Germany."[24] Such discussions reinforced Hitler's belief that Britain would acquiesce. It is no wonder that Hitler began to pressure Austria. On 12 February 1938 Austria's Chancellor Schuschnigg visited Hitler at the Berghof, Hitler's mountain retreat in Bavaria, but for at least two weeks before, the British had pursued discussions among themselves on how the coming *Anschluss* could be arranged. "During the week, discussions took place...for a general settlement to include something about Austria, Czechoslovakia," said Harvey's diary for 6 February. For 16 February his diary reads: "*Anschluss* (which hasn't yet occurred), or at least a satellite Austria, is probably inevitable." This matched the attitude of the British press. From "16 February, there was a striking assumption that

Austria was a closed case, that war in her support would be out of the question."[25]

The psychological role of Austria needs to be carefully studied, but while contemporary western statesmen, diplomats, and journalists saw the *Anschluss* as rape, German historian Hans Rothfels later observed that "rape has seldom been accompanied by such frantic rejoicing on the part of the victim." Even at the time, some people understood there was a difference between western fantasies and Austrian realities. In reaction to the cheering Austrian crowds they were watching together, Hitler purportedly turned and asked journalist Ward Price "Is this a rape?"[26] For their part, British guilt over Britain's unconscious and overt clues compelled Chamberlain to begin his speech after the *Anschluss* in the House of Commons on 14 March by denying that his government had had anything to do with it. Such a disclaimer might not have been needed in any case; as one historian puts it, "there was remarkably little stir in England."[27]

Conversations in the Cabinet and in the British press turned immediately to Czechoslovakia, thoughts that had been tending that way for some time. One month before the *Anschluss*, General Ironside had anticipated events, writing in his diary on 16 February that: "the next to be attacked will be Czechoslovakia." On 19 March the *Times* reported a speech by Alan Lennox-Boyd, Parliamentary Secretary to the Ministry of Labor, in which he said that "he could countenance nothing more ridiculous than a guarantee that the frontiers of Czechoslovakia should not be violated... and from what he knew of Mr. Chamberlain, he did not think he would make a move to give a guarantee of that kind. Germany, he said, could absorb Czechoslovakia and Great Britain would remain secure." According to one historian, Lennox-Boyd's words "were an accurate reflection of the last Cabinet discussion of Czechoslovakia. No doubt Lennox-Boyd had picked up the tone of the meeting from those Ministers who attended." His speech was immediately broadcast to the Czechs by the Germans.[28]

Throughout the Czech Crisis the press continued to telegraph the wishes of the British people to Europe and to Hitler as much as to 10 Downing Street. "It is impossible that the British Government should pledge us to fight to hold together the ramshackle state of Czechoslovakia," said the *Daily Express* to its 2,329,000 readers on 29 April 1938. On 21 May it alerted the world: "Britain does not undertake to look after Abyssinia, Austria, China, or Czechoslovakia. And we are happy to inform the *Daily Herald* that the first three clients are off our books, and the fourth may be off, too, anytime now." A week earlier, Chamberlain had told a group of Canadian and American journalists, as reported in *The New York Times*, that he favored a "separation of the German districts from the body of the Czech republic and the annexation of them to Germany." In addition to the *Times*, his views were reported in the *Montreal Gazette* and the *New York Herald-Tribune*, and, since it amounted to Chamberlain letting the cat out of the bag, his words caused a stormy debate in Parliament.[29]

Even when the British did send a warning to Germany during the Czech Crisis, historian Larry Fuchser says, "everything possible was done to nullify its effect," and the diplomatic documents confirm it. The French were cabled that they were not to "read more into those warnings than is justified." British Ambassador Nevile Henderson was apologetic in Berlin, and Allied pressures were redoubled on the Czechs. Throughout these months, British attitudes can be followed in Harvey's diary. On 22 February he believed Chamberlain's speech "was an open intimation that Great Britain would do nothing to protect the small nation from the dictators." On 11 March, Halifax told the departing German ambassador Ribbentrop, "if it was Austria today it might be Czechoslovakia or what not tomorrow." Ten days later, the Foreign Affairs Committee "considered further the Czech memo and a draft statement for Parliament to be made Thursday....It is of course as good as an invitation to Hitler to step into Czechoslovakia," wrote Harvey. On 11 May Harvey had lunch with Charles Peake and W.N. Ewer, editor of the *Daily Herald*. "Latter said he thought Sudeten would have to go." On the next day: "I lunched with King-Hall....He also regards Central Europe as written off."[30] About that time, second-in-command to Ambassador Henderson, Ivone Kirkpatrick, was telling a German official: "If the German Government would advise the British Government confidentially what solution the Sudeten German question they were striving after...the British Government would bring such pressure to bear in Prague that the Czechoslovak Government would be compelled to accede to German wishes."[31]

Should the Czechs resist, German armies might eventually overwhelm them, but this became a certainty were the Sudeten areas ceded, as the Czech defenses were strongest there. That outcome was precisely what the British press had been suggesting for months. Journalists wondered in private correspondence as early as 27 February 1938, two weeks before the *Anschluss*: "Is there anything at all to the suggestion from the 'Church Times' that Czechoslovakia would be better off all around if it lost its German minority?" Throughout the summer of the crisis the British press repeated the idea—especially the *Times*, which several times suggested the possibility of revising frontiers. The *New Statesman* proposed revision again on 27 August, and declared, "the strategical value of the Bohemian frontier should not be made the occasion of a world war." According to Elizabeth Wiskeman, the Czech Ambassador to Britain, Jan Masaryk, "was shattered by the *Statesman* article."[32] When the *Times* published its famous go-ahead in early September, Hitler finally reacted.

Although the Sudeten Germans had not yet asked to join Germany, and although Hitler had not yet claimed the Sudeten areas, the *Times* on 7 September 1938 suggested that Czechoslovakia should consider "the cession of that fringe of alien populations who are contiguous to the nation to which they are united by race"—namely, the Sudeten Germans.[33] The Germans believed the *Times* was a semi-official organ used for *ballons d'essai*.[34] For the first time, in a violent speech five days after the *Times* article, Hitler demanded Sudeten self-determination.[35]

The significance of the *Times* article was understood at the time. "It was broadcast to Germany," wrote Harvey in his diary the day after it appeared, "and has been interpreted everywhere as a *ballon d'essai* and as foreshadowing a fresh surrender by H.M.G."[36] Coming as it did after the months-long statements of the press and various communications from British officials, it seems clear enough that these messages, not Hitler's "misreading" of the situation, account for what Weinberg concludes was "Hitler's absolute conviction in the summer of 1938 that he could attack Czechoslovakia without precipitating a general war."[37]

Ambassador Nevile Henderson and Horace Wilson, Chamberlain's special envoy, met with Hitler in Berlin on 26 September. When Hitler began to verbally abuse the Czechs Henderson interrupted: "the British Government would see to it that the Czechs did hand over the territory." Suddenly, writes historian Martin Gilbert, "Hitler was incredulous."[38]

He was incredulous because Henderson had done nothing less than give the show away. It was one thing to suggest by subtle cues, another to extend open invitations. Henderson had broken the rules of the unconscious game. Or perhaps Gilbert is wrong, and maybe Henderson was too: Hitler was not so much incredulous as feeling stymied and frustrated, and was thrown by Henderson's words because he did not want to act under British tutelage—that is, with parental consent.

Of course, Hitler did get the Sudeten territories at Munich instead of the war he wanted, and the missed opportunity filled him with anger. Kirkpatrick saw the signs as Hitler signed the Munich Agreement, "as if he were signing away his birthright." The war that had offered the promise of escape from his internal emotional chaos and the British governess's parental control had eluded him. With those internal intra-psychic defenses still crumbling in the winter of 1938-39, and the imperative to separate and individuate as pressing as ever, war was as much if not more a necessity than ever before. By mid–March 1939, as predicted by several commentators in the press and in the British government, Hitler marched on Prague. Within two weeks the British had guaranteed the borders of Poland, which was understood, long before the hyphenated Czecho-Slovak state's demise, to be Hitler's next target. Did Hitler believe that the British would fulfill their obligations this time around? Probably not: Britain had guaranteed the state of Czechoslovakia, too, but when reminded of that fact Chamberlain tried to absolve Britain by telling the House of Commons: "We never guaranteed the frontiers as they existed." It seems clear that the British had expected this ending all along as they withheld loans to the rump-state following the Munich Agreement until the situation "clarified"—which meant they were not about to throw money down a rat hole knowing as they did that it was only a matter of time before Germany absorbed the rest of Czechoslovakia. As historian H.L. Rowse later judged: "Hitler can hardly be blamed for thinking, with these people to deal with, that there was no point at which they would stick."[39]

The British and French military negotiations with the Soviet Union, which began in the summer of 1939, seemed to hold out the prospect of thwarting Hitler's plans for Poland. But the British and French dragged their feet, and the Poles were uncooperative, saying, perhaps suicidally, that they would fire on any troops crossing their borders even if they were Soviet troops trying to save them. In order to forestall any possible Anglo-French-Soviet accord, with the invasion for Poland set for 1 September, Hitler sent

Ribbentrop to Moscow on 22 August. The resulting Nazi-Soviet Non-Aggression Pact was meant to assure that Britain and France would not move to save a Poland whose fate was sealed beyond Great Britain's reach. It would be strategically foolhardy for Britain (and, the French believed, for France, too) to try to save Poland without Soviet assistance. This was not quite the case for the French, for if they had invaded Germany (as their pact with Poland obliged them to do on the fifteenth day of any German invasion) they could have marched on Berlin virtually unopposed—or else forced Hitler to recall troops from Poland to halt the French advance. But the clues he had received from the family of nations let Hitler know he did not have to consider this as a real possibility. He told his Commanders-in-Chief on 22 August: "The danger of the Western Powers intervening in a conflict is not great." He based his arguments on what had come before: "It appears to me, therefore, inconceivable that a responsible English statesman would in this situation incur the risk of war."[40]

That is why the British reaction to the Nazi-Soviet Pact, presented to Hitler in a note of 23 August, came as such a surprise. The note was firm. It said: "Apparently the announcement of a German-Soviet Agreement is taken in some quarters in Berlin to indicate that intervention by Great Britain on behalf of Poland is no longer a contingency....No greater mistake can be made. Whatever may prove to be the nature of the German-Soviet Agreement, it cannot alter Great Britain's obligation to Poland....If the case should arise, they are resolved, and prepared, to employ without delay all the forces at their command....Having thus made our position perfectly clear, I {Chamberlain} wish to repeat to you my conviction that war between our two peoples would be the greatest calamity that could occur."[41]

Had the British made their position perfectly clear? The note went on to describe—in seven more paragraphs—how the parties could still negotiate: "I cannot see that there is anything in the questions arising between Germany and Poland," it said, "which could not and should not be resolved without the use of force....We have been, and at all times will be ready to assist creating conditions in which such negotiations could take place," and so on.

The firm tone of the note's first part was compromised by the conciliatory tone of its second part. British ambivalence and contradictory clues had surfaced again. This time Hitler could not make sense of what mother Britain really wanted. The ensuing conversation with Henderson, who had delivered the note, shows Hitler to be angry and confused. He was trying, by subtle cues, to get clarification.

Few who have studied this famous meeting have been able to make much sense of a familiar phrase Hitler seemingly pulled from nowhere and used here for the first time. Claiming that the British guarantee to Poland had given the Poles a free hand, he said: "If you have given a blank cheque you must also meet it." "England had given a blank cheque for all this," he said again, "and now she must pay for it."

The phrase "blank cheque" had, of course, a historical referent, Wilhelm II's famous blank cheque to Austria in July 1914, which, by Germany's failing to restrain Austria, was understood (or misunderstood) by the Austrian government as Germany's permission to move against Serbia, with World War I the result. On the face of it, Hitler meant that Britain had now given Poland a similar blank cheque: he was threatening Britain if Britain did not reign in Poland. Unconsciously he also meant something else: that Britain had all along given *him* the blank cheque. His invocation of that earlier dramatic event was not merely a political ploy to bully the British into inaction, but was an unconscious effort to let the British know he was appealing to them for consistency. When the British would not comply he became angry. Henderson, dutifully reporting back to London, added: "I denied the 'blank cheque' but this only started Hitler off again."[42]

Later events were to corroborate Hitler's earlier confusion and his belief that Britain would not act. Two days after the invasion of Poland, Hitler's interpreter, Paul Schmidt, walked from the Foreign Office to the Chancellery carrying the British ultimatum demanding that Germany end the invasion. As he entered the anteroom outside Hitler's office, he pushed through the crowd of Nazi officials who shouted questions about the contents of the British text. He remained silent, then, stepping into Hitler's office, saw that "Hitler was sitting at his desk and Ribbentrop stood by the window. Both looked up expectantly as I came in. I...slowly translated the British Government's ultimatum. When I finished, there was complete silence. Hitler sat immobile, gazing before him....He sat completely silent and unmoving. After an interval, which seemed an age, he turned to Ribbentrop....'What now?' asked Hitler."[43]

Here, in one of history's most dramatic moments, the sadistic, "iron-willed" dictator was confused, the uncharacteristic words "What now?" clashing with the world's image of the ruthless Führer who had long planned war and would stop at nothing to achieve it. Hitler's shock came from Britain's sudden reversal (which contradicted Ribbentrop's assurances that Great Britain would not budge); after a prolonged period of British encouragement the British were now actually ready to punish him. Like the delinquent child suddenly confronted with parental disapproval following frequent unconscious encouragements, Hitler was bewildered.

It was not what he wanted. If anything, Hitler wanted to feel less confusion, less emotional turmoil. That was, after all, the promise of going to war. Finding an enemy meant projecting bad feeling into others; going to war meant one's inner turmoil was now safely on the outside. Paradoxically—for the British and for all of Europe—war would bring inner peace.

In the months preceding the outbreak of war, the emotionally charged words in Hitler's rhetoric show a marked increase in intensity, suggesting that he was in this kind of emotional upheaval, his intra-psychic defenses continuing to crumble. One can sense this in the same way that the bizarre inner world of the schizophrenic can be sensed, from carefully listening to and looking at the schizophrenic's images and distorted "logic." As a historical method, this may not be as far-fetched as it at first might seem since it sounds something like the technique of content analysis long used by literary critics and social scientists, and even has the endorsement of a "no-nonsense" historian. In *The Hitler of History*, John Lukacs, who generally has little use for psychological approaches, finds what he calls the "psychological statements" of prominent German historian Friedrich Heer to be "proper and penetrating." He approvingly quotes Heer's statement that: "Some of Hitler's own words we may consider as expressions that were not only the results of deliberate speaking but that in moments of fatigue or high stress break out, carrying his wishes, hopes, anxieties as they surge up to the surface of his consciousness,"[44] This somewhat confusing translation doesn't quite catch the full meaning of Heer's statement, which is exactly what has been and is being proposed here: that under heavy stress, Hitler's words not only reveal his unconscious; they embody —they become, they in some ways *are*—his unconscious.

Virtually all Hitler scholars agree that from 1937 on his words and actions show an increasing sense of urgency: his desire—indeed, need—for war accelerated. This new urgency, as we have seen in the last chapter, is most often attributed to his accompanying preoccupation—some call it "morbid" —with his own mortality, a concern, runs the standard argument, stimulated by the removal of a benign polyp from his vocal chord and the celebration of his fiftieth birthday, both producing in him a feeling that time was running out.

These are important and real external markers on Hitler's road to war, but are not isolated things in themselves. They are best understood as additional stressors coming as they did on top of the domestic and international pressures, which added to and helped further undermine his steadily eroding intra-psychic defenses.

The host of painful and worrisome physical symptoms mentioned in the last chapter both influenced and were exacerbated by these internal processes. As 1939 unfolded, Hitler's words give evidence of his increased stress, and show that more and more of his repressed material was coming to the surface. In this respect, his 28 April 1939 Reichstag speech is especially revealing. Ostensibly a reply to President Roosevelt's appeal for restraint and a call for Germany's promise to respect the integrity of a whole host of enumerated states, Hitler's speech gave him an opportunity to publicly humiliate Roosevelt, the entire Reichstag laughing hilariously every time he mentioned one of the many states Roosevelt had cited as a possible Nazi target. The speech was broadcast to Germany, Europe, and the rest of the world, and was widely covered in the world press. In it, Hitler once again showed how irrational he was beginning to sound, especially to those who knew him well. Several months before, while witnessing Hitler's Sportpalast speech of 26 September 1938, William Shirer had written in his diary, "for the first time in all the years I've observed him he seemed tonight to have completely lost control of himself." The 28 April speech was another such example, members of the German Foreign Ministry feeling that Hitler had indiscriminately "lashed out all over the place." When he had finished his two-and-a-half hour harangue, he was bathed in sweat.[45]

How can one grasp the essential unconscious and emotional meanings embedded in Hitler's words? There is no simple formula. Any rigid set of analytic rules can easily lead to projections of one's own conscious and unconscious fantasies into the material, what psychoanalysts call "counter-transference." The best the psychological historian can do is to "feel" one's way into the material. It is more art than science, what psychotherapists call "listening with the Third Ear."

Hitler's speech was filled with images of things collapsing, of "internal disruption," "isolation," and "disintegration," of the need to defend frontiers and have strong fortifications, both symbolic of his own need to restore his disintegrating internal defenses. There was "tension," " threat," and a "rising tide of distress." He said: "I myself am a child." He said things were "destroyed...split up." There was "bloodshed," " blood flow," "bloody war" and "inevitable blood-lust."

He projected crazy feelings onto Britain and France, predicting "madness for Paris or London." He projected onto the continent by speaking of "disturbances of the European atmosphere." He spoke of a "danger of immense explosives," and of a "danger in Central Europe." He said there was "general chaos," and "chaos in Germany." He spoke of "sacrifice," and mentioned the word "war" forty times.[46]

These images either reveal Hitler's emotions, or they do not. For those hearing him, some took open pleasure, others a secret pleasure in his threats and humiliation of Roosevelt. But on another level, all of Hitler's audiences, assaulted by images of his raging inner conflict, were left with a sense of disquiet and dread—or even excitement—as his images stirred their own unconscious impulses. For those who did not hear him, that sense of dread (or excitement) could be picked up through later reports of his speech in the world press. In these ways, Hitler's words mirrored Britain and Europe's out-of-control feelings while at the same time provoking and reinforcing them.

Other documents in the late summer of 1939 show Hitler's continuing emotional crisis. His August 1939 meetings with Ciano struck a tone reminiscent of the 28 April Reichstag speech, his language filled with images of "disintegration," "flooding," "dykes breaking," "war," and "sacrifice." To his Commanders-in-Chief in late August he spoke of "tension," "strain," "hysteria," and "intolerable stress." On 23 August,

Henderson found him "excitable," his language "violent and exaggerated." In the next few days Hitler spoke of "intolerable" conditions, "tension," "strangulation," and of "conflagration," "sacrifice," and "blood."[47]

The flood of intolerable feelings was accompanied not only by a wish to discharge them in war, but also by the contradictory wish to get them under control. This seeming inconsistency arises from the same wish that drives the ambivalent, out-of-control child whose pleasure in acting out is partly offset by the terror of his own imagined omnipotent rage. Like the acting-out adolescent, the out-of-control child's ranting is in some ways a plea to be restrained, and one can sense in Hitler a struggle to restore some outer controls.[48] In international affairs this was concretized by the word "encirclement."

"Encirclement," like *carte blanche*, had, of course, a historical referent, harking back to Germany's pre-World War I claim to have been encircled. In the late-1930s the British were again discussing the possibility, the word often being used in the press and in the House of Commons. As late as 21 April 1939 Churchill's earlier notion of a "Grand Alliance" was still deemed by Harvey to be a sensible option, and he used the word "encirclement" to characterize it.[49]

On 30 March 1939 the British had seemed to send Hitler a firm message by guaranteeing the frontiers of Poland. Thus, in his Wilhelshaven speech of 1 April Hitler complained about encirclement, and not just for strategic and propaganda effect. A few days before Hitler ranted in his 28 April speech, Henderson returned to Berlin and reassured Ribbentrop that there was no attempt to encircle Germany. On one level, it was not what he wanted to hear, for Hitler nevertheless complained about the "policy of encirclement" in his 28 April speech. That complaint was, again, a conscious, calculated propaganda tactic meant to gain political capital, but was also driven by internal personal needs. For the next week, the British press did not co-operate, and continually denied all charges of encirclement,[50] which must have made Hitler even angrier. In any event, restraints were long overdue, and it is doubtful if anything could have stopped him by the spring of 1939.

It is worth repeating that his feelings, as much as his ideology, had already turned him to war by late-1937, as historians have seen in the Hossbach Memorandum, notable, as mentioned several times, as "an expression by Hitler of a new sense of urgency."[51] Now, in the summer of 1939, he was frustrated. The promise of the emotional release he had sought through war with the Czechs had been thwarted by the British at Munich; as a result, he was even more distressed. Speer reported that by 1939 Hitler "tended to be angry and impatient more often than in the past." When crowds called for him to appear he snapped: "Stop bothering me with that." He began to fear the possibility of riots: "Suppose there should be some disturbances!" he wondered. By the "last days of August Hitler was in an unwonted state of nerves," reported Speer, "and at times completely lost the reassuring air of infallible leader."[52]

The Pact of Steel, forged with enabler Mussolini on 22 May 1939, allowed Hitler, and Europe, the possibility of relief at last. Although contingency plans for war against Poland had been drawn up on 11 April in Operation White, he immediately decided on a final date for the war with Poland. "Further successes can no longer be won without bloodshed," he told a secret meeting of senior army commanders on May 23. "We cannot expect a repetition of Czechia. There will be war." He then turned his words to Britain: "the showdown with England is a matter of life and death," he said. "England is the motive force driving against Germany....The *aim* will always be to force England to her knees,"[53] which, although the stated target was Poland, continued as his underlying theme. It marked a dramatic change and final break from his earlier plans for some kind of alliance with Britain, now abandoned for a new goal—"to force England to her knees."

Throughout the summer of 1939 he continued to rage. His 31 August 1939 Directive No. 1 for the Conduct of the War began: "exhausted" by the "intolerable situation....I have determined on a solution by force."[54] On 1 September the first part of his speech justifying the war to the Reichstag ended by asserting that an "intolerable state of affairs" had created "suffering" and "pressure" and that "intensified pressure" was causing "strangulation." The second half of his speech called for "sacrifices," for "unlimited sacrifices," and for "personal sacrifice." The "struggle" was "for the rebirth of Germany," which demanded "sacrifice" after "sacrifice" after "sacrifice" after "sacrifice."[55]

These repeated references to sacrifice call for at least mention of a theory of war, which holds that wars are periodic "cleansing sacrifices."[56] In this conceptualization, the youth of one's own country become containers for the group's projected bad feelings, and when they are sent off to war, people's bad feelings are symbolically killed off with them.

It is a provocative idea, but one with several problems. For example, sacrifice means giving up something of value. If a group like youth is really a symbolic substitute for one's own despised parts, it would mean that people's despised parts are in some way valued—something of a contradiction (even though contradictions can exist in the unconscious). Are youth, or what youth represents, then, consciously valued but unconsciously despised? Are these feelings ambivalently experienced, with one winning out over the other? And while it is true that the word "sacrifice" becomes a central part of the rhetoric of war, that does not happen only for unconscious reasons, but because wars have to be won and can be won only at a price. Personal goals, life itself, must be set aside for the common good. This is obvious.

This theory owes something to an idea proposed fifty years ago by the French sociologist Gaston Bouthoul who said then that wars are ways of carrying out delayed infanticide, since the one thing all wars have in common is that older men send younger men to their deaths.[57] This may make some kind of strange sense in the context of interwar diplomacy if one remembers Hitler's fantasy role as raging child. The anger, sometimes the murderous rage, of adults towards children is not often understood or fully appreciated except by therapists and by the children of angry parents. If millions of Europeans were regressed to the point where infantile rage was breaking into their consciousness, it is theoretically possible that it could be temporarily escaped by projecting that rage onto the youth of Europe (and onto enemy youth), which could then be symbolically killed off when those youths died in war.

In this symbolic slaughter, Hitler could serve as Europe's delegate. The idea sounds far-fetched, except that he was quite capable of killing off such "container groups"—and everyone knew it. That had been dramatically shown to Germany, Europe, and the world by the June 1934 Blood Purge, or The Night of the Long Knives, when the murder of scores of Storm Troopers at Hitler's orders had "cleansed" Hitler and Germany of their own bad feelings. Hitler, said Rebecca West, "at one and the same time fed his appetite for murder, and enacted a fantasy that all of us have played with in our infancy"; in the bargain he had carried it out, she said, with a "baby ferocity." Although the purge was prompted by domestic political issues having to do with leadership, the S.A. and the German army, it alerted the world that what had been domestic could go international. The "blood-bath of 30 June precisely revealed the true nature of Hitler's Germany," wrote historian A.L. Rouse: "if this was what they would do to their comrades think what they would do to their enemies, and did! I understood this in my bones."[58]

The possibility of Hitler's having the potential to carry out a symbolic "delayed infanticide" by war seems to have been well understood in Germany as well as Europe. Symbolic sacrifice was unconsciously acted out all over the

Third Reich in the interwar years. As recounted by SS-Brigade Leader Julius Schrenk in a popular German picture book of 1936, everywhere Hitler went mothers would gather with their children. "Women with babes in their arms could not reach him. They held up their little ones, Germany's future, over the heads of the enthusiastic crowd, as if they wanted to say: You belong to him!"[59] Such scenes, graphically captured in the 1935 Nazi-propaganda film *Triumph of the Will*, were repeated throughout Germany countless times. One observer recalls how "on numerous occasions" large numbers of German women would march through the streets shouting in unison: "We want to beget children for the Führer!"[60] The mothers and mothers-to-be may have understood their role as part of this unconscious sacrifice through the stream of popular films with the theme of how youth had been martyred for the cause, and by a Nazi ideology—carefully reconstructed by historian Jay Baird—filled with death themes and calls for youthful martyrdom.[61] Even traditional historians have noticed this strand in Hitler's personality. Historian Felix Gilbert, translator of the document collection *Hitler Directs His War*, says in the book's introduction: "It would seem that the records contain material that demand the diagnosis of a trained psychiatrist, for even the layman is struck by the strange attraction that talking about deaths and sacrifices seems to have had for Hitler."[62]

And Hitler was certainly capable of carrying out this task. Erich Fromm saw him as the embodiement of wanton human destructiveness, and, in the words of one recent scholar, Hitler "experienced destruction as an aesthetic pleasure." It seems clear that whatever rationalizations he offered for his aggression, Hitler could wage war purely for the sake of waging war. He envisioned Europe as a vast necropolis, commissioning architect Wilhelm Kreis to design a series of hugh stone structures (*Totenburgen*, or Citadels of the Dead) scattered in scores of sites across the

Reich to house the remains of the German war dead. It was as if a mass murderer had captured a continent and was preparing to bury his trophy victims around him. When, during the war, he was informed of the astonishing losses sustained by newly commissioned officers he said: "Isn't that what the young people are there for?" and once said, "I insist I have a right to send the youth to their death."[63] For their own conscious and unconscious reasons, the other members of the European family were prepared to help him.

VII FRANCE

THE GOVERNMENT'S GREAT FEAR WAS THAT ONE DAY
FRANCE WOULD FIND HERSELF FACING GERMANY ALONE.[1]
—*Prime Minister Herriot*, 1932

France, a great power, did not act like it in the 1930s. Ambivalence toward resisting Hitler meant that the French would retreat into inaction, regularly subordinating themselves to Great Britain by 1936.

Many historians have noticed this trend and painted the same picture. William Rock has said: "The French Government abdicated all initiative in…foreign affairs to the British." Telford Taylor notes: "the loss of Italy's friendship made France more than ever dependent on Britain, and seriously limited her future freedom of action….French foreign policy was largely determined in London." Anthony Adamthwaite concludes: "The policy of Chautemps, like that of Baldwin, was one of drift. Inevitably, therefore, the key decisions were made for him and France was taken in tow by her British partner." "The French were at a loss what to do," wrote A. J. P. Taylor; "they therefore decided to let things happen. Decisions thus rested exclusively with the British government." It meant: "France found herself the junior partner of the Western democracies."[2]

Many answers have been offered as to why the French allowed this to occur—a failure of nerve; internal dissent; parliamentary indecision; collective decadence; the loss of *élan vital*; military weakness; a Maginot-Line mentality; a stupidity, ineptitude, or defeatism bordering on treason; a socio-political system which allowed twenty-four ministerial changes in a decade; the devastating demographic consequences of the First World War; a bad conscience over Versailles and the Ruhr invasion; and more.

Complex processes have multiple causes and several of

these factors are doubtless important, including the largely unmentioned role of fantasy. What fantasies were operating most powerfully at any given moment is hard to determine since one major tendency of French diplomacy was always to operate in secrecy and in ways the French sometimes hid even from themselves. Lord Strang noted this in general: "While the declared policy of France was to stand by her obligation{s}," he wrote "a very different impression was given by what French Ministers said behind the scenes, whether in social gatherings or to foreign representatives."[3]

The British operated behind the scenes too, Sir Eric Phipps encouraging Daladier to fire Paul-Boncour by sending "messages {which} were quite indirect"; as Sir Eric said: "I can always disavow them." But the French made a habit of the practice, using many unofficial intermediaries during the Czech Crisis. At other times, they passed on "impressions" that they would give Mussolini a free hand in Ethiopia, or Hitler a free hand in Central Europe.[4] When in March 1939 the *Union des Intellectuals Français* called for an inquiry into Foreign Secretary Bonnet's covert activities—alleging he had "consistently pursued a secret diplomacy detrimental to France's interests"[5]—it was an accusation that said as much symbolically about France's general diplomatic techniques as Bonnet's specific policies.

If this is so, how can historians be expected to recapture meaningful feelings and fantasies from behind-the-scenes undertones, gestures, and nuances, especially since they were not consciously acknowledged and have since been lost to history because they were never recorded in the first place? The answer is, of course, that they cannot.

For evidence of fantasies, psychological historians must look elsewhere—to people's behavior—because it is possible to identify feelings and fantasies from what people do, not just from what they say. This is really not as unorthodox a method as it might seem, for nearly all historians recognize that what people do can sometimes be symbolic.

Behaviors result from fantasies as well as from rational choices since people act according to their beliefs, including those that are not conscious, or are only partly conscious. One must in addition look at outcomes, since people sometimes unconsciously arrange circumstances to get what they unconsciously want, and loudly oppose.

How did the French behave? As in Britain, many consciously understood what Germany was doing and predicted what would happen, yet little was done to prevent it. In October 1932, Premier Herriot commented: "I have no illusions. I am convinced that Germany wishes to rearm.... We are at a turning point in history. Tomorrow it will be a policy of territorial demands."[6] (He was speaking several months before Hitler came to power.) Also in 1932, Alexis Saint-Léger, a key figure in the foreign office, outlined a future scenario to a British colleague: "If Germany were now allowed to take the law into her own hands in the armaments question, and were not brought to book, her next move would assuredly be to proceed to some flagrant act....The only way...to meet the situation...was for the British and French Governments to unite in saying to Germany: 'Thus far and no further,' they must speak their mind clearly and make it plain that there would be no wavering. Otherwise a situation would develop in which war in the relatively near future was absolutely inevitable."[7]

In 1936, the political director of the Quai d'Orsay, René Massigli, had warned that strategic dominance would follow from German economic dominance over the states in central and eastern Europe which, "already dependent on the Reich economically...{were} now menaced by its military influence. Having begun its intensive rearmament, Germany can offer arms in payment of its commercial debts. By doing so she can also keep her arms factories running and improve her own matériel."[8] In early 1936, General Gamelin—warned by intelligence that German troops would move into the Rhineland "in the near future"—recommended "nothing to counter the threat even as he pointed out with great lucidity that the loss of the Rhineland guarantee would put France's eastern allies at Germany's mercy,"[9] a behavior that begins to look like a choice specimen of asking for it. (Three years later, Gamelin's memo in September 1939 on why France should not invade Germany from the west looks like a continuation of France asking for it.) In March 1938, after Germany had seized Austria, French Foreign Minister Paul-Boncour told the British ambassador in Paris that "a definite warning to Germany by the two countries...would be the best means of avoiding war.... Time was not on our side, for Germany was getting stronger and stronger, until she would finally attain complete hegemony in Europe."[10]

In the face of these predictions, the French pursued their policy of "drift," while, as elsewhere, other options were available.

Adamthwaite believes: "If a military alliance had been constructed in 1936 instead of 1939, a European war might have been averted." Renouvin states: "if France's political leaders had adopted a firmer attitude, public and parliamentary opinion would undoubtedly have supported them." Historian Jean-Baptiste Duroselle believes that during the Rhineland Crisis leaders "wanted to avoid action by France alone," but "did not realize that if she did act, France's allies would be obliged to follow suit."[11]

Whether these things could have actually worked is not history, but speculation. The point, however, is that alternatives did exist though none were taken. What the French did—and did not do—worked against their great power status, undermined collective security, encouraged Hitler, and contributed to the feeling that the French were "alone," a condition which, by their behavior, they brought on themselves.

This process was not new, and seems to have gone back to at least the immediate post-World War I era when the French made several diplomatic decisions which isolated them.[12] That sense of isolation in turn helped create a "Maginot-Line" mentality, but it is not clear, if it can ever be proven, what came first, whether the actual Maginot Line fortifications were more cause or consequence of the psychological state they symbolized. What is clear is that the Maginot Line left the Franco-Belgian frontier wide open to easy assault in May 1940.

By the mid-1930s, the French feeling of isolation led them to act like the British, who, for their own reasons, were leaving it to Hitler to act out their own aggressiveness, and encouraged him by sending Europe mixed signals. In April 1934, the French government reacted strongly to news of a large German defense budget by denouncing further armament negotiations, asserting that France would undertake "security through her own means." Then the French undercut their words by their behavior. "What made the French government's gesture so extraordinary," says D. C. Watt, "was that instead of accompanying it with a programme of rearmament…it cut French defense expenditure still further."[13]

Throughout the period, the French continued to act in other ways that undermined collective security and assured their own sense of isolation. They concluded a mutual assistance pact with the Russians on 2 May 1935. A Russo-Czech agreement followed two weeks later.The Russo-Czech agreement was made contingent on the functioning of the Franco-Czech alliance already in place, which meant if the French did not support the Czechs, neither would the Russians.

Governments normally conclude such quid pro quo agreements, but in this instance, what was being constructed contained a hidden, unmentioned "domino-effect" clause. The fate of Czechoslovakia—hence the functioning of the whole system—became dependent on an "unseen partner," Great Britain, since the French refused to act unless Britain, with whom they had no formal alliance, acted first. Europe's governess still ran the show. But the

French contributed to the situation themselves since "the staff talks which might have given life to the Franco-Soviet pact were studiously avoided by the French."[14]

By mid-1935, the stage was thus set for one of the most significant turning points in the interwar period. The Versailles Treaty had prohibited German troops from entering the Rhineland, and Germany had freely re-confirmed this prohibition in the Locarno Pact. Remilitarization was not only illegal, but was fraught with strategic consequences. German fortifications on the French frontier would mean that France would be unable to protect its eastern allies by threatening to attack Germany in the west.

The French had been discussing the possibility of a German move from at least the summer of 1935. A.J.P. Taylor is not the only historian who has noted that "the reoccupation of the Rhineland did not take the French by surprise."[15] By November 1935, Ambassador François-Poncet was proposing a conference with Germany to discuss the Rhineland. Did Hitler hear these things as unconscious calls to act?

By 18 February1936, the French General Staff had already written off the Rhineland. In anticipation of later capitulations, it recommended the French create a British alliance "as compensation" for what had not yet happened—the loss of the Rheinland "no man's land." Duroselle finds it "abundantly clear that, through blindness or unwillingness, the leaders in charge of national defense had not, before March, planned a single measure or prepared a single move toward a response in terms of force....Although it was fairly well warned, the French government was absolutely unprepared for action."[16]

One could blame this on incompetence, but it was neither blindness nor unwillingness that left France unprepared: it was an unconscious complicity, which joined the larger European-wide fantasy process. This can be seen in the actions of individuals at a meeting at the Ministry of War on 7 February 1936. The meeting had been called to talk about the Rhineland, but there was a long discussion of minor matters. Finally, Flandin tried to re-focus the group on its declared agenda: "It is time to define in a very clear manner the probable means of {German} remilitarization," he said, "and, on the other hand, what countermeasures we can assume we should take." In response, "the military ministers merely changed the subject."[17] (Such sabotage is familiar to all students of the psychodynamics of small groups.)

When Hitler finally moved in early March, France's Allies called for French firmness. Many promised their support. The Romanians proposed economic sanctions against the Germans. A high Austrian official, who thought "next time it will be our turn," said Austria's faith in France depended on the "vigor" of France's "counteraction." The Poles reaffirmed their solidarity, the Czechs said they "would adopt exactly the same attitude as France," and the Belgians promised the same. Léger believed the British would accept a fait accompli, and "will have to follow us" if France acted vigorously. Churchill thought that if France remained firm, Hitler would have to withdraw. The Germans even expected it, their generals anticipating the worst, their London embassy staff was as nervous as Hitler, who later told Speer: "If the French had taken any action, we would have been easily defeated."[18]

At this crucial point, the French did nothing. One of the things that kept them from doing anything—and throughout the years after 1936—was the constant tendency to overestimate German strength. As Watt notes, intelligence reports in 1938 judged the Siegried Line to be "manned with more divisions than were in the whole German army." Similar overestimates were made for the German air force. In reality, with Poland and Czechoslovakia, France could have mustered 160 divisions against Germany's 120, and alone the French air force was stronger. "Surprisingly, no account was taken of the potential contributions of Czechoslovakia and Poland."[19]

Even so, France could still have acted by itself. But the key figure in French inaction was once again the do-nothing General Gamelin. Telford Taylor notes that although the other Locarno powers, Britain and Italy, were then "at swords point over Ethiopia…Gamelin continued to harp on the notion of bringing British and Italian troops to France." It was not going to happen; Taylor calls it "a fantasy."[20] In addition, Gamelin created a scenario of such difficulty that it paralyzed the French government. Resisting the Germans, he said, meant "the mobilization of 1.2 million men, the expenditure of 30 million francs per day," and in any case nothing could happen for a week.[21] The French had a legal right to act quickly by Article 4 of the Locarno Treaty, but vacillating only meant that discussions began at the League of Nations a full week later. By that time, it was already psychologically and diplomatically too late.

The result was that doubts were thrown onto France's resolve. An emotional environment was created which made the French feel isolated. The Romanian Foreign Minister said: "If on 7 March you could not defend yourself, how will you defend us?" French weakness worried the Czech Foreign Minister and shook the Little Entente. Belgium pulled out of the French alliance the following October. The Austrian Foreign Minister predicted: "If Germany is allowed to fortify the Rhineland, we are lost." Léger now told his subordinates "war was inevitable. It was only a matter of time and Germany's choosing."[22]

And after Hitler's march into the Rhineland, the French did little to counter Germany's increased aggressiveness. Military talks with the Russians in the summer of 1937 came to nothing. Help could have come from the east—or at least some efforts could have been made to turn Stalin into the ally he was on record as saying he wanted to become. Yet during the Czech Crisis contradictory messages were sent to the Soviets, Ambassador Coulondre telling the Russians in Moscow that France would stand by the Czechs, while Bonnet told them in Paris the matter would have to be studied. Was this conscious manipulation, incompetence, or unconscious intention? Four days after the Munich Agreement, the *Moscow Daily* asked, "Who will still believe France's word, who will remain her ally?"[23]

When Hitler turned then to threaten Poland it was clear that if Poland was to be defended the Franco-Polish Alliance of 1921 had to be updated and confirmed. It was not. Moreover, part of the diplomatic offensive during the summer crisis of 1939 should have been to begin talks with the Germans, but the French refused even to speak with them. "The absence of any Franco-German dialogue was significant," says one historian: "Hitler had decided that France was not worthy of attention."[24] Apparently, the French had decided for their part that Hitler was not worthy of their attention, and, even for propaganda purposes, weren't willing to keep up appearances.

All along the British helped France play its suicidal game. A number of times during the Czech Crisis they had restrained the French by warning them not to over-interpret Britain's concern for Czechoslovakia. The British documents on the origins of the war confirm it.[25] So does Harvey's diary: "I must record my view that Phipps in Paris has done his utmost to discourage the French from anything resembling positive action."[26] Chamberlain had similarly pressed Daladier mercilessly at their 25-26 September 1938 London meeting.[27] Harvey believed: "Had we been robust, the French would have been robust too."[28] But this was a mutually reinforcing system and things worked both ways. Chamberlain, says one historian, was in turn "strengthened in his resolution to appease Hitler by the pathetic condition of the French government and the Premier"[29] a condition the British had themselves encouraged. Both sides blamed the other.

Harvey had understood the consequences of France's fear of being alone when he speculated about Austria months before: "Will Hitler be tempted to make a fresh 'coup' because he believes...France would not dare to move without us?"[30] The answer was yes. Hitler had long before intuited the workings of the European diplomatic system, predicting in the secret Hossbach Memorandum of November 1937: "Without British support a warlike action by France against Germany was not to be expected."[31]

Attempts to explain why the French acted this way were abandoned in the immediate aftermath of the Second World War. Instead of historical understanding there was a rush to find scapegoats. What took place was a "race on all sides in France to pass the buck,"[32] and Daladier was a central figure in the effort. He "blamed everyone else for the sins of France: British lack of armaments, Britain's refusal to support France, Polish hostility towards Czechoslovakia, Russian legalism over the alliance, and United States isolationism." The French seemed to be doing what they always did when things went wrong. "During the Rhineland Crisis," said Paul Reynaud, "the government of the time was happy to find in British resistance a cover for its own fainthearted-ness." And when in August 1939 news came of the Nazi-Soviet pact, France's leaders blamed the Russians and the Poles, never themselves.[33]

Others in France blamed France's leaders, and there is something to this since they were the ones ultimately responsible for carrying out France's policies. Bonnet has been characterized as "appeasement personified," and Daladier seems to have been hired mainly to keep up appearances. "There were many of us in the party and outside," wrote Bertrand de Jouvenel, "who considered that once in power Daladier would be capable of taking vigorous action to restore the prestige of the state." His image of strength was his cover. In reality he was France's delegate. According to one historian, "he knew from the outset that Munich was a disaster for French diplomacy and a national humiliation," while another sees him as merely "following the ebb and flow" of public opinion. As A.J.P.Taylor put it:

"on every occasion he spoke decisively against appeasement and then acquiesced in it." It was not easy to play the role of public deceiver, and the stress of events was also taking its toll, Daladier apparently turning more and more to self-medication after Munich. A November 1938 entry in Harvey's diary reads: "Daladier, who is said to be drinking heavily and certainly looks it, has much deteriorated."[34]

Why France's leaders were capable of acting on group wishes, while paying the emotional price for it, is still unclear. (Some historians, when at a loss to explain behavior, look for ways to excuse it.)[35] Even with detailed psychological biographies, it would be easy enough to scapegoat France's leaders by focusing on them alone, which, since they do seem to have been carrying out the wishes of the French people, would only cloud their role as group-fantasy delegates.

That role was already well understood by Jacques Maritain when he wrote from his American exile in 1941 that the French people had created with their leaders "what might be called in biological parlance a relationship of parasitical symbiosis," using "them as scapegoats to curse at when things went too badly." People "took an interest and a vicarious part in their {leaders'} game...ironically conniving with them...in their performance"[36] never acknowledging that this was what they were doing. It is, of course, a characteristic not confined to France in the 1930s.

The historical evidence corroborates Maritain's intuition that France's leaders were carrying out the mandate, including the unconscious mandate, of the French people. During the Rhineland crisis, for example, "neither parliamentary leadership nor the press did anything to arouse public opinion," and, with rare exceptions, "the Parisian newspapers... ruled out the possibility of a resort to force."[37] The Left denounced the German moves, but argued that action should only take place through the powerless League of Nations, an idea tantamount to capitulation. "From one end to the other of the political spectrum the cry for peace was unanimous; no important voice was raised...to push the Germans back from Strasbourg."[38] Twice, writes Renouvin, "the majority of the members of the Council of Ministers declared themselves in favor of negotiations...the lead article of *L'Echo de Paris* was entitled 'Pack on the back? No!' and *L'Action Française* played the same tune....The dominant tendencies of public opinion at the time were an inclination toward inaction and a desire to maintain unity with Great Britain....This fact was obviously not overlooked by the majority of the Council of Ministers."[39]

French historical writing has tended to overlook this consensus. Instead: "Ministers and diplomats have been divided into sheep and goats: resisters and appeasers....In reality such sharp clear-cut differences did not exist. For example, in September 1938 the majority of Ministers and diplomats favoured some agreement with Germany at the expense of Czechoslovakia." As Daladier put it: "The French Government met...September 19 at the Elysée, and I did not hear one voice raised in opposition—not one. We all deplored what we called the 'sad necessity,' but no one in the Council of Ministers supported an opposite policy—no one."[40] Later, when he saw large crowds beneath his circling aircraft as he returned from Munich, he expected to be lynched; instead, he was cheered.

What emotional factors, conscious and unconscious, might have led the French to act in these ways?

Several themes found in Britain and Germany were at work in France too where many people openly admired Hitler and Nazism. Ambassador François-Poncet had long admired Mussolini and was considered by American Ambassador Dodd "not far from a fascist," and there seems something almost seductive in his regularly sending Hitler chocolates from Paris. In March 1939—when the Germans were complaining about encirclement—he warned against giving the impression that the democracies were "ganging up" on Germany.[41]

The motto "Better Hitler than Blum" was not only an anti-Semitic, anti-socialist, right-wing slogan aimed at the Popular Front, but was for some people a transparent semi-conscious fantasy that Hitler should be ruling France. As in Britain, people resonated with Nazi power, violence, and sadism. The foreign editor of *Figaro* was not the only one who called Hitler and his henchmen "gangsters,"[42] and, again, they *were* gangsters. But as with some Britons who experienced a secret vicarious thrill when denouncing the Nazis, some French men and women must have too, and some of those on the Left who consciously opposed right-wing groups like *Action Française* could unconsciously identify with Hitler as the embodiment of their own repressed sadism.

Underneath this sadism, as usual, was a powerful masochism which, as much as in Britain, was one of the catalysts for the policy of appeasement: the French, too, wanted to be humiliated. Historian Eugen Weber has found that during the 1930s (the decade he calls "the hollow years") the French were awash in the theme of decadence. Neither defeating Germany in 1918, constructing the Maginot Line fortifications, nor remaining one of the great powers were sufficient realities to keep these depressive feelings at bay, and it seems likely that the feeling was caused in part by their paralysis against Hitler and the dependency they felt, and were themselves encouraging, by allowing their foreign policies to be made in London. A masochistic impulse would have shown up in the "fear-as-wish" principle anyway. For whatever reasons, the French wanted to be punished, but only, it seems, as prelude to a larger scenario.

French historian Marc Bloch's *Strange Defeat*, written at fever pitch in the months immediately following June 1940, blended the tools of his trade with his experience as a soldier, and found fault with many French institutions. It contained some stunning psychological insights and concluded: "events…in the last analysis, are dictated by human psychology." Bloch acknowledged the irrational (the "history of the Ministry of Munitions reads like a lesson in unreason"), quoted a Belgian friend ("You've no idea of the amount of damage done to the French cause by your great Weeklies. They declare in every issue that France, as a nation, is in an advanced stage of putrescence"), and judged that the French "set off for the war haunted by these gloomy prognostications," believing "it was perfectly natural that they should be beaten," that it would be a just "punishment meted out by Destiny to a guilty nation." Historian-journalist Alexander Werth noted in 1942 that for years "—particularly after Munich—writers like M. Detoeuf had liked to play about with...ideas of the inevitable regeneration of France through {its} conquest and humiliation." Two historians who have worked separately on Pétain's psychobiography agree that his rise to power had something to do with the notion of "regeneration through suffering," a deeply personal issue which helped his popularity because it resonated so well with the larger French community. In July 1943 Camus wrote in *Revue Libre* that France's right to wage war had been "paid for...with humiliations and silences, with bitter experiences...and, above all, with humiliation of our human dignity." He was right, but that feeling was abroad in France even before the humiliating defeat of 1940. Adamthwaite finds the language of sacrifice appearing in the rhetoric of French leaders in the 1930s, while among intellectuals the idea of "Rebirth through masochistic surrender"—to the point of martyrdom and death—was a notion central to many whose writings helped form French opinion, among them Simone Weil. She put the theme best in 1943 when she fantasized what would have happened if France had embraced Gandhi-like passive resistance: "far greater numbers would have perished," she wrote approvingly. "This would have been an imitation of Christ's passion realized on a national scale."[43]

These themes were not very different from those found in

other countries. What made the French unique was their preoccupation with being alone.

The sentiments of Prime Minister Herriot quoted at the beginning of this chapter were echoed by others.[44] As German remilitarization of the Rhineland loomed immediately ahead, General Maurin had written: "We risk appearing as the aggressor and finding ourselves left to face Germany alone." On 7 March 1936 the French premier asked what would happen "if we were alone, without allies." During the Czech Crisis, Léger "believed that France stood alone, without allies among the Great Powers, and that alone it would have been nothing short of folly for her to fight."[45] If symbolic behavior means anything, during the Four Power talks at Munich Hitler and Mussolini always ate together, while the British and French delegations invariably took their meals separately. In the summer of 1939 during the Polish Crisis both Britain and France each asked Mussolini to restrain Hitler without telling the other of their plans.

Although they could have effectively acted alone or, at times, with other states, the perception that they were alone even when they were not allowed the French to become psychologically dependent on Great Britain. This was telegraphed to the world long before Hitler came to power, the Poles being informed as early as 1928 that if Germany attacked Poland the French response depended on the attitude of the British government.[46] The appraisals of the general staff consistently followed this dependency. In April and May 1937 they emphasized that there had to be prior agreement with London before concluding military accords with other states. Regressed by the stressors of the period, France sought comfort in the arms of Mother Britain and could then blame the British for what they unconsciously knew they were going to do—encourage Hitler. The documents are filled with statements like: "French security rested above all on a close entente with Great Britain."[47] For the same reason, no warnings were issued to Hitler during the 1938

Austrian crisis. "Apparently, it was mostly because the government—on this occasion as on so many others—did not want to take a stand without being assured of the assent and cooperation of Great Britain, and because it waited in vain for a British response."[48] After the *Anschluss*, the Committee of National Defense met to discuss Czechoslovakia and was told by General Gamelin that a French attack on Germany could be launched only through Belgium, for which "British diplomatic support was necessary."[49] Bonnet forcefully stated the case for French dependency at a March 1939 London meeting: "If the people of France thought it was impossible to look to Great Britain for any really substantial measure of military help...the consequences might be profound and irretrievable." Historian Paul Renouvin sums up these separate examples by saying: "Not one government had contemplated taking a forceful stand without being assured in advance of British support."[50]

At bottom, the fear of being alone was irrational since France at times could have acted independently. The root of the obsession was that the French were not only feeling isolated, they were feeling abandoned.

This is not surprising considering how strongly abandonment themes played in French society during the interwar years. Drieu La Rochelle who, before becoming a fascist was a regular contributor (along with Gide and Malraux) to France's most prestigious literary journal *La Nouvelle Revue Française*, filled his novels with abandonment themes and phrases like: "Yves...felt...his abandonment....He broke into sobs." La Rochelle's autobiographical novel states his mother's "departure was the frivolous climax of a cruel drama which existed in my head....I so bitterly anticipated the evening of tears, of fear and of despairing solitude that awaited me....I told her of all the pain those evenings had caused me...she...felt moments of remorse....Did she stay?...I no longer know. Maybe she left." Many protagonists of his later novels are orphans.[51]

Orphans also figure prominently in the popular cinema, and were one of the reasons why particular films became popular. Historian Paul Monaco found the French films of the 1920s filled with themes of orphanage and abandonment, and argues that although it was not necessarily a predictor of specific decisions, this figured in France's overall domestic and international posture. One can say, although Monaco doesn't, that this feeling would have had to work its way into foreign policy. Historian Faris Kirkland has shown how the French military in particular was demoralized by the actions and attitudes of the French people, as well as by several French governments, with the result that by the 1930s the French military felt, in his word, "abandoned."[52] The shift reflected the mood of the larger society and went hand in hand with what was happening in diplomacy.

The origins of France's preoccupation with abandonment are not hard to find, and are rooted, in part, in the consequences of the First World War.The years 1914-1918 saw millions abandoned as fathers and husbands went off to war, Sartre noting in his autobiography that: "At that time, we were all more or less fatherless orphans. The male parents were dead or at the front; those who remained behind lost status, were less manly, and wanted their sons to forget about them."[53] When the war was over, one million three hundred thousand Frenchmen had been killed, an astonishing thirty percent of all males between the ages of eighteen and twenty-seven, including the heads of 646,000 families which, as late as 1931, remained fatherless. On top of that it must be considered that the fathers of one million three hundred and twenty-two thousand children had been mutilated or wounded, children who must have come to feel abandoned in part because many of their mangled and mutilated fathers, and the women who took care of them, were unavailable for sufficient parenting in the postwar era.

How could these statistics not be psychologically significant? Yet they do not tell the whole story. There was considerable loss of life among Germans too, but the orphan theme does not appear with regularity in the German cinema of the 1920s.[54] While the proportion of French orphans was considerable—given a population of 40 million—the fear of abandonment was nationwide and cannot be explained by the historical experience of a specific cohort alone.

In fact, Monaco points out, the orphan theme was already "common in French novels, particularly in the last few decades of the nineteenth century." Another historian has connected the abandonment theme to common practices in French childrearing in general. Stephen Ryan has written that "French children were loved but at a distance; firm discipline, often severe, was the norm, and French children were expected to comport themselves like little adults. Mothers—the disciplinarians in the French family—were supportive but intrusive and controlling. Within the family circle adults remained aloof, the child isolated, so that traumatic experience of painful abandonment was likely even as the child's conduct was carefully regulated."[55] So it appears that parental loss in the First World War mingled with childhood experience and earlier trauma. But these factors do not seem to tell the full story either. Historian George Sussman, without discussing psychological causes or drawing any psychological conclusions, has uncovered a startling historical fact with psychological implications: the wet-nursing business in France prospered until 1914.

Sending infants and newborns away from their parents' home to wet nurses who lived at far distances in the countryside was an old practice which went back centuries in Europe, and is central to the very high infant mortality rates (upwards of 50 percent) recorded well into the early modern period. Indeed, wet-nurses were nicknamed "the killing nurses."[56] Infants stayed with them for upwards of a year or more with no, or rare, visits from their mothers. Those infants who survived had thus experienced early parental abandonment and generally poor care at the hands of their wet nurses.

Sussman's explanations for the practice in France down to 1914 are cultural, technological, and socioeconomic, all valid in their own ways, each combining to produce important psychological consequences.

In the late nineteenth century in some French regions fully two-thirds of the children were sent away to wet nurses for a year or more in conditions not much different from those of earlier centuries: they "lived in poor, rural, often mountainous or swampy regions, usually at such a distance that their parents could rarely have visited their babes during the year or more they were away."[57] Sussman concludes that about 10 percent of the total infant population, or about 88,000 French babies per year in the 1890s, were affected. Even accepting Sussman's conservative figures would mean that in the fifteen years from 1890-1914 over half a million French babies were abandoned to wet-nurses. Since the percentage of those sent to wet nurses declined in the late-nineteenth century, it would mean that babies who had been wet-nursed made up a large proportion of the older adult population in the 1930s. More research is needed, especially for specific French leaders, but it seems likely that a good number of the older statesmen, politicians, soldiers, and diplomats, that is, those influencing and making decisions in the 1930s, had been abandoned to wet nurses in the nineteenth century.

Millions of French men and women—abandoned to wet-nurse, orphaned by the Great War, emotionally abandoned by their parents, or all three—thus made up a population compulsively driven to reenact their feelings through foreign policy. Millions of Europeans outside France had experienced various kinds of abandonment too, or, if not actual abandonments, they sometimes felt emotionally abandoned, even those within intact families. The result was that abandonment feelings lay buried everywhere. Victims in childhood, the French, like everyone else, had become victims of that childhood, a childhood which—for them especially was reinforced by the traumatic consequences of the First World War and led to their manipulation of the "real world" through diplomacy in order to match their inner needs. Playing the abandoned child—the fantasy role assigned to them by the European family system—also allowed not only the French, but millions of other Europeans to vicariously experience the repressed abandoned child within themselves, thereby moving Europe along the path to Hitler's War. And, at a critical juncture, and for some of the same reasons, Belgium, France's neighbor to the north, adopted the same position.

VIII BELGIUM AND ITALY

MUSSOLINI WAS BEHAVING LIKE A CHILD
AND THE CHILD WAS DREAMING OF SOME LARGE NEW RATTLES.[1]
—*Neville Chamberlain*, 1932

After World War I Belgium became the lynchpin of the French alliance system. Guaranteed by the great powers in the nineteenth century, Belgium's neutrality had failed to prevent a German invasion in 1914. After the war, King Albert I sought to keep Belgium safe by tying into France's post-war alliance system.

This made good sense in the 1920s when Germany was weak. It made even better sense in the 1930s when Germany was getting stronger. Yet the alliance with France was suddenly, precipitously, disastrously discarded, and, in October 1936, Belgium's neutrality was reestablished. This hampered France's ability to act, as Belgium now shielded Germany from French attack, while Belgian neutrality prevented the French from building Maginot-Line-like fortifications on the Franco-Belgian border. Thus: "Belgium's neutrality of 1936-1940 played entirely and perhaps decisively into Hitler's hands."[2]

What caused this dramatic turnaround lies with the new king Leopold III, who had succeeded his father after Albert's sudden death in a mountaineering accident. At first Leopold focused his attention on the Congo; soon he shifted to Europe and induced a "responsive Council of Ministers" to accept armed neutrality, a policy which was "applied thereafter under his strict personal surveillance." This view is played down, or entirely ignored, by most historians. Telford Taylor provides the narrative details in a more traditional mode, the *flamand-wallon* schism, a changed international environment, the intitiative of the Ministers, all combining as causes with Leopold hardly appearing in his account until he "stamped the royal seal on the new policy." Renouvin explains the shift entirely in terms of strategic consequences: "when the Belgian government saw that France had allowed the reoccupation of the demilitarized Rhine territories…it wished to avoid being drawn into a war between powerful neighbors," and hence turned to neutrality. Historian Brian Bond agrees that the neutrality policy owed virtually nothing to the Belgian king. Doubtless, decisions were made in the context of the Flemish wish to have closer ties with Holland, but as Telford Taylor says, "the *Flamands* were congenitally opposed to the Government's ties with France" in any case, so this was their traditional stance and could not have had a sudden impact on foreign affairs. As for the changed international environment and the German reoccupation of the Rhineland, any increase in German power, as noted above, made a French alliance more, not less, desirable. Besides, neither Taylor nor Renouvin nor Bond even mention the dramatic personal events in Leopold's life, which preceded Belgium's shift in policy. [3]

Historian Rudolph Binion has shown how and why neutrality was Leopold's and not his Minister's initiative and how his actions were unconsciously meant to encourage war, a war, Binion argues, that Leopold unconsciously wanted. This was apparent in the contradictions inherent in Leopold's 14 October 1936 statement on neutrality, as Binion's analysis proves: "The King's policy of 1936-1940 was self-refuting as well as self-defeating—and not merely in retrospect, but within the perspective that was then his."[4] Leopold's later statements "taken together, betrayed a secret persuasion that the prospective {German} attack was inevitable, that it would be irresistible, and that Belgium would succumb to it." Buried in this belief in inevitability was Leopold's secret wish for those things to happen. His minister Paul Henri Spaak, for one, almost recognized it, saying: "With hallucinatory prophetic prescience the King had long since seen what was due to happen." Binion concludes: "the King contrived to make his foreboding prophetic. His policy conduced to the catastrophe....His premonition concealed a guilty project, as is the way with premonitions. The neutrality policy, ostensibly his means of warding off a dread fatality, was in actuality the very opposite."[5] The question remains: what motivated him?

Binion argues persuasively that the answer lies in Leopold's personal unconscious agenda established by a deep trauma suffered only the year before. It was not the death of his father Albert that counted most for him, but the death of his beloved Queen Astrid and, especially, the circumstances of that death. On the morning of 29 August 1935, "an open roadster driven by Leopold, in alpinist's apparel, with Astrid beside him and his chauffeur in the rumble seat, accidentally veered off the road just outside the Swiss village of Küssnacht near Lucerne and coasted uncontrollably down the bank of the Lake. Leopold and the chauffeur escaped serious injury, but Astrid, projected head-on against a tree part way down, succumbed a few minutes later in Leopold's arms. Leopold's shock at Albert's ghastly death was as nothing compared with his shock at Astrid's. And Astrid's affected the whole Belgian nation as grievously as did Albert's, for Flemings and Walloons alike idolized the gracious and beautiful queen."

Leopold was in "shock," unable to talk, his suffering, it was said, was "dreadful to behold." Astrid's death was called a "national catastrophe," and Leopold "must have felt the incrimination behind the myriad compassionate gazes directed at him as he left the train in Brussels; he must have overheard public rumor thereafter even from his great remove," all of which fueled his own feelings of responsibility, for he was, after all, the driver. "Throughout the funeral procession all eyes were upon him, while his own eyes remained fixed upon the coffin. 'His jaws {were} contracted in an effort of will power,' *Le Temps* related. He was, one could feel, at the end of his strength, and pain was ravaging his face."[6]

Earlier painful events were nothing like this. As Binion notes, "Albert's death had not prostrated him for a single moment;" he got over it "in the normal course." Astrid's death was different. A late March 1936 visit to the king from Harold Nicolson confirms Binion's judgment: Nicolson found him "terribly pathetic," a "poor lonely young man." As with severe trauma, Leopold was now primed to unconsciously relive the experience, the second time symbolically, with his ministers as chauffeur-substitute, and Belgium as a stand-in for Queen Astrid. As he said in 1938, a peaceful country is like "a motorist who is calmly driving along a road, but is exposed to the possibility of an accident produced out of a byroad." And "if the catastrophe comes... streams of blood will flow." Rhetoric like this betrays the unconscious wish behind the neutrality policy. It led, in May 1940, to a second scenario when, as Binion says, "Astrid died a second death in his arms" as "the nation—signifying Astrid—succumbed with its army."[7]

Although some historians who are unfamiliar with the notion of trauma, or who have difficulty in accepting the existence of repression, the power of the unconscious, the compulsive need to relive, and the possibility of acting out unconscious impulses will not be convinced, Binion's breakthrough study has clearly shown the unconscious personal agenda behind Leopold's neutrality policy. But as is the way with breakthrough studies, it leaves some questions unanswered. Although he works hard to prove that Albert's death was without crucial emotional significance for Leopold, it is hard to dismiss it as a possibility just because the outward expressions of Leopold's grief for his father were less dramatic than his grief for Astrid. Strivings against father—if not always a full-blown Oedipus Complex—and guilt over those strivings are certainly part of life for men, or some men, or at least some of the time, and it is difficult to avoid the thought that Astrid's death loaded onto Leopold an additional burden of guilt from his sudden accession after his father's untimely death. Moreover, one wonders if Astrid's death—experienced in part as abandonment—called forth repressed memories of earlier childhood abandonments.[8]

Binion notes the important fact that Leopold's needs were not his alone and that his "delusive, disastrous policy was democratically sustained."[9] The Belgian people had also felt abandoned by Astrid's death. In this respect, Leopold was enacting the Belgian people's wishes as well as his own by assuming the unconscious delegate role seen in leaders in other countries. What is not so clear is whether there was an experience of childhood abandonment among many Belgians before Astrid's death. A full-scale study of Belgian child-rearing is needed to see if it differed at all from its French, Dutch, and German neighbors, and how that may have helped prepare the Belgians to play their decisive group-fantasy role. Chances are, however, that Belgian childhoods were not much different from those of the peoples living around them.

It is possible (some would say proven by clinical evidence) that with imperfect parenting the rule, no one escapes feelings of abandonment—it is part of the human condition—and that various kinds of parental neglect have produced in everyone deeply frightening memories of having been abandoned, or fears of being abandoned once again, even if people have not been physically abandoned. These are the repressed reservoirs being tapped when people cry at abandonment scenes in movies. Could not the same feelings be tapped by diplomatic cues coming from the European family? And it seems that another crucial factor for the Belgian people's need to follow Leopold's neutrality policy is connected to the dual traumas of their 1914 defeat and the devastations of 1914, both of which may have driven a need in the 1930s to relive the pre-World War I neutrality policy which had ended so disastrously in August 1914.

For Leopold specifically, Binion's judgment seems right when he writes that he "was not reacting to the general

European situation at the same time he was abreacting Küssnacht; he was abreacting Küssnacht within the context of European politics, which is quite another matter."[10] That is the argument here too. Leopold's grief was operating in a specific political situation at a specific historical moment as he tried to use the public stage to resolve his inner conflict. Only a careful search of the sources will reveal the ways in which the international community, especially Britain, France, and Germany, may have cued Leopold and the Belgians to act out their own feelings of abandonment. By producing a policy which led, in fantasy, to Belgium becoming the European system's second abandoned child, Belgium's military and diplomatic isolation helped France continue to feel alone while encouraging Hitler to play his role as Europe's bad boy. But, as everyone knows, Hitler had come late to the game: playing Europe's bully was a role he had assumed from its earlier bad boy, Italy's dictator, Benito Mussolini.

Prior to Hitler, Mussolini had been the raging, out-of-control child of the interwar years. He acted the part, with his outrageous rhetoric, grandiose boasting, and absurd posturing. He provided the European family with an opportunity of projecting its aggression into him. He was, said contemporaries, a "swashbuckler," a "freebooter," a "criminal," a "gangster," a "blackmailer," a "bully," and, occasionally, "mad." He accommodated these images by such things as ordering the Italian press, within months, to print verbal attacks on thirty different countries.[11] Chamberlain was grasping for this fantasy function when he said: "Mussolini was behaving like a spoiled child, and the child was dreaming of some large new rattles." And he even looked the part when he showed off his bald head—rationalized as hiding "the aging process"[12]—which made him look unconsciously to the world and himself like a newborn child.

As with other fantasy leaders, the Duce was able to play several roles at once. Italian playwright Luigi Pirandello saw him as "essentially an actor pretending to be the person the Italians wanted him to be." One of his leading English biographers agrees, characterizing him as "an actor, a dissimulator, an exhibitionist who changed his role from hour to hour to suit the occasion." It was as if "he never knew his genuine self and was always striving after some counterfeit impersonation."[13] Because the actor needed a script, it was all the easier for the great powers to cue him.

Among the several masks he wore—"father," "brother," "husband," macho sex symbol—the one that played best, "violent aggressor," doubled for the international community. It was the role with which he was most comfortable since he had played it continuously since the early days of his very angry childhood.

Mussolini's newest political biographer pays scant attention to his childhood so that one needs to look elsewhere for the origins of his anger. It seems to have come from two early sources: maternal neglect and paternal beatings. Biographer Laura Fermi suggests an early abandonment, noting that it was Rosa's mother Marianne (Benito's maternal grandmother) who was the family caretaker. She lived with them and "looked after the children while Rosa taught school." Fermi asserts that although Rosa had become "deeply worried" over Benito's childhood "wildness," she "was too busy with family and school chores to give sufficient attention to her unmanageable son."[14] (How Fermi knows this is unclear.) Mother seems to have been involved with the children only to the extent that she took them to church every Sunday—an outing Benito despised and continually rebelled against. Three separate times he was sent away to boarding schools. Responding with anger and autism to his early treatment, he withdrew from the world, worrying his parents for many months by his inability to speak. One biographer induces from his behavior a marked ambivalence toward his mother. "Although Mussolini always claimed to be deeply fond of his mother," writes Denis

Mack Smith, "he hardly acted toward her with much consideration."[15] Later attitudes, relationships, and acting out with many other women, including his wife, suggest displacement from his repressed rage towards her.

Like Hitler, Mussolini thought of the masses as a "woman," and referred to public opinion as a "harlot." Like Hitler, he believed: "The crowd likes strong men. The crowd is like a woman." Ciano's diary records him as saying that the people were "'a whore'...who simply ran after a conquering male." As a young man he visited prostitutes, boasted of rape in his autobiography, and described one scene in graphic detail. He declared that women "prefer brutality in a man." These clear sadistic messages apparently stimulated sexual excitement in some Italians and non-Italians, including, as Bosworth shows, the occasional wife of a British diplomat. He once stabbed his partner—a married woman with whom he was having an affair. And although he was later able to marry and father four children, he was never emotionally close to his wife: she called him "Duce" (even at home); they lived in separate rooms; he ate alone; and when they exchanged anniversary greetings, it was by telephone or telegraph. Although, as his wife admitted, it hurt her feelings, he had several mistresses. Even with them the core anger at women prevailed, one biographer finding "a manifest element of sadism in his treatment of Clara Petacci and his many other mistresses."[16]

Another adult characteristic, Mussolini's grandiosity, suggests the extent of his deep childhood hurt. He unconsciously tried to make up for the nurture he had failed to receive by surrounding himself with sycophants who had to continually flatter him. He compared himself to Napoleon and Julius Caesar, declaring himself an even greater leader. He staged massive rallies where thousands could steadily cheer him. His narcissism even found its way into a Hemingway short story: "On the walls of the houses {in Spezia} were stenciled eye-bugging portraits of Mussolini."[17] American journalist Louis Fischer noted the same phenomenon. Passing through Milan in 1935, he found it "plastered with... Mussolini pictures. Mussolini scowling, frowning, pouting, smiling; Mussolini fencing, shooting, swimming, strutting, flying, speaking, fiddling; Mussolini on a canon, on a tank, on a horse, on a balcony; Mussolini bald, Mussolini in a Roman helmet, in a steel helmet, in a flier's cap; Mussolini, Mussolini." One estimate puts the number of photographs of him distributed to the Italian people during his years in power at 30 million, with him striking 2500 different poses.[18]

These propaganda images were, of course, for political effect, but they sound like the mandated expressions of a needy child starved for attention and reveling in it. All of his biographers comment on his vanity and egotism; others, including some who knew him well, also speak of his "inferiority complex." (This included the theorist of that complex, Alfred Adler.) Egotism and inferiority can be two sides of the same coin. The need to be the center of attention was compensatory, an intra-psychic strategy designed to make up for "a poor self-image." In poor bonding with his mother and inadequate nurture from her and other maternal caretakers one finds the rage and narcissism which also animated several narcissistic rituals in his fascist state.

But Mussolini's rage was not just displaced from Rosa. As a child he was beaten by his father, Alessandro. "A thick leather strap played a part in the family's upbringing," writes one biographer. Another says there was "strong paternal discipline with his father in the smithy," and he "was beaten if he was careless or allowed his attention to wander." Later, he was severely punished and beaten in several schools by priests. As an adult his idea of a proper upbringing recapitulated those early years: he said that children should be "lined up in uniform from morning to night, and give them stick, stick, stick."[19]

His rage expressed itself in many acts of childhood violence, as would later be the case for the European family.

He stoned people at church and once stabbed a fellow student. The records of the Salesian school at Faenza describe him as "passionate and unruly; and he cannot adapt himself to the life of the school, where, he is convinced he has been sent as a punishment....He places himself in opposition to every rule and discipline....He feels sadder and more alone....He rebels against every punishment and correction." Mack Smith sums up Benito's violent childhood: "A perhaps untrustworthy legend has it that he plucked live chickens and blinded captive birds. He was remembered for pinching people in church to make them cry. As a gang leader he used to bully others into joining his escapades, and a close disciple confirmed that he was always the one to start a fight. As he had a pronounced sense of vendetta, no insult was allowed to pass without his enacting vengeance, but he also sought quarrels for their own sake and because he needed to dominate....In later years he used to smile with pleasure at the thought that his school fellows would still carry the scars of wounds he had inflicted."[20]

It seems possible that Benito's lawlessness and bullying, his violence of word and act as both child and adult, were encouraged—even delegated—by father Alessandro, who in an act of conscious symbolic delegation named him after three famous revolutionaries, Benito Juarez, Andrea Costa, and Ailcare Cipriani. Indeed, Alessandro, a lifelong socialist who had earlier been a follower of the anarchist Bakunin, had himself spent time in jail. Benito listened at his father's knee to political discussions with other socialists and revolutionaries, understanding from these cues what would win father's approval. Later, his brother Arnaldo continued in the role of father-substitute when "he secretly sometimes encouraged Benito to acts of severity and aggression,"[21] as Mussolini would later encourage Hitler. After Arnaldo's death in 1931, the consummate actor Mussolini—filled with rage and violence, and used to the role of delegate from childhood—could continue to look to

Europe for parental substitutes and cues on how and when to play the bad boy.

People at the time sensed it. In 1935, the British ambassador felt: "My own constant impression is of a man who is the victim, not the master, of his destiny," a destiny, in part at least, controlled by the Italian people. As one prominent Italian historian argues, Mussolini's foreign policy, at least until 1937, was a manifestation of Italy's popular will. But he was also Europe's delegate, like Hitler the sometime container of Britain's "crazy" feelings when he was often called "a madman" in public.[22] Yet the British were also ambivalent, unconsciously identifying with his violence as they did with Hitler's, sometimes expressing open admiration for him, as was the case in the approving words used by Chamberlain's sibling rival Austen, or with the King of England, who knighted him. Still, what mostly came from Europe was the message that he was a bully, and as the frequency of the images intensified were unconsciously understood by him as "commands" as he had earlier understood similar cues from his father in childhood. Europe as much as Italy (and when Italian public opinion moved away from a desire for war after 1937, increasingly Europe alone), was driving Mussolini. Earlier he had become "fascinated and almost obsessed with the prospect of leading his country in a victorious war. He repeated earlier statements that 1935 was the year when he would be ready for war, and fascism must seize its chance to capture another colony as proof that Italy under his leadership had become a great power."[23]

This fitted his earlier childhood family role, providing an outlet for his—and Italy's—adult "inferiority complex." And there was historical precedent: it had been Italy's tradition, noted by many historians since Italy's unification in the nineteenth century, to act the role of self-styled great power striving to be recognized as such in the European state system. Feelings of inferiority had continued to plague Italy following the terrible sacrifices of the Great War, what

Italians called "the mutilated peace." Italy's striving thus combined with Mussolini's striving, collective wish with personal agenda. The bully role was one both could enjoy. So could Europe.

Several examples from the diplomatic history of the period illustrate these points, with Great Britain, sometimes aided by France, again leading the way. The twists and turns of Italy's interwar diplomacy are well known, and one need only focus on two aspects of the story to understand its underlying psychodynamics: first, Italy's relationship with the Allies: and second, Mussolini's relationship with Hitler.

In January 1935, French Foreign Minister Laval visited Rome for agreements on colonial and other issues. Mussolini later claimed that at this meeting Laval had given him a free hand in Abyssinia; Laval maintained that no assurances had been given. Perhaps both were right. It is worth remembering that several observers felt French diplomacy was frequently filled with covert clues and hidden meanings, and on this occasion, while no overt permission had been offered on Abyssinia, Laval seems to have unconsciously communicated French (and European) wishes by his silences, body language, and various non-verbal cues. French statesman Paul-Boncour thought so: "what was said in the *tête-à-tête* during the evening party at the Palazzo Farnese?" he asks. "We shall never know. Perhaps they said nothing to each other....But if they did speak of Abyssinia, and if then....by a shrug of the shoulder or a wink of the eye—Vandervelde who knew them both well was sure it was thus that it must have happened—M. Laval allowed M. Mussolini to understand that he would not be too severe should a military expedition be attempted."[24]

Thus cued, Italy began sending troops to Somaliland. Mussolini was preparing to fulfill his prediction and Europe's unconscious hope that Italy would be at war by 1935. In March 1935 Hitler announced rearmament, and by April British, French, and Italian leaders were meeting at

Stresa to "act in close and cordial collaboration" by way of opposing the acts of aggressors "which may endanger the peace of Europe." The "Stresa Front" which emerged was designed to keep Hitler in check, but also, paradoxically, gave the Allies an opportunity to encourage Mussolini's aggression. British diplomat Sir Ivone Kirkpatrick wrote in his Mussolini biography that "neither during the six sessions of the conference nor in the lobbies did any Briton breathe a word to the Duce about Abyssina....The original draft spoke of peace in general, but Mussolini demanded and secured an amendment to 'peace in Europe.' This significant modification passed unobserved or at least it was not contested by the British delegation....Thus Mussolini left Stresa with the clear conviction that Britain, which was fully aware of his military preparations, attached little importance to Abyssinia." Later manipulations encouraged him to move towards friendship with Germany. The author of the recent study *Mussolini as Diplomat* finds that: "British policy threw Mussolini into Hitler's arms."[25]

It was as if he were a juvenile delinquent convincing himself—along with his parents convincing him—that they were about to accept his behavior since the British said nothing to restrain the lawlessness they knew he was planning and guessed would soon be unleashed. (Indeed, as a recent popular biographer has noted, "in contrast to all the other twentieth century dictators...Mussolini had the unique distinction of having been a juvenile delinquent.") Thus, along with Laval's earlier "assurances," the cues from Britain encouraged the Duce to feel he now had a free hand. In October Italian troops invaded Ethiopia. Publicly, and consciously, the Allies were outraged. The League applied sanctions. Neville Chamberlain wrote in his diary that sanctions were not enough, and told Hoare: "If we weakened now because of Mussolini's threats we should leave the Americans in the air....It was inevitable that in such circumstances U.S.A. would decline in future to help in any way, sanctions crumble, the league would lose its coherence, and our whole policy would be destroyed."[26]

Nevertheless, oil sanctions were not applied, even though by his own later admission Mussolini would have been compelled to withdraw from Ethiopia if they had been. Instead of applying sanctions, the British rewarded his negative behavior, and alerted Hitler, Mussolini, and Stalin that their protests were mere empty gestures, by concluding a January 1937 "Gentleman's Agreement" with Italy on the status quo in the Mediterranean.

It will be remembered that Chamberlain's turnabout from anti-appeaser to appeaser came immediately after his elevation to Prime Minister and the death of his brother Austen. It was earlier suggested that unconscious guilt over attaining what had eluded both his father and brother somehow unconsciously figured in his policy change. And it will be remembered that father Joseph as Colonial Secretary had earlier sought an accommodation with Germany and that by pursuing peace with Germany Neville seems to have been trying to "out-Joseph" Joseph. As for Italy, Neville's appeasement policy after 1937 seems to have been unconsciously designed to "out-Austen" Austen, his major sibling rival, who, as Britain's Foreign Minister in the 1920s had sought accommodation with Italy, popularized the word "appeasement," and admired Mussolini as his "friend." In fact, Chamberlain virtually said as much when he wrote Mussolini directly in 1937, "summoning in his support," writes one biographer, "the ghost of his brother Austen {who} had always viewed Mussolini," as Nevelle's letter put it, "as 'a good man to do business with.'"

Before that, however, the same Samuel Hoare whom Chamberlain had tried to embolden about oil sanctions stirred up a hornet's nest. The event in December 1936 involving Hoare foreshadowed the policy of appeasement, and in the process revealed Britain's real intentions so glaringly that they could not be covered over with rationalizations. Due to outraged public opinion, they had to be temporarily abandoned until (because groups tend to be amnesiac) the public at large forgot about the episode. The British government had pledged full support to the League's sanctions policy against Italy, but at the cabinet meeting of 2 December, Foreign Secretary Hoare, fearing Mussolini might be driven to a "mad dog" act by oil sanctions, proposed a negotiated settlement. On his way to Switzerland to offer generous terms to Italy, Hoare stopped to get Laval's consent in Paris. Both agreed that Italy should receive economic and territorial cessions—more even than Mussolini's armies had yet taken. On 8 December, the British Cabinet approved the plan, but when it was leaked to the press there was such a public outcry that Hoare was forced to resign. The plan nevertheless sent a message, which had far-reaching consequences despite its never being implemented. Telford Taylor sees it clearly: "It was an impossible basis for a settlement under which the nation condemned an aggressor was to be substantially rewarded for its aggressions.... the...proposals had effectively undermined Britain's leadership at Geneva, and it was too late to retrieve the situation....The League Committee...refer{red} the oil sanctions proposals to a committee of experts....The Germans marched into the Rhineland, and the question of oil sanctions was drowned in a sea of other trouble....Britain got the worst of all possible worlds—an arrogant, resentful Mussolini thrown into ominous combination with an increasingly confident and acquisitive Hitler, a League of Nations damaged beyond repair as an engine of collective security, and a national image badly tarnished at home and abroad."[27] It was all the British could have unconsciously hoped for, and more.

The leak that had turned public opinion around and foreshadowed the appeasement to come turned out to be the "family secret" revealed. At the moment it was revealed, the threat of European war was not severe enough, nor the "moral position" of the Allies sufficiently prepared. Conscious awareness of Europe's unconscious wishes could therefore not be rationalized. The scapegoat Hoare had to go.

The second thing illustrating the psychodynamics of Italy's diplomacy in the period is the connection between the Duce and the Führer. By the mid-1930s, Mussolini's relationship with Hitler began undergoing a change. At first the Führer, who had openly admired the Duce in the 1920s and built elements of Nazi ritual and practice on the fascist model, subordinated himself to the Duce's well-established dictatorship—and felt and acted like a disciple. But as Hitler increasingly moved to center stage and eclipsed Mussolini's role as Europe's out-of-control, raging child, the Duce, like the flattered adolescent gang leader whose preeminence is challenged by a younger usurper, became angered and more and more ambivalent: he alternately encouraged, then restrained Hitler's aggression. He too used Nazism as a container for his own projected craziness, calling Göring an "ex-inmate of a lunatic asylum," Hitler a "buffoon," "mad," and "a horrible sexual degenerate," and Nazi Germany "a racialist lunatic asylum."[28] Because of these feelings, he eventually encouraged Hitler's aggressive intentions towards Austria—or at least Hitler thought so at their June 1934 Venice meeting. When Austrian Nazis then shot and killed Chancellor Dollfuss, Mussolini turned the tables and played the role of outraged neighbor, sending Italian troops to the Brenner Pass. Later, as described above, German rearmament led Mussolini to help create the "Stresa Front" against Hitler, but Allied reaction to his Ethiopian venture prompted him in May 1935 to suggest a "mutual press truce" with Germany. This beginning of improved relations with Germany was followed by Italian and German assistance to Franco in the Spanish Civil War, the "Rome-Berlin" Axis (Mussolini's phrase), a trip to Germany, Hitler's trip to Rome, and Mussolini's eventual acceptance of the *Anschluss* in March 1938.

What seems apparent in all of this maneuvering is that the displaced Mussolini was becoming Hitler's enabler. During the Czech Crisis he stated that he was ready to support Germany militarily if war should come. In 1939, he became Hitler's enabler again by concluding the "Pact of Steel."

The Pact of Steel in May 1939 was a crucial turning point in Europe's road to war. It was preceded by a meeting between the Italian and German foreign ministers in early May. On the eve of Ciano's meeting in Milan with Ribbentrop, Mussolini had sent a set of instructions which began: "It is my firm conviction that the two European Powers of the Axis require a period of peace of at least three years. It is only after 1943 that a war effort will have the best prospects of victory." These instructions were shown to Ribbentrop, then resurfaced on 21 May when they reappeared, verbatim, in a memorandum sent to Hitler "which gave at great length Mussolini's reasons for wishing to see peace preserved for at least three years." It is not surprising then that the bellicose Ribbentrop had "reassured" Ciano on the eve of the signing of the treaty by telling him of Germany's expectation of peace "for at least three years."[29]

This has been used by historians to "confirm" Mussolini's peaceful intentions: by concluding the Pact of Steel, it is said, he thought he was working to keep the peace–Italy's intentions had been made clear to Hitler. That is on the conscious level. Mussolini's unconscious intentions were linked to his fantasy role as Hitler's enabler, and are better reveled by his novel notion of having the pact announced before its terms were settled. Because Mussolini bound Italy to an agreement before knowing what its details were, he was in effect talking peace while actually leaving it to Hitler to start war whenever he chose, with Italy obliged to come in on Germany's side whenever the war began. This could have been a "mistake" on Mussolini's part, the result of poor judgment, some kind of momentary lapse, a lack of attention to unforeseen consequences, or even an unconscious wish. The latter is suggested by the last line of the German memorandum, quoting Ciano quoting Mussolini, that "the future policy of the Axis Powers must be: 'Toujours parler de la paix et préparer la guerre.'" Unlike Mussolini, Hitler did not consciously delude himself over the meaning of the agreement, understanding it as a message to proceed with his war plans. The day after the Pact was signed he informed his generals: "War is inevitable," and decided "at the first suitable opportunity to attack Poland." Unconsciously, Mussolini knew this too: his first impulse had been to call their new agreement "the Pact of Blood."[30]

Thus, from the dominant "partner" capable of independent action Mussolini had become Hitler's encouraging subordinate. "Italy, like France, was now on the sidelines; the fate of both countries determined by the actions of their greater partners."[31] How could Mussolini have so thoughtlessly surrendered Italy's choices? The compulsion to war was now so great that it pressed to be acted out at all costs. For Italy, the outcome was the consequence of a process begun at least four years earlier. Although Hitler had secretly sent supplies to Ethiopia in order to keep Mussolini tied down there longer, several German actions had a reverse impact on Mussolini's policies. Telford Taylor describes the interactions of how the Italo-German friendship unfolded:

> In 1935, Mussolini's Ethiopian venture had helped Germany by deflecting international attention from Hitler's denunciation of Versailles, and Germany's neutrality and economic support had given Mussolini comfort and support in carrying through his program in the face of sanctions. In 1936 the German march into the Rhineland helped Italy by putting the Ethiopian war into the shade, and Mussolini's refusal to support the French helped Hitler to survive the initial crisis and turn the Rhineland occupation into a fait accompli....By the summer of 1936 it had become apparent even to Mussolini himself, that his efforts to pursue an independent European policy had failed. In 1934,

> Hitler, by his crudely overt support of the Austrian Nazis, had thrown Mussolini into the arms of France. In 1935, Britain, by her hostile but indecisive sanctions policy, pitched him...to Hitler.[32]

Thus, Taylor agrees with the author of *Mussolini as Diplomat* that, "British policy threw Mussolini into Hitler's arms." It helps explain externals, but what of "internals," those psychological changes that made Mussolini's diplomatic transformation possible? The evidence seems clear enough. Italy's foreign policy shifts were accompanied by—even pre-dated—Mussolini's growing identification with Hitler: first Hitler had modeled himself on Mussolini; now the Duce was becoming the Führer.

This growing identification can be seen, for example, in Mussolini's reaction to news of the "Night of the Long Knives." He was openly repelled by the Röhm purge: Hitler, he said, was "a cruel and ferocious character who calls Attila to mind." But he also began to hint at a secret admiration when he said: "Those men he killed were his closest collaborators, who hoisted him to power." In the outrage was the subtle admiration of one bully for another, followed by the thrill of a more explicit identification: "It is as if I came to kill with my own hands Balbo, Grandi, Bottai!" (Anyway, had not Mussolini helped prompt Hitler at their Venice meeting to get rid of the uncouth S.A. types in Hitler's entourage?) He was identifying with Hitler when he suddenly decided that he wanted to become the Commander-in-Chief of Italy's armed forces. He sought to instill more courage in Italian soldiers by introducing the goose step from the German army, and at "its first public appearance, Mussolini surprised everyone by jumping down from his podium and leading the parade to show how it should be done." He shocked the world by imposing Racial Laws modeled after Nazi Germany's: "Even in September 1937, he was still insisting that the 40-70,000 Jews in Italy constituted no problem...but by the beginning of 1938, the press was encouraged to inform the public that the Jews have wormed their way into strategic positions in Italian life." By summer, the "Charter of Race" was promulgated.[33] His identification with Hitler had gone so far by the time of the Czech Crisis that he was serving as the Führer's puppet, misrepresenting Germany's demands, telephoned to him from Berlin the day before, as his own. His 1939 seizure of Albania not only looks like, but was inspired by Hitler's invasion of Czechoslovakia.[34] These facts make it abundantly clear that Mussolini, once Hitler's model, had become his ardent follower.

These efforts to be like Hitler—in fantasy, to "become" Hitler, to enjoy his power and influence by proxy—were not without their psychological dangers. Not only was there the fear of the loss of self, there was also the prospect of encountering one's own repressed homosexual proclivities.

The evidence, indirect, seems conclusive enough. While not so openly homophobic as the Nazis, Mussolini's macho posturing, the sexualized aggressive fascist rhetoric, the Duce's Don Juanism and generalized contempt for women all suggest that the militant strutting was in part a personal defensive strategy to cover over, deny, and keep in check fear of homosexual longing in himself. The Duce admitted later in life that he had never had any male friends. Biographer Mack Smith notes: "He used to talk of a protective wall being necessary to keep others away and even of a 'physical revulsion' at human contact. When he abolished the handshake and replaced it with what he called a 'more hygienic' Roman salute, this derived in part from an almost morbid dislike of physical touch." He stated that "war was for men what maternity was for women," and believed, contemptuously, that Hitler wore rouge.[35]

The kind of fantasies circulating around Italy's growing ties with Germany must have stirred homosexual fears even more. The British by late 1938 were concerned that Italy would be "thrown into the arms of Germany," which their policies were creating, although one official thought that in regard to the Duce, "Hitler was getting much too big to be a comfortable bed-fellow." In February 1938, political cartoonist David Low concretized the image when he drew them in bed together, armed and suspiciously eying one another.[36] Their macho posturing is what in part allowed them to join together, the Italo-German connection being aptly called "the brutal friendship." To the extent that the Nazi alliance, even détente, was experienced as a fantasy "marriage"[37] it can be hypothesized that such approaches would almost invariably be accompanied by even greater macho posturing to prove one's "masculinity." Of course, the homosexual material threatening to break into consciousness could not be entirely covered over and would have to be handled in some other way, and it was–by being projected onto the British.

Mother Britain, already governess to Europe's fantasy system, was the ready-made container for these projections. There was a tradition among Europeans that homosexuality was particularly British, and celebrated cases, like that of Oscar Wilde, seemed to confirm it. For his part, Mussolini thought the British "weak," "impotent," and "effeminate."[38] During the Czech Crisis he believed they were suffering from a "menopausal disorder;" at Munich, he said, Chamberlain had "licked his boots." Britain was "a decadent country with four million surplus women. Four million sexually unsatisfied women," he said—a theme he returned to again and again with a vehemence that surprised his listeners.[39]

These fears, not just homosexual "panic," joined with other stressors to exhaust his intra-psychic defenses, and repression began to break down. Mussolini's public and private statements, like those of others in the European "family"—Hitler, Chamberlain, the British press—reveal how that unconscious repressed material was flooding, or threatening to flood, his consciousness. There would be "war," "explosions," "the destruction of everything that passes for civilized life:" "Europe is going up in a blaze," he said. Mack Smith notes: "By the beginning of 1939 there was something increasingly frenzied and irrational about Mussolini."[40] The kind of destructive fantasies he was expressing would somehow rid him (as well as Europe) of the out-of-control raging child within through a symbolic "delayed infanticide" by sacrificing a new generation of youth in a new war. As much as Hitler, he wanted war, saying that Italy needed one every twenty-five years to keep healthy.[41] Hints of this as a symbolic sacrifice are found in many symbolic acts—infants a few months old photographed in black shirts, military instruction being made compulsory for children of eight. At least one Briton was consciously repelled. Harvey found "the sight of little boys with their miniature rifles...rather revolting."[42] As with Hitler, Italian mothers held up their children in symbolic sacrifice to be "blessed" by the Duce as he passed by, and Mussolini seems to have left no doubt about his future intentions when he stated publicly how he wished that more Italians had been killed in the Ethiopian war.[43]

Still, despite his encouraging Hitler and helping to trigger Hitler's immediate plans for a September 1939 invasion of Poland by concluding the Pact of Steel in May, Mussolini did not go to war alongside his Axis partner until the next year. One experiences here an eerie sense of *déjà vu*. Historians saw early on that it all seemed to have happened before.

In 1953 historian Felix Gilbert wrote: "There is irony in the fact that in September 1939 Fascist Italy...ended up roughly in the same position in which parliamentary Italy had found herself at the beginning of the first world war."[44] In late December 1938, Harvey had already predicted Mussolini's course: "if there is a war he would most certainly betray the Germans anyway, as Giolitti did in 1914." This seems consistent with the wishes of the Italian people who didn't want war in 1939, thus allowing Mussolini—despite his disintegrating defenses—to serve once again as their unconscious delegate.[45] Nor was this all. According to Overy and Wheatcroft: "Since the signature of the Pact of Steel, he had been sending belligerent messages to Berlin, reassuring Hitler that the two fascist states would 'march together.'" As enabler Mussolini was recreating one of Italy's roles in the pre-World War I Triple Alliance. Michael Palumbo has shown how some of Italy's actions in the years before the First World War were understood by its Austrian ally as signals encouraging Austria to go to war.[46] Now Germany, not Austria was being consciously and unconsciously encouraged, but the end result was the same. Germany was in a sense "Austria" this time around since the *Anschluss* had made Austria part of Germany. What unconscious forces might compel Italy to play the same fantasy role again, with the Austrian Hitler's Germany in the role of the Austria of 1914, is still unclear, but Mussolini's "repeat performance" of 1939 may suggest here too a need to replay an earlier collective trauma. World War I was a horrific bloodbath for Italy, after which the Italians felt they had been robbed of the spoils. Was Mussolini delegated to nominally avenge Italy's humiliation of 1918-1919 while actually staging a bigger and better replay?

When Mussolini finally went to war it was after months of accumulating stress. He felt his regime was weakening, the Germans were increasingly highly critical of his lack of "hardness," there were rumors that his physical abilities and health were disintegrating, he was experiencing "deepening anger," Ciano noted his mood swings, and Bosworth reports that in his February 1940 visit to Italy Sumner Wells found "the Duce visibly suffering from being the leader of a non-belligerent Italy, a country with no place to go." These stress indicators sound familiar, and have been found in Britain, France, Germany, Chamberlain, and Hitler. As in those other countries and leaders, it is probable that this time too Mussolini's move to war was a reaction to the wishes of the Italian people. Bosworth found that many Italians were then "ending their war doubts," concluding: "There is every reason…to think that…Mussolini had made a 'decision' from which few demurred."[47]

Whatever one makes of these several psychodynamic processes, it is clear that Mussolini had helped Europe to war by 1939. A key event in that process, one not yet explored, occurred one year earlier. In the images and actions of the great powers can be found the deep unconscious wishes of the European family as it turned in 1938 to settle the fate of the young state Czechoslovakia.

IX CZECHOSLOVAKIA

DON'T SHOOT CZECHOSLOVAKIA, STRANGLE HER.[1]
—*Anonymous Briton*,
(Reported by Ambassador Dirksen to Berlin, 1938)

Thomas Masaryk and Eduard Beneš, it was commonly said, were the founding fathers of Czechoslovakia. Both had been distinguished academics in the Austro-Hungarian Empire before beginning their revolutionary-patriotic activities as exiles during World War I. In the final days of the War, they helped form the new Czechoslovak state from parts of the old Habsburg Empire.

The new state was looked upon as occupying a central place in the European family of nations since—using an organic metaphor—it lay, it was repeatedly said, "in the heart of Europe." Its frontiers with Germany, Austria, Poland, Hungary and Rumania gave it strategic significance, while the efforts of President Masaryk and Foreign Minister Beneš to help its many nationalities live together harmoniously made it a major experiment in democracy. One of the groups that had lived in reasonable quiet with the others was the Sudeten Germans, a ready-made minority excuse for Nazi intervention.

Immediately after the *Anschluss* with Austria, the "Sudeten Question" became an international issue. Hitler wanted it that way: the Hossbach Memorandum of 5 November 1937 and Plan Green of 21 April 1938 said as much. In the Memorandum Hitler imagined "the blow against the Czechs" coming "even as early as 1938;" Plan Green arranged for the invasion.[2] Through the spring and summer of 1938 Hitler's pressures on Czechoslovakia stimulated the activities of the Nazi leader of the Sudeten Germans, Konrad Henlein. Europe was pushed into a seven-month long crisis, which threatened to plunge the continent into another Great War.

The details of the crisis are well known. It only needs recalling here how the crisis was finally resolved in September 1938 by Chamberlain's visits to Hitler in Berchtesgaden and Godesberg and then, with Daladier and Mussolini, in Munich.[3]

As detailed in Chapter III, the Munich Agreement was experienced in Britain as a humiliation. Virtually every historian since has seen it as a turning-point, signaling the eventual end of Czechoslovakia, encouraging Hitler to believe the Allies had given him yet another free hand, and creating conditions which seemingly made World War II a certainty.

Two things about these events are of interest: first, the fantasies people had about them at the time; and, second, the question of whether those fantasies were in any way acted out.

Comments by nearly all participants (and by virtually all later analysts) repeatedly refer to the pressures on the Czechs and the eventual union of the Sudetenland with Germany as the "sacrifice of Czechoslovakia." On 20 September 1938, the *Times* of London spoke of the "Czech Government's sacrifice." The next day, a Czech communiqué stated: "Our friends have advised us to pay for peace with our sacrifice." Masaryk's son, Jan Masaryk, Czech Ambassador to Britain, revealed to William Shirer that he had told Chamberlain and Halifax: "if you have sacrificed my nation to preserve the peace of the world, I will be the first to applaud you. But if not, gentlemen, God help your souls." Beneš, who had succeeded Thomas Masaryk as President after Masaryk's death a year before the crisis, later declared his government had accepted the Munich solution as a "sacrifice for world peace." The anti-appeasers said the same, as did the British press. Thomas Mann's 1940 book, *This War*, asserted that the Nazis "could not be stopped even by the terrible sacrifice of Munich."[4] The theme continued into the present with historians having spoken this way for sixty-five years.

Intellectually, the word "sacrifice" means giving up something of value, but it may be understood in fantasy as a real sacrifice.[5] Chapter II has shown how the fantasy language used at the time spoke of Czechoslovakia's "amputation," how it was thought that an "operation" was underway, of how it was imagined that the powers had begun to "rend bits...from the flesh of the stricken country."

Since countries may be understood in unconscious and conscious fantasy as human bodies, it is at least theoretically possible that the sacrifice of a country can be understood on deep fantasy levels as an actual human sacrifice, and, in any case, the frequent use of the sacrifice metaphor could have been enough to induce a climate of opinion, an unmentioned assumption encouraging people to feel, think, and act that way. Was this the case with Czechoslovakia?

Clues come from the words most often attached to Czechoslovakia in the media, along with the words used by politicians and statesmen at the time. Czechoslovakia, they said, was "small" or "weak." In fact, the words "small" and "weak"—and British contempt for being small and weak—went back at least to the 1920s and early 30s when the British repeatedly spoke of Czechoslovakia (and other smaller countries) as "wretched little places...half the size of Yorkshire," "snuffling little countries," and "funny little people." A December 1938 *Punch* cartoon had "Czechy" as one of the seven dwarfs (with Hitler as Snow White). A more positive tone was struck in a personal note written in October 1938 by American diplomat George Kennan who called the Czechs "a remarkable little people." Chamberlain told a worldwide radio audience it was a "small nation" confronted by a "big and powerful neighbor." On 8 October, Harvey wrote in his diary: "The western democracies have bought 'peace' by sacrificing a small nation." In criticizing Chamberlain's policies, Eden told the House of Commons that Munich had been a "grave injustice to a small and friendly nation." Sir Archibald Sinclair thought that Munich had brought "injustice to a small and weak nation." The organic metaphor connected perfectly to the theme of size when German Foreign Minister Neurath, echoing Göring's words, told Poland's Beck that sooner or later the Czechoslovak "appendix" would have to be cut out.[6]

Of course, Czechoslovakia was not an "appendix," but a country. Since in reality it was small in comparison to Germany, the widespread use of the word "small" is an apt description. But what is at issue is what the word small meant in fantasy. One can hypothesize from the evidence that on some level Czechoslovakia was being imagined in the 1930s as a child, in particular, a young child or infant.

A leading French statesman, Paul Reynaud, wrote that "Czechoslovakia was one of the new-born states and delicate like all the newly born." In the late 1920s, perhaps anticipating the future, Churchill wrote of Czechoslovakia that: "It is always unlucky to be born in the central regions of any continent." Hitler himself denounced the "birth" of the Czech state at the hands of "democratic midwives." In his study of the British press, Gannon notes that both the *Daily Express* and the *Daily Mail* were hostile to Czechoslovakia because, in their words, it was the "spawn of the Versailles system." In his popular 1939 book, *Disgrace Abounding*, British journalist Douglas Reed said that although "no blood relationship existed between London and Prague...France and England were the godparents of the free Czech State." The French Military Mission, "in Czechoslovakia for twenty years," was there, he said, "since the birth of the Republic;" it was France "whose darling child was Czechoslovakia." Even after the Munich "amputation," the new Czecho-Slovak state was experienced that way, Edith Summerskill saying to Parliament on 2 November 1938: "The Prime Minister went to Munich in the role of European obstetrician...and produced a monstrosity of which we were asked to be godparents."[7]

After Munich, Czechoslovakia began to break apart. The

Slovaks demanded independence. The Czechs "accepted with remarkable equanimity," wrote Kennan at the time, dismissing the Slovak behavior "outwardly as the pranks of a headstrong child who has been given a new toy." On 8 December 1938 he had written: "It is not surprising that the birth of a new form of government should have been a hard one. There were even some tense days, at one time, when it looked as if Adolf—who was after all the father in a sense—was getting impatient and was about to take a direct part in assisting the delivery—a development which might have produced a lusty child with commendable promptness but would have been hard on the mother."[8]

So pervasive was the fantasy of Czechoslovakia as an infant or small child that the image became the central metaphor in Godfrey Lias's book on Beneš. Published in 1940, but written before the outbreak of war, the book's chapter headings—such as "Conception of a State," "Birth Throes," and "Weaning Time"[9]—seem even today to have more to do with Lias's fantasies of Czechoslovakia as an infant than with Beneš's life.

World War I in Lias's fantasy language was a time when "new states were leaping into the womb of history." It was then that "the babe that was to become Czechoslovakia" had its "conception." The state was "a composite idea...born in the heart of two great men." It was Masaryk who "sired a state and saw it through infancy;" and although he was of central importance, "Masaryk's grandiose architectural conception would have been still-born without Beneš." The role of Beneš's wife "in the genesis of the Czechoslovakian State has been less spectacular than her husband's but the republic was her child almost as much as Eduard's and Masaryk's. She has been denied other children." During the war Masaryk's absences "threw chief responsibility as midwife for the unborn Czechoslovakian State on to the shoulders of Beneš." This took place "between the formation of the National Council and the actual birth of the new State."

As World War I reached its decisive phase, "the destiny of the embryo Czechoslovakian State was trembling in the valance of great events." At last "the infant Czechoslovakian State officially saw light on October 28, 1918." For Beneš and Masaryk, "the child of their dreams had not only been safely delivered, but even duly recognized by its contemporaries in advance of its actual birth." But now it faced new dangers. "For young States....There is apt, in the first place, to be violent disagreement among its political nurses about its mode of life. In the second place, there are generally several wolves around to gobble it up if the nurses show any sign of carelessness." Earlier Lias had said: "A wrong step...might have killed the Baby State before it was born."[10]

Britain and France, the fantasy "midwives of Versailles," had become, in fantasy, the "careless nurses" of the 1930s, where "wolves" still lurked about to gobble up the "baby state." This language is key to the central fantasy of what was about to happen to Czechoslovakia. On the eve of Munich, Churchill gave a statement to the press in which he noted the "fatal delusion" of believing "that security could be obtained by throwing a small state to the wolves." Churchill was invoking the fable of those who escaped a wolf attack by throwing their baby to the pack. He had invoked the imagery already in Parliament in his 14 March 1938 speech calling for a Grand Alliance. As he said then: "let those who wish to reject it ponder well and earnestly upon what will happen to us if when all else has been thrown to the wolves, we are left to face our fate alone." The image was used again and again by others, and even extended to other countries. On 2 November 1938, a Laborite Member of Parliament said: "The Government are engaged in a crazy policy...they have already sacrificed Austria; and within recent days they have sacrificed Czechoslovakia. Today they are in effect throwing Spain to the wolves."[11]

In January and February 1939, before Germany had annexed all of Czechoslovakia, Kennan used a different metaphor, which captured the same meaning: "As one Czech put it to me yesterday," he wrote on 6 January, "they are dangling Bohemia over the abyss." On 1 February he noted that Hitler "is still dangling Czechoslovakia over the abyss." A Low cartoon for Christmas 1938 captured these behaviors as an abduction fantasy: Hitler as Santa Claus places frightened babies ("Austria-Czechoslovakia-Poland," and so on) into a sack labeled "Deutschland über alles," collecting them from a bed called "Ex French–British Family." It seems that most Britons were then thinking along the lines enunciated by Sir John Wheeler-Bennett, who wrote *Munich: Prologue to Tragedy* about the events he witnessed. After the German occupation of Prague, said Wheeler-Bennett, the Allies could no longer afford to repeat the same policy of "fending off calamity by throwing another baby to the wolves." As usual, Low caught the underlying meaning of events in a 2 December 1938 cartoon, which showed a stretcher-bearing Chamberlain as part of a "First Aid Unit" arriving at the edge of a wood. "Excuse me, but did you hear a piercing scream?" asks the caption: four fat-bellied wolves, licking their chops, sit before a few scattered bones labeled "Czechoslovakia."[12]

All this made it fairly clear to the Germans exactly what the European family, or at least the British, intended. As Ambassador Dirksen wrote to Berlin in June 1938, as quoted at the beginning of this chapter: "most brutal, but also most characteristic, is the advice given to a German acquaintance by an influential Englishman: 'Don't shoot Czechoslovakia, strangle her'."

But if the end of Czechoslovakia was imagined in unconscious fantasy as Europe's infant or child sacrifice, the Czechs imagined it to be their own mass suicide. "Are we to commit suicide?" asked the headlines of Czech newspapers on 29 September 1938. It was a rhetorical question since they already knew the answer.[13]

Sensing the underlying unconscious meaning of Munich

and its aftermath, some historians have called these events Czechoslovakia's "suicide." Writing years after the events he lived through, Kurt Weisskopf noted how the "Czech government had at first been reluctant to commit hara-kiri," then recalled how the events of those days impacted on his psyche, saying "at times I felt almost schizoid." In 1940, Lias condemned Britain and France who had "presented the Munich pistol at Beneš's head." Reed said Munich meant that "about a million Czechs, in the name of self-extermination, now live under German rule." Harvey, in his diary, also grasped what was about to happen. As early as 5 June 1938 he feared British policy was "compelling Beneš to commit suicide in order to forestall murder."[14]

That summer the British, not unexpectedly, suddenly became fascinated with the issue of collective suicide itself. Although the *Anschluss* had taken place months before, the *Daily Telegraph* suddenly reported on 6 July that there were 800 Jewish suicide attempts in Vienna within a few days. Three weeks later, Josiah Wedgwood, speaking against concessions to Germany, told Parliament: "Directly Nazi rule comes along what happened in Austria will be repeated in the Sudeten Deutsch territory—another 20,000 suicides.... Every time you sacrifice one of your potential allies to this pathetic desire to appease the tyrants you merely bring nearer and make more inevitable that war which you pretend you are trying to avoid."[15] But Wedgwood was articulating exactly what thc powers unconsciously wanted, and such statements clued the Czechs that this was to be their fate.

The Czechs seemed willing to be sacrificed. When Jiri Mucha returned home from abroad in 1938 he found a "feeling of euphoria," a feeling confirmed, perhaps for others too, by Reed's journalistic account. When Beneš ordered mobilization on the night of 24 September 1938, he wrote: "The Czechs were born again," that "magnificent mobilization" was the act "of a small nation doomed to the sacrifice and exulting in its fate." He could remember "no example in history of a small nation that was not only ready, but clamorously eager to...deliberately sacrifice itself," an impression confirmed by a recent BBC television documentary which mentions that many in Prague had engaged in mass rallies demanding weapons while "the powers were intent on making Czechoslovakia commit suicide." When mobilization was ordered, there was a "tremendous willingness to die for the country."[16]

That "willingness to die," that "euphoria" Reed spoke of, may have been for some Czechs an intra-psychic defense, the manic side of the real fear stirred by the prospect of war. And it was also anger, a rage directed against the self, which came to be expressed in depression and self-loathing just as soon as the external "cause" for war was removed by the Munich Agreement. Kennan's personal letter of 8 December 1938 captures that post-Munich mood of depression and despair: "I spent weekends in the country where the guests did nothing but toss down brandy after brandy in an atmosphere of total gloom and repeat countless times: 'How was it possible that any people could allow itself to be led for twenty years by such a *Sauhund*...as Beneš? Such a people don't deserve to exist. It ought to be annihilated."[17]

That is precisely what the Czechs allowed the powers to do after Munich by helping along the demise of the newly hyphenated Czecho-Slovak state, although by then it was already too late for the Czechs to help themselves. The Munich Agreement had given the Sudetenland to Hitler, and when the Poles demanded Teschen, Teschen was granted. At a Rome meeting on 2 November, Ribbentrop and Ciano agreed on a new Hungarian-Czech frontier, and the Czechs accepted it without a word. The Russian and French alliances were abandoned. Domestically, a changed constitution gave the Carpatho-Ukranians and Slovaks autonomy.

When the Slovaks later demanded independence, it was granted. Czecho-Slovakia, it was said, was "breaking apart at the hyphen." How many Czechs matched their country's destruction by actually committing suicide is not known, but, as with the annexation of Austria, there seem to have been more suicides, certainly more suicidal thoughts, when the Germans came to Prague. "At home for breakfast," wrote Kennan in March 1939, "I had a refugee, a Jewish acquaintance who had worked many years for American interests. I told him that I could not give him asylum....For twenty-four hours he haunted the house, a pitiful figure of horror and despair, moving uneasily around the drawing room smoking one cigarette after another, too unstrung to eat or think of anything but his plight. His brother and sister-in-law had committed suicide together after Munich, and he had a strong inclination to follow suit."[18]

But suicides do not take place in a vacuum, and here the political conditions of the time make them understandable. Even so, suicides are not simply the result of despair, "weakness," or personnel self-loathing. Elaborate fantasies are connected with them—for example, the wish to punish and hurt loved ones. Research has shown that these fantasies can also serve a family function. The family often denies this.

In a brief but important paper based on clinical experience, M. Duncan Stanton has shown how these processes work. In "The Adduct as Savior: Heroin, Death, and the Family," he argues that the "high mortality rate among drug addicts" is "a suicidal phenomenon with a family basis. The death wish, or instruction for the addict to die, is often quite clearly expressed by the family." The addict's "death is seen as a noble, cleansing sacrifice in which he is often a willing participant."[19] Stanton offers several case studies to prove his conclusions.

As in Haley's findings for schizophrenics, the "sick" or addicted family member—the designated patient—"helps to keep the Family, particularly the parents, together through allowing them to unite over his incapacitation." More ominously: "We find that death issues are a part of the hidden agenda of these families. Often such issues take the specific form of a death wish towards the addict usually expressed most openly by the mother." Other family members collude in the process: the addict "becomes the receptacle of the family's pain, suffering, and perhaps 'baser' instincts." Like the ancient Greek *pharmakos*, he becomes a sacrificial scapegoat whose death "is viewed as a cleansing of other's sins." There is almost a religious fervor to the sacrifice, and the victim is a participant in the process. As Stanton says: "He is suicidal more in the sense that a martyr is suicidal."[20]

This seems to be the kind of process the European family had arranged for Czechoslovakia. In the dynamics described above, the death wish "is usually expressed by the mother," in this case mother Britain, with the suicidal partner, as Stanton says, an unconscious "willing participant." In Masaryk and Beneš, Czechoslovakia and the family of Europe had found the perfect leaders to carry out their sacrifice.

The personalities of Masaryk and Beneš made them especially suitable candidates for Europe's delegated suicidal commands. Psychological historians have shown how, for some individuals, it is not only on the public stage, but also in their chosen life work that people attempt a partial or even lifelong working through of intra-psychic conflicts.[21]

This was clearly the case with Masaryk whose life was obsessed with one central theme—suicide. His first published work was *Suicide and Civilization.* He regularly returned to the theme, in his essay on "Modern Suicidism" in *Modern Man and Religion*, and in his essays on Dostoevsky's views of suicide, and on the views of Tolstoy and Turgenev, in *The Spirit of Russia* in 1896. In what was a projection of his own depressive feelings, he claimed that: "My psychological and sociological analysis of suicides has taught me that the number of suicides is a direct mathematical measure of the real mood of a society, that society is deep down in the depths of its soul excited, perturbed, sick."[22]

Masaryk's scholarship was preoccupied not only with what makes an individual commit suicide, but with suicide as a group process. "The purpose of this work," he wrote in the Preface to *Suicide and Civilization*, "is to show how suicide as a general or 'mass' phenomenon has developed out of and as part of modern culture." He concluded that suicide is "an escape from the despair engendered by one's own guilt. Almost every suicide, as we see from the efficacy of its causes, has been prepared long in advance." Masaryk identified Silesia, Bohemia, and Moravia—all territories that would later become Czechoslovakia—along with Lower Austria, as having "the highest suicide frequency."He believed that "on the whole, it is higher in free states, and smaller in enslaved states." Basically, the "mass phenomenon of suicide manifests itself…as an historical process, as a collective guilt of society." He found that "revolution appears as an indirect mass suicide, as a sort of powerful purification." He concluded that: "*Suicides are the bloody sacrifices of the civilizing process.*"[23] It seems likely that the free Czechoslovakia he was about to create already existed in his unconscious fantasies as an example of such a sacrifice.

In his personal life as much as in his scholarship, Masaryk seems equally preoccupied with suicide, sacrifice, and martyrdom. He believed, he said, in "the life of Christ as the supreme experience of practical religion." One of his life-guiding principles was: "A life without sacrifices is no fine life." He admired the martyrs Jan Hus and Socrates, and seems to have attracted suicidal individuals. "In 1881 came the following incident," he told Karel Čapek. "I had a pupil in Vienna called Flesch, the son of a well-known Brno manufacturer. He followed me to Prague and continued to attend my lectures. He was a strange, melancholy youth. By and by he went away to Berlin, and there he shot himself. In his will, he left me his money."[24]

Masaryk's personal and professional preoccupation with these themes is further corroborated by two books published by distinguished writers in the 1930s, Emil Ludwig's *Defender of Democracy*, and Karel Čapek's *President Masaryk Tells His Story*. Both books contain extensive quotations based on long interviews. Masaryk speaks in both places of the "small" Czech state, which, like the "birth" of the United States earlier, was now a "newborn." He identified with Jesus, with the late-medieval religious martyr Jan Hus, and with people who commit suicide. He invoked in his interviews the name of Socrates, revealing that he had been charged with the same crime as the ancient Greek philosopher. ("In Vienna I was again denounced on a charge of corrupting the youth through my lectures," he said.) Although in his interviews he reported being beaten as a child, (and also hints at some possible sexual abuse), Masaryk focused on one traumatic event which left a deep negative impression on him. After a stable boy had hanged himself, he said: "Suicide became a great problem for me. Even as a boy I used to analyze...persons who were disgruntled with life. Later I discovered how it permeates so much of literature." This hints at a traumatic preoccupation, an effort at mastery that could not die. He told Čapek: "My book on suicide is an answer to that childish experience." He was also fascinated by the literature on Catholic Martyrs. Some people sensed that he wanted others to act out his own impulses: "The clerical and liberal parties accused me of advocating suicide," he said. Masaryk seems to have dimly understood how much his scholarship revealed about his unconscious fantasies when he told Čapek: "Anyone who understands how to read will find me between the lines of my books."[25]

This was the man to whom Eduard Beneš was attracted. Historians have judged that in the course of their collaboration, one became virtually indistinguishable from the other. "In reality the two saw eye to eye on almost every detail of policy," wrote historian R.W. Seton-Watson in the early 1940s. "Let there be no doubt about it...the policy of Czechoslovakia, right on till 1937, was a joint policy shared between them.... In a word, it is impossible to separate Beneš and Masaryk." As Masaryk earlier told Emil Ludwig, the "relationship between myself and Beneš had been and still is an ideal one, that of father and son." A.J.P. Taylor's view near the end of the Second World War went beyond a fantasy union of both men to a merger of the whole Czech people with Beneš: "The man made the country, and the country made the man, the history of one entwined with the life of the other. History records no other example of such a complete identification....Dr. Beneš...has been the embodiment of Czechoslovakia in Europe." These images of Beneš merging with Masaryk and with the Czech people are corroborated by Beneš's interview with Compton Mackenzie during World War II where his words sound exactly like Masaryk's forty years before, implicitly and explicitly confirming the missions of martyrdom he had been delegated to fulfill.[26]

A.J.P. Taylor meant that the connection between Beneš and his people was political, intellectual, and cultural, but intuitively captured a deeper psychological union, which joined the Czechs to Masaryk through Beneš. Robert Pynsent has studied Czech and Slovak ideas of personality and nationality, noting that "perhaps Masaryk's only contribution to assessing Czechness was his observation... that Czechs had a predisposition to martyrdom...what in intellectual discourse has come to be labeled the 'Czech martyr complex.'" Pynsent goes on to show that numbers of influential nineteenth and early twentieth century writers reflected the collective belief that Slavs felt there was "an exceptional claim to fame in the fact that they have been eradicated, suppressed, deslavicized everywhere," that, for Czechs in particular, in the words of "the popular *fin-de-siècle* novelist, Emil Tréval...'You Czechs are flagellants... born suicides.'"[27]

Beneš did not seem as preoccupied with suicide as was Masaryk, but he was fully capable of carrying out acts of martyrdom himself, perhaps even suicide through martyrdom. When he escaped from Austria in 1915 to join Masaryk in Switzerland, the first thought his mentor had was to wonder who was going to take his place in the secret revolutionary movement for independence back home. "He even wanted Beneš to go back to Prague again....Beneš pointed out that his return meant absolutely certain arrest, but added that he was quite ready to go....Masaryk, after sleeping on his idea, found it a bad one." Masaryk seems to have delegated Beneš to continue his suicidal work after his death, telling Emil Ludwig that in the politics of the 1930s, Beneš "must drink the hemlock for me."[28]

Beneš's fascination with, and even identification with, the role of the suicide-martyr in history matched Masaryk's own, and, like Masaryk's, began early in life. Edward Hitchcock's biography, based on interviews with Beneš, mentions how "when he was between eight and nine years old, Eduard wrote a poem. It was an ode to Jan Hus, the great Czech preacher who led the Protestant Reformation {sic} in that part of the world. However, it was not because of his religious activities that this Catholic boy eulogized him, but because he was burned at the stake by the Germans."[29] In Masaryk, in Beneš, and apparently in all of Czechoslovakia, Europe had found willing martyrs who could be called upon to sacrifice themselves when it was unconsciously agreed that such a sacrifice was "needed."

Europe and the Czechs did not have to go down this path, however. Gerhard Weinberg has argued that if the Czechs had taken the initiative by making concessions in May 1938 they would have exposed Hitler's plans. Instead, by letting policy be determined by the demands of the Sudeten German Party, the Czechs were "unintentionally falling in with the strategy Hitler had prescribed." Pierre Renouvin believed that the Czechs would have resisted given the support of France and Britain. Indeed, several alternatives to the destruction of Czechoslavia had been advocated at the time, in Britain and throughout Europe, including the implementation of existing alliances, creating new ones, and bringing the Soviet Union into the mix. The stress of the crisis understandably produced a fantasy reaction, rumors that the Germans possessed a Death Ray, that the Wehrmach had a secret weapon which could "immobilize any combustion engine," and that Hitler was dying of throat cancer. But despite these regressive retreats into magical thinking, the evidence is clear: in the face of the Nazi threat, all of Czech society was ready to fight—until it became understandably demoralized by the Allied betrayal.[30] Ultimately, as with other realistic assessments of how to stop Hitler, the Allies concluded that no alternatives were feasible. Telford Taylor has calculated that the combined forces of the Allies with Czechoslovakia would have outnumbered the Germans in 1938 and would have offered a good chance for victory, concluding: "they would have been better off had they fought in support of Czechoslovakia in 1938 instead of throwing her to the wolves."[31] In retrospect, and for some who said so at the time, abandoning the Czechs was a suicidal gesture, and not just for the Czechs.

Clearly, alternatives had to be rejected or denied. If sacrifice was to happen illusions had to be maintained, Chamberlain already having told his sister in late March 1938 that "Czechoslovakia cannot be defended," a theme he repeated several times later, including a meeting with Daladier in late April where he said "he himself could not see any possibility of saving Czechoslovakia, of avoiding the destruction of that county, or of its being overrun by the aggressor." At a meeting with the French on 18 September he mercilessly pressed Daladier to accede to Germany's demands. Eventually, a plan was concocted to give Hitler all the Czech lands with a German population of over 50 percent. "Most of us disliked the idea," wrote Secretary of War Hore-Belisha in his diary, but "in the end there didn't seem to be any alternative."[32]

Even though they had deluded themselves, the Allies knew on some level that things were not inevitable, and that they had kept the Czechs from uttering a single word during the negotiations. Consequently, they felt guilty. The American Ambassador to Britain reported that Chamberlain believed people would probably charge him with the rape of Czechoslovakia, while Kirkpatrick attributed Daladier's irritability to "a guilty conscience."[33] But Allied guilt was not going to be felt for very long, at least not in the short run. The British, of course, tried repressing it, and succeeded in part, but what they had done to the Czechs produced feelings so powerful that some additional intra-psychic defenses needed to be called into play. Guilt was dealt with in the same way that the unconscious accomplices in a pathological family manage the unconscious guilt they feel for the family suicide they helped arrange—by blaming the victim. Historian Paul E. Zinner's early post-war study concluded: "the testimony of available documents is clear on one point. Neither France nor Britain treated Czechoslovakia as if moral right were on her side." Elizabeth Wiskeman reported that Bobby Stopford, financial expert of the Runciman Mission and an old friend, had come to her for advice on behalf of the Mission. "He expressed the prevalent feeling of veiled guilt towards the Germans and distaste for the Czechs," she said. Harvey recorded on 19 September 1938 how "Runciman…has nothing good to say of the Czechs and adds his influential voice to the chorus of blame and abuse which is now their lot." These defensive strategies worked, at least for the victimizers. Chamberlain, for one, was not at all distressed by what he had helped bring about. When the Munich accord was finally read to the Czech representatives, who were only then learning of its provisions, "Mr. Chamberlain yawned without ceasing and with no show of embarrassment," said Masaryk's report.[34]

The compulsion to "kill off" Czechoslovakia through its "own" suicide created as a "family sacrifice" had been so great as to outweigh all rational considerations of military and strategic importance. The British had achieved their wished for humiliation, and had frustrated Hitler's desire for war only to press him on with greater urgency. Allied responsibility was denied, Allied guilt absolved by blaming the Czechs.

Two days after Munich, "Atticus," imagining that the old forms of power politics had been now suddenly changed for the better, wrote in the London *Sunday Times* how he was "going home to take all my books on Europe, place them in a garden trench and have it filled in."[35] It was clear that some people felt the benign atmosphere of a new diplomatic order meant the old books were suddenly obsolete. His intention was to fill his readers with the joy of peace. Instead, he was inviting Europe to a symbolic funeral. Buried in the trench along with his books were the "babe" Czechoslovakia and the peace of the continent. Poland was next.

X POLAND AND THE SOVIET UNION

WE DISLIKE THE POLES. THEY ARE AN AWFUL NUISANCE.
—*Sir Horace Wilson*, 1939

STALIN IS STEALTHILY AND CUNNINGLY PULLING THE STRINGS BEHIND THE SCENES TO GET US INVOLVED IN WAR WITH GERMANY.[1]
—*Neville Chamberlain*, 1938

In the late 1920s Churchill had written: "the intention of those who framed the Treaty of Versailles had been to create in Poland a living, healthy, vigorous organism." Poland, said Louis Fischer in the 1930s, was "born of the 1919 peace." "A child of Allied victory," it had been "hatched in the incubator of Versailles."[2] The Soviet Foreign Minister Molotov called it "the ugly offspring of the Versailles Treaty."[3]

Organic and family images like these helped leaders, people, and statesman forget that Poland, like Czechoslovakia, was not a newborn, but a country with a history centuries old and helped the European family prepare Poland as the next sacrifice. Like the Czechs, the Poles were willing if unconscious accomplices in their own suicide.

There are some indications that this strain of self-sacrifice runs deep into the Polish past. When nineteenth-century patriot Adam Mickiewicz published his *Pilgrimage of the Polish Nation* in 1832, it was to prove that Poland's "resurrection" would bring with it a millenarian order of world joy. The book's Preface by the Count of Montalembert identified Poland as "the Christ of nations," a "{sacrificial} victim chosen from Above to wash off with its blood the sins of modern society, and to buy that liberty for which the world thirsts."[4] Did this notion intertwine with and reinforce the phrase "self-sacrificing generations" in the Polish Constitution of 1921, and influence Polish diplomacy in the interwar years? Does the perpetual idea in Polish history of an eventual sacrifice suggest the possibility that a sacrifice was implicit in the very creation of the modern Polish state? If so, was it an expression of an unconscious wish to re-enact the traumas of the late eighteenth-century Partitions of Poland, which themselves had never been far from Polish consciousness? These ideas may be too speculative an explanation and need further study, but the issue is not only the long-term causes and outcomes of Polish diplomacy, but actual practices in the 1930s.

Polish policy had been engineered equally by Marshal Pilsudski, whose abilities, after developing cancer, do not seem to have been compromised, and by Foreign Minister Colonel Josef Beck, an alcoholic whose judgment was at least partially impaired, which would have become especially important after Pilsudki's death in 1935. What confronted Pilsudski, Beck, and the Poles, historians agree, was a particularly difficult geopolitical reality: Poland lay between two great powers, Germany and the Soviet Union. Supporting one, it seemed, would naturally mean alienating the other. Poland was, in the terminology of the time, "sitting between two stools."[5] Despite several treaties, it remained isolated and vulnerable.

Given these conditions, what, after all, could the Poles do? Little, some historians have said, and by saying this have reinforced the notion of Poland's inevitable "victim position." This sense of things comes from assertions such as: "the Poles could exercise only a marginal control over their destiny."[6] In reality, there were several alternatives. One alternative, summarized by historian Bohdan Budurowycz, deserves to be quoted at length. Immediately after the First World War:

> With Germany defeated and disarmed, and with Russia only slowly emerging from the revolutionary chaos, the nations of East Central Europe had a unique opportunity to create and consolidate a bloc of middle and small powers able to resist the encroachments of both Berlin and Moscow and thus to restore

> the system of equilibrium in that part of Europe which became unbalanced as a result of the dissolution of the Austro-Hungarian Empire. By uniting their forces and establishing a community of interest, they could play a role in international affairs that went far beyond their individual possibilities and afforded invaluable advantages for each and all partners. Unfortunately, Poland and her neighbors failed to grasp this great historical chance and let it pass—perhaps forever.[7]

These notions corresponded somewhat to Beck's idea of making Poland the center of a Third Europe, "a bloc of independent, non-aligned States stretching from the Baltic to the Mediterranean, a counter weight to the German and Soviet Colssi."[8]

The bloc never materialized, in part because Poland's obsession with its two giant neighbors prevented it. Alternatives were ignored since only one course seemed inevitable. Pilsudski admitted to having "had ideas for five Polands—but they could be fulfilled to measure only one." One recent historian says: "The 'Doctrine of the Two Enemies' was engraved in Polish strategy." It led to paralysis. Pilsudski's advice to "stay idle and wait to see what all the others {were} going to do"[9] was Beck's idea too, and in a dynamic situation, Poland remained essentially reactive.

Thus, the idea of a Third Europe was not so much a road not taken as much as it was a road never seriously considered. Given the selfish nationalistic aspirations of the several non-aligned states, and the continuing force of *Realpolitik* in international life, such an undertaking could not have been easy. But in the end, the inability to seek out more alliances in order to create that Third Europe proved to be self-defeating because "Polish pursuit of an independent line led not to greater power, but to isolation." One recent scholar has shown that the Poles' main fear was that any security system would lead to Poland becoming a battleground. Since it can also be argued that the lack of a security system made that prospect more, not less, likely, and since Poland did become a battleground, it is possible, even if unlikely, that the expression of the fear was somehow an expression of an unconscious wish. This possibility was recognized as early as the mid-1950s by historian Henry L. Roberts who argued that Beck's "prophecies tended to be self-fulfilling ones which his own activities and outlook helped bring about." [10]

What caused Poland to act in these ways, to avoid alliances and become—as another small state born in the "incubator" of Versailles—a "willing victim" in another family sacrifice is difficult to tell with any certainty. There is little evidence beyond some vague hints of hidden fantasies found in statements uttered by some of Poland's leaders at the time. The well-known words of Marshal Smigly-Rydz for example, "With the Germans we risk losing our freedom, with the Russians we lose our soul,"[11] seem to contain hints of a deep regression under stress to an infantile victim position. Was it that Nazi Germany and the Soviet Union, "the German and Soviet Colossi," were seen through the prism of regressed childhood terror, with both states being experienced—and fantasized—as two giant, raging "parents," each ready to tear small, helpless Poland apart? There was, of course, a historical referent for that fear, the aforementioned three partitions of Poland, a trauma that in the 1930s still preoccupied Beck. As he said: "History teaches us: 1) that the greatest catastrophe of our nation has been the result of concerted action by these two powers and 2) that in this desperate situation there was not to be found any Power in the world to bring us assistance." [12]

Beck's prophetic words echo not only from Poland's tragic past, but also, perhaps, from fears of the child, and hint at a felt need to repeat the trauma while serving as a prediction, or wish, for what was about to happen. When the secret parts of the Nazi-Soviet Pact actually came into effect in late-September 1939, Poland was duly divided again, this time between Nazi Germany and the Soviet Union. Beck's fears and independent policies, along with Europe's overt and covert assistance, had helped create the very thing the Poles most feared. Many, not just Beck, had predicted it. Again and again, as in other countries, leaders and observers expressed a clear understanding of how events would unfold.

Marshal Pilsudski, for example, had predicted that both Austria and Czechoslovakia would disappear; the "only important point was to know which would disappear first," he said. Beck called the course of the Czech Crisis correctly when he "assumed that the Czechs would not fight, that the Western Democracies were unprepared, and that Soviet Russia would offer only symbolic protest." Before the *Anschluss*, General Sosnowski predicted that after Hitler took Austria it would be Czechoslovakia, after Czechoslovakia, Poland. "The fate of Poland depends upon the fate of Czechoslovakia," wrote Swencicki during the Czech Crisis: "The defeat of Czechoslovakia would mean the defeat of Poland....Czechoslovakia today—Poland tomorrow." Writing in the *Kurien Warszawski* after Munich, Stanistaw Stronski said that he saw only two possibilities for Poland: Britain and France would serve either as its "specialists in amputation," or as its "undertakers." As it turned out, they did both. Immediately after Munich, Soviet Vice Commissar for Foreign Affairs, Vladimir Potemkin, confirmed the Poles' own worst fears when he told French ambassador Robert Coulondre: "My poor friend, what have you done? For us I see no other outcome but a fourth partition of Poland."[13]

It had been the Poles' actions in specific instances, not just in general attitudes, which had helped bring this about. They were not able to help the Czechs against Hitler because of their short sighted wish to grab a slice of Czech territory, a very popular policy sanctioned by the Polish people as a whole, which, one historian judges, was supported by the Polish press "to an extent...unknown since the pre-1934 era." During the crisis, Hitler had fed Europe's regressed oral incorporation fantasies, saying that "those who wished to share in the meal would have to help with the cooking." An outside observer, William Shirer, found it hard to make sense of "the blind stupidity of the Poles in the crisis, helping to carve up Czechoslovakia."[14] Since many had correctly predicted the course of events, it can be argued that the popularity of the policy in Poland was not only short sighted, and not just blind nationalism, but was unconsciously desired, fulfilling the wish of many Poles to move Poland down a dangerous road toward the possibility of its own destruction.

What helped the Poles act out the hidden impulses caused by the traumas of Polish history were cues sent by the members of the European family, which, as they had done with Czechoslovakia, encouraged Poland's self-destructive behavior.

The central role of Mother Britain was symbolically expressed before the 1930s by the widespread but untrue belief in Poland that the British Foreign Office had been responsible for Marshal Pilsudski's May 1926 coup d'état. For its part, the West generally saw Poland as a greedy revisionist power, anti-Semitic, pro-German, and anti-liberal. Foreign Minister Beck was seen as "treacherous" and a "menace." Cadogan called him a "brute." On 26 September 1938, Daladier told the American ambassador that he hoped to "pay Poland back" for Poland's role in the Czech Crisis land-grab by proposing a new partition of the country. Sir Horace Wilson summed up the sentiments of many Britons by saying that the Poles were "an awful nuisance," Lord Dawson of Penn hoping "Poland would...wither away and suffocate." Fantasy wishes were alive in France as well where Daladier said: "The Poles must sacrifice Danzig." Everywhere in Europe Poland had become the new container for Europe's projections, and it wasn't just propaganda when the Nazi press office said in late-March 1939 that, "Poland carries within her the seeds of death."[15]

More than just sending cues, the powers acted in ways

that worked to assure Poland's sacrificial destruction. After Munich, Britain and France both let Hitler know that they expected Poland to be next. Ambassador Kennedy reported to Washington in October 1938 that Halifax was inclined "to let Hitler go ahead and do what he likes in Central South Eastern Europe," adding, "there is no question in Halifax's mind that reasonably soon Hitler will make a start for Danzig, with Polish concurrence...it is Halifax's idea that England should mind her own business."[16] In France, Flandin called for the French to abandon Poland. From Warsaw, French ambassador Noel advised Paris in October that it should terminate agreements with Poland. Out of Brussels came rumors that France was considering ending its Polish alliance. In late-November, *Le Temps*—regarded as the semi-official mouthpiece of the Quai d' Orsay—published an article, which stated that the Western powers should be less interested in conflicts in Eastern Europe.[17] Hitler's inclination to turn eastward was being encouraged. On 3 March 1939, Chamberlain told the House of Commons that Britain had never guaranteed the frontiers of Czechoslovakia. Hitler marched on Prague on 15 March. That event led directly to Britain's unilateral guarantee of Poland's borders on 31 March.

Immediately upon the occupation of Prague, the British press was filled with speculations about a German advance on Poland. In the next two weeks, speculation became "fact," as the British projected their own aggression into Hitler, whose own desperate emotional needs to move against the Poles and have the war that until now had eluded him, just happened to make the British guess correctly. By "29 and 30 March the press was full of rumors about an imminent German attack on Danzig....There is no doubt that the press was in a belligerent mood. It is probable that Halifax was receptive to it, even though he often proclaimed his immunity from public opinion." As shown in Chapter IV, the British guarantee to Poland was greeted with widespread popular support, and when on 1 April the London *Times* said, "the new obligation which this country yesterday assumed does not bind Great Britain to defend every inch of the present frontiers of Poland," there were howls of outrage in Parliament. But even as Hugh Dalton wondered if "another Slav victim {was} to be sacrificed on the altar,"[18] his alarm was sounding the unconscious wish of Mother Britain: it was precisely what the European family had ordered up.

This time, "in strange contrast to earlier crises," wrote A.J.P. Taylor, "there were no negotiations over Danzig." There were hardly any Anglo-German diplomatic exchanges. From the end of March to the middle of August, the British ambassador "never saw Ribbentrop, let alone Hitler."[19] If Poland were to be protected, the Franco-Polish alliance of 1921 would have to be updated and reconfirmed. But in May, Bonnet kept postponing his signing of a new Franco-Polish protocol. American Ambassador Bullet cabled home: "As soon as he had ascertained that the British had not yet entered into serious negotiations for a political accord... Bonnet flatly refused to sign the agreement."[20] The French were again using Britain as a scapegoat so they could escape their own responsibility and continue to feel like the abandoned child. Meanwhile, the British governess continued to control events.

The Poles had asked for a loan of 60 million pounds. By early July, the Polish Finance Mission left Britain "in a state bordering on despair at attitude of H.M.G. and Treasury toward financial assistance," Harvey recorded in his diary. "They were told we did not regard it as of great urgency, and we wished to attach all sorts of conditions."[21] The British were treating Poland as they had treated the Czecho-Slovak state after Munich, and were not about to waste money on a country on the verge of disappearing.

The Poles were being set up. At first assured of Franco-British support, when it came down to honoring the pledges, the French and British reneged. "In May the French promised to begin an offensive against Germany on the fifteenth day after a German attack on Poland 'with the bulk of her forces.' Both Britain and France promised to begin bombing attacks on Germany immediately war broke out to weaken German morale."[22] On 22 August, to universal applause, the British Cabinet determined to stand by its obligation to Poland, and when news of the Nazi-Soviet pact arrived in Paris, General Gamelin said the French army was "ready." But the French did nothing except ask the Poles to postpone mobilization for several hours. Britain's last act before war came was to pass on Hitler's demands to Warsaw at 12:25 on 31 August; it came twenty-five minutes after the German ultimatum had expired. The Polish ambassador to Paris reported that Daladier had told him on 6 September that, "the French air force had expressed its readiness to go into action against Germany but was unable to realize their desire because of the refusal of the British."[23] Daladier was again blaming the British, who still ran the show. But it was the Poles who suffered. As it turned out, Britain's sole "military action" to assist Poland was to send the RAF to drop leaflets over Germany calling for Germany's surrender.

The British had made a show of support; privately they had written Poland off. Even before the guarantee, Halifax admitted "there was probably no way in which France and ourselves could prevent Poland from being overrun."[24] The promise to bomb Germany was later ruled out by an agreement between Britain and France to avoid provoking aerial counterattacks on their own populations.[25] Sir John Slessor wrote in his memoirs that from the time of the March guarantee on, the British and French general staffs were in agreement that "there was nothing either of us could do to save Poland."[26] Chamberlain's actions echoed half-brother Austen's words, themselves paraphrasing Bismarck, who said that Poland would never be worth the bones of a single British

Grenadier. In any case, Chamberlain told Ambassador Kennedy that Great Britain could do nothing to save the Poles.

Anyone who was listening could hear what was about to happen. By late August, the British were quite open about their intentions. The "overwhelming unanimity of opinion" was summed up by William Dims in the journal *Nineteenth Century*—and it had nothing to do with Poland: "If war should breakout" he wrote, "we should be fighting...for no other purpose than to repel danger to ourselves...our lives, our security, our property, our national existence." Almost the whole of the British press, from the *Glasgow Herald* to the *Economist*, struck the same tone: "If war comes, it will not be fought for Danzig or Poland."[27] Once more the Poles were to be betrayed, as they would be again during the war, and have been, tragically, so often throughout their history. Britain's unconscious, sometimes semi-conscious goal seems clear enough: war with Germany, with a sacrificial Poland as the excuse. In Stalin, the brutal dictator of the Soviet Union, Britain, Europe, and Hitler found someone ready and waiting to help them complete their goals.

The Soviet Union entered the 1930s a pariah among the powers. It was still excluded from the League of Nations, but, of course, was not excluded from the European fantasy system.[28]

The language, metaphors, and images of the Soviet sources parallel those used throughout the west. Taking cues from Hitler's use of the phrase "the British governess," the Soviet press admonished Poland not to listen to the instructions of its Berlin "governess," proving once again that the governess metaphor and fantasy was widespread and malleable, and that countries and leaders could play several contradictory but related roles at once. Throughout the period, the language of the Soviet press and members of the Central Committee of the Communist Party expressed the realities of Nazi aggressiveness by using the terms "lawlessness" and

"Nazi gangsters" that were being used in the west, and, as in the west, used regressive images of devouring monsters and expressed fears of oral incorporation. Stalin's words to the Eighteenth Congress of the Communist Party in March 1939 invoked images of monsters and feelings of loathing and craziness when he said the powers were trying to "poison the atmosphere," and spoke of "madmen" who thought of "annexing the elephant...to the gnat."[29]

For its part, the Soviet Union played an active and complicated role in the fantasy life of the west. At once idealized as the center of the great socialist experiment, it was also condemned and feared as the exporter of revolution. It was perceived as the only consistent foe of fascism, but was also used as a container for the West's projections, as in the "infected," "poisoned," "plague-bearing" Russia of Churchill's rhetoric. As pariah it remained an easy target. In March 1939 Chamberlain could state, perhaps projectively: "I must confess to the most profound distrust of Russia. I distrust her motives." In his conscious mind it was not Britain, but—in words echoing his being bullied as a boy—distant Russia, which seemed intent "only with getting everyone else by the ears."[30]

Chamberlain, of course, meant the Soviet Union, and while he was employing the common usage of "Russia" in place of the Soviet Union, he also meant Stalin, by any reckoning one of the most brutal dictators of the twentieth century. In Stalin's totalitarian state, and in the absence of any clear-cut understanding of Soviet public opinion, it has been understood by historians that foreign policy was Stalin's policy, which means that all the psychological historian can do at present is try to assess Stalin's personality and the role it played in the formation of that policy with only a few brief excursions into the ways Stalin seems to have served as the Soviet people's delegate.

In the first instance there is the issue of how Stalin and the Soviet Union fit into Europe's family fantasy scenario.

Robert C. Tucker's psychologically oriented study *Stalin in Power* (called by George F. Kennan "the most significant single scholarly contribution made to the history of Soviet Power") argues that: "Many have seen Stalin as a power seeker. That view is not so much wrong as incomplete" because the "political motive alone does not provide a sufficient explanation." Stalin "needed a cult as a prop for his psyche."[31] The same psychic need is seen, or implied, in the totalitarianisms of Mussolini and Hitler, political systems with the cult of the leader also at their core, which helped everyone hide, deny, channel and finally act out the terrified, raging child in themselves. In this respect, Stalin's tyrannical system wasn't any different.

As with other leaders, his childhood helps provide some clues to his personality, while his adult behavior offers additional symbolic clues as to the nature of that childhood. His chosen revolutionary name ("Steel") sounds compensatory, a hard cover for deeper feelings of weakness and insecurity. His ability to ruthlessly initiate actions resulting in the deaths of millions, and the impulse to lawlessness which he put at the service of the revolution, show, like Hitler, a sociopathic brutality based on repressed rage, which, from the documented evidence, probably originated in his childhood.

Tucker finds a "wretched childhood, particularly the beatings inflicted on him and his mother in his presence by {his father} Vissarion."[32] Many biographers have recognized these beatings as important. Adam Ulam writes that Stalin's daughter "Svetlana Alliluyeva passes on the family tradition (i.e., what she heard from her mother's sister) that young Soso {Stalin} was frequently beaten and that he had to witness many a scene between his parents." Robert Payne says: "The boy's father was a drunkard...who possessed a violent temper, with no feeling for his wife or his son; he beat them unmercifully....Sometimes poverty drove Ekaterina close to madness, and we hear of her wandering through the streets with her hair disheveled, crying, praying, singing and muttering to herself....According to Iremashvili, who knew the family well...the father beat the son vengefully, remorselessly, with a kind of brooding, deliberate passion without pleasure and without any sense of guilt or wrong doing....'I never saw him crying,' Iremashvuli relates... 'His face and body were covered with bruises, but he was determined not to surrender.'" Historian Edvard Radzinsky quotes the testimony of N. Kishidze: "One day when his father was drunk he picked him up and threw him violently to the floor. There was blood in the boy's urine for days afterwards."[33]

In his earlier psychologically oriented study, *Stalin as Revolutionary*, Tucker notes that things were so violent at home that the boy sometimes "found refuge with neighbors, who hid him," a tip off that even among the brutal childhoods experienced by those around him, Stalin's beatings were above the community's social norm. And it was not only his father who administered beatings: "According to Svetlana," says Tucker, "Stalin...recalled that {his mother} used to 'thrash' (*kolotila*) him when he was small." Tucker perceptively concludes: "the horror that the beating of his mother inspired in him may help explain why in later life he thought of beating—symbolic or real—as a form of punishment merited by the worst of offenders."[34] Although Tucker doesn't say it, this helps explain the rhetoric Stalin sometimes used for historical and economic processes, a rhetoric not solely based on its obvious metaphorical meaning: "To slacken the pace," Stalin once said, "would mean to lag behind; and those who lag behind are beaten. We do not want to be beaten. No, we don't want to. The history of old...Russia {was that}...she was ceaselessly beaten for her backwardness. She was beaten by the Mongol Khans, she was beaten by Turkish Beys, she was beaten by Swedish feudal lords, she was beaten by Polish-Lithuanian Pans, she was beaten by Anglo-French capitalists, she was beaten by Japanese barons, she was beaten by all—for her backwardness. For military backwardness, for industrial backwardness, for agricultural backwardness. She was beaten because to beat her was profitable and went unpunished." This confirms the thought advanced by one of Stalin's recent biographers that the beatings he experienced in childhood meant "the verb to beat lodged forever in his subconscious."[35]

Stalin's childhood was not much different from that of other Georgians, and, by extension, other ethnic groups in the region. The very limited available evidence suggests that his experiences were repeated in millions of Russian homes. Historian David Ransel has shown that abandonment was widely practiced in the nineteenth century. Domestic violence seems to have been the norm well into the twentieth century, along with abandonment to wet nurses. Swaddling, while on the wane, was still practiced in some parts of the Soviet Union as late as the 1980s. And swaddling alone suggests that millions of Russian children had been continuously used as containers for massive parental projections. The adult feelings behind these practices are captured in the title of Patrick Dunn's groundbreaking article on Russian child rearing: "That Baby is the Enemy."[36]

As with the history of childhood in other areas of Europe, more research is needed before convincing generalizations can be made. But if nineteenth-century Russian child rearing was as terrible as now seems probable, it may help answer some elusive questions, including, for example, why the innocent victims of Stalin's purges exhibited such astonishing co-operation with their persecutors.

Adam Ulam identifies the mysterious nature of this behavior: "We may find in Stalin's personality some clue as to why he dealt with his closest friends and associates in the way he did, but not why he was served unquestioningly by men whose brothers had been tortured and executed, whose wives had been exiled, whose sons were imprisoned, all at his orders, and why none of them felt he could express his anguish by raising his hand or his voice against the dictator. No incident in Stalin's childhood, no personality trait of his can explain such behavior on the part of Orjonikidze, Molotov, or Mikoyan."[37] Ulam's obsevations, while telling, slightly miss the mark: the behavior *can* be explained in the sense that Stalin's experiences matched the childhood experiences of others. The family dynamics and child abuse characteristic of millions of Russian homes drove them to play a group-fantasy role as Stalin's "willing" sacrificial victims, and indirectly corroborate that child abuse.

Stalin's purges in the mid-to late-1930s are well known, and historians have offered many reasons to account for them. With few exceptions, scholars have been reluctant to include a diagnosis of Stalin's paranoia among them. But it seems likely that psychological factors, including Stalin's paranoid-like thinking, played some role.

While the sources show that Stalin is certainly the central figure in the purges, a recent study based on extensive research in newly opened Soviet archives has found that "at every step of the way, there were constituencies both within and outside the elite that supported repression of various groups, sometimes with greater vehemence than Stalin did. The terror was a series of group efforts...rather than one man intimidating everyone else." Indeed, there was "no grand plan for terror," nor did it follow a straight line, going instead in "zigzags and circles." The study, *Road to Terror*, sub-titled the *Self-Destruction of the Bolsheviks*, contains a section provocatively called "The Party Commits Suicide" explaining how class, attitudes, beliefs, and bureaucracy worked toward these ends, but offering no psychological perspective. Understanding that a "self-destructive" "suicide" was underway connects, however, to a well-known and remarkable feature of the purges: the need to produce confessions from the innocent. Tucker accounts for this on Stalin's side when he notes that, "his urge to unmask, his overpowering need for confessions, was at bottom a need for reassurance, *for proof* that he was right."[38] Did his need for proof flow from his certain knowledge that nearly all of his purge victims were innocent? (An example of the principle: "I am right, *they* said so.") Yet, Ulam is correct as well: a remarkable feature on the victim's side was the willingness of the innocents to admit their guilt. Some of this behavior was doubtless a simple capitulation to force, the wish to end the intense pain of intolerable torture. But another part is psychological, and lies in the tangled web of childhood experience and adult fantasy.

Repressed murderous rage toward their fathers, felt by millions of Soviet citizens who had been brutalized as children, was displaced onto father figure Stalin. Wishing him dead made them feel guilty. Playing the fantasy-father seems for Stalin to have been a comfortable role, reinforced, as it was in other regimes, by the Soviet propaganda machine. "Photos of him appeared daily in the Soviet Press now surrounded by young pioneers, now in a country setting with an arm around his ten-year-old daughter Svetlana. He was shown holding little girls who were invited to the reviewing stand atop the Mausoleum during events in Red Square." Henri Barbusse's book, *Stalin: A New World Seen Through One Man* (1935), called him "the Lenin of today," and when Barbusse went on to call Lenin "our father and mentor" his word signified ("by the canons of the dual cult," notes Tucker) that "Stalin was the father and mentor of today."[39] He was widely "known as the children's best friend." Many, besides Ehrenburg, must have thought him "a kind of Old Testament god." One hears echoes of the fantasy that the Soviet people were his children when Fadeyev declared: "We are children of the Stalin era." Stalin's own murderous rage at his own brutalized childhood seems to have made him into an exemplar of the hate-filled father many Soviet citizens had experienced in their own childhoods. He expressed a murderous rage against symbols of innocence, displaced, and symbolically enacted again and again, in one of his favorite pastimes, the "occasional diversion of shooting at hares illuminated by automobile headlights." He beat and kicked his son Vaska, habitually called his other son Iakov "my fool," and passed a decree in 1935 that all Soviet children above the age of twelve could be arrested and punished as if they were adults—including the death penalty. Like other victims of brutal parenting, the Soviet people had to repress, deny, and idealize: he was their "good father," they were his "bad children." The fantasy of the Good Father had to be desperately retained; at the height of the Terror Pasternak's denial spoke for millions when he said of Stalin: "If *he* only knew." The psychological study of Daniel Rancour-Laferriere, *The Slave Soul of Russia*, sheds more light on some of these issues, arguing for the central role of moral masochism.[40] In addition, the Soviet people's thralldom recalled their thralldom as children to their tyrannical fathers, whom they both feared and hated, and whose selves, as in the authoritarian German family, had been stolen.

Those caught in Stalin's net during the purges thus punished themselves for complex reasons buried in their own unconscious, making themselves into new, symbolic "child sacrifices" at Stalin's command. Looked at this way, the Purge resembles a "self-inflicted wound," a "wished for," unconsciously arranged event dependent not just on Stalin, but also on the unconscious complicity of the victims, in what, it is helpful to remember, *The Road to Terror* calls the Bolshevik's "self-destruction" and "suicide."

On the level of the international family system, these purges weakened the Soviet state and armed forces, making it difficult if not impossible for Stalin to join the West against Hitler's aggression. A few scholars have suggested that this was one of the intentions of the purges. Within the framework of common-sense thinking it seems unlikely that such a goal could ever have been Stalin's conscious intent, but there is a kind of tortured logic to the argument, which, in any event, fits neatly into the pathological process of the family of nations and certainly could have been unconsciously motivated.

As Tucker puts it with subtle psychological clarity, the purge trials were a "vehicle of exculpation in advance for his contemplated coming accord with Hitler." Stalin was punishing himself and the Soviet Union for the coming arrangement with their most hated ideological rival. Paradoxically, smearing the accused Soviet Party leaders as Nazi collaborators and as pro-fascist "was preparation for Stalin's collaboration with them." It sent the message that Communism was not "antifascist in principle." Mussolini, for one, saw a direct connection when he wrote in the fascist paper *Popolo d' Italia* on 5 March 1938, "Stalin is doing a notable service to fascism by mowing down in large armfuls his enemies who have been reduced to impotence." Only "in the context of a contemplated agreement with Hitler's Germany," writes Tucker, "is Stalin's slaughter of the Russia-based leadership and militants of German Communism politically intelligible." In Stalin's typically paranoid way, he blamed others for what he was doing; "even while prisoners in the dock were confessing under duress to mythical efforts by Trotsky and other conspirators to reach an accord with the Nazis, Stalin was methodically engaged behind the scenes in actual efforts toward that end."[41] As is often the case in history, the accuser's accusation is a tip off for what the accusers themselves are actually doing.

In reality, the Nazi-Soviet "courtship" was not as consistent as these insights suggest, but waxed and waned according to the shifting ambiguities of the 1930s. Still there is something to the notion, for despite the real hatred each found in the other and despite the anti-communist and anti-Nazi rhetoric of leaders on both sides, the possibility of a Nazi-Soviet collaboration was expressed by many people, even from the time the Nazis had first come to power. In some ways these thoughts continued an association that went back to the secret German-Soviet military ties of the 1920s. For many months after Hitler became Chancellor, for example, the Soviet Union continued to make "desperate attempts to maintain the connection with Germany which had been the center of her strategy since 1922." Some Germans were responsive. As Bulow wrote in late 1933: "good German-Soviet relations are of essential importance to Germany." Hitler was not the only German at the time preoccupied with countries protecting their "rears." In early April 1933, German Foreign Minister Neurath asserted: "We cannot do without Russia's cover for our rear."[42]

Even when German forces occupied the Rhineland in March 1936, Stalin let it be known that while there existed "a tendency among certain sections of his Soviet public towards an attitude of thoroughgoing irreconcilability to the present rulers of Germany, the chief tendency, and the one determining the Soviet Government's policy, {is that he} thinks an improvement in Soviet-German relations possible." On 29 January 1937, Stalin, through a public statement by Kandelaki, announced that he was prepared for negotiations with the Reich.[43]

But it was Stalin's 10 March 1939 speech to the Eighteenth Communist Party Congress that fully signaled, to those who could hear between the lines, that he was ready to negotiate in earnest. Only five days later, Hitler occupied Prague. Ribbentrop and Molotov believed that Stalin's 10 March speech "brought about {a} reversal in political relations" between the two countries. Stalin had given "no major public addresses for two years" after March 1937, and "spoke for publication only twice more in 1937 and only once in all of 1938," so it was clear that his 10 March speech was meant to be understood by everyone as important. Stalin claimed that a new imperialist war was already two years old, with the Allies making various attempts to provoke a conflict between Germany and the Soviet Union. He said their strategy would not work. The Soviets would continue to do business with anyone so long as their business partners acted appropriately. In a famous phrase, Stalin stated that he would "not allow our country to be drawn into conflicts by warmongers who are used to having others pull chestnuts out of the fire for them," a phrase the psychoanalytically inclined might find deeply significant. Three days later the *Manchester Guardian* used the same image, but applied it to Germany—"She has several chestnuts on the fire." On 29 June 1939 the image was still in the mind of the Italian ambassador in Berlin, who reminded Rome, "Stalin had no intention of pulling others' chestnuts from the fire." The phrase went back at least to the late 1920s, Masaryk telling the German Foreign Minister in March 1927 that in a conflict between Poland and Germany he did not want to "pull Poland's chestnuts out of the fire." Chamberlain had used the image in a private letter of 16 January 1938, a year before Stalin's speech, in which he said he did not "want or expect America to pull our chestnuts out of the fire." Mussolini had used the phrase two months later; so had Hitler, earlier in *Mein Kampf* and again in his 1 April 1939 Wilhelmshaven speech.[44] The image, which was circulating and had been circulating for some time, shows that everyone knew perfectly well what Stalin meant. He was talking of Britain and France.

When Stalin "attributed to the democracies a plan of embroiling the fascist states in war with the Soviet Union," writes Tucker, "he was projecting onto them a scenario that had been in his own mind since at least 1925." As Stalin put it to the American ambassador on 5 June 1938: "the Chamberlain government were determined upon a policy of making Germany strong and thus place France in a position of continually increasing dependence upon England; also with the purpose of ultimately making Germany strong against Russia." Chamberlain, at least by early 1939, thought he had abandoned all illusions as to Stalin's game, saying that Russia's aim was "to see the 'capitalist' Powers tear each other to pieces while they stay out themselves," exactly the same idea which had been long circulating in the British Foreign Office, except with Nazi Germany and Communist Russia as the protagonists and Britain and France as bystanders. Was everyone projecting their own wishes onto everyone else? The Soviet press seems to have missed the meaning of Stalin's words, but, as historian Jonathan Haslam points out, the German ambassador didn't: "this was the moment that Schulenburg had long been waiting for." Stalin followed his speech by replacing Foreign Minister Litvinov, a Jew, with Molotov, a non-Jew, thus signaling the Germans and the world that he was ready to deal. On 17 April the new Soviet Ambassador to Berlin told the German Foreign Office that ideological differences did not have to inhibit better German-Russian relations. On 5 May Hitler was wondering if Stalin might be ready for an understanding. Ribbentrop told the German ambassador that he should inform Molotov that in the case of a war between the Third Reich and Poland, the Nazis were prepared to make far-reaching concessions. By mid-June 1939, the Soviet Chargé d' Affaires in Berlin was telling the Bulgarian ambassador that the Soviets were poised between three choices, one of which was a *rapprochement* with Germany, and that if Berlin signed a non-aggression treaty with Moscow, there would be no Soviet treaty with Britain. All of this suggests that historians who try to find which of the two parties first "wooed" the other are missing the point. It was classic *folie à deux*, a mutual circling till the embrace could be joined. Alan Bullock puts it best: "There is little profit in debating whether the Russians or the Germans made the first approach. There were hints and probes by both parties in the spring of 1939."[45]

These approaches between Germany and the Soviet Union continued during the summer when rival Soviet and Anglo-French military negotiations began in Moscow. Both sets of events unfolded in parallel. Beck believed the

Russians were "playing a double game." Again, historians have hampered themselves when dealing with the dichotomies of these related but separate activities by seeing them in either/or terms. Gerhard Weinberg's rationalist approach has to believe that Stalin was stringing the Western Powers along "in public in order to put pressure on the Germans to raise their efforts in private." Since logic dictates you can't have it both ways, one was lever for the other. But in the psycho-logic of the unconscious one *can* have it both ways, and that is why the position of Soviet foreign policy expert Jonathan Haslam makes perfect sense. "If anyone is too taken in by the...notion that the individual cannot hold two entirely incompatible ideas in his mind at the same time," he says, "they should take a look at Stalin." When the British and French began their military talks with the Soviets they could thus trick themselves, as Stalin had, into believing they were entering into negotiations in good faith, and they probably were, despite the countervailing impulse to arrange things so that the talks would ultimately fail. After Hitler seized Prague, it became immediately apparent to the Allies, as it was to many people for many years before, that if Poland was to be saved, the cooperation of the Soviet Union was essential. Geographic realities meant that a British-French-Soviet connection had to be made, but it was not to happen. Some forty years ago, A.J.P. Taylor showed the ways in which the British and French worked to sabotage the negotiations: by allowing the discussions to be "conducted with a lack of secrecy remarkable even at a time when old-style secret diplomacy had everywhere broken down"; by not sending top-level negotiators, and, in a climate of urgency, by not sending them by airplane; in addition, the negotiators were unable to make on-the-spot decisions, having to check back on every detail with London and Paris; and, despite obvious geographic realities, the British and French governments could not sway their Polish ally from its policy that it would fight Stalin even if Soviet armies entered Poland to resist a German invasion, which looks like another example of Poland's self-defeating, self-sacrificing behavior. Taylor found all of this "a curious puzzle," and concluded "it is impossible to discover a rational answer to these questions."[46]

When the negotiations ended in failure, each side blamed the other. The British, at least, derived some unconscious secondary emotional satisfaction during the talks, a Foreign Office veteran calling them "humiliating." When they ended, British Ambassador Seeds thanked London for allowing him to express an emotion "after months of patience and self-control," reporting how thrilled he was at being finally able to momentarily drop the passive exterior demanded of diplomats and discharge the smallest bit of anger by telling the Soviets they had "acted in bad faith." Historians have been at it ever since, the debate over where to place the blame apparently continuing well into the future, unless, that is, historians eventually come to see the merits of the final judgment offered by one of the talks' major participants. In a lecture delivered at the University of Leeds thirty-five years ago, Lord Strang concluded reluctantly "everybody had been at fault."[47]

By dragging their feet, the western powers had apparently reinforced Stalin's suspicion that they were trying to turn Hitler eastward. Britain was again manipulating events. If a military alliance between the West and Stalin was formalized, theoretically at least, war could be averted; instead, these delaying tactics helped push Hitler and Stalin into each other's arms.

In late August 1939, Hitler, fearing that Stalin might actually sign an agreement with Britain and France at the last minute, took up the general suggestion that Stalin had initiated in his 10 March speech and sent Ribbentrop to Moscow to conclude a Nazi-Soviet Non-Aggression Treaty.

It was not only Hitler who consciously believed the pact had thwarted Britain and France. In the Soviet Union,

Manuilski said: "Only suicidal maniacs would dare to unleash a war against Germany and the USSR to defend Poland!" He was right, but only if everyone was operating on a conscious, rational level. Like many others, Manuilski was hiding the awareness that it was precisely this unconscious suicidal mania that was driving events. The words of British diplomat Clifford North may be symbolically revealing here: he had earlier written from Warsaw that the only way to "diminish the risk of hanging separately seems to me by hanging together." The hanging fantasy—or at least the metaphor—was in the air, the 31 March 1939 British *Daily Herald* saying that unless "Europe faces its own peril and bands together to resist the common menace then nothing is plainer than that the free States of Europe will 'hang separately.'" When Germany presented its terms to Poland, Sir Howard Kennard said to Henderson that they would probably be understood "as an attempt to strangle her under the cloak of legality." In July, Lord Dawson of Penn had said to a friend that if Poland lost Danzig Poland would "wither away and suffocate," thus reinforcing the fantasy expressed by the Polish press and leaders as long ago as 1930 that Danzig made up the "lungs" of the Polish economy.[48] It may not be too much of a stretch to suppose that North's obvious play on words and the *Daily Herald*'s more open invitation to a coming collective "suffocation" and Kennard's words to Henderson, and Lord Dawson of Penn's words to a friend are not far removed from Chamberlain's 1931 fear that "the suicidal embrace...will finally drown the lot of us," a notion made all the more likely by the public and private expression of the strangulation and smothering fantasies being applied to Poland. The sources show that in the earlier Czech Crisis only one anonymous Briton had called for Czechoslovakia's "strangulation." The Czech sacrifice had begun instead with imagery of an "appendix," with the Sudeten "amputation" fantasized as a medical "operation" before the "young state" was "thrown to the wolves." Could it be that the fate of the "new-born" Poland, and perhaps Europe through Poland, would be sealed not by an "operation" but by an imaginary "suffocation," or by suffocation through hanging? It seems far-fetched, but again, even if these images are mere metaphors and not fantasies, they must be taken into account since they helped create a certain atmosphere in which diplomatic action, and thinking about diplomatic action, took place.

What was unfolding was in any case what many people had predicted, especially after Munich. In the autumn of 1938 Trotsky had written: "We may now expect with certainty Soviet diplomacy to attempt rapprochement with Hitler." Coulondre wrote Bonnet from Moscow: "What other course remains for her (USSR) but to return to the policy of entente with Germany?" On 27 January 1939 an article by the diplomatic correspondent of the *News Chronicle*, Vernon Bartlett, forecast a deal between Germany and the Soviet Union, and throughout 1939 French diplomats warned of an impending *rapprochement*.[49]

On 4 May 1939 Harvey wrote in his diary: "News of Litvinov's resignation came as a complete surprise....Does it mean Russia will turn from the West toward isolation? And if so, won't she inevitably wobble into Germany's arms?" On 7 May he wrote that although there had been assurances there would be no change in Russia's policy, he didn't quite believe it: "I do not like it and there are hints here and there that it may mean a Russo-German rapprochement." On 20 May he recorded the words of a visitor from Paris who came "to warn me of the importance of clinching matters with Soviet Russia" (that is, creating a military alliance) "as there already were contacts between the Soviets and Germany."[50] At the time, British journalist Oliver Reed had noted in his early-1939 book *Disgrace Abounding* that "if the avoidance of war was really the paramount aim...it could have been achieved by combining with Russia to confront Germany with overwhelming force...now it is too late. The development has passed that stage. Now the only question is whether Hitler will attack Russia or make terms with Russia before attacking the west;" he concluded that a German-Soviet alliance was the more likely possibility.[51] A British foreign policy memo from the summer of 1939 predicted that "unless the required cooperation of Poland...is secured, negotiations...will break down. The effect of this on Soviet policy cannot be foreseen, but the possibility of a policy of accommodation with Germany should not be excluded. In that event Russia might either share the spoils with Germany at the expense of Poland...or remain neutral and constitute the chief menace when the war was over."[52] A David Low Cartoon from 29 June entitled "If the British Don't, Maybe We Will" shows a group of patient Nazis seated on a bench outside Molotov's office, one holding a briefcase with the words "Proposal for a Nazi-Soviet Pact." In late August, before any agreement was actually reached, headlines in a Special issue of the Basel *Nationalzeitung* announced "Conclusion of a German-Russian Non- Aggression Pact Near." Walter Bringolf at once wrote a commentary in *Volksrecht*, which appeared on 22 August, one day before the pact was signed. Headlined "Agreement Berlin-Moscow," it said: "Poland is abandoned....Poland has been delivered up to the German invasion."[53] Because of this and like predictions, it is astonishing to read in Harvey's diary for 23 August: "News of German-Soviet Russian non-aggression pact announced today came as a complete shock to H.M.G."[54]

How can this "shock" be explained, especially for those politicians, statesmen, and diplomats who had been closely following developments? It is not difficult to see it for what it really was, another example of the denial and self-deception the British, and other members of the European family, had used to hide from themselves their own unconscious intentions and complicity. But British denial was nothing as compared to the denial employed by Beck and the Poles. They were convinced that the pact had no real significance. "Beck was one of the few statesmen who professed to believe that this development, which actually destroyed the very formulation of his policy of balance, did not really change the situation." British diplomats reported from Warsaw that Polish public opinion was "surprisingly calm." And the "Polish press tended to discount the importance of the German-Russian rapprochement, emphasizing that it would not change the existing relationship of forces in Europe."[55] This is not so astonishing considering that several sources show the agreement in the context of the family fantasy. *Pravda* ran a two-page photograph of Molotov receiving Ribbentrop: "A charming family group" remarked Katya Rotminstrovskaya, a prisoner in the Magadan labor camp who was shot six months later for "anti-Soviet agitation." Cartoons depicting Stalin as either Hitler's bride or groom appeared all over the east and west, Hitler speaking of the pact as a "marriage," and historians speaking of a "marriage of convenience" ever since.[56]

Hitler's motives for the pact seem clear enough. Why did Stalin accept it? The argument advanced over the years has been that with the Red Army devastated by the Great Purge, Stalin needed time to rebuild the Soviet military. That argument has merit, but seems to some only a partial answer, or no answer at all. One communist observer stated that: "The theory that Stalin was merely playing for time while feverishly arming against the Nazis was invented much later, to cover up the Kremlin's tragic blunder in trusting Germany." Another has said: "the huge loses of manpower, civilian population and resources suffered by the Soviet Union in the surprise attack {by Germany in 1941} make a shambles of the old apologetic argument that it gave time for preparation. What preparation?"[57]

Tucker's more reasoned explanation is that Stalin thought Hitler would invade Poland and get into war with Great

Britain and France while the U.S.S.R. could sit back and wait for the kill after the adversaries were exhausted. It will be remembered that this was what Chamberlain feared as well, and is indeed what happened.

Some historians have argued that what was at work was less strategic and more personal, that Stalin was flattered by Hitler who, unlike the western powers, took him more seriously. Hitler won him over by treating him as an equal, wasting no time when he was ready to deal by sending the German Foreign Minister Ribbentrop, not minor diplomats, to Moscow by air. This argument has the merit of containing at least an emotional dimension. But what seems to have been driving Stalin was something more than just the Führer's flattery, perhaps the same thing that drove Mussolini to likewise become dependent on him.

Observers even in the 1930s saw many similarities between Stalin and Hitler. Mussolini wondered after the purges if "Stalin could secretly have become a fascist." The Romanian communist Grigore Gafencu "was struck by the number of aspects that the regime of Hitler and Stalin had in common." A French cartoon from November 1939 shows Stalin before a map of Europe standing on six copies of *Mein Kampf* as he reaches for Finland. A David Low cartoon from 1936 had suggested Stalin's conscious intentions as, trimming his moustache, he tries to become Hitler.[58]

Recently, historians have remarked on the many similarities between the two dictators. By the time of the purge, writes Tucker: "Stalin's regime was surreptitiously becoming, like German fascism, a terroristic dictatorship headed by a Führer." Walter Laqueur's book *Stalin, The Glassnost Revelations* draws several comparisons by arguing that both dictators were similar in many ways. Historian Louis Rapoport's *Stalin's War Against The Jews* demonstrates the existence of an unstated collusion between Hitler and Stalin to rid both countries of the Jewish populations under their control. And historian Sir Alan Bullock's 1992 thousand-page comparative treatise *Hitler and Stalin,* draws many other comparisons, including recognition of what sounds like the notion of a delegated leader. As Gordon Craig put it in his book review of Bullock's study in *The New York Review*: "They were driven by an inner force that was more than individual and represented 'a mysterious coincidence' between personal egotism and mass will; they spoke both to the yearnings and to the fantasy of their age."[59]

The evidence suggests that at least some of these similarities were neither accidental nor circumstantial, but were consciously and unconsciously wished for. Historian Klaus Hildebrand notes how Stalin "was thoroughly acquainted with Hitler's thoughts after having studied the {Nazi} Programme carefully when Hitler came to power in 1933." It is well known that Stalin spoke approvingly of "The Night of the Long Knives," saying of the Röhm purge: "Have you heard what happened in Germany? Some fellow that Hitler. Knows how to treat his political opponents."[60] And it has long been argued that The Night of the Long Knives served Stalin as a model for his own later purges.

These do not seem separate, parallel political processes carried out by leaders driven to act alike due merely to the similar inner structures of their dictatorships. Stalin's deep personal identification with Hitler is suggested by a remark made to his daughter after the war: "Ekh, together with the Germans we would have been invincible."[61]

It has been argued above that the British vicariously experienced their own sadism thorough Hitler. More openly, Mussolini, and other Europeans, also came to identify with Hitler's power. For his part, Stalin, like the others, seems to have been driven by an intra-psychic defense known as identification with the aggressor.[62] This is a way of warding off fear. By becoming the aggressor—verbally, physically, or by gesture or in imagination—the self as the target of aggression disappears in fantasy, and anxiety is reduced. This may help explain a persistent mystery that has perplexed scholars for decades, that is how, despite ample warnings, Soviet forces failed to prepare for the German assault they knew was coming in the summer of 1941. Overy and Wheatcroft say the cause of that failure "remains obscure,"[63] but part of an answer to Stalin's denial, his astonishing refusal to believe any of the intelligence reports of the Nazi buildup and the immediate realities of the June attack, seems based on his near-total identification with the Führer.

Whatever happened later, the Nazi-Soviet Pact of August 1939 allowed Stalin to grab the eastern part of Poland at the same time that it allowed him, as the Pact of Steel three months earlier had allowed Mussolini, to become one of Hitler's enablers. With it, Stalin achieved another of his long-term goals. For years, according to Tucker, "Stalin was assisting events to take their course toward a European war. An accord with Germany remained a basic aim because it would offer an opportunity to effect a westward advance of Soviet rule while turning Germany against the democracies in what Stalin envisaged as a replay of World War I."[64]

It has been argued above that Mussolini slipped into the role of enabler after being supplanted by the younger upstart Hitler, who became Europe's new rage-filled child. Was Stalin understood in Europe's fantasy life to be another enabling sibling, or displaced gang leader? If not, what was his fantasy role?

Therapists who treat pathological families often find that the fathers of such families are distant, absent, or quiescent. Father is a kind of never-mentioned shadow figure, who in fantasy, even in reality, does not exist for family members. For the family to have an effective father would mean that family members would be restrained, would follow some rules, would be less prone to acting out. The role of ineffective, shadowy father would be perfect for a fantasy family working toward an outburst of violence "provoked" by the family's designated, out-of-control, raging child.

There is evidence which circumstantially points to Stalin

as Europe's absent or distant father. Although the fantasy of Mother Russia predominated for centuries, it was the tsar, imagined as The Little Father, who was said to have "married" the country upon assuming the throne, an idea solemnized in ceremony. These ideas did not suddenly die out with the coming of the Bolsheviks. In *Mother Russia*, Joanna Hubbs has shown how deeply these mythical images ran in the Russian people's minds and emotions, concluding that "in Soviet literature, art, and life {Mother Russia's} iconographic presence continues." Richard Wortman has shown how the tsars remained "fathers" and how the mythic idea of the tsar's "all-national betrothal with Russia" maintained its ceremonial hold in the Russian monarchy right up until 1917.[65] Despite communism's avowed hatred of royal, autocratic rule and the murder of the Romanoff dynasty during the Revolution, Stalin must have unconsciously inherited those Russian traditions: he was the new "Little Father." Centuries had embedded it in people's minds, and it was a way of collective thinking that could not be abandoned overnight. Moreover, it was reinforced by Stalin's paternal public image, and carried through from the Russian past to the whole of the Soviet Union.

Indeed, it seems that Russia's rulers had long served others in Europe as masculine fantasy figures. Masaryk told Emil Ludwig the Czechs had expected protection from a masculine figure, no matter how remote: "As a nation we were Russophiles. We believed that the Big Uncle would not sacrifice us to the Austrians." But Masaryk also said: "The idea of the Czar {as} the 'Little Fathers,' the father of his country and the like, is merely a metaphorical exaggeration."[66] He was speaking of real fathers and not symbolic "uncles," of course, but one hears hints of some unconscious realities beneath his conscious denial. Another indication of a fatherly fantasy, which must have continued into the Soviet era and naturally connected to Stalin and the Soviet Union, is found in Nicolaus Sombart's essay on pre-World

War I Germany, which shows that the associations—or fantasies—of German men in the Wilhelmine era contained an interesting array of images: "England came to be identified with the female in the imagination of German men," Sombart says, while in their fantasies of Eastern Europe, "male features prevail, {especially in} the autocratic Tsarist regime in Russia."[67] Mother Britain in the west, Father Tsar in the east, Mother Russia *in* Russia, Father Tsar in Europe.

Was the fantasy of the Russian Father embraced not only by Germans (and Russians) but by other Europeans as well? Did it continue into the 1930s and beyond? Was Stalin's nickname "Uncle Joe,"–which echoed Masaryk's "Big Uncle"–meant to symbolize the feelings of familiarity with and yet the sense of distance from a recognized family member who isn't much around?

More research into the language and images in the diplomatic documents may reveal some answers. But what seems clear enough now is that Stalin's crucial choices, as with the decisions made and not made by the leaders of other countries, were inspired partly by his own emotional needs and partly by Europe's conscious and unconscious promptings, both of which emerged from long term stressors which had produced the irrational decisions that made the outbreak of war among the European family a virtual certainty by September 1939.

XI SOME CONCLUSIONS

EUROPE...HAS TORN ITSELF APART SUICIDALLY A SECOND TIME IN A WAR OF BROTHER AGAINST BROTHER.[1]

—*Stefan Zweig*, 1941

Hitler wanted war. The powers helped him. With war imminent, the Führer, raging for months, was suddenly at peace. "Fuehrer calm, has had good sleep," reads a Halder diary entry for 31 August.[2] Hitler was not alone.

With rage and bad feelings now safely contained in enemies "out there," a strange calm settled over Europe. The usually astute William Shirer observed the behavior but missed its full import. As he moved through the streets of Berlin on 1 September he found people "apathetic."[3] What he meant was that he found no cheering, nothing like the manic joy that had swept Europe in 1914. Historian Pierre Renouvin sensed a different mood when he observed what Hitler must have understood: "the signs of unrest...in public opinion the preceding year were absent this time."[4] It was not so much apathy as calm, resignation mingled with relief.

As war approached, the British fantasized a popular uprising in Germany they expected would topple Hitler's regime, but were not at all surprised by the actual turn of events. "I met Nevile Henderson and Embassy staff on arrival from Holland at Victoria {Station} last night," says Harvey's diary for 8 September. "They all testify to calm in Berlin and lack of any hostile demonstrations."[5] In the very earliest days of the war, people quietly packed the restaurants, cafés, pubs and beer halls in London and Berlin[6] as Europeans naturally sought comfort from food, drink, and each other as they faced a common fate.

The same mood of relief prevailed throughout Europe partly because the coming of war was no surprise. Calm reigned in part due to the simple release of tension: a long diplomatic crisis had finally terminated. It was the same type of release Cadogan had hoped for prior to the *Anschluss* a year and a half earlier when he had written in his diary, "I almost wish Germany would swallow Austria and get it over."

When Germany did "swallow" Austria he wrote: "Thank goodness Austria is out of the way." During the Czech Crisis which followed, the London *Times* reported Chamberlain's flight to meet Hitler at Berchtesgaden had, for "the great bulk of the public," given relief from "an intolerable sense of impotence and tension." Yet the tension was only renewed with Hitler's new demands until the Munich Agreement a few days later offered what seemed to be relief at last. But it too was only temporary. Not until September 1939 when general war finally came did the ongoing diplomatic crisis of several years end for good. Over that time, the general tensions had taken their toll, prompting many irrational, or at least emotional, decisions from Europe's leaders. In the spring and summer of 1939, with war still in the future, the popular slogan "*Il faut en finir*" ("There must be an end to this") had circulated through France.

As the people of Paris awaited the expiration of the French ultimatum on 3 September, their behavior once again symbolized Europe's feelings. Lukacs puts it best: "By early afternoon the boulevards and the Champs-Elysées were filled. In the crowded cafés people sat, rather quietly. They were looking at their watches. Five more minutes; one more minute: and we are at war."[7]

The British had enjoyed premature relief the year before when it seemed that war would break out over the Czech Crisis, as Hitler had intended. In September 1938, taking leave of the Führer, Sir Ivone Kirkpatrick later remembered, as "I grasped {Hitler's} podgy hand I felt an overwhelming sense of relief that war would come and that I should never have to see him again. In the Embassy the feeling was the same." With war imminent, Harold Nicolson wrote to his wife that "everyone is calm, resolute and cheerful;" he wondered if she had "found the same psychological experience going on in yourself as I am finding during these dreadful days: a sort of strange calm and resignation." A year later, on 30 August 1939, he wrote in his diary, "today when war seems a matter of hours, the absolute despair of a week ago seems to have changed into determination, the gloom of anticipation melting into the gaiety of courage. It is as though we had taken our fill of apprehension and sadness and can absorb no more."

On 3 September 1939, Cadogan, echoing the sentiments he had expressed over Austria a year earlier, wrote in his diary: "In a sense there is relief, doubts resolved." Churchill experienced it as well: "a very strong sense of calm came over me...I felt a serenity of mind and was conscious of a kind of uplifted detachment." Britain as a whole reacted with a businesslike: "Let's get this over with." So did the French. As their armies marched, the American ambassador to Paris recorded: "The men left in silence. There were no bands, no songs....no hysterical weeping of mothers, sisters and children. The self-control and quiet courage...had a dreamlike quality." One year later, with Italy tumbling into war, a retired Italian diplomat wrote, "strange to say, the general feeling is one of relief. The trying period of uncertainty is over."[8]

And a year after that—following the shock, surprise, and shame of Pearl Harbor—the same reaction overcame Americans as they transformed World War II into a "good war." Many remembered it later, as they had experienced it at the time, as filled with romantic excitement, an idealization which has continued into the twenty-first century through films, television, the histories of Stephen Ambrose, and the several books by Tom Brokaw on *The Greatest Generation*, recently joined by Larry King's best-selling *Love Stories of the Second World War*.[9]

For the European diplomatic community in August 1939

there was, as Bullock aptly puts it, "an unreal atmosphere about all of {the}…eleventh-hour negotiations, an air of urgent futility in the telegrams passing between London and Warsaw, Berlin and London, London and Paris, Paris and Rome. Even at the time those who were engaged in these diplomatic activities found it difficult to believe that they had any point. As in a badly managed stage play, anti-climax had preceded the denouement, and there was only relief when the curtain finally came down."[10]

There was relief, in part, because the build up of repressed murderous feelings and suicidal impulses ready to be enacted were now officially sanctioned. All the intolerable feelings, only partly contained in Hitler which had threatened to make, or were making, people feel "crazy," were now safely lodged in an external mortal enemy it was their duty to kill. Churchill's paradoxical words in the House of Commons on 3 September bear repeating: "Outside the storms of war may blow, and the lands may be lashed with the fury of its gales, but in our own hearts this Sunday there is peace."[11]

Still, it should not be misunderstood that in the interwar era people only wanted emotional release through war; they also rationally wanted peace. In the inner struggle between the two, war finally triumphed, winning out over what emotionally was peace in name only. Paradoxically, relief came with an end to ambivalence when inner tensions became outer conflicts.

Besides the sense of relief, Europe's unconscious "need" for war seems corroborated by the widespread attitude that war was inevitable, a feeling which came to prevail more and more in the last interwar decade. As the 1930s progressed, hopes for peace slipped away and were replaced by a persistent sense of foreboding. The idea of automatic historical Progress had been dealt a near-fatal blow by The Great War, and matters were not helped by novels such as H.G. Wells's *The Shape of Things to Come* (1933), or its popular film version *Things to Come* (1936), which graphically predicted massive air assaults and a civilization-ending war by 1940. As the 1930s began, Freud sensed the coming storm, adding to the pessimism when his writings returned to the theme of how difficult it was for human beings to renounce impulse in favor of civilization.

In *Civilization and its Discontents* (1930) he asked: "How has it happened that so many people have come to take up this strange attitude of hostility to civilization," and wondered if people would ever "succeed in mastering...the human instinct of aggression and self–destruction," which was the "fateful question for the human species." His vision was prompted as much by the emotional currents of his time as by his earlier clinical findings, and his prophetic observation that "men have gained control over the forces of nature to such an extent that with their help they would have no difficulty in exterminating one another to the last man"[12] seemed all the more ominous by 1939.

Some of those closer to power accurately foresaw the disintegration of the European state system. The warnings of many who were operating on more realistic rather than purely fantasy levels—Coulondre, Churchill, Ambassador Dodd[13]—were intended as calls for preventative action. But, as noted several times, because no coalitions were ever formed to resist Hitler, such warnings only served to feed a sense of fear, powerlessness, and gloom.

The growing sense of inevitability was found to be an important interwar theme in earlier studies of prewar diplomacy too[14] but has largely disappeared from most of the newer histories. In those earlier studies, Felix Gilbert observed "in Ciano's Diary how, in his discussions with Mussolini, the decadence of the democracies and the inevitability of war became recurrent themes."[15]

In a study of Polish diplomacy, Henry L. Roberts connected Beck's views to the European-wide sense of doom: "The feeling, so apparent in his memoirs, that there were no feasible alternatives, was characteristic of a general European mood which was creating, and being created by, the approaching catasrophe."[16] Gordon Craig's study of German diplomacy noted an atmosphere of fatalism at the German Foreign Office: "Even those officials who were dismayed by what was obviously a headlong rush toward war and the probable destruction of Germany were powerless to influence the course of policy....they could only go about their customary dignified business of indicting notes and sealing diplomatic pouches, while they waited for the inevitable to happen."[17]

In Britain, the theme of inevitability was as widespread as it was elsewhere, and, as seen in Chapter III, circulated in the press, government memos, and, even as he denied the possibility, in the speeches of Neville Chamberlain. Germans in Britain wrote home about the feeling, foreign journalists found it common throughout the country, and by late-March 1939, Halifax was regularly expressing the idea in Foreign Policy Committee meetings.[18]

The notion ran through the British press, German Foreign Office, and British Foreign Office and is found in the public and private words of Leopold III, Ciano, Beck, and a host of other leaders, diplomats, and statesmen. Again, for some people these forebodings were based on the reality that unless policies changed, war was likely; for others, the fearful sense that war had to happen was the expression of a fantasy, even a wish.

Because Hitler was clearly bent on war some have argued that the European expectation of war was justified since nothing could have stopped him. Given the evidence for the extent of his out-of-control feelings in the years 1938-39, it seems likely that he could not have been stopped by August 1939. Yet this cannot be known for certain. Such assertions are not history, but "virtual history"—that is, speculation. What is certain is that, alternatives were never tried, although there had been a good likelihood of military success against him in 1936, even as late as 1938.

Historian Keith Eubank puts it correctly when he says: "it would have been impossible for Britain and France to have entered any kind of war...before 1939, because neither the people nor the governments of the two countries were conditioned to the idea of war. The only way they could accept war after 1918 was for it to be thrust upon them by a series of crises."[19]

Those crises were absolutely essential to the process; and that is why they were in part unconsciously arranged. A.J.P. Taylor's view that "the war of 1939, far from being premeditated, was a mistake, the result on both sides of diplomatic blunders,"[20] misses the mark. Alternatives were never tried or were repeatedly sabotaged precisely so that a series of crises could ensue. Almost all concerned hid their intentions from themselves and masked their actions by clever rationalizations, so that when allied "peace gestures" failed, the French, and especially the British, could comfortably feel they had now reached a higher moral plane—and, given the evils of Nazism, they had.

Of course, none of it had been necessary, since the Allies stood on a higher moral plane already in 1935 when they could have acted within the framework of international law and the Locarno and Versailles Treaties. Instead, they tragically put themselves and Europe through an elaborate diplomatic charade. A.J.P. Taylor's statement that statesmen are "too absorbed by events to follow a preconceived plan. They take one step, and the next follows from it,"[21] is doubtless sometimes the case, but diplomatic drift is only one process in diplomacy and overlooks the power of suppressed and repressed feelings. Wars, like family fights, can be unconsciously prepared; statesmen, like family members, know precisely what steps to take, what buttons to push, so that the next step, predictably, will follow.

This, at least, is one of the findings of the preceding study.

There are, however, a number of important gaps, missing pieces, and unresolved issues.

The statement made by Sir Ivone Kirkpatrick at the beginning of Chapter III ("History will wonder how it came about that any Government should have deliberately closed its eyes and those of the nation to so clear and imminent a peril") was in fact not all that new; it had been made in a slightly different form by journalist Douglas Reed in his popular book *Disgrace Abounding* in the spring of 1939. Reed invited his readers to ponder over "Czecho-Slovakia and Spain. Why, if England is in danger, have these two small nations been sacrificed, why are Englishmen to be sent to be killed in the most unfavourable circumstances possible...why has everything been done in advance to reduce the chances of victory and of life itself for this new generation of Englishmen that is being told to prepare for the slaughter?"[22]

Reed's questions get to the heart of the matter, and carry with them the notion that some of what was going on—the sacrifice of small nations, preparing for the slaughter of the next generation—was in some way wanted. That all of it (or much of it) comes down to an unconscious need for the British to feel humiliated must seem to narrative historians extremely unlikely (if not altogether impossible), and raises the question of why the British needed to feel humiliated in 1939 but not in 1914.

If childhood trauma produced such an urgent need to re-experience humiliation in the interwar years, why was the same need not part of Britain's road to World War I? Insofar as one can tell, there was no marked difference between the childhoods of one generation over the next, and if humiliation was so compelling in the 1930s, one should naturally expect similarities, if not exact parallels, to show up in the earlier documents as well. At this point, no answer can be given to this question beyond the suggestion that the road to World War I has not been studied from the standpoint of feelings, fantasies, and family systems. There may indeed be something there, although judging by what is known, the British did not prepare humiliations as an excuse for themselves in the decade before 1914.

In any case, the current study is not in the business of trying to find universal laws for all wars, or explain World War I by reference to the psychological causes of World War II. Whatever other reasons one may find to have driven British behavior in 1937-1939—commands from the European family which asked them to play that masochistic role, guilty feelings over the desire to go to war to avenge the unmourned dead, or additional factors yet to be uncovered—one must conclude from the documents that in this particular diplomatic scenario the British were compelled, at this moment in the interwar decade, to behave in this way simply because the evidence points to these causal connections. World War I has to be studied on its own.

An additional issue on the British side is the question of their concern for the continued existence of the British Empire, a serious matter for the Foreign Office, much of the electorate, and hence British politicians. Hankey was asked to prepare a position paper on the topic after his retirement, spoke twice on the BBC, and had his views printed in *The Listener*, Chamberlain was aware, as he wrote in a private letter in early 1938, that "we are a very rich and vulnerable Empire," and in the midst of the Czech Crisis Britain's apparent weakness prompted Cadogan to ask: "How can we hold Egypt, India, and the rest?" Did, on the one hand, "good enough" parenting create conscience enough in some people so that guilt about the Empire's very existence—the perceived and actual general contempt for and brutal treatment of the colonial peoples—create another stream feeding the national need for masochistic humiliation, as Rebecca West suggested?[23]

It seems unlikely, but needs examining. On the other hand, there is the more likely possibility, as hinted at by

Cadogan's words, that semi-consciously, even consciously, the wish for war was a way for some to prove to themselves and others—even if they didn't admit it—that the British were still robust, and that they would *not* be humiliated because, strong in military potential and committed to protecting their commitments, the Empire in the long run could not slip away. These contradictory considerations—guilt on the one side, aggression on the other, with perhaps each feeding off the other—seem psychologically significant, but lie beyond the scope of the present study.

Another significant loose end, one connected to Britain as to all the powers, is the question of Spain. The Spanish Civil War is almost universally understood to have foreshadowed World War II. Its outbreak triggered rumors in Berlin of a European wide war. As Europe's first killing field of the 1930s, it was a clear dress rehearsal for what was to come, and reveals, as surrogate for Europe, the seething, pent-up, murderous rage at the heart of the continent.

"At the outbreak of the civil war, republicans, anarchists, socialists and communists—caught in enclaves controlled by the extreme right—were murdered by the tens of thousands. On the other hand, nuns, priests, conservatives and extreme right-wingers in enclaves controlled by the extreme left were also murdered by the tens of thousands. The exact number of unarmed victims has never been certified."

And the war chillingly foreshadowed other atrocities to come: "It was not unusual…for killing squads of the right and left to murder their victims in cemeteries—it was more convenient that way." Spain was the place where ideologically justified rage could be enacted and vicariously experienced by Europe's millions. Salvador de Madariaga saw it clearly: "Spain is thus suffering vicariously the latent civil war which Europe is—so far—keeping in check." Spain was Europe in microcosm, complete with communism versus fascism, death from the sky, and civil war. Echoing and elaborating Madariaga, historian Piers Brendon has recently written: "The Spanish Civil War brought home to contemporaries…not only the horror but the imminence of a European…civil war." It was a "small nation" also "sacrificed" by the powers, and became an arena into which mature statesmen could project childish fantasies by playing at soldier on the map of Spain.[24]

Other omissions from the preceding pages include the United States and Japan. It is generally agreed that American disinterest in both the League and Europe helped shape an environment favorable to Hitler's aggression. Did the United States act toward Europe in ways similar to the ways in which Britain acted? Did it do so for some of the same reasons? Was U. S. policy toward Japan influenced by similar fantasies?

Historian John Dower has shown how images of the enemy in both Japan and the United States helped prolong the Pacific War.[25] What prewar images helped create it? Did the Japanese, perceived in the West as a "childlike little people,"—or, as Secretary of State Stimson put it, "puppies" who would run "if a whip were swished firmly before their eyes"—serve the United States in the same fantasy role as the "child" Hitler served Europe? Was America Europe's "sister," Britain's "cousin," Britannia's "adolescent offspring," or all three? Was Uncle Sam, like Uncle Joe, a distant, disengaged, enabling "father?"

The unconscious fantasies which were circulating in American cartoons images during the 1930s show that the same metaphors were being used on both sides of the Atlantic—devouring monsters, Germania as mother, young countries as children being sacrificed to wolves, Europe and America as a family, diplomatic marriages, and regular humiliations. What did it mean when thousands of American college students spontaneously identified with Hitler and Nazism by donning Hitler mustaches and Nazi uniforms at prewar Halloween frat parties? Did Orson Welles's famous 31 October 1938 "War of the Worlds" radio broadcast, which pretended a real Martian invasion was underway, reveal a "paranoid projection," or was it merely the technical brilliance of the broadcast (or both) that produced the nation-wide panic? What about the *Life* magazine article published during the same week as Welles's broadcast which told the world: "The U.S. Prepares for War with Germany, Italy, and Japan"? Was F.D.R. responding to, or trying to work through, "group wishes" communicated to him via the media when he dreamt before the war that he was being bombed by the Germans?[26]

What suicidal impulses propelled the Japanese to attack Pearl Harbor? Admiral Nagano's words to Emperor Hirohito sound strikingly similar to those organic fantasies being uttered at the time in Europe: "Japan was like a patient suffering from a serious illness," he said. "Should he be left alone without an operation, there was a danger of a gradual decline. An operation, while dangerous, would still offer some hope of saving his life."

A recent study has argued persuasively that the details of a Pacific War against the U.S. were planted in Admiral Yamamoto's mind when he served as Japanese Naval Attaché in Washington during the 1920s. At the time, the writings of journalist Hector Bywater, especially his book *The Great Pacific War*, were widely known and debated. In them, Bywater outlined the strategic blueprints almost exactly followed by Japan in 1941-42. Translated and published in Japan in Japanese, Bywater's influence went beyond Yamamoto and fed the ever growing number of novels depicting a future Japanese-American war, a very successful sub-genre in the Japanese popular culture of the 1920s and 30s which its historian Shōichi Saeki calls "enormous." Saeki concludes that long before Pearl Harbor, "on the unconscious level, Japan was prepared for war with the United States."

As for Bywater, his book predicted that the Japanese would lose the war. These facts point to the possibility at least, no matter how improbable, that the expectation of defeat may have been one of the unconscious motives in the Japanese decision to attack Pearl Harbor. That decision apparently came after several of the committees, which had been discussing the question in the spring, summer, and fall of 1941, correctly guessed at the probability of short-term success but were also deeply concerned about the very real possibility, and considerably higher risks, of a protracted conflict (namely, the likelihood that Japan might lose a war with the United States).

Feeling that war was inevitable, imagining that America was an aggressor, and projecting their own wishes onto the United States (they believed the U.S. would attack first), they decided to risk everything in a war against "the cancer of the Pacific," removing "the arrogant Americans" by "wielding the big knife," although the long-term odds were not in their favor, or were at best fifty-fifty. General Tojo summed up what may have been the group's secret wish when he said in an often quoted statement: "There are times when we must have the courage to do extraordinary things—like jumping, with eyes closed, off the veranda of the Kiyomizu Temple!" (Anyone doing so risked almost certain death on the rocks hundreds of feet below.)[27]

Given the importance of suicide in Japanese culture, Tojo's words fit neatly into a familiar pattern of thinking. But was it mere metaphor, or an invitation to everyone, including the United States, to join in a kind of Asian "suicidal embrace"?

On the United States side, a recent study again argues for the long-standing suspicion held by some that the U.S. was aware of the Japanese attack, and may even have provoked it. Oil sanctions were seen by Japan as an act of war, and with the Japanese diplomatic and naval codes broken, it is possible, perhaps even likely, that Roosevelt knew some kind of attack was planned, yet no one at Pearl Harbor was forewarned, and its military and naval commanders were later scapegoated. At the same time, it is abundantly clear that no one consciously thought a carrier-based air attack on the Hawaiian Islands was remotely possible. Most historians, therefore and with good reason, rely on the standard studies of Samuel Eliot Morison, Gordon Prange, and Roberta Wohlstetter (who also has some interesting psychological things to say about the character of Japanese decision making), and reject the notion of Roosevelt's foreknowledge and complicity. They point, in addition, to the massive flood of contradictory raw data at the time, and the usual difficulties always encountered in intelligence work in distinguishing real signals from background noise: how could the few crucial facts be separated from the mass of other material, except in retrospect?[28]

To skeptics, such observations will forever remain part of a massive cover-up (which would now be more than sixty years old). Whichever side one comes down on—even on the side of mainstream scholars who have shown that Roosevelt was not complicit—it is hard to believe that people in the United States, alone among the powers, were immune to their own internal stressors and were somehow able to remain indifferent to the fantasy messages circulating in the European family system. While the jury is still out and may always be out, the fantasies connected to Pearl Harbor, before and after the attack, deserve careful study.

Preceding pages have neglected other issues—some implied, others never elaborated, some not mentioned: the details of the group fantasies of Belgium, France, Italy, Czechoslovakia, Poland, and the Soviet Union; the roles of Austria, of Ethiopia and Albania, of Hungary and Romania; the question of misperceptions among diplomats.[29]

Many psychological biographies remain to be written. And scant attention has been paid here to traditional economic, political, and strategic factors. It is not that those traditional factors are unimportant, but the study's intent was to get at feelings and fantasies, not strive for a full-scale synthesis. Then, of course, all histories are in some ways out of balance. Economic historians are not faulted for leaving out psychological factors; why should psychological historians be faulted for leaving out economic ones?

Another consideration is the role of incomplete mourning, briefly mentioned in Chapter IV. Mourning as a collective as well as individual process is intuitively understood by nearly everyone as an important part of life, and it seems clear that the need to mourn was at least partly responsible for the extraordinary number of monuments and annual commemorations which followed the end of World War I. Historian Eric Hobsbawm finds it curious that "the much smaller {death} figures of the First World War were to make a much greater impact than the vast quantities of the Second World War, as witness the much greater prominence of memorials and the cult of the fallen of the First World War. The Second World War produced no equivalent to the monuments to the 'unknown soldier,'" he says, "and after it the celebration of 'armistice' day gradually lost its interwar solemnity."[30] But these behaviors are indicative of a truly profound trauma. They are "curiosities" only if one fails to fully appreciate the nature and significance of repression, symbolic re-enactment, the need to mourn, the wish not to mourn, and the enormous impact of the First World War, which psychologically, can be called The Great Wound.

To break free of past trauma, and the compulsion to relive it, mourning is necessary. Wondering what the consequences might be for groups if they fail to mourn was an idea most scholars first encountered in the work of German social psychologists Alexander and Margarethe Mitscherlich in their study *The Inability to Mourn* (1967), which focused on post-World War II Germany, not interwar Europe. In the last decade, psychiatrist Vamik Volkan has stressed in his historical work the general importance of individual and group mourning, but while historians have worked increasingly and compellingly over the past fifteen years in the realm of "historical memories," they have done little on individual and collective mourning itself, for either post-1914-1918, or post-1939-1945, although a study by Stéphane Audoin-Rouzeau and Annette Becker, *14-18: Understanding the Great War*, has a number of important things to say on both narrative and psychological levels.[31]

It is presently unclear to what extent the trauma of 1914-1918 drove Europeans to unconsciously re-enact that war in 1939, although there has always been a sense that the outbreak of the Second World War recapitulated the outbreak of the First in a number of direct and symbolic ways. The need for traumatic re-enactment, as much as strategic and geopolitical realities, needs to be seriously considered. In any event, common sense alone tells us that for the many who had fought in World War I, as well as for those who had lost loved ones, the existence of unfinished, partial mourning meant that seething hatreds, and the wish for revenge, could not have been far from the surface—and not just among Germans.

There is also the question of the course of World War II itself. What events during the war might be better understood by a deeper understanding of the psychology of the war's diplomatic prelude? These issues include the war's strategic and tactical aspects: studies of the military, of battles, and of tactical and strategic decisions should reveal deep, irrational fantasies, including Hitler's "blunders" which a few scholars have seen as unconsciously motivated. Then there is the creation and dropping of the first atomic bombs, which one guesses should be filled with rich veins of unconscious fantasies.[32]

Historians love facts and especially in their diplomatic histories are prone to writing dense volumes filled with the myriad details necessary to allow us to begin to understand complex phenomena. This study, more of an interpretive essay, has tried to be more simple and direct, to catch hold of the outlines of an inner process. It has meant sacrificing nuance and complexity. Since there is more to interwar diplomacy than feelings and fantasies, the picture painted above is necessarily incomplete. Decision-makers and statesmen did not always inhabit a never-never world of perpetual fantasy. Rational and irrational thought processes moved along in tandem, one above, one beneath the surface. People moved back and forth between the real world and wishes about it.

Sometimes the two intersected; sometimes the irrational overwhelmed the rational. Fantasies were acted out not by everybody at all times, but by important people at crucial times. At any given moment the historian's question should be: "Was this one of those times?"

The study's focus on emotions was meant to get at this inner core of events. It has included many quotations from the documents, more than is perhaps usual in diplomatic history, since it is the actual words and images used by leaders, statesmen, and the media, which reveal those emotions. Since many of the essay's arguments are non-traditional, it has also included many more quotations from historians than is usual: the intention was to show that many of the facts, ideas, and interpretations used here are a normal part of standard historical explanation, which, when assembled according to a set of accepted psychological criteria, reveal the outline of a puzzle only dimly perceived, or usually not seen at all. Despite its limitations, gaps, and missing pieces, the general contours of that inner core seem clear enough.

Emotions count, especially when they are repressed. Emotions are contained and expressed in fantasies, even in international affairs, and sometimes acted out under stress. If the evidence presented here is not enough to convince the most died in the wool traditionalist that metaphors are fantasies, it must be remembered that the repeated and widespread use of those specific metaphors—aggressive, organic, regressive, and familial—which clustered in the period of the 1930s, doubtless created a certain emotional climate in which diplomacy actually took place, a climate which needs to become more acknowledged as part of the historical record.

Diplomacy, it seems, is not confined to the policies created in capitals, and for the period 1930-1939 included a vast subterranean network of feelings and fantasies. In his autobiography, Arthur Koestler hints at the extraordinary web of exquisite sensitivity which spanned Europe when he describes the continental impact of Stalin's purges: "The Terror was roaring across Russia," he wrote, "like a tidal wave drowning everybody on its way, and even a small distant ripple of it made the cup tremble in ones hand in a Paris café." It seem obvious that in addition to those things which normally pass across borders—information, threats, lies, misperceptions, goods, credits, people, and ideas—so too did fears, wishes, and fantasies. They moved from country to country by means of various informal networks, through formal networks of business and diplomacy, and through the media.

Fifty years ago, Gordon Craig saw how the professional diplomats of the time had been more and more "excluded from important discussions," how "the advice of trained observers in the missions abroad were neglected in favor of the intuitive judgments or chance impressions of tourists who possess{ed} the ear of the political ministers." Craig noted the process but did not try to explain it. Intuitive judgments and chance impressions actually carried and reinforced shared fantasy messages, allowing statesmen, leaders, and peoples another way of telling each other what they were really thinking, feeling, and doing, or planning to do, or were about to ask someone else to do. It kept the process from consciousness while allowing it to be "intuitively" understood. Craig also noted a second trend, a "growing tendency by home governments to give attention, and preferment, to those diplomats who reported what their superiors wanted to hear."[33] People are no doubt universally aware of the value of agreeing with their bosses, which then, as now, helped produce consensus through complicity in the fantasy system.

The evidence has shown that some interwar leaders were sometimes delegates, acting out their people's unconscious wishes. Under stress, important decisions were made which had more to do with inner, emotional needs than with external, objective realities. One of the central fantasies of statesmen and peoples was the fantasy of the family of nations. Because it was a derivative of past realities—that is, the pre-World War I marriage alliances of European royalty—the political leaders, intellectuals, and media, as much as the statesmen of the 1930s, sometimes thought and acted as if the states of Europe were actual members of a pathological family system writ large, one in which each country acted out a particular fantasy role.

While the evidence remains inconclusive, it does appear that some relationship existed between the unconscious fantasy roles played by each country and particular aspects of European childrearing. Britain, where humiliations played a relatively large part in childcare, served as Germany's masochistic partner, and sometimes, even often, played a maternal role. Germany, a land of beaten children, was encouraged to play the sadistic, bad-boy bully and in abused-child Hitler, Germans and Europeans alike found someone well suited to act the out-of-control, raging child.

In France, where hundreds of thousands had been sent to wet-nurse, where over a million had been orphaned by the Great War, and millions more had been in part emotionally abandoned by their mothers, it was easier to embrace the role of abandoned child. So—after the trauma of Queen Astrid's death—did Belgium. Europe's first post-World War I raging child, Italy, became Europe's displaced gang leader then acted like Germany's enabling older sibling. Czechoslovakia and Poland, Europe's fantasy newborns, became

Europe's infant sacrifices. The Soviet Union served as absent father, the image of Uncle Joe a thinly disguised way of symbolically connecting the disengaged Stalin to the pathological family he let run wild.

Of course, Britain was no more a mother than Stalin was an uncle or Germany a child, except in people's unconscious imaginings. On the face of it, and without the corroborating evidence presented above, these observations sound strange, even bizarre. Yet these are the ways in which Europeans actually spoke about themselves, and sometimes acted.

Everyone in Europe, not just the British, could unconsciously identify with Hitler and vicariously indulge violent wishes through him, but, for reasons delineated above, most often it was the British who cued Hitler. A.J.P. Taylor is wrong when he said that Hitler was only an opportunist who sat back and waited for things to happen. Hitler was not merely reactive, but was "pro-active;" he initiated events, at least until 1941. But there was a reciprocal relationship between Britain and Germany—as among all the states. It is hard to determine who was "cause," who consequence in the European "family" since the fantasy structures created a mutually reinforcing system.

As in pathological families with absent or disengaged fathers, roles were sometimes fluid, interchangeable, and inconsistent. One or another country could embrace two or three roles simultaneously, or one role after another in quick succession. It was the maintenance of the family fantasy itself, even unconsciously, which kept the system cohesive.

And when Europe went to war, the conflict was unconsciously, sometimes consciously, understood as a family destroying itself. Many people before and after 1939 saw events in the same way that Spanish philosopher Ortega y Gasset saw them, as a civil war, a brutal "fratricide" in Europe. One eyewitness felt that a common political society, a *civitas Europae*, was being destroyed. Others, like Stefan Zweig, echoed and reinforced Chamberlain's feelings of 1931 by adding the notion of collective suicide. One scholar has spoken of the Holocaust as "social cannibalism," and, from his vantage point in the mid-1980s, George Steiner concluded: "In their origin and in much of their suicidal unfolding, both World Wars were European civil wars."[34]

A decade of diplomacy, amounting to a suicide pact, had set the stage. The European "family" was tearing itself apart.

Freud's authority never needs to be invoked to account for human aggression: history is bloody enough. War seems to have come in 1939 to discharge Europe's collective rage as much as to "stop" Hitler. One can call again on the authority of French sociologist Gaston Bouthoul who found all other explanations mere rationalizations: the social function of war, he believed, is "purely and simply destructive."[35]

The powers had not stopped Hitler, and now had to defeat him. Having loosed the raging child within, they had to destroy its embodiment without. This allowed them to unleash their own aggression and sadism. Because Hitler alone was to "blame," they were guilt-free.

Over the years, many historians have seen how the actions of the powers resulted in bringing about the very things they were designed to prevent; some have been quoted above. They include T. Desmond Williams, who noted that "the attitude of the {British} foreign office was a kind of self-fulfilling prophecy" which "had proved itself right insofar as its own policy was partly responsible for Hitler's decision to go to war after Poland in 1939," and Henry L. Roberts, who said of Poland that Beck's "prophecies tended to be self-fulfilling ones which his own activities and outlook helped bring about."

Adding to this chorus of early post-war scholarship is Gerhard Weinberg who calls the U.S. policy of non-involvement a "self-reinforcing process" which ended up destroying "resolution in the face of danger," Rudolph Binion who says of the Belgian King, Leopold III, that the "King's policy of 1936-1940 was...self-defeating...{even} within the perception that was then his," military historian Donald Kagan, who writes that Chamberlain "had created what proved to be a vicious circle: commitment to appeasement prevented adequate disarmament and the resulting military weakness supported the case for more appeasement," and historian Piers Brendon, who, in a recent synthesis of the interwar period, writes that Chamberlain's "signals invited the aggression they were designed to prevent."

Historian Ian Kershaw sees the story of Hitler's Germany as one "of national as well as individual self-destruction, of the way a people and their representatives engineered their own catastrophe—as part of a calamitous destruction of European civilization."[36] Everyone, it seems, acted in ways that brought about "the very things they were designed to prevent."

Once begun, violence escalated. It is hardly possible to underestimate the murderous rage that was unleashed everywhere, or the open and secret pleasures some derived from it, despite (or because of) the untold misery of millions. The killing frenzy reached levels of unimaginable brutality. Civilian populations suffered. Massive exterminations began. Europe went barbaric; so did the world. The bombing of London followed the bombing of Berlin, both a prelude to the massive air attacks on Japan and the entire Reich. Not all of these events were the direct result of out of control rage, of course, and some rational decisions had to be made in terms of strategic and tactical necessities. On the other hand, Jonathan Glover is just one of many writers who have shown how violence escalated incrementally, until ever more destructive thresholds were reached, and then, more easily crossed.

D.C. Watt, among others, has found strong evidence supporting the notion that some strategic and tactical decisions were motivated not by military contingencies but by a pure desire to destroy, Watt saying that the needless destruction of much of Europe's cultural heritage amounted to a "partial pre-frontal lobotomy." It is hard to look at pictures of Europe's massive devastations, encounter the statistics, or read W.G. Sebold *On the Natural History of Destruction* without agreeing.[37] Senseless slaughter at Stalingrad, the destruction of Lidice, the firebombing of Dresden, Hitler's command for all Germans to follow him in suicide, his orders to leave the Reich a ruin were all part of the story. So were Hiroshima, Nagasaki, and the Holocaust.

It does not trivialize the Holocaust's victims to acknowledge that part of Europe's killing frenzy was directed against Jews. The Holocaust more properly belongs to the course of the war than its origins, for few in the 1930s could have foreseen the destruction of Europe's Jews—unless, since Hitler never expressly said so in public until late January 1939, it was somehow unconsciously understood. The coming of the war made the Holocaust possible.

Historians are in disagreement over whether the Holocaust was central to the war's outbreak. Was the destruction of the Jews a motive for the conflict or an unfolding later opportunity? [38] That question cannot be answered here, but one can address at least one possible link between the Holocaust and interwar diplomacy. If the outbreak of war was in part an unconscious, collective wish, could the Holocaust, too, have been a European-wide unconscious, collective wish?

A number of scholars have denied this. Psychological historian and Holocaust specialist George Kren, has written: "Though it makes history appear very senseless…the decision to kill Europe's Jews must be located in Hitler's individual private pathology." Rudolph Binion has argued that "the radical Jew-kill" was Hitler's personal agenda. Everyone agrees that Hitler was responsible for the policy. Without him it would not have happened, although once the

Holocaust began he found many ordinary people to serve as his willing executioners.[39]

The evidence for this position is overwhelming and conclusive. *Mein Kampf* and Hitler's early speeches are filled with the rhetoric of Jews as "vermin," "cancers," and "blood poisoners," organic notions owing something to the ideas of *Volksgemeinschaft* and crude Social Darwinism, as well as fantasies of Germany as Klara's body, or as his own. In this organic thinking, Jews became containers for his own split-off, projected bad feelings he could then destroy in fantasy by destroying them. But the wish to destroy Jews was not the only option, and competed in Hitler's mind with the idea of expelling them right up until the end of 1938.

Only early in 1939 did he begin for the first time to openly express his murderous wishes: "We are going to destroy Jews," he told the Czech ambassador, going public a few days later in his 30 January Reichstag speech. "Today I will be a prophet," he said in words little noticed by non-Jews at the time buried as they were in the flood of his other rhetoric. "If international finance Jewry within Europe and abroad should succeed once more in plunging the peoples into a world war," he said, "then the consequence will be...the destruction of the Jewish race in Europe."[40]

All of this is old news and well known to scholars of German, Holocaust, and European history. But what has not been sufficiently appreciated is the extent to which Hitler as Europe's delegate was expressing the sentiments of millions of others, not just Germans. The scholarly studies of Bartov, and Browning, as well as the arguments popularized by Goldhagen, despite some of his misrepresentations and distortions, have demonstrated beyond doubt what some have understood intuitively for many years: Hitler wanted to kill Jews, but when war came hundreds of thousands of normal Germans willingly, many enthusiastically, followed him, as did hundreds of thousands of Europeans. Collaborators were everywhere. On orders of the German authorities, it was the Parisian police who rounded up the Jews of Paris; indeed, the French National Police had prepared lists of Jews in advance just in case the German occupying forces might need them. Somewhere in Amsterdam a Dutch citizen denounced the Frank family for forty guilders. Anti-Semitism was widespread throughout the British Foreign Office and in the U.S. State Department. Many throughout the world who did not actually work for the Nazis applauded in private those who did, and, given the extent of anti-Semitism everywhere, simple logic forces the conclusion that for each active collaborator, there were hundreds of thousands of sympathetic, if silent, accomplices.

These facts are also well known, but the Holocaust scholarship of the last twenty years clinches it. Some perpetrators and collaborators were attracted by the opportunity of bureaucratic advancement, some by the chance to steal property, others because of the power they came to wield over the victims, and some, at least in part, because the sadistic tortures and mass executions they were now allowed to carry out were just so much "fun." Kurt Franz, Commandant of Treblinka, kept a scrapbook of photos from his death camp: he called it "The Good Old Days." Scores of shocking other examples show how the mass killings drew crowds of spectators—including the wives of killers invited to watch their husbands "work." It became a kind of "popular entertainment."

Studies of the Jews in Poland, France, Bohemia, Hungary, Holland, and Italy, studies of the Red Cross, the Catholic church, of the Pope, and of Vatican diplomacy, studies of the Baltic and the Ukraine, Switzerland, and Romania[41] show the extent of Europe's complicity, and, despite a few courageous rescuers, the Holocaust has begun to look more and more like a Pan-European event.[42]

The same perspective holds if one looks beyond Nazi-occupied Europe. Here historians have found an equally sordid tale of indifference, amounting, it can be argued, to unconscious complicity. Recent studies have confirmed one horrifying fact: no one, or only a very few, wanted to save Jews. Except in a few instances, Jews were denied visas and were turned away everywhere, Churchill and Roosevelt never spoke out in public, and, although Churchill gave the order, since its blueprints were unaccountably "lost," Auschwitz was never bombed. There is one inescapable conclusion: Hitler's murderous agenda was, consciously and unconsciously, embraced by millions.

At least some of those who were "silent" or "indifferent," who made "mistakes" or failed to act at crucial times, must have been unconsciously motivated. The findings of historians in the last twenty-five years support the suppositions of people like theologian Eliezer Berkovits who had only the studies of Lewy and Morse to go on when he suggested in the early 1970s that the world's "apathy" was an "actual genocide-encouraging silence."[43]

Which part of the European "family" were the Jews—Europe's unwanted foster child? Possible future research may show what family roles they, and other victims of Nazi atrocities, such as Gypsies and homosexuals, played before, during, and after the war.

But is it really possible that the killing frenzy called World War II took place because the repressed wish to destroy the family of one's own childhood had bubbled to the surface and was being symbolically acted out? It is hard to believe that this was the cause even in the face of the evidence. On the other hand, a *Journal of Social History* article by Rudolph Binion has shown how the theme of family hate dominated European fiction writing in the generation before World War I.[44]

The article closed by wondering where those fantasies of family destruction went after World War I. The evidence presented in the current study has shown that part of it—and it looks like a major part—went into the diplomatic preparation for the destruction of the European "family" in World War II. But again, is it possible for repressed murderous rage displaced from the family of one's own childhood to alone account for the enormity of the killing and the savagery of the torture and destruction?

The orgy of bloodletting prepared by the interwar diplomatic Dance of Death—under the influence of regressive impulses unleashed by long-term, persistent stress—may go beyond the repressed tensions remembered from one's own family and, in its psychological origins, have been even more primitive. Given the bloody history of the twentieth century, it seems appropriate to at least consider the views of psychoanalyst Melanie Klein, whose ideas have found their way into the thinking of some modern psychoanalysts.

From a lifetime of clinical practice with children, Klein was able to trace a variety of hostile fantasies back to infancy, including the desire to "scoop out" the mother's body, and bite, tear, and destroy objects inside it. Comparing Klein's ideas with Freud's, historian Peter Gay has written: "the internal world of the small child is a mass of destructive and anxious fantasies, redolent with unconscious images of mayhem and death. For Freud, the child is a selfish savage; for Klein, it is a murderous cannibal."[45]

Did the pressures of stress push European regression beyond repressed memories of family to such early primitive levels? Was "Europa," personifying the whole continent, somehow associated with the primitive mother, whose body Europeans now wanted to bite, destroy, and mutilate? It sounds bizarre, but is at least possible. Still, as in other theoretical constructs, one can hardly expect to conclusively prove a hypothesis which sounds more like speculative meta-psychology than history.

More fruitful is careful attention to what people actually said and did. In psychological history, as in any history, care has always to be taken to guard against "wild analysis," for psychological history is in the first instance history after all, and the same scrupulous criteria should always be used which guide any history, which means that conclusions should arise from sources, not the other way around.

Even though the findings presented here, and the evidence for them, may nevertheless strike some readers as "wild analysis," a cautious approach has guided the present study throughout. As in any history, one must first immerse oneself in the sources, and it was here where the fantasy life of interwar diplomacy was found embedded in the words and images of people at the time. One must tread cautiously, for some psychologically oriented historians have been, and remain, not only too theoretical, but have asked symbols to carry more unconscious meaning than they can comfortably contain. This study has operated instead on the principle that image making takes place at specific moments, in specific places, for specific reasons, and that fantasies are rooted in the history and linguistic formulations of a particular group at a particular moment, not just in an individual's psyche. Images are constructed out of fragments from external reality and inner necessity, part from the world and part from the mind.

Still, a somewhat unorthodox method was used to identify these fantasies. A first principle was that people mean what they say; a second was that people get what they want: both reveal unconscious wishes. Words and behaviors have to be taken seriously since they can embody unconscious feelings. If people said Hitler was a devouring monster, they meant they *felt* as if he was a devouring monster. Hitler certainly was an aggressor, and external reality confirmed and mingled with their fantasies, but it was an external reality European diplomacy had also helped create. Whether that image was wish, projection, or "just a manner of speaking" has to be confirmed or disconfirmed by context and by what people later said and did. Either there is unconscious process, or there is not. Either the unconscious influences behavior, or it doesn't.

One may not want to go so far as psychoanalyst Erich

Fromm who said that "most of what we are conscious of is not real; most of what is real is not in our conscious."[46] But if one then concludes that historical fantasies never influence behavior, one is left with the untenable conclusion that people never meant what they said but only acted that way.

The major finding of this study—the central fantasy of the family of nations—has been supplemented by the introduction of several methods, theories, and findings from the psychological history of the past thirty years. It has been this study's intention all along to produce a synthesis, to integrate those things that would better help explain some of the contradictions found in the historical record. This meant the introduction of the themes of regression under stress, of trauma, of traumatic reliving, of the influence of childhood experiences and conditioning, of psychological biography, of the history of childhood, of how people use the public stage to try to resolve inner conflicts, of the unconscious significance of images and words, of the notion of groups and leaders as projective containers, and of leaders as group delegates. This effort at synthesis may, at times, have seemed to shift the focus away from the influence of the family fantasy, but in a world in which psychological history has been sometimes rightly criticized as being overly simplified, it is important to see that psychological history can try to be, and ideally should be, as complex as the processes it tries to explain.

Several years ago, historian Paul Kennedy, author of a best selling diplomatic history of modern Europe, wrote a short essay on the Allies' appeasement policy. He concluded that only "historical work which investigates the two distinct levels of causality—that is, the nebulous, sometimes confused mentality of the appeasers on the one hand, and the cluster of 'objective' military and economic motives which justified, *or served to justify*, concessions to the dictators on the other—will manage to pin down this phenomenon."[47]

One wonders exactly what Kennedy meant by "nebulous"? Did his readers sense that the rationalizations for the "confused mentality" he mentions extended to, and were part of, deeper irrational processes? Of the "two distinct levels of causality" Kennedy identifies, the current study has, of course, tried to make sense of the "nebulous" one, and has concluded that the "confused mentality" of the appeasers was not so confused, that it contained the unconscious goals of the appeasers, and that it was itself part of an intra-psychic defense system used by the historical actors to hide their unconscious motives from themselves, each other, and from us. Psychological historians can only welcome Kennedy's recognition that more was at work in interwar diplomacy than external "objective" factors.

Because the current study has looked at the neglected area of emotional causality, some confusing and contradictory behaviors seem to have been better understood. Yet, historians are fond of saying that ultimately there are no final conclusions, only more paths to follow.

While that is true, it is also clear from the evidence that a set of shared, shifting, and powerful feelings and fantasies—some conscious, some semi-conscious, many unconscious—were an integral part of the origins of the Second World War.

WE ARE ALL LOCKED IN A SUICIDAL EMBRACE
WHICH WILL PROBABLY DROWN THE LOT OF US!

—*Neville Chamberlain*, 1931

David Low's popularity among historians—he is often cited and reproduced in their books and articles—owes much to his ability to get things just right. He had an uncanny ability to sum up a feeling, a thought, a situation with a few words, a single image, and in just a few strokes of brush and pen. People still recognize something deeply important in his work, perhaps something universal, and his popularity can be measured by the publication of his many books, even an immediate post-war edition in German published in Switzerland in 1946.

He began his career in New Zealand, moving to Australia before migrating to Great Britain, where he went to work for the London *Evening Standard* in 1927. Some of his cartoons appeared from time to time in other publications, including the London *Star*, Britain's *Picture Post*, and *Collier's Magazine* in the United States. Although his fame began reaching a peak in the 1930s, he was sometimes criticized by those who disagreed with his political views, including one prominent writer and politician who revealed a prejudice when in the later stages of the war he felt it "heart-rending that such irresponsible conceptions {of}...Colonials like...Low are able to influence British opinion."[1]

Yet Low's extraordinary insight joined with an immediately recognizable individual style and a powerful sense of composition to do what all political cartoonists are trying to do: tell the story so that people almost feel they don't have to read it. And if the story is read, meanings become clearer and more profound.

Those who look today at various collections of his selected cartoons almost always come away with a deeper sense of what was taking place in the interwar years, not just in England, but for the whole of Europe. Sometimes that understanding cannot be easily articulated because it goes beyond words. As the back flap of his *Cartoon History of*

Our Time put it so clearly in 1939: "He shows...situations that reflect the true inwardness of contemporary events."

Some contemporary political cartoonists seem able to capture the "true inwardness" of things too even though they do their work without thinking much about it. Rigby senior once said: "I read *The New York Times* and watch the eleven o'clock news just like everyone else, then an idea hits me." Others are more introspective, Ben Sargent of the *Austin American-Statesman* saying: "we are speaking to the unconscious of the nation."[2] It might also be that the unconscious of the nation is speaking to the cartoonist. This is, of course, not true all of the time, but some of the time, and when it does happen, what is taking place is more of a dialogue than a monologue. The unconscious wishes, fantasies, and impulses of the group can be expressed through cartoons, not only by the artist telling the nation what to think and feel, but by the nation telling the artist what it thinks and feels.

It is well known—and intuitively understood—that one image may carry several meanings. Conversely, varied images may sometimes point to the same meaning. Low used both techniques. There are the typically stormy seas representing political and economic problems as well as various dangers to international security. One image he favored was of countries as courting couples sitting on park benches; another, of allies and potential allies as strange bedfellows, echoing the practice in families at the time of siblings sleeping in the same bed together. As did many of his contemporaries, Low drew aggressors as threatening, devouring monsters, or captured the infantile behaviors of leaders and countries in childish images. He recognized how regressed Europe and Great Britain were, calling Chamberlain's policy of appeasement a "fairy tale" in his 1957 autobiography.[3] Other themes, such as the family of nations, appear frequently in his work.

Like many others, he saw World War II as a continuation

of World War I. It arrived in 1939, Low said, "after an interval of twenty years for a change of moustache."[4] In the interwar years he was often able to apply that sense of humor to the serious business of international affairs. What follows is a representative sampling of Low's vast output from the 1930s.[5] The images, roughly corresponding to the sequence of chapters above, illustrate some of the central findings of this study and the ability of an exceptional artist to map some of the sources of the inner emotional meanings of his time.

"HOW MUCH WILL YOU GIVE ME NOT TO KICK YOUR PANTS FOR, SAY, TWENTY-FIVE YEARS?"

Commenting on Germany's unopposed remilitarization of the Rhineland one week before, Low played with the double meaning of "Stand Together." He showed how the policies of nations can be as self-defeating as the actions of individuals, while implying that if they only banded together the cowering Allies could easily resist the bully Hitler.

First published in the *Evening Standard* on 13 March 1936

CONFERENCE TO DECIDE WHETHER EVERYONE SHALL PULL TOGETHER.

With Hitler in power for only a few months, the numerous stresses of the interwar years—diplomatic crises, threats of war, the danger of economic chaos—continued to set countries adrift in what felt like tumultuous seas. The emotional result was disorientation, irrational thinking, and feelings of powerlessness.

First published in the *Evening Standard* on 12 June 1933

DO STUFFED ANIMALS MAKE GOOD GIFTS FOR NERVOUS CHILDREN?

Regressive images, including Peace as a young child, appeared long before the advent of Hitler, with the nationalisms of Germany, Italy, Britain, France and the U.S. producing feelings of a world peopled by threatening adults aggressively brandishing devouring monsters—if only in the form of terrifying toy animals.

First published in the *Evening Standard* on 8 December 1927

PLAYTIME IN THE EUROPEAN NURSERY.

Two months after the World Disarmament Conference ended in failure, Low played with the double meaning of "Blocs," as Europe's statesmen—now regressed to the level of small children—are in danger of tumbling the unbalanced world they have made onto their own heads.

First published in the *Evening Standard* on 20 July 1934

THE CONFERENCE EXCUSES ITSELF.

With the failed Disarmament Conference adding to the long-term stressors of the interwar years, childhood terrors were no longer symbolized as frightening stuffed animals but became fantasies of countries as dangerous biting and devouring monsters, which, for good measure, project their own aggressive feeling onto the peaceful peoples of the world.

First published in the *Evening Standard* on 23 May 1934

"EUROPE CAN LOOK FORWARD TO A CHRISTMAS OF PEACE." — Hitler

On 10 October 1938, with German troops occupying the Czech Sudetenland, Low criticized the Munich Agreement, signed ten days earlier, by showing how the absence of "adults" from the Family of Nations had allowed the trickster, Hitler-as-St. Nicholas, to abduct Europe's newborn states from the safety of the British–French family bed.

First published in the *Evening Standard* on 10 October 1938

STEPPING STONES TO GLORY.

The deep sense of shame following the 1938 Munich Agreement was not new. Many in the Allied countries had long experienced giving in to Hitler's demands as intolerable humiliations. Months after Germany's 1936 march into the Rhineland, Low reminded his readers that Hitler's contemptuous quest to become "Boss of the Universe" was aided by the Allies who provided a red-carpet treatment on their own backs. These images fed the messages that Allied obeisance could continue for some time to come.

First published in the *Evening Standard* on 8 July 1936

"SORRY, BUT WE DON'T WANT TO BURN OUR FINGERS."

Symbolically representing repressed emotions actually exploding or threatening to explode into consciousness, images of volcanic eruptions began to show up frequently in 1938 and 1939. Here, nine days after Hitler seized Austria, Chamberlain, who began to use the word "volcano" more and more in his speeches, letters, and diary, suicidally rejects Litvinov's offer of Soviet aid.

First published in the *Evening Standard* on 21 March 1938

WOULD YOU OBLIGE ME WITH A MATCH PLEASE?

Chamberlain, who had sounded alarms of a suicidal embrace seven years earlier, appointed the appeaser Halifax as Foreign Secretary on 20 February 1938. Three weeks later both capitulated to Hitler's seizure of Austria with scarcely a word. Here Low showed Chamberlain distracted from admiring his own image long enough to provide a polite Mussolini/Hitler with the means of his own destruction. As Rebecca West later said: "the instrument of our suicidal impetus {was} Neville Chamberlain."

First published in the *Evening Standard* on 25 February 1938

LITTLE ADOLF TRIES ON THE SPIKED MOUSTACHE.

Low was but one of many who sensed that a major role for the Führer in the fantasy life of Germany and Europe was to be that of an out-of-control child. He depicted Hitler here, two and a half years before he came to power, as a tiny would-be Kaiser competing to win Mother Germania's approval.

First published in the *Evening Standard* on 27 September 1930

LEAP YEAR—THE WRONG WAY TO PROPOSE.

Instead of resisting Germany's march into the Rhineland on 7 March 1936, France, the Great Power that did not act like one, seeks refuge in the arms of its cowering "protectors" Britain and the Soviet Union. Hitler (as the child Cupid) fires arrows from his toy gun, while Mother Germania, now a blustering Brunhilda, brandishes a handful of Manged Treaties in the faces of the frightened Allies.

First published in the *Evening Standard* on 30 March 1936

THE MAN WHO HEARS VOICES.

The Czech Crisis began to reach its zenith with Hitler's "sudden" demand—five days after The Times *of London had first suggested it—that the Sudetenland should be ceded to Germany. Low saw Hitler's aggression as prompted in part by a combination of feedback from his own words and encouraging cues coming from the Great Powers.*

First published in the *Evening Standard* on 12 September 1938

"HE ONLY WANTS TO LIE DOWN WITH YOUR LAMB"

Two days before Hitler demanded the Sudetenland, Low depicted a devouring Nazi monster licking its chops in anticipation of dining on the sacrificial lamb Czeco Democracy, an innocent childlike victim whose isolated and helpless leader Beneš can do little more than impotently comfort it.

First published in the *Evening Standard* on 10 September 1938

"EXCUSE ME, BUT DID YOU HEAR A PIERCING SCREAM?"

Two months following The Munich Agreement, Low was one of its many critics who predicted the coming end of the Czeck state. In his version, the British Rescue Team arrives too late—in an image used widely at the time—after Czechoslovakia had been thrown to the wolves.

First published in the *Evening Standard* on 2 December 1938

"IT'S QUEER HOW YOU REMIND ME OF SOMEONE, JOSEF..."

Many believed that Hitler's murder of the S.A. leadership in June 1934—The Night of the Long Knives—had inspired Stalin's purges of the mid-to-late 1930s. When Stalin copied Hitler, some thought, as in this Low cartoon, that he was becoming Hitler, a view shared by Mussolini and others. It also sent the message that Communism was "not anti-fascist in principle," a necessary step toward the Nazi-Soviet Pact of August 1939 which helped unleash World War II.

First published in the *Evening Standard* on 28 August 1936

ALL BEHIND YOU, WINSTON

Churchill, not yet universally admired, replaced Chamberland as Prime Minister on 10 May 1940. Low's cartoon four days later called for national solidarity, but also reflected the sense of calm, relief, and business-like determination that had arrived with the outbreak of war eight months before. Britain, like other members of the Family of Nations, was united in the task of carrying out the last phase of the suicidal embrace as the immense killing frenzy of World War II began in earnest.

First published in the *Evening Standard* on 14 May 1940

NOTES

The quotation following the Table of Contents is from Rebecca West, *Black Lamb, Grey Falcon. A Journey Through Yugoslavia* (Harmondsworth, Eng.: Penguin Books, 1994), p. 27, first published in 1940.

PREFACE

1 James L. Stokesbury, *A Short History of World War II* (New York: William Morrow, 1980), the quotation is from the HarperCollins Perennial edition (2001), p. 54. D.C. Watt, *How War Came. The Immediate Origins of the Second World War, 1938-1939* (New York: Pantheon, 1989), pp. 2-3. Richard Overy and Andrew Wheatcroft, *The Road to War* (New York: Random House, 1990), p. xii. Ian Kershaw, *Hitler 1936-1945: Nemesis* (New York and London: W.W. Norton, 2000), p. 224.

2 Jean-Paul Sartre, *Nausea*, translated by Lloyd Alexander (Cambridge, Mass.: Robert Bentley, 1979), p. 4.

3 *The Historikerstreit* can be followed in Charles S. Maier, *The Unmasterable Past. History, Holocaust, and German National Identity* (Cambridge Mass.: Harvard University Press, 1989), and Richard J. Evans, *In Hitler's Shadow: West German Historians and the Attempt to Escape from the Nazi Past* (New York: Pantheon, 1989). For German historiography since 1990, see Bill Niven, *Facing the Nazi Past. United Germany and the Legacy of the Third Reich.* (London and New York: Routledge, 2002). Ernst Nolte, *Der Europäische Bürgerkrieg, 1917-1945. Nationalsozialismus und Bolshewismus* (Berlin: Propyläen Verlag, 1987).

I FEELINGS AND FOREIGN AFFAIRS

1 Chamberlain, 6 December 1931, quoted in Keith Feiling, *The Life of Neville Chamberlain* (Hamden, Conn.: Anchor Books, 1970), p. 201.

2 John Harvey, ed., *The Diplomatic Diaries of Oliver Harvey, 1937-1940* (New York: St. Martin's, 1970), p. 187; André François-Poncet, *The Fateful Years: Memoirs of a French Ambassador in Berlin, 1931-1938* (New York: Harcourt, Brace, 1949), p. 273.

3 The "Baltic Sea," Ambassador Kennedy to Department of State, 27 June 1939, *Foreign Relations of the United States* (hereinafter cited as *FRUS*), 1939, I, 276, quoted in William Rock, *Appeasement on Trial* (Hamden, Conn.: Archon Books, 1966), p. 278; Bonar Law to Poincaré "go to hell," Robert Rhodes James, ed., *Memoirs of a Conservative: J.C. Davidson's Memoirs and Papers, 1910-37* (London, 1969), p. 143, quoted in Anthony Adamthwaite, *France and the Coming of the Second World War* (London: Frank Cass, 1977), p. 22; Paul Schmidt, *Hitler's*

Interpreter (New York: Macmillan, 1951), p. 151; the British official on Poincaré as "Frog" was Vansittart, quoted in J. Cairns, "A Nation of Shopkeepers in Search of a Suitable France," *The American Historical Review*, Vol. 79, no. 1 (1974), 722-723; Daladier on Chamberlain, reported by U.S. Ambassador Bullit, O.H. Bullit, ed., *For the President. Personal and Secret Correspondence between Franklin D. Roosevelt and William C. Bullit* (London, Boston: Houghton Mifflin, 1972), pp. 309-310; Daladier as drinker, Sir Alexander Cadogan, *The Diaries of Sir Alexander Cadogan*, David Dilkes, ed. (New York: G.P. Putnam's Sons, 1972), entry for 24 November 1938, p. 126. Galeazzo Ciano, *Ciano's Hidden Diary, 1937-38* (London: Methuen, 1952; New York: E.P. Dutton & Co., 1953), p. 165, entry for 28 September 1938, states that during the Czech Crisis British Ambassador Perth's "face quivers and his eyes are red....he bursts into a sobbing laugh and rushes off to his embassy." For the *tono fascisto*, Felix Gilbert, "Ciano and his Ambassadors," *The Diplomats, 1919-1939*, Gordon Craig and Felix Gilbert eds. (Princeton: Princeton University Press, 1953), p. 523, reissued in paperback in 1994. (All citations used in the current study are from the original 1953 hard-cover edition.)

4 Gains Post, Jr., *Dilemmas of Appeasement. British Deterrence and Defense, 1934-1937* (Ithaca and London: Cornell University Press, 1993), p. 341. Gerhard Weinberg, *The Foreign Policy of Hitler's Germany*, 2 vols. (Chicago: University of Chicago Press, 1970-1980), II, *Starting World War II*, 369. The raw data alone refutes Weinberg. See Ian Kershaw, *Hitler 1889-1936: Hubris* (New York: W.W. Norton, 1998), which lists 13 pages of "rages" in its index (p. 817), while the index to Kershaw's *Hitler: Nemisis*, lists 24 pages of "rages", p. 1095 (to which should be added other indexed categories, such as Hitler's "profound contempt for human existence").

5 Raymond J. Sontag, *A Broken World, 1919-1939* (New York: Harper & Row, 1971), p. 250. D.C. Watt, "The Historiography of Appeasement," *Crisis and Controversy: Essays in Honor of A.J.P. Taylor*, Alan Sped and Chris Cook, eds. (New York: St. Martin's, 1976), p. 124. Uri Bialer, *The Shadow of the Bomber: The Fear of Air Attack and British Politics 1932-1939* (London: Royal Historical Society, 1980). William M. Reddy, *The Navigation of Feelings: A Framework for the History of Emotions* (New York: Cambridge University Press, 2001) points out that the implicit Cartesian duality in the accounts of historians means that rational explanations almost always take precedence over emotions. Gordon Craig and Alexander George, *Force and Statecraft*, 3rd ed. (New York and Oxford: Oxford University Press, 1995), p. 61. There are only a few psychological studies of diplomacy: they include the non-psychoanalytic Caroline E. Playne, *The Neuroses of the Nations* (London: G. Allen & Unwin, 1925); Judith M. Hughes, *Emotion and High Politics: Personal Relations at the Summit in Late Nineteenth-Century Britain and*

Germany (Berkeley, Los Angeles, London: University of California Press, 1983); and the more theoretical, Vamik D. Volkan, *The Need to Have Enemies and Allies. From Clinical Practice to International Relationships* (Northvale, N.J.: Jason Aronson, 1988). See also Vamik D. Volkan, Joseph V. Montville, and Demetrious A. Julius, eds., *The Psychodynamics of International Relations*, 2 vols. Vol. I, *Concept and Theories*; Vol. II, *Unofficial Diplomacy at Work* (Lexington, Mass.: Lexington Books, 1990-1991).

6 Pierre Renouvin, *World War II and Its Origins: International Relations, 1929-1945* (New York: Harper & Row, 1969), pp. 3-4. Gordon Wright, *The Ordeal of Total War, 1939-1945* (New York: Harper and Row, 1968), p. 1.

7 For the particulars on why history needs psychology see: Peter Gay, *Freud for Historians* (New York and Oxford: Oxford University Press, 1985); William Langer, "The Next Assignment," *American Historical Review*, Vol. LXII, no. 2 (January, 1958), 283-304; Thomas Kohut, "History as Psychohistory," *The American Historical Review*, Vol. 91, no. 2 (April, 1986), 336-354; and Carl N. Degler, "Should Historians Be Skeptical About Using Psychological Methods?" *The Chronicle of Higher Education*, May 7, 1987, p. 80. Recent issues of the *American Historical Review* suggest that some historians are showing a little more interest in emotions: Barbara H. Rosenwein, "Worrying about Emotions in History," Vol. 107, no. 3 (June, 2002), 821-845; Ruth Leys' review of William Ian Miller, *The Mystery of Courage* (Cambridge, Mass.: Harvard University Press, 2000), Vol. 106, no. 5 (December, 2001), and Barbara Rosenwein's review of Reddy's book *The Navigation of Feelings* (cited above in endnote 4), in Vol. 107, no. 4 (October, 2002), 954, although the last three issues of the *AHR* have avoided emphasizing any emotions. See also Peter N. Stearns with Carol Z. Stearns, "Emotionology: Clarifying the History of Emotions and Emotional Standards," *American Historical Review*, Vol. 90, no. 4 (October 1985), 813-36, and Peter N. Stearns and Carol Z. Stearns, *Emotion and Social Change: Toward a New Psychohistory* (New York: Holmes & Meier, 1988). For the early development of psychological history see William J. Gilmore, ed., *Psychohistorical Inquiry: A Comprehensive Research Bibliography* (New York: Garland: 1984), and Henry Lawton, *The Psychohistorian's Handbook* (New York; Psychohistory Press, 1988) for an introduction to some early scholarship. Psychological history has been published in various scholarly journals, including the *American Historical Review* and *The Journal of Interdisciplinary History*, whose web page states, among other things, that the journal is "the home for quantitative and demographic articles in psychohistory." Specialized periodicals include: *The Journal of Psychohistory* (1973-present) published by the Institute for Psychohistory; *The Psychohistory Review* (1976-2000), published by the Group for the Use of Psychology in History, an affiliate of the American Historical Association; *Political*

Psychology: Journal of the International Society of Political Psychology (1980-present); *Mind and Human Interaction*, published by the Center for Mind and Human Interaction at the University of Virginia (1991-present); the *Jahrbuch für Psychohistoriche Forschung*, (1987-present), a publication of the Deutsche Gesellschaft für Psychohistorische Forschung; and *Clio's Psyche* (1994 –present), a quarterly published by the Psychohistory Forum. For an early overview of psychological biography, William McKinley Runyan, *Life Histories and Psychobiography. Explorations in Theory and Method* (New York and Oxford: Oxford University Press, 1982). Anthologies of essays are too numerous to cite here. All the writings of Bruce Mazlish are significant, but see in particular *The Leader, the Led, and the Psyche: Essays in Psychohistory* (Hanover and London: Wesleyan University Press/University Press of New England, 1990), pp. 59-76, 127-138, and 249-266. Robert Jay Lifton's numerous works are also important; three specifically related to the current study are Lifton and Eric Markusen, *The Genocidal Mentality: Nazi Holocaust and Nuclear Threat* (New York: Basic Books, 1990), Lifton, *The Nazi Doctors* (New York: Basic Books, 1986), and Lifton and Greg Mitchell, *Hiroshima in America: Fifty Years of Denial* (New York: Putnam's Sons, 1995). For group-fantasy models see Daniel Dervin, *Enactments. American Modes and Psychohistorical Models.* (Madison, Teaneck, N.J.: Fairleigh Dickinson University Press; London: Associated University Presses, 1996). For the role of childhood, Lloyd deMause, ed., *History of Childhood* (New York; Psychohistory Press, 1974), and, for several topic areas, Lloyd deMause, ed., *The New Psychohistory* (New York: Psychohistory Press, 1975). For a theoretical synthesis, Lloyd deMause, *The Emotional Life of Nations* (New York and London: Karnac, 2002), and for a critical symposium on the book, Paul Elovitz, *et al.*, *Clio's Psyche*, Vol. 10, No. 2 (September, 2003), 33-55. See the important work of Peter Loewenberg, *Fantasy and Reality in History* (Oxford: Oxford University Press, 1995), and Peter Loewenberg, *Decoding the Past*, cited below. For an assessment of Loewenberg's studies, David R. Beisel, "Peter Loewenberg's Psychohistories," *The Journal of Psychohistory*, Vol. 27, no. 1 (Summer, 1999), 124-135. For a general introduction to the field, Jacques Szaluta, *La Psychohistoire* (Paris: Presses Universiaires de France, 1987), and his enlarged English edition, *Psychohistory: Theory and Practice* (New York: Peter Lang, 2000). For some of the ways psychological historians think about war, Paul Elovitz, "Perspectives on Teaching About War Making—in 2002 America," *Clio's Psyche* Vol. 9, no. 3 (December, 2002), 125, 140-144, reprinted as "Teaching About War in Bush's 21st Century," {Sympoium Essay, with Replies by David Beisel, Peter Petschauer, Jerrold Atlas, Jennefer Mazza, Jacques Szaluta, Alice Eichholz, Rudolph Binion, and Robert Pois}, *The Journal of Psychohistory*, Vol. 31, no. 1 (Summer, 2003), forthcoming. All of Rudolph Binion's important studies relating to the relevant subjects in this book are cited below and throughout.

8 Hans Seyle, *The Stress of Life* (New York: McGraw Hill, 1978), Leo Goldberger and Shlomo Brenitz, eds., *Handbook of Stress: Theoretical and Clinical Aspects*, 2nd ed. (New York: The Free Press, 1993), and Richard S. Lazarus, *Stress and Emotion: A New Synthesis* (New York: Springer, 1999). For an up-to-date popular survey, see the long article by Erica Goode, "The Heavy Cost of Chronic Stress," *The New York Times*, Science Times, December 17, 2002, F1-F4.

9 Alan Bullock, *Hitler, A Study in Tyranny*, rev. ed. (New York: Harper & Row, 1962), p. 344; Gordon A. Craig, "The German Foreign Office from Neurath to Ribbentrop," *The Diplomats*, p. 426; Alan Bullock, "Hitler and the Origins of the Second World War," *Proceedings of the British Academy*, LIII (1967), reprinted in E. M. Robertson, ed., *Origins of the Second World War* (London: Macmillan, 1971), p. 215.

10 Harvey, *Diaries*, p. 302; Sir Ivone Kirkpatrick, *The Inner Circle* (London: Macmillan, 1957), pp. 113, 102.

11 Bella Fromm, *Blood and Banquets: A Berlin Social Diary* (New York: Harpers, 1942), p. 280; Harvey, *Diaries*, p. 186; Chamberlain's letter of 2 October 1938 quoted in Feiling, pp. 375-377; Keith Middelmas and John Barnes, *Baldwin: A Biography* (New York: Macmillan, 1969), pp. 929-931, 960, 962-943, and also Telford Taylor, *Munich, The Price of Peace* (Garden City: Doubleday & Co., 1979), pp. 535-536. For Stalin's "collapse" Adam B. Ulam, *Stalin, The Man and His Era* (New York: Viking Press, 1973), pp. 536-542, disputed by Anthony Read and David Fisher, *The Deadly Embrace: Hitler, Stalin, and the Nazi-Soviet Pact 1939-1941* (New York and London: W.W. Norton, 1988), p. 643, and by Edvard Radzinsky, *Stalin*, H.T. Willets trans. (New York: Doubleday, 1996), pp. 460-474, who argues unpersuasively that it was a conscious tactic modeled after his hero Ivan the Terrible. Robert Conquest, *Stalin: Breaker of Nations* (New York: Viking, 1991) argues more persuasively for Stalin's "paralysis," pp. 236-239, and Roy Medvedev, *Let History Judge: The Origins and Consequences of Stalinism*, rev. and expanded ed., George Shriver, ed. and trans. (New York: Columbia University Press, 1989) concludes that the evidence confirms that he was "incapacitated," pp. 751-757. Gordon Craig agrees with Alan Bullock that the night of 21 June 1941 was "a rare moment in the life of the Soviet *Vozhd* when he was utterly unhinged," Gordon Craig, "Above the Abyss," *The New York Review of Books*, April 9, 1992, p. 5 {review of Alan Bullock, *Hitler and Stalin: Parallel Lives*, cited below}. On Churchill, Anthony Storr, *Churchill's Black Dog, Kafka's Mice and Other Phenomena of the Human Mind* (New York: Grove Press, 1988), especially pp. 8-9,16-17, 24-25, 32-33.

12 Louis Fischer, *Men and Politics: Europe Between the Two World Wars* (New York: Harper & Row, 1966), pp. 3, 23. Renouvin, pp. 9, 10.

William Shirer, *20th Century Journey: A Memoir of a Life and Times*, Vol. II, *The Nightmare Years, 1930-1940* (Boston and Toronto: Little, Brown, 1984); *Berlin Diary. The Journal of a Foreign Correspondent, 1934-1941* (New York: Alfred A. Knopf, 1941), p. 149. Stefan Zweig, *The World of Yesterday: An Autobiography* (Lincoln and London: University of Nebraska Press, 1964), pp. 400, xxi-xxil. According to David Clay Large, the 1930s have also been called the Pink Decade, the Devil's Decade, the Threadbare Thirties, the Hungry Thirties, the Decade of the Dictators, and by W.H. Auden, the "Low dishonest decade," and the "rotten decade," *Between Two Fires. Europe's Path in the 1930s* (New York and London: W.W. Norton, 1990), pp. 13-14, all of which leads Large to conclude the period "was no oasis of tranquility," p. 14.

13 A.J.P. Taylor, *The Origins of the Second World War* (New York: Atheneum, 1962). Despite some of Taylor's convincing evidence, he made little impact on "official" versions of the story in Germany and elsewhere: see Earl F. Ziemke, "Germany and World War II: The Official History?" *Central European History*, Vol. XII, no. 4 (December, 1983), 398-407; Theodore S. Hamerow, "Guilt, Redemption and Writing German History," *American Historical Review*, Vol. 88, no. 1 (February, 1983), 53-72.

14 A.J.P. Taylor, "Accident Prone, or What Happened Next," *Journal of Modern History*, Vol. 49, no. 1 (March, 1977), 14. The Taylor controversy can be followed in: Wm. Roger Louis, ed., *The Origins of the Second World War: A.J.P. Taylor and His Critics* (New York: John Wiley, 1972); E. M. Robertson, ed., *The Origins of the Second World War* (London: Macmillan, 1971); Keith L. Nelson and Spencer Olin, Jr., *Why War? Ideology, Theory, and History* (Berkeley: University of California Press, 1979), pp. 136-137; and W.H. Dray, "Concepts of Causation in A.J.P. Taylor's Account of the Origin of the Second World War," *History and Theory*, II (1978), 149-174

15 Winston Churchill, *The Second World War*. Vol. I, *The Gathering Storm* (Boston: Houghton Mifflin, 1948), p. xxxiv.

16 Gerhard Weinberg's *Foreign Policy of Hitler's Germany* agrees in various places that the Allies helped Hitler (see my text). See also Gordon Craig, "Prewar Diplomacy in Europe," *The New Republic* (December 9,1981), p. 32; Gordon Craig, *Germany 1866-1945* (New York and Oxford: Oxford University Press, 1978), pp. 673-713; Craig and George, *Force and Statecraft*, pp. 43-86; Simon Newman, *March 1939: The British Guarantee to Poland* (Oxford: Oxford University Press, 1976), p. 6; and Gordon Martel, ed., *The Origins of the Second World War Reconsidered: the A.J.P. Taylor Debate After Twenty-Five Years* (New York: Allen & Unwin, 1986).

II FANTASIES AND FOREIGN AFFAIRS

1 Jose Ortega y Gasset, *History As a System and Other Essays Toward a Philosophy of History* (New York: W.W. Norton, 1941), pp. 54-55.

2 Melanie Klein, *Narrative of a Child Analysis* (New York: Delta, 1975).

3 William Niederland, "Psychogeography: A New Science," unpublished paper; see the account in *Behavior Today*, April 21, 1980, pp. 5-7; Avner Falk, "Border Symbolism," *Psychoanalytic Quarterly*, Vol. 43 (1974), 650-660, and Avner Falk, "Border Symbolism Revisited," *International Review of Psychoanalysis*, Vol. 10 (1983), 1-6.

4 Howard Stein, *Developmental Time, Cultural Space. Studies in Psychogeography* (Norman: University of Oklahoma Press, 1987). Howard Stein and William Niederland, eds., *Maps From the Mind: Readings in Psychogeography* (Norman: University of Oklahoma Press, 1989), which reprints several essays, including those cited in endnote 3 above.

5 Alex Strachey, "Psychological Problems of Nationhood," *The Year Book of World Affairs, 1960* (London: Stevens and Son, 1960), p. 279.

6 Father Jahn quoted by Louis L. Snyder, *German Nationalism: The Tragedy of a People* (Harrisburg: Stackpole, 1952), p. 34.

7 John of Salisbury, *Policraticus, The Statesman's Book* (New York: Frederick Unger, 1979), 60-61, the same passage in *The Portable Medieval Reader*, James Bruce Ross and Mary Martin McLaughlin, eds. (New York: The Viking Press, 1949), pp. 47-48.

8 Winston Churchill, "The Poison Peril from the East," 28 July 1920 *Evening News*, quoted in Martin Gilbert, *Winston Churchill: A Stricken World, 1916-1922* (Boston: Houghton Mifflin, 1975), 417, 419. Winston Churchill, *The Aftermath: The World Crisis—1918-1928* (New York: Macmillan, 1929), pp. 274, 288.

9 Masaryk quoted in R. Bruce Lockhart, *Jan Masaryk: A Personal Memoir* (London: Putnam, 1956), p. 18, quoted by Piers Brendon, *The Dark Valley. A Panorama of the 1930s.* (New York: Alfred A. Knopf, 2000), p. 620. Samuel I. Rosenman, ed., *The Public Papers and Addresses of Franklin D. Roosevelt*, 13 vols. (New York: Russell & Russell, 1938-1950), 1937, 406-411 for the full speech. Several of FDR's advisors claimed credit for the word "quarantine," suggesting the image was subconsciously shared by many: see Benjamin Wells, *Sumner Wells: FDR's Global Strategist* (New York: St. Martin's, 1997), pp. 204-205, where he reprints Sumner Wells' reply to a query from Samuel I. Rosenman in which Wells, convincingly, takes credit.

10 George F. Kennan, *From Prague after Munich: Diplomatic Papers, 1938-1940* (Princeton: Princeton University Press, 1968), pp. xiv-xv.

11 See B.H. Liddel Hart, *The Real War, 1914-18* (London: Faber & Faber, 1930), pp. 89-94, 503. Danzig as "lungs" quoted by Renouvin, p. 155. Richard Overy, *Why the Allies Won* (New York and London: W.W. Norton, 1996), p. 341, n. 19, p. 106.

12 Harvey, *Diaries*, pp. 185, 146.

13 Göring on "appendix," quoted by François-Poncet, p. 257. Chamberlain 3 October 1938, in *Parliamentary Debates, House of Commons*, (hereinafter cited as *Parl. Debs.* H.C.) 5, Vol. 339, 41-42, 45, 47-49.

14 *The Guardian* quoted in Franklin Ried Gannon, *The British Press and Germany, 1936-1939* (Oxford: Clarendon Press, 1971), p. 204. Edmund Ironside, *Time Unguarded: The Ironside Diaries, 1937-1940*, R. Macleod, ed. (New York: David McKay, 1962), p. 62. César Saerchinger, *The Way Out of War* (New York: Macmillan, 1940), pp. 109-110. For the "poison" in Europe's "maimed body," Zweig, p. 127; additionally, the notion of "Europe's" suicide runs throughout his autobiography. Watt calls Chapter Two of his *How War Came* "Preliminaries to Europe's Suicide," p. 11.

15 Gordon A. Craig, "The Historian and the Study of International Relations, " *American Historical Review*, Vol. 88, no. 1 (February, 1983), 8.

16 On Nazi-Deutsch see Victor Klemperer, *The Language of the Third Reich. L T I Lingua Tertii Imperii: A Philologists Notebook,* Martin Brady trans. (London, New Brunswick, N.J.: Athlone Press, 2000), a translation of his *L (Lingua) T (Tertii) I (Imperii): Notizbucheines Philogen* (Leipzig: Reclam, 1957), reprinted in 1996. For survivals of Nazi-Deutsch into the present see Karen Doerr, "German that is Not Taught: How Holocaust Survivors Remember," paper presented at the 29th Annual Conference on the Holocaust and the Churches, Nassau Community College, Garden City, N.Y., March 6-9, 1997. Haushofer quoted by Dan Diner, *Beyond the Conceivable. Studies on Germany, Nazism, and the Holocaust* (Berkeley, Los Angeles, London: University of California Press, 2000), pp. 29, 28. For Hitler's rhetoric see Adolf Hitler, *Mein Kampf*, Ralph Manheim trans. (Boston: Houghton Mifflin, 1971), pp. 398, 155, 329; N.H. Baynes, ed., *The Speeches of Adolf Hitler*, 2 vols. (New York: Oxford University Press, 1942), I, 188; II, 1253, 995. For convenience, Hitler's speeches throughout are cited from this edition. Scholars, of course, will want to consult the standard collection, Max Domarus, ed., *Hitler. Reden und Proklamationen 1932-1945. Kommentiert von einem deutschen Zeitgenossen*, 2 vols. (Neustadt a d. Aisch: Schmidt, 1962).

17 Rudolph Binion, *Hitler Among the Germans* (New York and Amsterdam: Elsevier, 1976), which elaborates on his first published findings in

Rudolph Binion, "Hitler's Concept of Lebensraum: The Psychological Basis," *History of Childhood Quarterly: The Journal of Psychohistory*, Vol. 1, no. 2 (Fall, 1973), 187-215, with a Symposium discussion by seven commentators, 216-258. Germany as maternal object independently corroborated by Richard A. Koenigsberg, *Hitler's Ideology. A Study in Psychoanalytic Sociology* (New York: Library of Social Science, 1975). On ideology, see the too few thoughts of Erik Erikson, *Young Man Luther: A Study in Psychoanalysis and History* (New York: W.W. Norton, 1958), where he argues that ideologies derive from an inner conflict, the need for groups to find leaders to master collective identity crises, p. 22. For the best psychological work on Nazi ideology see Jay Y. Gonen, *The Roots of Nazi Psychology. Hitler's Utopian Barbarism* (Lexington: University Press of Kentucky, 2000).

18 Hitler, *Mein Kampf*, pp. 14, 3, 124.

19 David R. Beisel, "The Group-Fantasy of Early German Nationalism, 1800-1815," *The Journal of Psychohistory*, Vol. 8, no. 1 (Summer, 1980), 1-19, and the Symposium discussion by Boyd Shafer, Louis Snyder, Donald Dietrich, Peter Petschauer, Robert Pois, John Hanson, and the author in *The Journal of Psychohistory*, Vol. 9, no. 3 (Winter, 1982), 321-353. The article reprinted in German as "Kindheit und Staatsidee. Die Gruppenphantasie führen deutschen Nationalismus, 1800-1815," *Jahrbuch der Kindheit: Kinderleben in Geschichte und Gegenwart*, Vol. I. Christian Büttner and Aurel Ende eds. (Weinheim and Basel: Belz Verlag, 1984), 195-208. On the fatherland as feminine, John Lukacs, *The Hitler of History* (New York: Alfred A. Knopf, 1997), p. 60. See also Janine Chasseguet-Smirgel, "Blood and Nation," *Mind & Human Interaction*, Vol. 7, no. 1 (February, 1996), 34, 35.

20 The literature on small groups is enormous. As a beginning, W.R. Bion, *Experiences in Groups* (New York: Ballantine Books, 1974) where he writes: "My impression is that the group approximates too closely, in the minds of the individuals composing it, to very primitive phantasies about the contents of mother's body." p. 147. See also Graham Gibbard, John J. Hartman, and Richard D. Mann, eds., *Analysis of Groups* (San Francisco: Jossey-Bass, 1974).

21 Quoted by Gordon A. Craig, *The Politics of the Unpolitical* (Oxford: Oxford University Press, 1995), p. 132, and quoted by him again in "The Magic Circle," *The New York Review of Books*, December 5, 2002, p. 36 {reviewing Amos Elon's *The Pity of It All: A History of Jews in Germany, 1743-1933*}.

22 It has been that way for at least the last twenty years. Since the current study is not about organic fantasies in the post-World War II era, a few scattered references will have to suffice. For Europe as a whole, the image has been reinforced over the years by such things as Friedrich

Heer's book, *Europa, Mutter der Revolutionen* (Stuttgart: W. Kohlhammer, 1964), and was kept alive, in the mid-1980s, by such headlines as "Europe as Little Old Lady" in a *New York Times* editorial (January 20, 1984, p. A22), and by Michael Howard's lead *New York Times Book Review* of Paul Kennedy's *Rise and Fall of the Great Powers* which contains a cartoon reading: "Britain: She could no longer pay for the control and protection of her imperial possessions. Germany: She failed to achieve her manifest destiny and led the countries into two utterly destructive wars. United States: She now finds herself in the position of Spain and France before her" (January 10, 1988, p. 1). Groups besides countries—and individuals—can serve as maternal images, Thomas Friedman recently calling U.S. troops in Israel a potential "midwife of the Palestinian state" (*The New York Times*, April 3, 2002, A19). A *Times* obituary called Alexander Ledbed a "Midwife of Russian Democracy" (April 29, 2002, A23). On January 23, 2003, p. A1, the *Times* headlined an article about Russian immigrants buying furs as "Embracing Mother Russia, Warmly."

23 Henderson on Czechoslovakia, 22 July 1938, *Documents on British Foreign Policy, 1919-1939*, Third Series, I, No. 534, hereinafter cited as *DBFP*; the London *Times*, 1 April 1939, p. 1; Sir Nevile Henderson, *The Failure of A Mission: Berlin 1937-1939* (New York: G.P. Putnam, 1940), p. 294; for the press, see Gannon, pp. 94-95.

24 Despite several decrees to call it the fatherland, "peasants continued to think of Holy Russia as a goddess, and repeated the proverb, 'Your fatherland is your mother'," Marina Warner, "My Love Has Butter on Her Hair," *The New York Times Book Review*, March 5, 1989, p. 28, {review of Johanna Hubbs, *Mother Russia*}, see Hubbs's full study, *Mother Russia: The Feminine Myth in Russian Culture* (Bloomington: Indiana University Press, 1989); Churchill's words were quoted in the London *Times* from his 11 December 1917 speech at Bedford, *Winston S. Churchill: His Complete Speeches, 1897-1963*, 8 vols. Robert Rhodes James, ed. (New York and London: Chelsea House, 1974), III, 2580; Blum quoted in Gordon Wright, *France in Modern Times* (Chicago: Rand McNally, 1960), p. 484; Courcoural of the Action Française to Pétain quoted in Jacques Szaluta, "Apotheosis to Ignominy: The Martyrdom of Marshal Pétain," *The Journal of Psychohistory*, Vol. 8, no. 2 (Fall, 1980), 438; Austen Chamberlain quoted by Anthony Eden, *The Memoirs of Anthony Eden: Facing the Dictators* (Boston: Houghton Mifflin, 1962), p. 7; the Polish Constitution of 17 March 1921 can be found in Krystyna M. Olszer, ed., *For Your Freedom and Ours: Polish Progressive Spirit from the 14th Century to the Present*, 2nd ed. (New York: Frederick Unger, 1981), p. 196; Victor Dyk quoted in Howard Stein, "Culture and Ethnicity As Group-Fantasies: A Psychohistoric Paradigm of Group Identity," *The Journal of Psychohistory*, Vol. 8, no. 1 (Summer, 1980), 41.

25 Goebbels in *Der unbekannte Dr. Goebbels. Die geheimen Tagebücher 1938*, David Irving, ed. (London, 1995), p. 53, quoted by Kershaw, *Hitler: Nemisis*, p. 72. Sir Orme Sargent was still talking about "rape" in an unpublished letter in December 1946: see Martin Gilbert's handy collection of excerpted documents, *Britain and Germany between the Wars* (London: Longmans, Green, 1964), p. 128.

26 For these repressed infantile fantasies in children see Dorothy Block, *"So the Witch Won't Eat Me: Fantasy and the Child's Fear of Infanticide* (Boston: Houghton Mifflin, 1978). Watson Kirkconnell, *Canada, Europe, and Hitler* (Toronto: Oxford University Press, 1939), p.v. Maurice Baumont, *The Origins of the Second World War*, Simone de Couvreur Ferguson trans. (New Haven: Yale University Press, 1978), p. 3. Eric Ambler, *Cause for Alarm*, in *Intrigue*: *Four Great Spy Novels: Journey Into Fear; A Coffin for Dimitrious; Cause for Alarm; Background to Danger* (New York: Alfred A. Knopf, 1943), p. 367. Despite Ambler's later partial rewrites for the American edition cited here, comparisons with the original 1938 London edition show no change in his metaphorical language, which is also the case for the U.S. edition of the 1938 Ambler novel cited below in Chapter III, endnote 57. See also Peter Lewis, *Eric Ambler* (New York: Continuum), 1990.

27 Daladier's words to Bullitt from *FRUS*, 1939, I, 301-302. Joseph E. Davies, *Mission to Moscow* (New York: Simon & Schuster, 1941), p. 60. Gannon, p. 165. *DBFP*, Third Series, I, 431. *Ibid*. Appendix II, 27 February 1939.

28 Kennan, pp. 40-41. Hitler quoted by Weinberg, *Foreign Policy of Hitler's Germany*, II, 337, and his footnote 87.

29 *DBFP*, Third Series, III, No. 515. Pilsudski from Adam C. Rosé, *La Politique Polonaise entre les Deux Guerres* (Neuchâtel, 1944-45?), p. 46, cited by Anna Cienciala, *Poland and the Western Powers 1938-1939: A Study in the Interdependence of Eastern and Western Europe* (London and Toronto: Routledge & Kegan Paul and University of Toronto Press, 1968), p. 16. Gannon, p. 210. Prince Ernst Rüdiger von Starhemberg, *Between Hitler and Mussolini* (London: Hodder & Stoughton, 1942), p. 26. Paul Reynaud, *In the Thick of the Fight, 1930-1945* (New York: Simon and Schuster, 1955), p. 198. Chamberlain's diary entry quoted by Iain Macleod, *Neville Chamberlain* (New York: Atheneum, 1962), p. 214. For the political cartoons see Svend Bahnsen, ed., *Verdensdram aet in Karkaturen* (Copenhagen: Commodore, 1945), pp. 20,114. For Czechoslovakia, follow the syndicated cartoons of Carghill for the years 1938-1939 in U.S. newspapers like the {Rockland County} *Journal-News*, Nyack, New York, especially during September 1938, and for 31 January 1939 which show that on the local level, not just in the big cities, images and fantasies of international affairs were being circulated

and understood. Other cartoon images of Czechoslovakia can be found in Ernst Herbert Lehmann, ed., *Mit Stift und Gift: Zeitgeschichte in der Karikatur* (Berlin: Carl Stephenson, 1939), especially p. 53, reprinted from the *St. Louis Globe-Democrat*, 7 November 1938.

30 Churchill's words quoted in William Manchester, *The Last Lion, Winston Spencer Churchill: Visions of Glory 1874-1932* (Boston, Toronto: Little, Brown, 1983, p. 689, and in Gilbert, *Churchill*, IV, 441. *The New York Times*, September 19, 1938, p. 1, quoting the *Daily Mail*, quoting Hitler from the 17 September 1938 G. Ward Price interview in the 19 September *Daily Mail*, reprinted in Baynes, II, 1501.

31 Joachim Remak {book review}, *The Journal of Modern History*, Vol. 44, no. 3 (September, 1972), 441. Renouvin, p. 153. Carl Schorske, "Two German Ambassadors: Dirksen and Schulenberg," *The Diplomats*, p. 505. Telford Taylor, *Munich. The Price of Peace* (Garden City: Doubleday, 1979), p. 167.

32 F.G. Stambrook, "'Das Kind'—Lord D'Abernon and the Origins of the Locarno Pact," *Central European History*, Vol. I, no. 3 (September, 1968), 233.

33 Harvey, *Diaries*, pp. 137, 57, 93. Emil Ludwig, *Talks With Mussolini* (Boston: Little, Brown, 1933), p. 156.

34 "Contents," *Foreign Affairs*, Vol. 82, no. 1 (January/February 2003), II. As in endnote 22 above, the current study is not about post-World-War-II fantasy, so only a few examples over the past thirty years will have to suffice. Scattered references include Anthony Burgess in *The New York Times Magazine*: "America is no longer Europe's daughter nor her rich stepmother; she is Europe's sister" (November 7, 1971). Family metaphors are found everywhere, from letters to *Aviation Week and Space Technology* (May 31, 1982, p. 82), to the Op-Ed page (October 8, 1983, p. A 23), and "News Of the Week in Review" section (July 31, 1988, p. 3) of *The New York Times*. A casual glance through recent *Times* editions finds statements such as: "Romania Wooed by the U.S.," (October 23, 2002, p. A 3). On the European Union, "Europe is Jittery as the Wedding Nears," (October 27, 2002, Week in Review, p. 4). On Saudis and Americans, "Can This Marriage Be Saved," (November 1, 2002, p. A 31). Earlier, South Korea and Japan were seen as an "odd couple," (May 12, 2002, p. A 3). Another headline announced: "In Quietly Courting Africa, White House Likes Dowry," (September 19, 2002, p. A 1). *The New Yorker* magazine (June 17 & 24, 2002) called Pakistan "India's estranged younger brother," (p. 47). In the early 1990s, people were saying that the Velvet Revolution had become, for Czechs and Slovaks, the "Velvet Divorce." Iain Bamforth's review of a new edition of Kafka's *Amerika* in *The New York Times Book Review* speaks of the United States as having tried to "make a radical break with its colonial father,

to orphan itself." (Sunday, January 26, 2003, p. 23.) Thomas Friedman speaks of rebuilding post-Gulf War II Iraq as "the mother of long hauls....We just adopted a baby called Baghdad and this is no time for the parents to get a divorce." (*The New York Times*, Week in Review, Sunday May 4, 2003, p. A 13).

35 Henry L. Roberts, "Maxim Litvinov," *The Diplomats*, p. 344.

36 Lynn Hunt, *The Family Romance of the French Revolution* (Berkeley and Los Angeles: University of California Press, 1992), p. xv. Balzac quoted by Ortega y Gasset, p. 55.

37 Robert A. Kann, "Dynastic Relations and European Power Politics (1848-1918)," *The Journal of Modern History*, Vol. 45, no. 3 (September, 1973), 389, 397.

38 Theo Aronson, *Grandmama of Europe: The Crowned Descendants of Queen Victoria* (London: John Murray, 1984), p. xiii.

39 Stephen Hunter, "War Movies: Illusion and Reality," *The Baltimore Sun*, January 18, 1987, Section H, pp. 1-6.

40 Ortega y Gasset, p. 49. Leo Amery, *Parl. Debs.* H.C., 23 October 1935. Lloyd George, *Daily Express*, 17 September 1936, p. 12. Chamberlain's speech in Francis L. Loewenheim, ed., *Peace or Appeasement? Hitler, Chamberlain and the Munich Crisis* (Boston: Houghton Mifflin, 1965), p. 55.

41 Bonnet quoted in Raymond J. Sontag, *A Broken World, 1919-1939* (New York: Harper & Row, 1971), p. 380. Beneš quoted by Reynaud, p. 183. *Documents on German Foreign Policy 1918-1945*, Series D, III, 529 17 February 1938 for Ribbentrop's memo (the German documents hereinafter cited as *DGFP*). Göring to Czech ambassador Vojtech Mastny, cited in Keith Eubank, *Munich* (Norman: University of Oklahoma Press, 1963), p. 28. Hitler to the Czechs, quoted by Reynaud, p. 183.

42 *The Observer* said it is "a family issue within the German race," 6 March 1938, quoted in Gannon, p. 164.

43 D.C. Watt, *Too Serious a Business: European Armed Forces and the Approach of the Second World War* (Berkeley and Los Angeles: University of California Press, 1975), pp. 14, 15.

44 John Toland, ed., *Hitler: The Pictorial Documentary of His Life.* (Garden City, N.Y.: Doubleday, 1978), p. 282 (Toland's incomplete reference for the cartoon is simply "Library of Congress"). Bahnsen, p. 23.

45 Watt, *Too Serious*, pp. 15, 14.

46 Jan Jacobson, "Is There a New International History of the 1920s?"

American Historical Review, Vol. 88, no. 3 (June, 1983), 622. See Arno J. Mayer, *Political Origins of the New Diplomacy, 1917-1918* (New Haven: Yale University Press, 1959), and his *Politics and Diplomacy of Peacemaking: Containment and Counterrevolution at Versailles, 1918-1919* (New York: Alfred A. Knopf, 1967).

47 Letter to Lord Lothian cited by Klemens von Klemperer, "Adam von Trott zu Solz and Resistance Foreign Policy," *Central European History*, Vol. XIV, no. 4 (December, 1981), 357.

48 R.D. Laing, *The Politics of the Family and Other Essays* (New York: Random House, 1972), pp. 8-9.

49 Martin Grotjahn, *Psychoanalysis and the Family Neurosis* (New York: W.W. Norton, 1960), pp. 283, 184, 217, 91, 185, 188, 200, 23, 127, 123, 122, 30-31.

50 Helm Stierlin, *Separating Parents and Adolescents: A Perspective on Running Away, Schizophrenia, and Waywardness*, rev. ed. (Northvale, N.J.: Jason Aronson, 1981), and Helm Stierlin, *Psychoanalysis and Family Therapy: Selected Papers* (Northvale, N.J.: Jason Aronson, 1977). For children enacting the unconscious wishes of their parents, see also the work of Adelaide Johnson on super-ego lacunae, David B. Robinson, ed., *Experience, Affect, and Behavior. Psychoanalytic Explorations of Adelaide McFadyn Johnson* (Chicago: Chicago University Press, 1969).

III GREAT BRITAIN

1 Kirkpatick, *Inner Circle*, p. 132.

2 *Ibid*. pp. 137-139.

3 James J. Barnes and Patience P. Barnes, *Hitler's* Mein Kampf *in Britain and America: A Publishing History 1930-39* (Cambridge, Eng.: Cambridge University Press, 1980), p. 17 for sales, p. 18 for reviews, and p. 49 for the Prime Ministers. Eubank says: "Chamberlain did not read *Mein Kampf* until after his return from Munich," and "Henderson had not read *Mein Kampf* until appointed to Berlin as ambassador in 1937," *Munich*, pp. 17, 18.

4 Wheeler Bennet, *Disarmament Deadlock*, p. 249. *The Observer*, 2 June 1935. Vansittart's warnings can be followed from his papers, amply quoted in Ian Colvin, *Vansittart in Office* (London: Victor Gollancz, 1965), throughout, p. 35 for the quotation from 7 April 1934. Five articles on Vansittart have been published in a recent issue of the journal *Diplomacy and Statecraft*, Vol. 6, no 1. Eden's words, 25 March 1936, CAB 23/83, quoted in *Neville Thompson, The Anti-Appeasers: Conservative Opposition to Appeasement in the 1930s* (Oxford: Clarendon Press, 1971), p. 108. For a historiographical overview of much

of the major scholarly literature to 1993 see Robert J. Caputi, *Neville Chamberlain and Appeasement* (Selinsgrove: Susquehanna University Press; London: Associated University Press, 2000).

5 Eden, 25 March 1936, CAB 23/83, quoted in Thompson, p. 108. Churchill, 26 March 1936, *Parl. Debs.* H.C., 5, 1523-30, and *Complete Speeches*, VI, 5720.

6 Ironside, p. 49. Winston Churchill, *The Gathering Storm* , reprints his press statement, p. 238. For the "bitter cup," Churchill, 5 October 1938 House of Commons, *Complete Speeches*, VI, 6013. For Nicolson, Tawney (in the *Manchester Guardian*), and Grenfell statements see the quotations in Gilbert, *Britain and Germany Between the Wars*, pp. 141,123, 126. Chamberlain to Ida, 15 July 1939, quoted by Beattie, pp. 258-259.

7 Newman, p. 217.

8 Gannon, p. 96.

9 Wiskeman, "Czechoslovakia Prepares," Appendix in *The Europe I Saw*, pp. 246-249, quote from p. 246.

10 Cabinet minutes, 14 September 1938. CAB 23/95, quoted by Newman, p. 92.

11 "British diplomats" quote from Weinberg, *Foreign Policy of Hitler's Germany*, II, 55. One of the journalists who kept sounding warnings was Douglas Reed, *Disgrace Abounding* (London: Jonathan Cape, 1939), p. 60, who, keeping in mind his anti-Semitism, is a valuable source for opinion, feelings, and fantasies. Taylor quote from, *Origins*, p. 72.

12 From the London *Times* archives, quoted by Gannon, p. 289. Brigadier Temperley quoted in Vansittart's memoirs, *The Mist Procession: The Autobiography of Lord Vansittart* (London: Hutchinson, 1958), p. 478, where Vansittart also reveals: "I sent his memorandum to the Cabinet, and to no effect."

13 Quoted in William R. Rock, *Appeasement on Trial. British Foreign Policy and Its Critics, 1938-1939* (Hamden Conn.: Archon Books, 1966), p. 135.

14 Harvey, *Diaries*, pp. 297, 113.

15 Chamberlain Diary entry, 28 July 1938, quoted in Feiling, p. 253. See also Macleod, pp. 176-177. Chamberlain's statement in spring 1934 quoted by Feiling, p. 252, and Macleod, p. 176, and for air force, 1 July 1934, Feiling, p. 253.

16 Chamberlain Diary entry, 29 November 1936, quoted in *Ibid.* p. 272.

Macleod, p. 182. *Ibid.* pp. 188-189.

17 *Ibid.* p. 191.

18 Stephen Roberts, *The House that Hitler Built* (London: Methuen, 1939). Chamberlain's conscious denials quoted by Feiling, p. 328. Statement to Eden on "encirclement" quoted by Harvey, p. 81.

19 Chamberlain's words in March 1935 quoted in *Ibid.* p. 256.

20 Chamberlain letter of 13 March 1938, quoted in *Ibid.* pp. 341, 342; on Schuschnigg, Chamberlain Diary entry quoted in *Ibid.*, p. 337, the same statement is quoted from the very long Diary entry, 19 to 27 February 1938, reprinted in Macleod, p. 214. Chamberlain Cabinet minutes quoted by Newman, *March 1939*, p. 124.

21 Henderson Braddick, *Germany, Czechoslovakia and the "Grand Alliance" in the May Crisis, 1938*, University of Denver Monograph Series in World Affairs, Vol. 6, no. 2 (Denver: University of Denver, 1968-1969).

22 Feiling, pp. 403, Chamberlain letter of 16 January 1938, quoted in *Ibid.* p. 323. On Halifax, Harvey, *Diaries,* p. 121. Feiling, p. 322. For Chamberlain's statement on Germany, 28 May 1938, *Ibid.* p. 354.

23 Calls for Grand Alliance in press, Gannon, p. 13. *News Chronicle*, 14 March 1938, Editorial, p. 1, quoted by Gannon, p. 158. Vyvyan Adams, *Parl. Debs.* H.C., 14 March 1938, Vol. 333, 4-168, quoted by Rock, pp. 53, 56. On the press, *Ibid.* p. 56. On Eden, Harvey, *Diaries*, p. 185. On encirclement, *Ibid.* p. 283.

24 On undermining disarmament, Lord Londonderry, *Ourselves and Germany* (London: Robert Hale, 1938), pp. 47-48. Wheeler-Bennett, *Disarmament Deadlock*, p. 164. Low, *Cartoon History*, p. 7.

25 On the many ways in which the League was sabotaged see Thompson, *Anti-Appeasers*, p. 66. Lothian to Lloyd George, quoted in Gilbert, *Britain and Germany*, p. 33. Parliamentary Debates on 6 May 1936 were filled with anti–League statements. Harvey's memo to Secretary of State, 7 June 1938, Harvey, *Diaries*, p. 130. Reed, *Disgrace*, p. 108. Harvey, *Diaries*, p. 265. Thompson, p. 38. On Peace ballot see Sontag, *A Broken World*, p. 251. Alfred Duff Cooper, *Old Men Forget: The Autobiography of Duff Cooper Viscount Norwich* (New York: Dutton, 1954), pp. 182-183. See also Hugh Dalton, *Hitler's War: Before and After* (London: Penguin, 1940), pp. 58- 60. Churchill, *Gathering Storm*, p. 104. Rock summarizes the public opinion poll called "The Peace Ballot," p. 9. For the document itself, Dame Adelaide Livingstone, *The Peace Ballot: The Official History* (London: Gollancz, 1935), pp. 49-51, reprinted in the documents section of Anthony Adamthwaite, *The Making of the*

Second World War (London: George Allen & Unwin, 1977), pp. 140-142.

26 Mistrust of Britain, see Craig, "German Foreign Office," *The Diplomats*, p. 424. Harvey, *Diaries*, pp. 74, 76, 68. Robert Dallek, *Franklin D. Roosevelt and American Foreign Policy, 1932-1945* (New York: Oxford University Press, 1979), p. 156.

27 Chamberlain entry, 26 March 1939, Chamberlain letter to Mrs. Morton Price, 16 January 1938 in Feiling, pp. 403, see also p. 323. For Halifax see Harvey, *Diaries,* p. 121. Feiling, pp. 322, 354.

28 For over estimation of military strength, Taylor, *Munich,* pp. 985, 989. On caving in, Harvey, *Diaries,* p. 198. See also Watt, *Too Serious*, p. 29.

29 Nigel Nicolson, ed., *Harold Nicolson, Diaries and Letters*, 2 vols. (London; Collins; New York: Atheneum, 1966-1969), I, 249-250.

30 Low, *Cartoon History*, p. 33.

31 Quoted in Rock, pp. 53, 124.

32 Larry William Fuchser, *Neville Chamberlain and Appeasement: A Study in the Politics of History* (New York and London: W.W. Norton, 1982), p. 138.

33 Voight's unpublished diary, 19 September 1938, quoted by Gannon, p. 8.

34 Nicolson, Diary entry 19 September 1938, *Diaries*, I, 360, 361. Ironside, Diary entry 20 September 1938, p. 62. For the Vansittart and 4 cheeks quotes, Brendon, p. 626. For Churchill, 5 October 1938, House of Commons, *Complete Speeches* VI, 6011. Attlee to House of Commons, 3 October 1938, quoted in Gilbert, *Britain and Germany*, p. 121. For Rathbone, Mary Stocks, *Eleanor Rathbone* (London: Gollancz, 1950), p. 250. For psychosomatic reactions, Nicolson Diary entry for 20 September 1938, *Diaries*, I, 362, which corroborates Norman Rose, ed., *Baffy: The Diaries of Mrs. Blanche Dugdale, 1936-1947* (London: Valentine, Mitchell, 1973), entries for 20 September-10 October 1938, also cited in Rock, p. 129. For later feelings of humiliation, Churchill, 11 December 1938, at Chingford, *Complete Speeches*, VI, 6050; and Sir Orme Sargent in an unpublished letter from 1946 in Gilbert, *Britain and Germany*, pp. 126-128.

35 Harvey, *Diaries*, pp. 213, 238, 202-203, 208, 218.

36 The {Rockland County} *Journal-News*, Nyack, New York, September 25, 1938, p. 25.

37 Judith Herman, *Trauma and Recovery* (New York: Basic Books, 1992). Bessel van der Kolk, *Post-Traumatic Stress Disorder:*

Psychological and Biological Sequelae (Washington, D.C.: American Psychiatric Press, 1984); Bessel van der Kolk, ed., *Psychological Trauma* (Washington, D.C.: American Psychiatric Press, 1987); and Bessel van der Kolk, Alexander C. McFarlane, and Lars Weisrath, eds., *Traumatic Stress: The Effects of Overwhelming Experience on Mind, Body, and Society* (New York: Guilford Press, 1996). For the history of the diagnosis see Ruth Leys, *Trauma: A Genealogy* (Chicago: Chicago University Press, 2000). Peter Loewenberg, *Decoding the Past: The Psychohistorical Approach*, with a new Introduction by the author (New Brunswick, N.J. and London: Transaction, 1996), p. viii. Binion's works relevant to World War II are cited throughout this study; see also the compulsion for traumatic reliving in his *Frau Lou: Nietzche's Wayward Disciple* (Princeton: Princeton University Press, 1968). For case studies on the question of intergenerational transmissions, individual and collective, see Vamik D. Volkan, Gabriele Ast, and William Greer, Jr., *The Third Reich in the Unconscious: Transgenerational Transmission and Its Consequences* (New York and London: Brunner-Routledge, 2002).

38 Jonathan Gathorne-Hardy, *The Rise and Fall of the British Nanny* (London: Hodder and Stoughton, 1972), p. 19.

39 Randolph S. Churchill, *Winston Churchill*, Vol. I, *Youth 1874-1900* (Boston: Houghton Mifflin, 1966), 33-34, 243-247, and for more detail, Martin Gilbert, *Churchill: A Life* (New York: Henry Holt, 1991), pp. 1-17, quote from p. 2. David Dilkes, *Neville Chamberlain, Pioneering and Reform, 1869-1929* (Cambridge: Cambridge University Press, 1984), p. 16.

40 John Chandos, *Boys Together. English Public Schools, 1800-1864* (New Haven and London: Yale University Press, 1984).

41 *Ibid*. pp. 224, 226-235, 80.

42 *Ibid*. pp. 284-311.

43 Ronald Pearsall, *Night's Black Angels: The Forms and Faces of Victorian Cruelty* (London: Hodder and Stoughton, 1975), p. 36.

44 Chandos, p. 37. Pearsall, p. 35.

45 Quoted by Rock, p. 132.

46 Lloyd George quoted by Frank Owen, *Tempetuous Journey* (London: Hutchinson, 1954), p. 737. Landsbury quoted by Gilbert, *Britain and Germany*, p. 102. G. Ward Price, *I Know These Dictators* (London: Harrap, 1937), pp. 21, 117. Londonderry, pp. 21-22. Winston Churchill, *Great Contemporaries* (London: Butterworth, 1937), p. 268.

47 Erich Fromm, *Escape From Freedom* (New York: Avon, 1965).

48 Wyndam Lewis, *Hitler* (London: Chatto & Windus, 1931), p. 202. Arnold Wilson, *Walks and Talks Abroad* (Oxford: Oxford University Press, 1936), p. 96. Lord Winterton in Gilbert, *Britain and Germany*, p. 79. Anthony Eden, *Facing the Dictators*, p. 69.

49 Rumbold quoted by Evelyn Wrench, *Geoffrey Dawson and Our Times* (London: Hutchinson, 1955), p. 334.

50 Dawson in a 23 May 1937 letter to Lord Lothian quoted in Gilbert, *Britain and Germany*, p. 82. A *Guardian* account is quoted in *Ibid*. p. 79. A.L. Rowse, *Appeasement: A Study in Political Decline, 1933-39* (New York: W.W. Norton, 1963), p. 42.

51 Words used in Gannon, p. 76 ("a kind of schizophrenia in the *Manchester Guardian*"), and Rock, p. 117.

52 Paul Addison, "Patriotism under Pressure: Lord Rothermere and British Foreign Policy," *The Politics of Reappraisal*, Gillian Peele and Chris Cook, eds. (New York: St. Martin's Press, 1975), p. 189.

53 The "jamboree" phrase is by Malcolm Muggeridge from the 10 January 1939 *Daily Mail*, quoted by Gannon, p. 1. See Rock on splits in families, and for the comment by Duff Cooper, p. 161.

54 Chamberlain to Ida, 13 November 1938, paraphrased by Fuchser, p. 171, n. p. 221. From the press, as early as 1937 journalist Vernon Bartlett had said war was "inevitable," quoted by Gannon, p. 40. For government memos, Harvey, *Diaries,* 131-132. For diaries, see 16 February 1938 entry in Ironside, p. 49, "I cannot see how war can be avoided in the next two years." See also Harold Nicolson, "Is War Inevitable?" *The Nineteenth Century* CXXVI (July, 1939), 2-4, cited in Rock, p. 328. For Chamberlain's use of the inevitability of war, Taylor, *Origins*, p. 103, and throughout his speeches, letters, and diaries quoted by Feiling, Macleod, and Fuchser.

55 *DGFP*, Series D, VI, Doc. 497, June 1939. As, for example, *New York Times* correspondent Frederick T. Birchall, *The Storm Breaks* (New York, 1940), pp. 344-345, quoted by Rock, p. 188.

56 Foreign Policy Committee Minutes, 27 March 1939, CAB 27/624, quoted by Newman, p. 149.

57 George Orwell, *Coming Up for Air* (New York: Harcourt Brace, 1950), p. 267. Eric Ambler, *Epitaph for a Spy* (New York: Alfred A. Knopf, 1952), pp. 185, 186.

58 Groundless rumors, *DBFP*, Third Series, III, No. 5, 24 January 1939. See Harvey, *Diaries*, pp. 245, 248; and Taylor, *Origins*, p. 200.

59 T. Desmond Williams, "The Historiography of World War II,"

Historical Studies, I (1958), reprinted in Robertson, p. 47.

60 Pointed out by Rock, p. 323.

61 *Manchester Guardian*, 16 September 1936, p. 8, quoted by Gannon, p. 30. *DBFP*, Third Series, II, No. 613.

62 Harvey, *Diaries,* pp. 278, 430.

63 Cadogan, *Diaries*, 20 March 1939, p. 102, and p. 161. Duff Cooper to Halifax, FO 88/315 f57, quoted by Newman, p. 134, footnote 1. Henderson to Halifax, CAC, HLFX, 410. 3. 2., 23 November 1937, quoted by Brendon, p. 616.

64 Johnson, *Viscount Halifax*, p. 520. For Halifax in the Lords, *Parl. Debs*. H.L., 1 September 1939, Vol. 114, 917-19, cited by Rock, p. 312.

65 Feiling, pp. 416, 415, 418.

66 Churchill, 3 September 1939, House of Commons, *Complete Speeches*, VI, 6152.

67 Orwell, *Coming Up for Air*, p. 186. The Chamberlain biographer is Fuchser, p. 126. A list for others in Europe needs to be compiled; in the meantime, Reynaud (who also spoke of volcanic eruptions), 12 November 1938, told a radio audience, "we are going blindfold toward an abyss," and Simone Weil said France waited "passively, like waiting for a tidal wave or an earthquake," Overy and Wheatcroft, pp. 134, 142. G.E.R. Gedye, *Fallen Bastions. Betrayal in Central Europe* (London: Gollancz, 1939). Gannon, pp. 184, 270. Reed, *Disgrace*, p. 241, and 430 for another "volcanic movement." (Also note, parenthetically, Reed's anti-Semitic statements in the next paragraph, p. 430.) Reed's *Insanity Fair* (London: Jonathan Cape, 1938), chapters 45-47 added after the second impression. Churchill, 5 October 1938, House of Commons, *Complete Speeches*, VI, 6013.

68 H.G. Welles on Hitler as a "certifiable lunatic" in the 23 January 1939 *News Chronicle* cited by Norman Mackenzie, *H.G. Wells: A Biography* (New York: Simon and Schuster, 1973), p. 415. Harvey, *Diaries*, pp. 29, 91, 179. On Cabinet members, Ambassador Kennedy to Secretary of State, London, Sept. 13, 1938, *FRUS*, 1938, I, 592, cited by Rock, p. 118. Chamberlain letter of 3 September 1938, quoted in Feiling, p. 357, entry of 11 September 1938, quoted in *Ibid*. p. 360, and Diary entry of 12 March 1937, quoted in *Ibid*. p. 279.

69 *Western Mail* quoted by Rock, p. 283. Kirkpatrick, *Inner Circle*, p.126.

70 Atmosphere of panic, Newman, p. 136. Acceptance of press, Rock, p. 230.

71 Duff Cooper *Old Men Forget*, pp. 259-60, for "bewildered rage." Halifax, *Fullness of Days*, pp. 214-215, also quoted in Rock, pp. 317-318, n. 56, p. 319. And Birkenhead, *Halifax*, pp. 446-447.

72 Churchill, 3 September 1939, House of Commons, *Complete Speeches*, VI, 6152.

IV CHAMBERLAIN AND BRITAIN

1 West, pp. 1121, 1125.

2 Chamberlain, letter of 10 September 1939, quoted in Feiling, p. 417.

3 J. Hermann, "Soviet Peace Efforts on the Eve of World War II," *Journal of Contemporary History*, 15 (1980), 585.

4 D. Dervin, *Enactments: American Modes and Psychohistorical Models.*

5 Feiling, pp. 2, 8.

6 Dilkes, I, 16. Feiling, p. 6.

7 *Ibid.* p. 120.

8 Jose Harris, "Chamberlain for our Time," *London Review of Books*, 20 December {1984}-24 January {1985}, p. 8.

9 Feiling, p. 6.

10 Dilkes, I, 9-10. Peter T. Marsh, *Joseph Chamberlain: Entrepreneur in Politics* (New Haven and London: Yale University Press, 1994), p. 141.

11 Iain Macleod, *Neville Chamberlain* (London: Frederick Muller, 1961), p. 20.

12 Quoted by Dilkes, I, 18-19; Feiling, p. 3; and Fuchser, the latter saying: "The author was unable to locate the source of this statement in the Chamberlain papers," p. 15, n. 6.

13 Feiling, p. 8.

14 "Bullies by nature" from Chamberlain's letter, May 1938, quoted in *Ibid.* p. 350.

15 Chamberlain letter to Sir Ernest Debenham, 2 June 1937, quoted in *Ibid.* p. 294. Chamberlain letter to Hilda, 30 May 1937, quoted in Macleod, p. 199.

16 Feiling, pp. 8, 7, and deference to Austen, Chamberlain Diary entry 19 March 1937, *Ibid.* p. 293. Harvey asked Eden if he thought Chamberlain "was jealous of Austen's career," Harvey, *Diaries*, p. 243.

17 Macleod, p. 35.

18 Feiling, pp. 8, 118.

19 *Ibid.* pp. 121, 143. Fuchser, p. 12.

20 Macleod quoting Chamberlain, p. 203; see pp. 119 ff. for growing contempt for the opposition based on evidence from his letters and diary. Eden quoted by Harvey, *Diaries*, p. 21.

21 Fuchser, p. 173.

22 Alan Beattie, "Neville Chamberlain," *British Prime Ministers in the Twentieth Century*. John P. Mackintosh, ed., Vol. I, *Balfour to Chamberlain* (New York: St. Martin's, 1977), 241.

23 Fuchser, p. 173.

24 Harvey, *Diaries,* pp. 212, 21. Londonderry, FO 800/328, Hal 39/29, quoted in R.A.C. Parker, *Chamberlain and Appeasement: British Policy and the Coming of the Second World War*, (New York: St. Martin's, 1993), p. 4. Harvey, *Diaries*, p.48.

25 Reed, *Disgrace*, p. 169, quoting the London *Times* during the Munich Agreement.

26 Gannon, p. 47. "Gauleiter" and "Führer" quotes from Gedye, pp. 307, 505.

27 Letter of 19 September 1938, quoted in Feiling, p. 366.

28 Fuchser, p. 22.

29 Macleod, p. 74. Feiling, pp. 77-78.

30 Fuchser, p. 21.

31 Macleod, p. 74. Quote from Fuchser, p. 22.

32 C.L. Mowat, *Britain Between the Wars* (Chicago: University of Chicago Press, 1961), p. 203.

33 Nora Newcombe and Jeffrey C. Lerner, "Britain Between the Wars: The Historical Context of Bowlby's Theory of Attachment," *Psychiatry*, Vol. 45 (February, 1982), 8. (Thanks to Brett Kahr for this source.)

34 Beattie, p. 227-228.

35 Colville quoted by Parker, p. 6. Chamberlain quoted by Feiling, p. 118. Harvey's diary on Chamberlain's reception in France, *Diaries,* p. 223.

36 Fuchser, pp. 173, 62 n., 15, 170.

37 The comment on 'major war...minor country" from the documentary film *Munich: The Peace of Paper*, Cate Haste producer and director, Brook Productions for Thames Television, 1988. Gannon, pp. 268, 270.

38 Rock, p. 167.

39 *Ibid*. p. 281. Harvey, *Diaries*, pp. 230-231.

40 Rock, p. 329.

41 Robert J. Wybrow, *Britain Speaks Out, 1937-1987: A Social History As Seen Through The Gallup Data*. (London: Macmillan, 1989), pp. 6, 5. George H. Gallup, ed., *The Gallup Poll: Public Opinion, 1935-1971*, 3 vols. (New York: Random House, 1972), I, 93, for strengthening of resistance to Hitler (Chamberlain's foreign policy was favored by only 24 per cent of the public already on 11 March 1938). For other statistics, George H. Gallup, gen. ed., *The Gallup International Opinion Polls, Great Britain, 1935-1975*, 2 vols. (New York: Random House, 1976), I, 8, 17, 21. For opinion in France, Overy and Wheatcroft, p. 135.

42 Churchill, *Gathering Storm*, p. 347.

43 Taylor, *Origins*, pp. 203-204.

44 Rock, pp. 241, 276.

45 Chamberlain's speech to Women's Conservative Association quoted by Fuchser, p. 125, and Fuchser's observations for Chamberlain's volcano images, *Ibid*. p. 126. For cartoon, Low, *Cartoon History*, p. 35.

46 Cadogan, pp. 94, 96, 97, 100, 101, 104, 105, 201, 127, 122, 190, 132, 105, 121, 112, 160, 112, 104. Chamberlain's letter of 2 October 1938, quoted in Feiling, pp. 375-377.

47 On his speaking of the "two Chamberlain's," Feiling, p. 401. On Trentano, Rock, p. 187, n. 55.

48 Feiling, p. 226. Fuchser, p. 48.

49 *Ibid*. p. 187. Chamberlain, 10 September 1939, quoted in Feiling, p. 417. Fuchser, p. 186. Chamberlain, 10 September 1939, quoted in Feiling, p. 416.

50 On Austen striving to be like his father, Marsh, p. 141.

51 Leo Amery, *My Political Life*, 3 vols. (London: Hutchinson, 1953), III, *The Unforgiving Years*, 324.

52 *DBFP*, Third Series, VII, 740.

V HITLER AND GERMANY

1 César Saerchinger, *The Way Out of War* (New York: Macmillan, 1940), p. 99.

2 The "early Nazi" is Otto Strasser, *Hitler and I*, trans. Gwenda Davis and Eric Mosbachen (Boston: Houghton Mifflin, 1940), pp. 64-65. Quote from Walter Langer, *The Mind of Adolf Hitler: The Secret Wartime Report* (New York and London: Basic Books, 1972), p. 205. The other quotes are from Binion, *Hitler Among the Germans*, pp. 50, 53, 114, 125, 118, 126, 127.

3 Erich Fromm, *The Anatomy of Human Destructiveness* (Greenwich, Conn.: Fawcett, 1975), p. 416.

4 Quoted by John Toland, *Adolf Hitler* (New York: Ballantine, 1977), p. 12, where Toland references "CIC interview with Paula Hitler, June 5, 1946. U.S. Army Military Research Collection, Carlisle Barracks, Pa.," no page (his note p. 926). Interview with "Paula Hitler, U.S. Army Intelligence Service Interrogation Report, Berchtesgaden 26 May 1945, National Archives" is the citation in psychiatrist Fritz Redlich, *Hitler: Diagnosis of a Destructive Prophe*t (New York: Oxford University Press, 1999), p. 384 n. 46, the same source for Paula Hitler quoted in Robert Waite, *The Psychopathic God, Adolf Hitler* (New York: Basic Books, 1977), p. 134, from the Hitler Source Book, National Archives, Washington, D.C., p. 925, cited as "interviews in OSS Source Book," 924, in Waite's Notes, p. 448 n. 22. As outlined in the text, the OSS Source Book must generally be used with caution, but judging by the number of times these passages have been cited by historians, it is widely accepted as a valid source for Hitler's regular thrashings. For virtually all the primary evidence on beatings, Kershaw, *Hitler: Hubris*, pp. 606-607, n. 60-64.

5 See below, endnotes 14, 17, and 20.

6 Quoted by Waite, *Hitler*, p. 134 from OSS Source Book, 924, Waite's n. 22 on p. 448. Quoted from the same source by Stierlin, *Hitler*, p. 25. Although Bridget Hitler's *The Memoirs of Bridget Hitler*, Michael Unger ed. (Dallas, TX: Duckworth, 1979) is virtually worthless for the historian—it is notoriously unreliable, contains several lies and many distortions, and must be carefully weighed before one can even think of citing it—it does contain several factual statements which corroborate Alois's harshness and violent temper, among them the report that he once "grabbed Adolf by the throat and held him against a tree until he half choked. Adolf dropped in a faint….For a week Adolf was more dead than alive," p. 170, which sounds like the same anecdote cited from the OSS Source Book above. (See Waite's discussion on the *Memoir's* unreliability, not for this but for other issues, in his section on "A Note on Spurious Sources" *Hitler*, pp. 432-433, and also Kershaw, *Hitler:*

Hubris, n. 235 on pp. 705-706, who likewise mentions the source only in regard to another matter and shies away from listing it in his bibliography.)

7 Toland, *Hitler*, p. 9, cites OSS Source Book, 924, 913; Toland's note on his p. 926 refers probably to Bridget's testimony, as quoted in text above and as accepted by Waite from the OSS Souce Book but not cited by Toland as such.

8 Waite, *Hitler*, p. 134, quoting Jetzinger's interview with Mayerhofer (see below), Waite n. 20, p. 448.

9 Franz Jetzinger, *Hitler's Youth*, Lawrence Wilson, trans. (Westport, Conn.: Greenwood, 1976), p. 51.

10 Toland, *Hitler*, pp. 12-13, quotes Zoller (below, n.11), but for some reason cites the French edition, *Douze ans auprès d'Hitler* (Paris: Julliard, 1949), p. 55.

11 Waite, *Hitler*, p. 137, quotes Albert Zoller, ed., *Hitler Privat: Erlebnisbericht seiner Geheimsekretärin* (Düsseldorf: Droste Verlag, 1949), p. 46 (See Waite's n. 28, p. 449).

12 Jetzinger, p. 61.

13 For those who feel Hitler can never be understood, see Ron Rosenbaum, *Explaining Hitler: The Search for the Origins of His Evil* (New York: Random House, 1998). For the television program on Hitler's youth, my text quotes Richard Bernstein, "The New Refrain: Adolf, We Hardly Knew Ye," *The New York Times*, News of the Week in Review, August 25, 2002, p. 3. See the news account, with the same themes, in *The New York Times*, August 20, 2002, The Arts Section, pp. E1, E3. Lukacs, *Hitler of History*, p. 55. Kershaw, *Hitler: Hubris*, p. 13.

14 Hitler, *Mein Kampf*, pp. 31-31. Among those authorities who have been convinced this passage reflects Hitler's own childhood are: G.M. Kurth, "The Jew and Adolf Hitler," *Psychoanalytic Quarterly*, Vol. 16 (1947), 11-32; Walter C. Langer, *The Mind of Adolf Hitler: The Secret Wartime Report* (New York and London: Basic Books, 1972), pp. 142-145; Waite, *Hitler*, pp. 162-168 (although his linking it to "Primal Scene Trauma" seems unconvincing); and two other authorities cited below, Alice Miller, *For Your Own Good. Hidden Cruelty in Child-Rearing and the Roots of Violence*, Hildegarde and Hunter Hannum, trans. (New York: Farrar, Straus, Giroux, 1983), p. 161; and Stierlin, *Hitler*, p. 67.

15 Bradley F. Smith, *Adolf Hitler: His Family, Childhood and Youth* (Stanford: Hoover Institution Press, 1967), p. 42 .

16 Waite, *Hitler*, pp. 168, 140.

17 Alice Miller, *The Drama of the Gifted Child* (New York: Basic

Books, 1990), originally titled *Prisoners of Childhood* (New York: Basic Books, 1981). Miller's work on Hitler and German childhood is found in *For Your Own Good*, pp. 181, 180-183. See also Miller's other relevant works: *Banished Knowledge. Facing Childhood Injuries* (New York: Doubleday, 1990); *Breaking Down the Walls of Silence* (New York: Dutton, 1991); and *The Untouched Key: Tracing Childhood Trauma in Creativity and Destructiveness* (New York: Doubleday, 1990).

18 E. Bloch, "My Patient, Hitler," *Colliers Magazine*, 15 March 1941, pp. 35-37, 22 March 1941, 69-73, quotes from p. 35. Bloch, "The Autobiography of Obermedizinalrat Eduard Block," *Leo Baeck Institute Year Book XLVII*, 2002, p. 226. Kershaw, *Hitler: Hubris*, p. 12.

19 *Ibid.* p. 33. Margaret Mahler, Anni Bergman and Fred Pine, *Symbiosis and Individuation: The Psychological Birth of the Human Infant* (New York: Basic Books, 1975). Stierlin, *Hitler*, p. 33.

20 For some statistics and regional variations see Jeffrey S. Richter, "Infanticide, Child Abandonment, and Abortion in Imperial Germany," *The Journal of Interdisciplinary History*, Vol. 28, no. 4 (Spring, 1998), 511-551. For the sweep of German childhood, part of which covers the nineteenth century, see deMause, *Emotional Life of Nations*, pp. 184-201, with the exception of his generalizing from Raffael Scheck, "Childhood in German Autobiographical Writings, 1740-1820," The *Journal of Psychohistory*, Vol. 15 (1987), 397-422, which stops in 1820 and therefore cannot be extrapolated into the nineteenth and twentieth centuries; likewise for the reproduced image of "German baby being assaulted with an enema," which, even though it correctly depicts one of the many horrors inflicted on German babies in earlier times, cannot be used as a source for the nineteenth and twentieth centuries judging from the style of clothing worn in the picture. For a convincing early overview (also cited by deMause), Aurel Ende, "Battering and Neglect: Children in Germany, 1860-1978," *The Journal of Psychohistory*, Vol. 7, no. 3 (Winter, 1980), 249-279, and Aurel Ende, "Bibliography on Childhood and Youth in Germany from 1820-1978: A Selection," *Ibid.* 281-287. Morton Schatzman, "Paranoia or Persecution: The Case of Schreber," *History of Childhood Quarterly: The Journal of Psychohistory*, Vol. 1, no. 1 (Summer, 1973), 62-88.

21 For an overview see John Wilkes, "Conversation. Ernest R. Hilgard. A Study in Hypnosis," *Psychology Today* (January, 1986), pp. 23-27. For the evidence see Josephine Hilgard, *Personality and Hypnosis. A Study of Imaginative Involvement* (Chicago: University of Chicago Press, 1970). See also Ernest R. Hilgard, *Divided Consciousness: Multiple Controls in Human Thought and Action* (New York: Wiley, 1977). For a theoretical discussion, see Jerrold Atlas, "Understanding The Correlation Between Childhood Punishment and Adult Hypnotizability as It Impacts on the Command Power of Modern Charismatic Leaders,"

The Journal of Psychohistory, Vol. 17, no. 1 (Winter, 1989), 309-318. On Hitler's hypnotic power see Binion, *Hitler*, pp. 121-127.

22 Documentary film, *Heil Hitler! Confessions of a Hitler Youth*, based on *A Child of Hitler* by Alfons Heck, Home Box Office (Round Hill Productions, 1991). David R. Beisel, "Europe's Killing Frenzy," *The Journal of Psychohistory*, Vol. 25, no. 2 (Fall, 1997), 200-211, and David R. Beisel, "Resistance to Psychology in Holocaust Scholarship," *The Journal of Psychohistory*, Vol. 27, no. 2 (Fall, 1999), 124-135 for some of the ways German childhood seems recapitulated in Nazi tortures. Miller, *For Your Own Good*, Preface to the American edition, pp. viii-ix.

23 *Ibid.* p. viii.

24 Adorno, Theodore, *et al.*, *The Authoritarian Personality* (New York: Harper, 1950). Bertran Schaffner, *Fatherland: A Study of the Authoritarianism in the German Family* (New York: Columbia University Press, 1948). Arno Gruen, "Surrendering Identity. Hermann Göring and Rudolf Hess," *Mind and Human Interaction*, Vol. 12, no. 1 (2001), 35-51. Interview with Junge in Gitta Sereny, *The Healing Wound: Experiences and Reflections on Germany, 1938-2001* (New York and London: W.W. Norton, 2001), p. 361. See also the Junge documentary film/oral history, *Blind Spot: Hitler's Secretary*, Andre Heller and Othmar Schmiderer directors, Danny Krausz and Kurt Stocker producers, Sony Picture Classics, 2002. Göring quoted from Joachim Fest, *The Face of the Third Reich: Portraits of the Nazi Leadership* (New York: Pantheon, 1970), p. 75, also quoted by Gruen, p. 43.

25 Peter Loewenberg, "The Psychohistorical Origins of the Nazi Youth Cohort," *American Historical Review*, Vol. 76, no. 4 (December, 1971), 1457-1502, reprinted in Loewenberg, *Decoding the Past*, pp. 240-283.

26 *Hitler's Fatal Attraction*, documentary film, Bill Treharne Jones, producer, BBC, 1989.

27 As father figure for Goebbels, Kershaw, *Hitler: Nemisis*, p. 33. Kindergarten poem printed in J. Noakes and G. Pridham, eds. *Nazism 1919-1945: A History in Documents and Eyewitness Accounts*, 2 vols. Vol. I *The Nazi Party, State and Society, 1919-1939:* Vol. II, *Foreign Policy, War and Racial Extermination* (New York: Schocken Books, 1988), I, 572, hereinafter cited as: Noakes and Pridham (1988), to distinguish it from the other edition (1975) also used in this study. The coloring book quotation is from Toland, *Hitler: Pictorial*, p. 224.

28 Omer Bartov, *Mirrors of Destruction: War, Genocide, and Modern Identity*. (Oxford: Oxford University Press, 2000), pp. 26, 25. See also Omer Bartov, *Hitler's Army: Soldiers, Nazis, and War in the Third Reich* (New York: Oxford University Press, 1991), especially Chapter 4.

29 Alison Owings, *Frauen: German Women Recall the Third Reich* (New Brunswick, N.J.: Rutgers University Press, 1993), pp. 172-184. Sereny, *The Healing Wound*, pp. 227-233. Hitler as "sex object" needs a full study. The sensual reactions of several people to him is seen in scenes from Leni Riefenstahl's film *Triumph of the Will* and in statements and behaviors of German women (see below, Chapter VI). Hitler's rationalization for not marrying is well known. For the judgment by George Victor, *Hitler: The Pathology of Evil* (Washington, D.C.: Brassey's, 2000), p. 105, and for a few sexually charged behaviors, pp. 105-106, valid here even though Victor's study needs to be used with caution due to its uncritical acceptance of a notoriously unreliable source, Bridget Hitler's memoirs (see my endnote 6, above), and by his overemphasis on the question of Hitler's father's so-called Jewish paternity, ably disproven by Kershaw, *Hitler: Hubris*, pp. 7-9, and by Kershaw's extensive notes on the subject, pp. 604-605. The issue remains open only if the anti-Nazi press charges that Hitler was secretly Jewish were, for him, more than a nuisance.

30 John Stoessinger, *Why Nations Go to War* (New York: St. Martin's Press, 1978), p. 60.

31 Erik Erikson, *Childhood and Society*, 2nd ed. (New York: W.W. Norton, 1963), p. 337.

32 First published in 1936, *Adolf Hitler: Pictures from the Life of the Führer, 1931-1936* (New York and London: Peebles Press, 1978), p. 3.

33 Quoted in Waite, *Hitler*, p. 212.

34 Martha Dodd, *Through Embassy Eyes* (New York: Harcourt Brace, 1939), p. 211.

35 Kirkpatrick, *Inner Circle*, p. 96.

36 Waite, *Hitler*, p. 48.

37 The documentary film *Hitler's Fatal Attraction* shows Hitler, as he prepares to speak to a large group, remaining quiet for a full minute, after which he begins to talk so gently and slowly as to be almost inaudible, thus creating a physical tension in his listeners as they strain to hear him. Only then does he theatrically rev up over time until he reaches the high intensity crescendo familiar to viewers of The History Channel.

38 Dorothy Thompson, *I Saw Hitler* (New York: Farrar & Rinehart, 1932), p. v.

39 David Low, *Europe Since Versailles* (London: Penguin Books, 1940), pp. 36, 59, 77, 79, 113, 137.

40 T.T. Heine quoted in W. A. Coupe, "Adolf Hitler and the Cartoonists," *History Today*, Vol. 33 (January, 1983), 26: Coupe says that showing

Hitler as an "absurd little fellow" was a way of proving he was not an "active threat," that is, it helped reduce Europe's anxiety. Anti-Nazi cartoons from abroad were published in Germany ostensibly to show the hostility of the world press: E. Hanfstaengel, ed., *Tat gegen Tinte: Hitler in der Karikatur* (Berlin: Verlag der brauner Bucher, 1934).

41 *Life Goes to War*, (New York: Simon and Schuster) p. 32.

42 The psychiatrist was Martin Wangh, cited by Waite, *Hitler*, p. 339.

43 *Ibid.* p. 329 argues that Fallada's book reflected the "despair and bewilderment of the middle class," but the popularity of the book and film suggest a broader identification, including the working and upper classes. See David Stuart Hull, *Film in the Third Reich: Art and Propaganda in Nazi Germany* (New York: Simon and Schuster, 1973), p. 40.

44 Louis Snyder, ed., *Hitler's Third Reich: A Documentary History* (Chicago: Nelson-Hall, 1981), pp. 282, 283. *Hitler's Secret Conversations 1941-1944*, Introduction, "The Mind of Adolf Hitler," by Hugh R. Trevor-Roper (New York: Farrar, Straus and Young, 1953), p., 178. The latter source must be used with care since later editions include some passages which may have been rearranged with some sentences paraphrased or slightly altered, and are associated with those who have openly admired Hitler (see Sereny, pp. 154-155, 190, 227, and 307). Lukacs, on the other hand, finds the source valid and usable: see his discussion of the historiography in *Hitler of History*, pp., n. 47-48; and Kershaw includes it in his List of Works Cited, *Hitler: Hubris*. In any case, for the quotation here, and in my text Chapter VI, endnote 9 for Wilhelm II, Hitler's statements are consistent with his thinking and with like statements he made throughout his life.

45 Quoted by Binion, *Hitler*, p. 132.

46 Baynes, II, 1612, 1609.

47 Waite, *Hitler*, pp. 8-12. For Mickey Mouse at Christmas, Kershaw, *Hitler: Nemisis*, p. 33. On lederhosen, The Editors of Time-Life Books, *The Third Reich: Storming to Power* (Alexandria Va.: Time-Life Books, 1989), p. 19 (no notes).

48 Waite, *Hitler*, pp. 9, 12-13.

49 O.S.S. Source Book, quoted in *Ibid.* p. 12.

50 Kershaw, *Hitler: Nemisis*, p. 229.

51 Hitler, *Mein Kampf*, p. 124.

52 Fromm, *Anatomy*, pp. 411, 420. Erikson, *Childhood and Society*, p. 328.

53 Binion, *Hitler*, pp. 20, 21, 137-138.

54 Waite, *Hitler*, pp. 197, 189, 359-360.

55 Stierlin, *Hitler*, p. 48.

56 *Ibid*. pp. 49, 51.

57 *Ibid*. pp. 45, 59-60.

58 Quoted in Fest, *Hitler*, p. 157.

59 Karl Alexander von Müller quoted by Binion, *Hitler*, pp. 1-2, and Waite, *Hitler*, p. 209.

60 See Binion, *Hitler*, throughout. Fest, *Hitler*, p. 153, quotes him as saying: "When you go through the halls…and everywhere people shout their enthusiasm for you—it is an uplifting feeling, you know."

61 *Ibid*. pp., 171, 179. For his hypersensitivity, Kershaw *Hitler: Hubris*, p. 162, and "pressure to act," *Ibid*. p. 202.

62 Bullock, *Hitler*, p. 105.

63 Toland, *Hitler*, pp. 143, 144.

64 William Carr, *Arms, Autarky, and Aggression: A Study in German Foreign Policy, 1933-1939* (New York: W.W. Norton, 1973), p. 65.

65 Ian Kershaw, *Der Hitler-Mythos Volksmeinung und Propaganda im Dritten Reich* (Stuttgart: Deutsche Verlags-Anhalt, 1980), and Ian Kershaw, *Popular Opinion and Political Dissent in the Third Reich. Bavaria, 1933-1945* (Oxford: Clarendon Press, 1983). M.G. Steinert, *Hitlers Kreig und die Deutchen Stimmung und Haltung der deutschen Bevölkerung im Zweiten Weltkrieg*. (Düsseldorf and Vienna: Econ Verlag, 1970), and in an abbreviated English version, *Hitler's War and the German Public Mood and Attitude During the Second World War* (Athens, Ohio: Ohio University Press, 1977). Bernt Engelmann, *In Hitler's Germany: Everyday Life in the Third Reich* (New York: Pantheon, 1986). Victor Klemperer, *I Will Bear Witness: A Diary of the Nazi Years*, 2 vols. Martin Chalmers trans., Vol. I, *1933-1941*, Vol. II, *1942-1945* (New York: Modern Library, 1998-1999). Eric A. Johnson, *Nazi Terror: The Gestapo, Jews and Ordinary Germans* (New York: Basic Books, 2000). James Scott, *Domination and the Arts of Resistance: Hidden Transcripts* (New Haven: Yale University Press, 1990), pp. 37-38.

66 Wolfram Wette, "Ideology, Propaganda, and Internal Politics as Preconditions for the War Policy of the Third Reich," *Germany in the Second World War*, Wilhelm Deist, *et al*., eds., Militär- geschichtliches Forschungsamt (Research Institute for Military History), Freiburg im Breisgau, Germany, 2 vols. (Oxford: Clarendon Press, 1990), I, *The Build-up of German Aggression*, 78. Hull, p. 117.

67 Harold C. Deutsch, *Hitler and His Generals: The Hidden Crisis, January-June 1938* (Minneapolis: University of Minnesota Press, 1974); see also Harold C. Deutsch, *The Conspiracy Against Hitler in the Twilight War* (Minneapolis: University of Minnesota Press, 1968). Richard Overy, "Germany and the Munich Crisis: A Mutilated Victory?" *The Munich Crisis, 1938: Prelude to World War II*, Igor Lukes and Erik Goldstein, eds. (London, Portland Or: Frank Cass, 1999), where Overy observes: "The more Hitler was obstructed by enemies abroad and doubters at home, the more determined he became," p. 207.

68 Harvey, *Diaries*, pp. 91-92.

69 *DBFP*, Second Series, VI, 152-153 where Hitler told Phipps on 5 December 1933: "Indeed there was a very real danger of some future weak French Government deciding to embark on a policy of foreign adventure to divert attention from its weakness at home."

70 T.W. Mason, "Labour in the Third Reich, 1933-1939," *Past and Present* (1966), 132.

71 All those who reject the syphilis charge rely on the negative Wassermann from Dr. Morell's records without considering that the test gives false negatives in 80 per cent of later stage cases, one of the compelling points in Deborah Hayden, *Pox: Genius, Madness, and the Mysteries of Syphilis* (New York: Basic Books, 2003), a book lauded by Natalie Angier, "Feared by All, Even Giants and Tyrants" in the 2 January 2003 *New York Times*. On "no syphilis," Kershaw, *Hitler*: *Hubris*, p. 618, n. 146, citing Maser; Waite, *Hitler*, pp. 353-354, 435; and Lukacs, *Hitler*, p. 43. For medical diagnoses see Leonard L. Heston and Renate Heston, *The Medical Casebook of Adolf Hitler: His Illnesses, Doctors, and Drugs* (London, William Kimber, 1979). Bert Edward Park, *The Impact of Illness on World Leaders* (Philadelphia: University of Pennsylvania Press, 1986), pp. 149-219, and "Comment on the Medical Historiography of Adolf Hitler," 343-353; for his comment on psychohistorians, p. 205. John K. Lattimer, *Hitler's Fatal Sickness and Other Secrets of the Nazi Leaders: Why Hitler "Threw" Victory Away* (New York: Hippocrene Books, 1999). (Thanks to Robert Wentland for this source.) For the "with paranoid tendencies," Norbert Bromberg and Verna Volz Small, *Hitler's Psychopathology* (New York: International Universities Press, 1983). The not-clinically-insane diagnosis, Fritz Redlich, in general, and pp. 332-341 in particular; also pp. 223-254 for a medical review, and the section on "The Alleged Syphilis," pp. 231-232. William Carr, *Hitler: A Study In Personality and Politics* (New York: St. Martin's, 1979), pp. 142-166, also deals with the issue of mental illness. "Hitler's doctor agrees," Richard Weber oral testimony from the documentary film *Hitler's Fatal Attraction*. Kershaw, *Hitler: Nemisis*, p. 94.

72 Albert Speer, *Inside the Third Reich*, Richard and Clara Winston

trans. (New York: Collier, 1970), pp. 103-106. See also David Irving, ed. *The Secret Diaries of Hitler's Doctor* (New York: Octagon Books, 1983), p. 30. Carr, *Arms*, p. 77.

73 *DGFP,* Series D, I, 29-38, also mentioned by Kershaw, *Hitler: Nemesis*, p. 47.

74 Hitler's 2 May 1938 Will and Testament, facsimile reproduction with English translation in Werner Maser, *Hitler's Letters and Notes*, Arnold Pomerans trans. (New York: Harper and Row, 1974), pp. 149-159.

75 Carr, *Arms*, p. 77. Neurath's testimony, 24 June 1946, International Military Tribunal, XVI, 641, quoted by John L. Heinemann, *Hitler's First Foreign Minister: Constantin Freiherr von Neurath, Diplomat and Statesman* (Berkeley and Los Angeles: University of California Press, 1979), p. 166.

76 See above, Chapter IV.

77 Braddick, p. 44.

78 For "Black rage," Bullock, *Hitler*, p. 447. Jodl wrote in his diary: "Because of Germany's self-restraint, its consequences lead to a loss of prestige for the Führer, which he is no longer willing to take. Therefore the new order is issued for 'Green' on 30 May," in Jeremy Noakes and Geoffrey Pridham, eds., *Documents on Nazism, 1919-1945* (New York: Viking, 1975), p. 541. A reminder that two editions of Noakes and Pridham are being used in the current study (1988), and this one (1975). On Revised "Operation Green," *DGFP,* Series D, II, 358.

79 Braddick, p. 45.

80 Gannon, p. 172.

VI BRITAIN AND GERMANY

1 *DGFP*, Series D, IV, 302-303.

2 Kershaw, *Hitler: Nemisis*, pp. 32, 105-106. Watt, *How War Came*, pp. 34-35. Zachary Shore, *What Hitler Knew: The Battle for Information in Nazi Foreign Policy* (Oxford: Oxford University Press, 2003) says that fear over what the Nazis had done and might do undermined the smooth functioning of the German Foreign Office (officials were afraid to tell Hitler the truth about certain things), while competition among various individuals and departments resulted in contradiction and confusion. But there is no reason to suppose that unconscious messages did not come through to Hitler; the evidence from his behavior shows him to have understood their meanings.

3 *DBFP*, Second Series, IV, 423. Taylor, *Origins*, p. 15.

4 Rock, p. 73.

5 George Orwell, *Burmese Days* (San Diego, New York, London: Harcourt Brace, 1962), p. 37.

6 For the nineteenth century, Michael Wynn Jones, *The Cartoon History of Britain* (New York: Macmillan, 1971), pp. 89-206. On *Punch*, Peter Mellini, "Not the Guilty Men? *Punch* and Appeasement," *History Today*, Vol. 46, 5 May 1996, p. 39. (Thanks to Don Kantrowitz for this source.) Political cartoons from: Lehmann, p. 53, reprinted from the *St. Louis Globe-Democrat*, November 7, 1938; Britain as lion, The {Rockland County} *Journal News*, Nyack, New York, September 7, 1938; "John Bull," Lehman, p. 205, reprinted from February 23, 1939, *Ken*, Chicago, Illinois.

7 Watt, *Too Serious*, p. 133. Klemens von Klemperer, "Adam von Trott Zu Solz and Resistance Foreign Policy," *Central European History*, Vol. XIV, no. 4 (December, 1981), 352, and especially his *German Resistance Against Hitler: The Search for Allies Abroad 1938-1945 (*Oxford: Clarendon Press, 1992). For the resistance in general, Peter Hoffman, *The History of the German Resistance, 1933-1945*, Richard Barry trans. (Cambridge, Mass.: MIT Press, 1977), and the search for foreign allies, in addition to von Klemperer cited above, Peter Hoffman, "Peace Through Coup d' État: The Foreign Contacts of the German Resistance, 1933-1944," *Central European History*, Vol. XIX, no. 1 (March, 1986), 3-44. See the symposium on the German Resistance in *Central European History*, Vol. XIV, no. 4 (December, 1981), 322-399, especially Harold C. Deutsch, "The German Resistance: Answered and Unanswered Questions," *Central European History*, Vol. XIV, no. 4 (December, 1981), 324, and, in general, Deutsch, *Hitler and His Generals*.

8 Theo Aronson, *Grandmama of Europe: The Crowned Descendants of Queen Victoria* (London: John Murray, 1984), p. 323.

9 Robert Waite, *Kaiser and Führer*. (Toronto: University of Toronto Press, 1999), p. 199. See Donald Dietrich, "Kaiser Wilhelm II: Crisis and the Failure of Leadership," *The Journal of Psychohistory*, Vol. 8, no. 4 (Spring, 1981), 465-484. Thomas A. Kohut, "Kaiser Wilhelm and his parents: an inquiry into the psychological roots of German policy towards England before the First World War," *Kaiser Wilhelm II: New Interpretations*, John. C.G. Röhl and Nicolaus Sombart, eds. (Cambridge, Eng.: Cambridge University Press, 1982), pp. 63-89, and Thomas Kohut, "Mirror Image of a Nation: An Investigation of Kaiser Wilhelm II's Leadership of the Germans," *The Leader: Psychohistorical Essays*, Charles B. Strozier and Daniel Offer, eds. (New York: Plenum, 1985), 179-229. See also Thomas Kohut, *Wilhelm II and the Germans: A Study on Leadership* (New York: Oxford University Press, 1991). Hitler's statements on Wilhelm from Hitler's *Secret Conversations*, pp. 412, 552,

525. See above, Chapter V, endnote 44, for a brief discussion of this source.

10 Hitler's 28 April 1939 speech to the Reichstag, Baynes, I, 1614, 1624.

11 Hitler, *Mein Kampf*, p. 140.

12 Andreas Hillgruber, *Deutschlands Rolle in der Vorgeschichte der beiden Weltkriege* (Goettingen: Vandenhoeck & Ruprecht, 1967,1979), p. 67, and Andreas Hillgruber, *Die gescheiterte Grossmacht: Eine Skizze des Deutschen Reiches 1871-1945* (Duesseldorf: Droste, 1980,1981), p. 106. The text quotes Holger H. Herwig, "Andreas Hillgruber: Historian of 'Grossmacht-politik' 1871-1945," *Central European History*, Vol. XV, no. 2 (June, 1982), 195.

13 Hitler, *Mein Kampf*, p. 140. Klaus Hildebrand, *The Foreign Policy of the Third Reich*, Anthony Fothergill, trans. (London: B.T. Batsford, 1973), p. 52.

14 Germany as Britain's "vassal" from the 28 April 1939 Reichstag speech in Baynes, II, 1624. The "sword on the continent" comes from the "memoirs" of Otto Wagener, published in English by Henry Ashby Turner, Jr., ed., *Hitler—Memoirs of a Confidant*, Ruth Hein trans. (New Haven and London: Yale University Press), p. 157. Despite the enthusiasm of the editor, Wagener's memoirs must be used with extreme caution since they were written in an Allied prison camp years after the "facts" they report: see also pp. 150, 151, 90, 173, 157. Overy and Wheatcroft, p. 45.

15 *DBFP*, Second Series, IV, 452. Harvey, *Diaries*, p. 136. Ashton-Gwatkin, unpublished document in Gilbert, *Britain and Germany*, p. 98. Lothian, unpublished letter, *Ibid*. p. 99. Ironside, p. 49. Halifax quoted in Birkenhead, p. 372. Galeazo Ciano, *Ciano's Hidden Diary, 1937-1938*, Andrea Mayor trans. (New York: E.P. Dutton & Co., 1953), p. 188.

16 Wheeler-Bennett, *Disarmament Deadlock*, p. 249. Rock, p. 214. Kirkconnell, p. 192. Wiskeman, pp. 22, 32. A.L. Rouse, *Appeasement: A Study in Political Decline* (New York: W.W. Norton, 1963), pp. 31, 43.

17 Goebbels in the *Völkischer Beobachter*, reprinted in Snyder, *Documents*, p. 307. Taylor, *Origins*, p. 109.

18 Dawson to Lord Lothian, Gilbert, *Britain and Germany*, p. 82, cited above, Chapter III, n. 50. Hossbach Memorandum in *DGFP*, Series D, I, no. 19.

19 Atlee to House of Commons, *Parl. Debs*. H.C., 21 October 1937. Journalist Charles Higham, *The Duchess of Windsor: The Secret Life* (New York: McGraw-Hill, 1988), p. 241, states that "the duke encouraged Hitler's ambitions to strike against Russia," but on little evidence. Two other writers feel the Duke said nothing along those lines during his twenty-minute private audience with Hitler: Michael Bloch,

Windsor: The Secret Files of the Duke of Windsor (New York: Harper & Row, 1988), and Philip Ziegler, *King Edward VIII: A Biography* (New York: Alfred A. Knopf, 1991). Testimony for Hitler's belief in the Duke of Windsor's sympathy for the Nazis comes from Hitler's translator, Paul Schmidt, pp. 74-75.

20 Harvey, *Diaries*, p. 57.

21 *Evening Standard* quoted in Gannon, p. 129.

22 Taylor, *Origins*, p. 137.

23 Weinberg, *Foreign Policy*, II, 379.

24 Reed, *Disgrace*, p. 205.

25 Harvey, *Diaries*, pp. 85, 91. Gannon, p. 145.

26 Hans Rothfels, "Resistance Begins," *The Road to Dictatorship: Germany 1918-1933*, T. Eschenburg, *et. al.*, eds. (London: Wolff, 1964), p. 146. Hitler quoted by G. Ward Price, *Year of Reckoning* (London: Cassell, 1939), p. 148.

27 Chamberlain to House of Commons, *Parl. Debs.* H.C., 14 March 1938, vol. 333, cols. 45-52, quoted in Thompson, p. 157. For "remarkably little stir," *Ibid*. p. 156.

28 *Ibid*. p. 166.

29 Quoted in Gannon, pp. 36-37. Fuchser, p. 127. Rock, p. 95, and n. 12.

30 Fuchser, p. 128. Harvey, *Diaries*, pp. 99, 113, 122, 138, 139.

31 Memorandum by Bismarck, 10 May 1938, *DGFP*, Series D, II, No. 151.

32 For suggestions in the press in the summer of 1938, Gannon, pp. 178, 179-183. On Masaryk's reactions, Wiskeman, p. 91.

33 The London *Times*, 7 September 1938, p. 1.

34 *DGFP*, Series D, II, No. 247.

35 For a long excerpt of Hitler's closing speech at Nuremberg, 12 September 1938, Baynes, II, 1487-1499.

36 Harvey, *Diaries*, p. 171.

37 Weinberg, *Foreign Policy*, II, 379.

38 Martin Gilbert, "Horace Wilson: Man of Munich?" *History Today* (October, 1982), p. 7. For the detailed reports on what passed between them see notes of a "Conversation between Sir Horace Wilson and Herr Hitler at Berlin on September 26, 1938," and "Notes of a Conversation

between Herr Hitler and Sir Horace Wilson at Berlin on September 27, 1938," *DBFP*, Third Series, II, 5543-557, 564-567. For the German version of events, *DGFP*, Series D, II, 934-935, 963-965.

39 Kirkpatrick, *Inner Circle*, also quoted by Taylor, *Munich*, p. 48. Foreign Policy Committee Meeting, November 1, 1938, FPC Minutes, CAB 27/624, quoted by Newman, p. 69. Chamberlain on never having guaranteed Czechoslovakia's borders, *Parl. Debs.* H.C., November 1, 1938, vol. 340, 79-80, quoted in Rock, p. 198. Rowse, *Appeasement*, p. 65.

40 Noakes and Pridham (1975), pp. 564, 565. See the versions in *DGFP*, Series D, VII, Nos. 192, 193; and in *DBFP*, Third Series, VII, No. 314, enclosure.

41 Text of British note 23 August 1939 in *DBFP*, Third Series, VII, No. 145. Also in *DGFP*, Series D, VII, enclosure, pp. 215-216.

42 *Ibid*. No. 200, pp. 210, 211. Henderson's account, *DBFP*, Third Series, VII, No. 200, pp. 162, 163.

43 Schmidt, pp. 157-158.

44 Lukacs, *Hitler*, p. 26 n. The quote is from Friedrich Heer, *Der Glaube des Adolf Hitler: Anatomie einer politischen Religiosität* (Munich: Bechtle, 1968); Lukacs cites the 1994 ed., p. 344.

45 Shirer, *Berlin Diaries*, p. 141. On comments from the Foreign Ministry and Hitler in a sweat, Kershaw, *Hitler: Nemesis*, p. 189.

46 Hitler's 28 April 1939 speech in Baynes, II, 1605-1656.

47 Galeazzo Ciano, *Ciano's Diplomatic Papers,* Malcolm Muggeridge, ed. (London: Odhams, 1948), account of two meetings with Hitler at Berchtesgaden on 12-13 August 1939, pp. 299-304. Hitler's speech to Commanders-in-Chiefs in Noakes and Pridham (1975), pp. 562-568. Henderson on Hitler's state of mind on 23 August, *DBFP*, Third Series, VII, No. 200. Directive No. 1 for the Conduct of the War, 31 August 1939, Noakes and Pridham (1975), pp. 568-569, and reported by Speer, p. 162.

48 Hitler's rhetoric in 1938-1939 was filled with "walls," "fortifications," and "frontiers" "crumbling" and being "invaded." He may have become preoccupied with the Westwall fortifications in part for symbolic as well as strategic reasons. See the details on the wall itself in John D. Heyl, "The Construction of the Westwall, 1938: An Exemplar for National Socialist Policymaking," *Central European History*, Vol. XIV, no. 1 (March, 1981), 66.

49 *News Chronicle*, 14 March 1938, quoted by Gannon, p. 158. Adams to House of Commons, *Parl. Debs.* H.C., 14 March 1938, Vol. 333, 47-168. Support for mutual defense, Rock, p. 56. Harvey *Diaries*, pp. 185, 183.

50 Hendeson's denials, *DBFP*, Third Series, V, Nos. 288, 289. For press, Gannon, throughout. Hitler's 1 April 1939 Wilhelmshafen speech, Baynes, II, 1591

51 Noakes and Pridham (1975), p. 522.

52 Speer, pp. 158, 165.

53 Noakes and Pridham (1975), p. 559 offers a brief excerpt of Rudolf Schmundt's notes, with a slightly longer exerpt in their later edition (1988), II, 736-738, both exclude important phrases: "England as motive force" and "force England to her knees" in the full document "Minutes of a Conference on May 23, 1939," *DGFP*, Series D, VI, No. 433.

54 *Ibid*. p. 569.

55 Excerpt from Hitler's speech to the Reich, 1 September 1939, Noakes and Pribram (1988), II, 755-756.

56 Lloyd deMause, *Reagan's America* (New York: Creative Roots, 1984).

57 Gaston Bouthoul, *Les Guerres: Eléménts de Polémologies* (Paris: Payot, 1951). These ideas are developed in Franco Fornari, *The Psychoanalysis of War*, Alenka Pfeifer, trans. (Garden City: Anchor/Doubleday, 1974).

58 West, p. 1112. Rouse, *Appeasement*, p. 30.

59 *Adolf Hitler: Pictures from the Life of the Führer*, p. 12.

60 Stoessinger, p. 62. See also Claudia Koonz, *Mothers in the Fatherland: Women, the Family and Nazi Politics* (London: Jonathan Cape, 1987).

61 Roger Manville, *Films and the Second World War (*South Brunswick and New York: A.S. Barnes, 1974), pp. 53, 57. Jay W. Baird, *To Die for Germany: Heroes in the Nazi Pantheon* (Bloomington and Indianapolis: Indiana University Press, 1990).

62 Felix Gilbert, ed. and trans., *Hitler Directs His War* (Oxford: Oxford University Press, 1950), p. 30.

63 Fromm, *Anatomy*, throughout. Frederick Spotts, *Hitler and the Power of Aesthetics* (Woodstock, N.Y.: Overlook Press, 2003.), pp. 116-117. The "young people" quote from Zoller, p. 196. "I have a right" quoted by Heer, *Hitler*, p. 293; also cited by Waite, *Hitler*, p. 18.

VII FRANCE

1 *Documents diplomatiques français, 1932-1939*, {hereinafter cited as *DDF*}, 1 Serie (1932-1936) (Paris, 1964-) Tomes I-VI; 2 Serie (1936-1939) (Paris, 1963-), Tomes I-VII. Herriot's words, I Série, I. no. 286, quoted by Adamthwaite, *France*, p. 30.

2 Rock, p. 118. Taylor, *Munich*, p. 125. Adamthwaite, *France*, p. 58. Taylor, *Origins*, pp. 266, 35.

3 Especially so during the Anglo-French discussions of 25 September 1938: see Lord Strang, *At Home and Abroad* (London: Andre Deutsch, 1956), pp. 135, 142.

4 Adamthwaite, *France*, pp. xiv, 43.

5 *Ibid*. p. 302.

6 *DDF*, I Série I, no. 286.

7 *DBFP*, Second Series, IV, 101-102.

8 Quoted by Gordon Craig, "Prewar Diplomacy in Europe," *The New Republic*, December 9, 1981, p. 34.

9 Taylor, *Munich*, p. 131.

10 Phipps to Halifax, 24 March 1938, *DBFP*, Third Series, I, no. 112.

11 Adamthwaite, *France*, p. xv. Renouvin, p. 111. Jean-Baptiste Duroselle, "France and the Crisis of March 1936," *French Society and Culture Since the Old Regime*, Evelyn M. Acomb and Marvin L. Brown, Jr., eds. (New York: Holt, Rinehart and Winston, 1966), p. 257, excerpted as "France and the Rhineland," in the text *World War II: Roots and Causes*, Keith Eubank, ed. (Lexington, Mass.: D.C. Heath, 1975), p. 88, which reprints half the article with neither references nor the "Commentary" by John C. Cairns, pp. 283-296, and disappears altogether in Eubank's revised second edition (1992). In contrast to Duroselle, Robert J. Young, *In Command of France: Foreign Policy and Military Planning*, 1933-1940 (Cambridge, Mass.: Harvard University Press, 1978) argues that French policy was realistic given the conditions and circumstances of the time.

12 For France's incoherent policies before the 1930s see Jan Jacobsen, "Is there a New International History of the 1920s?" *American Historical Review*, Vol. 88, no. 3 (June, 1983), 618-619, 623, n. 633.

13 Watt, *Too Serious*, p. 90.

14 Adamthwaite, *France*, p. 24.

15 Taylor, *Origins*, p. 97.

16 Duroselle, pp. 251-252.

17 *Ibid*. p. 81.

18 Churchill, *Gathering Storm*, pp. 170-171. Bullock, *Hitler*, p. 344. Craig, "German Foreign Office," *The Diplomats*, p. 426. Speer, p. 72.

19 Adamthwaite, *France*, p. 39. Watt, *Too Serious*, p. 94. Faris Kirkland, "Anti-Military Group Fantasies and the Destruction of the French Air Force," *The Journal of Psychohistory*, Vol. 14, no. 1 (Summer, 1986), 43.

20 Taylor, *Munich*, pp. 134-137.

21 *Ibid*. p. 138.

22 *DDF*, 2 Série, II, No. 85. Elizabeth R. Cameron, "Alexis Saint-Léger Léger," *The Diplomats*, p. 390.

23 On the summer talks, Adamthwaite says: "The negative attitude of Daladier, Minister of National Defence and War, and of his military advisors, virtually foredoomed the talks," *France*, pp. 48, 50. Coulondre, *De Staline á Hitler*, pp. 152-153. Franklin L. Ford and Carl E Schorske, "The Voice in the Wilderness: Robert Coulondre," *The Diplomats*, p. 567. *Moscow Daily* quoted by Taylor, *Origins*, p. 119.

24 Adamthwaite, *France*, p. 317.

25 *DBFP*, Third Series, I, 346-347.

26 Harvey, *Diaries*, p. 188.

27 Strang, *Home and Abroad*, pp. 141-142.

28 Harvey, *Diaries*, p. 188

29 Eubank, *Munich*, pp. 278-287.

30 Harvey, *Diaries*, p. 109.

31 *DGFP*, Series D, I, no. 19.

32 Cameron, p. 387.

33 Eubank, *Munich*, pp. 279-280. Reynaud quoted by Renouvin, p. 84. Adamthwaite, *France*, p. 338

34 The phrase "appeasement personified" is A.J.P. Taylor's, *Origins*, p. 157, also on Daladier's "acquiesence." De Jouvenal quoted by Adamthwaite, *France*, p. 97. Quote on Munich disaster and humiliation from Tony Judt, "France Without Glory," *The New York Review of Books*, May 23, 1996, p. 41, who cites Stanley Hoffman's foreword to Edouard Daladier,

Prison Journal 1940-1945 (Boulder: Westview Press, 1995). "Ebb and flow" from Brendon, p. 602. Harvey, *Diaries*, p. 223.

35 A.J.P. Taylor excuses Daladier who was "convinced that a firm policy could alone stop Hitler. But he was at a loss how to do it." *Origins*, p. 197. Adamthwaite excuses Bonnet: "muddle not machination was at the bottom of Bonnet's handling" of affairs, *France*, pp. 326, 320.

36 Jacques Maritain, *France, My Country Through the Disaster* (New York: Longman's Green, 1941), p. 221.

37 Renouvin, pp. 85, 83.

38 Taylor, *Munich*, p. 140.

39 Renouvin, pp. 82-83.

40 Adamthwaite, *France*, p. xiv. Daladier quoted in Reynaud, p. 187.

41 Adamthwaite, *France*, p. 25. W. E. Dodd, *Ambassador Dodd's Diary* (New York: Harcourt Brace, 1941), p. 347. Adamthwaite, *France*, p. 305.

42 *Ibid.* p. 25.

43 Eugen Weber, *The Hollow Years: France in the 1930s* (New York: W.W. Norton, 1999). Marc Bloch, *Strange Defeat: A Statement of Evidence Written in 1940*, Gerard Hopkins trans. (New York: W.W. Norton, 1968), pp. 173, 157, 168, 170, although the majority of Bloc's analysis is more traditional and faults, among others, the General Staff, an "exacerbated sense of inequality" in the working class, the bourgeoisie, a spirit of apathy, bureaucratic practices, the weaknesses of French education, "the vices of our military system," and older, instead of younger, leaders. Alexander Werth, *The Twilight of France, 1933-1940*, D.W. Brogan ed. and intro. (New York and London: Harper & Brothers, 1942), pp. 352-356. Judt, p. 41. David Carroll, *French Literary Fascism: Nationalism, Anti-Semitism, and the Idelology of Culture* (Princeton: Princeton University Press, 1996). Jacques Szaluta, "Apotheosis to Ignominy: The Martyrdom of Marshal Pétain," *The Journal of Psychohistory*, Vol. 7, no. 4 (Spring, 1980), 415-453. Stephen Ryan, "Pétain and Vichy: Abandonment, 'Love of Harlot,' and Repetition Compulsion," *The Journal of Psychohistory*, Vol. 8, no. 2 (Fall, 1980), 149-158. Camus in the second issue of *Revue Libre* (1943) reprinted in *Albert Camus: Resistance, Rebellion, and Death* (New York: Vintage, 1974), p. 8. Adamthwaite, *France*, p. 339. Simone Weil, *The Need for Roots: Prelude to a Declaration of Duties Toward Mankind*, Arthur Wills, trans. (New York: Octagon Books, 1979), p. 160. Weil's ideas evolved over time, of course, but the roots of her brand of "regeneration through suffering" can be found earlier, for example in her arguing for the sacrifice of Czechoslovakia, Simone Weil, *Formative Writings, 1929-*

1941, Dorothy Tuck Mcfarland and Wilhelmina Van Ness trans. and eds. (Amherst: University of Massachusetts Press, 1986), pp. 264-268, reprinted from *Feuilles libres de la quinzaine*, no. 58, May 25, 1938.

44 *DDF*, I Série, I, no. 286.

45 Maurin, *DDF*, 2 Série, I, no. 196, quoted by Duroselle, p. 251. Taylor, *Munich*, p. 134. Cameron, *Diplomats*, p. 394.

46 Adamthwaite, *France*, p. 25.

47 *DDF*, 2 Série, III, V no. 480. Adamthwaite, *France*, p. 49.

48 Renouvin, p. 107.

49 Taylor, *Origins*, p. 156.

50 Bonnet in London, *DBFP*, Third Series, IV, No. 507. Renouvin, p.171.

51 Quotes, translations, and analysis from Robert Soucy, "Psycho-Sexual Aspects of the Fascism of Drieu La Rochelle," *The Journal of Psychohistory*, Vol. 4, no. 1 (Summer, 1976), 71-92. Other leading fascists were literally orphans: see Robert Soucy, "Psychological Dynamics of French Fascism: The Case of George Valois," *The Psychohistory Review*, Vol. 12, nos. 2/3 (Winter, 1984), 19-23. Carroll (see n. 43 above) does not emphasize the orphan theme. See Soucy's other works for more details: *French Fascism: The First Wave, 1924-1933* (New Haven: Yale University Press, 1986), *French Fascism: The Second Wave, 1933-1939* (New Haven: Yale University Press, 1995), and *Fascist Intellectual, Drieu La Rochelle* (Berkeley: University of California Press, 1979).

52 Paul Monaco, *Cinema & Society: France and Germany During the Twenties* (New York and Amsterdam: Elsevier, 1976). F. Kirkland, "The French Military Collapse of 1940: A Psychohistorical Interpretation," *The Journal of Psychohistory*, Vol. 12, no. 3 (Winter, 1985), 313-337.

53 Jean-Paul Sartre, *The Words* (New York: G. Braziller, 1964), p. 227.

54 The themes of blood, clocks, and especially betrayal predominated in German films, Monaco, p. 122.

55 *Ibid.* p. 158. S. Ryan, "Reflections on the Psychohistory of France," *The Journal of Psychohistory*, Vol. 11, no. 2 (Fall, 1983), 226-227.

56 Lloyd deMause, "The Evolution of Childhood," *Foundations of Psychohistory* (New York: Creative Roots, 1982), pp. 1-83.

57 George Sussman, *Selling Mother's Milk: The Wet-Nursing Business in France, 1715-1914* (Champaign: University of Illinois Press, 1982), p. 174.

VIII BELGIUM AND ITALY

1 Feiling paraphrasing Chamberlain's words in spring 1938, p. 352.

2 Rudolph Binion, "Repeat Performance. Leopold III and Belgian Neutrality," *Soundings: Psychohistorical and Psycholiterary* (New York: Psychohistory Press, 1980), p. 15.

3 *Ibid.* p. 16. Taylor, *Munich*, pp. 472- 476. Renouvin, p. 137. Brian Bond, *Britain, France, and Belgium, 1939-1940* (London and Washington: Brassey's, 1990), where he asserts that neutrality was not sudden, but a gradual process of the entire Belgian Government, and that "the new policy owed little to King Leopold personally," p. 8. See also David O. Kieft, *Belgium's Return to Neutrality: An Essay in the Frustration of Small Power Diplomacy* (Oxford: Clarendon Press, 1972).

4 Binion, "Repeat Performance," p. 30.

5 *Ibid.* pp. 31, 32.

6 *Ibid.* pp. 16, 36-37, also referencing preceding paragraph.

7 *Ibid.* pp. 42, 38, 39. Harold Nicolson to his wife Vita Sackville-West, 22 March 1936, in Nicolson, *Diaries*, I, 253, 254.

8 Full psychological biographies, the details of Leopold's childhood, and the personalities of his ministers all need pinning down.

9 Binion, "Repeat Performance," p. 31.

10 *Ibid.* p. 43.

11 Harvey for the "mad" Mussolini, *Diaries*, p. 282. For press attacks see Mack Smith, *Mussolini* (New York: Alfred A. Knopf, 1982), p. 186.

12 Mack Smith, p. 106.

13 *Ibid.* p. 4.

14 R.J.B. Bosworth, *Mussolini. A Biography* (New York: Oxford University Press, 2002). Laura Fermi, *Mussolini* (Chicago: University of Chicago Press, 1961), pp. 5, 13, 16.

15 Mack Smith, p. 6.

16 Mussolini quoted by Ludwig, *Talks with Mussolini*, p. 62. People as "whore" from *Ciano, Diario, 1937-1943*, pp. 417-418, quoted by Bosworth, p. 367, n. 87. On his role as sex symbol and his sex appeal for the wives of British statesmen, Bosworth, p. 212. Mack Smith, p. 7. On women under fascism, Victoria de Grazia, *How Fascism Ruled Women: Italy, 1922-1945* (Berkeley: University of California Press, 1992).

17 Ernest Hemingway, "Che Ti Dice La Patria?" *The Short Stories of Ernest Hemingway* (New York: Charles Scribner's Sons, 1953), pp. 292-293.

18 Fischer, p. 273. On number of photos and poses, Bosworth, p. 211.

19 Mack Smith, p. 1. Kirkpatrick, *Mussolini*, p. 22. Mack Smith, p. 181.

20 Fermi, p. 15. Kirkpatrick, *Mussolini*, p. 25. Mack Smith, p. 3.

21 *Ibid*. p. 109.

22 Harvey, *Diaries*, p. 29. The historian Renzo De Felice is most closely associated with the notion of Fascism as a manifestation of the popular will, disputed by Paul Corner, "Italian Fascism: Whatever Happened to Dictatorship?" *The Journal of Modern History*, Vol. 74, no. 2 (June, 2002), 325-351, although neither view is really incompatible with the other. Kirkpatrick, *Mussolini*, p. 166.

23 Mack Smith, p. 189. Overy and Wheatcroft, p. 169. For the public's change of mind on war, Bosworth, p. 356.

24 Paul-Boncour, *Entre les deux guerres*, iii, 14-16, quoted by Sir Lewis Namier, *Europe in Decay* (Gloucester, Mass.: Peter Smith, 1963), p. 17.

25 Kirkpatrick, *Mussolini*, pp. 302-303. Richard Lamb, *Mussolini As Diplomat: Il Duce's Italy on the World Stage* (New York: Fromm International, 1999), p. x.

26 The popular biographer is Jasper Ridley, *Mussolini* (New York: St. Martin's, 1997), p. 13. Chamberlain Diary entry 29 November 1935, quoted in Macleod, pp. 188-189.

27 Taylor, *Munich*, pp. 231-233. In the proceeding paragraph of text, Chamberlain letter to Mussolini, 28 July 1937, in *I documenti diplomatici italiani*, 8s, 127, quoted by Bosworth, p. 329.

28 Mack Smith, pp. 183, 185, 186.

29 Mario Toscano, *The Origins of the Pact of Steel* (Baltimore, MD: Johns Hopkins University Press, 1967); for the full text of Mussolini's memorandum to Ciano on 4 May 1939, *Ibid*. 289-292. Report on the Ribbentrop-Ciano 6-7 May 1939 meeting, *DGFP*, Series D, No. 341. Ciano reports Ribbentrop's "three years" reassurance before signing the Pact of Steel in Galeazzo Ciano, *Ciano's Diaries 1939-1943*, Hugh Gibson, ed. (Garden City: Doubleday, 1946), p. 84. See *Ciano's Diplomatic Papers*, pp. 283-286, for Ciano's memorandum on the 6-7 May 1939 meeting, and p. 284 for Ribbentrop's reassurance of peace.

30 Craig and George see it as "a not inconsiderable amount of slipshodness in detail" as the Pact, as they put it, "imposed rigid conditions upon Italy without defining the *casus foederis*, providing escape clauses, or

stipulating the necessity of consultation," *Force and Statecraft*, pp. 82-83. Mussolini's "Toujours parler", *DGFP*, Series D, No. 341. Hitler on "war inevitable" and "attack Poland," *Ibid*. No. 433, reprinted in Noakes and Pridham (1975), p. 559. Inclination for "Pact of Blood," Overy and Wheatcroft, p. 173.

31 Taylor, *Origins*, p. 222.

32 Taylor, *Munich*, pp. 165-166.

33 Mack Smith, pp. 218, 221.

34 Taylor, *Munich*, p. 30. Mack Smith, p. 230.

35 *Ibid*. p. 110. On Hitler's rouge, G. Ciano, *Ciano's Hidden Diary, 1937-1938*, A. Mayor, trans. (New York: E.P. Dutton, 1953), p. 113.

36 Harvey, *Diaries*, pp. 209, 215. David Low, *Europe Since Versailles: A History in One Hundred Cartoons with a Narrative Text* (Harmondsworth: Penguin Books, 1940), p. 168, reprinted from February 11, 1938.

37 F.W. Deakins, *The Brutal Friendship: Mussolini, Hitler and the Fall of Italian Fascism* (New York: Harper & Row, 1962). In mid-February 1938, Harvey was concerned that "Italy would become still more wedded to Germany," Harvey, *Diaries*, p. 93.

38 Mack Smith, p. 224.

39 Entry for September 29-30, Ciano, *Hidden Diary*, p. 166.

40 Mack Smith, pp. 229, 195, 227.

41 *Ibid*. p. 191.

42 Mack Smith, p. 176. Harvey, *Diaries*, p. 240

43 Mack Smith, pp. 201, 202.

44 Gilbert, "Ciano," *The Diplomats*, p. 535.

45 Harvey, *Diaries*, p. 209. For popular opinion against war by 1939, Overy and Wheatcroft, p. 169, and Bosworth, p. 356.

46 Overy and Wheatcroft, p. 176. Michael Palumbo, "Italian-Austro-Hungarian Military Relations Before World War I," Samuel R. Williamson and Peter Pastor, eds. *War and Society in East Central Europe, Essays on World War I: Origins and Prisoners of War* {Atlantic Studies: Brooklyn College Studies on Society in Change, No. 14, Béla K. Király, editor-in chief} (New York: Columbia University Press, 1983), pp. 37-54.

47 Bosworth, p. 346, p. 501, n. 83-89; p. 364, n. 73; pp. 350, 369-370.

IX CZECHOSLOVAKIA

1 *DGFP*, Series D, II, 393.

2 *Ibid*. I, no. 19, for the Hossbach Memorandum; and II, no. 133, for Plan Green.

3 There is a large literature on Munich. Helpful works, in addition to the studies already cited and to be cited below, include, for the pre-Hitler period, F. Gregory Campbell, *Confrontation in Central Europe: Weimar Germany and Czechoslovakia* (Chicago: University of Chicago Press, 1975), and for the crisis itself, J.W. Wheeler-Bennett, *Munich: Prologue to Tragedy* (New York: Duell, Sloan and Pearce, 1962), which has the advantage of including some useful political cartoons.

4 The London *Times*, 20 September 1938, quoted in Gannon, p. 185. Masaryk quoted in Shirer, *Rise and Fall*, p. 411, who says in his n. 76, p. 1153: "Masaryk later described this scene to the writer, as he did to many other friends. But my notes on it were lost, and I have used Wheeler-Bennett's moving account in *Munich*, pp. 170-71." Anyway, Masaryk uttered almost exactly the same words publicly before a news-reel camera; it can be found in the documentary film, *Munich: A Peace of Paper*. Beneš's words from *Czechoslovak Sources and Documents*, 4 vols. (New York: Czechoslovak Information Service, 1942-194), II, 28-29. Thomas Mann's words from Thomas Mann, *This War* (New York: Alfred A. Knopf, 1940), p. 3.

5 Nigel Davies, *Human Sacrifice in History and Today* (New York: Dorset Press, 1981). Eli Sagan, "Toward a Theory of Human Sacrifice," *The Journal of Psychohistory*, Vol. 10, no. 2 (Fall, 1982), 115-140.

6 The phrases from the 1920s quoted in Erik Goldstein, "Neville Chamberlain, the British Official Mind and the Munich Crisis," *Munich Crisis*, Lukes and Goldstein eds., p. 282. *Punch* cartoon from Mellini, p. 42, the other "dwarfs" were Poly, Hungy, Jugy, Bulgy, Roumy, and Lithy. Kennan, p. 4. Harvey, *Diaries*, p. 210. Eden to House of Commons, 3 October 1938, and Sinclair to House of Commons, 3 October 1938, *Parl. Debs*. H.C., 3 October 1938, quoted by Gilbert, *Britain and Germany*, p. 122. Neurath—echoing Göring's words—to Beck that sooner or later the Czechoslovak "appendix" would have to be cut out, *DGFP*, Series D, V, no. 28.

7 Reynaud, p. 182. Churchill, *Aftermath*, p. 232. Hitler on the "child state" and "democratic midwives," speech at Saarbruchen, 9 October 1938, Baynes, II, 1611,1616, 1614. *Daily Express* and *Daily Mail* "spawn of Versailles" from Gannon, p. 225. Summerskill, *Parl. Debs*. H.C., November 2, 1938, vol. 340, 217, quoted in Rock, p. 166.

8 Kennan, pp. 19, 8.

9 Godfrey Lias, *Beneš of Czechoslovakia* (London: George Allen & Unwin, 1940).

10 *Ibid.* pp. 39, 11, 44, 17, 37, 84, 109, 123, 173, 110.

11 Churchill, *Gathering Storm*, 238. Churchill, 21 September 1938, Statement to the Press, *Complete Speeches*, VI, 6003. Call for Grand Alliance, Churchill to House of Commons, *Parl. Debs.* H.C., 14 March 1938, Vol. 33, 100, in Churchill, *Complete Speeches*, VI, 5927. Greenwood to House of Commons, *Parl. Debs*, H.C., 2 November 1938, Vol. 340, 217, quoted in Rock, p. 166.

12 Kennan, pp. 34, 10. Low, *Cartoon History*, p. 121. Wheeler-Bennett, *Munich*, p. 364. Low, *Cartoon History*, p. 167.

13 Reed, *Disgrace*, p. 110. See the attitudes described in the memoir of Kurt Weisskopf, *The Agony of Czechoslovakia '38/'68* (London: Elak, 1968), p. 73.

14 Taylor, *Origins*, pp. 161, 138. Weisskopf, pp. 110, 23. Lias, p. 241. Reed, *Disgrace*, p. 165. Harvey, *Diaries*, p. 149.

15 Reported by the *Daily Telegraph's* Vienna correspondent, cited in Gannon, p. 193. Wedgwood, *Parl. Debs.* H.C., 26 July 1938, vol. 338, 2293-2294, quoted in Rock, p 106.

16 Documentary film, *Munich: The Peace of Paper*. Reed, *Disgrace*, pp. 112, 152-153.

17 Kennan, p. 7.

18 *Ibid.* p. 86.

19 M. Duncan Stanton, "The Addict as Savior: Heroin, Death, and the Family," *Family Process*, Vol. 16, no. 2 (June, 1977), 191-197, 192, 196.

20 *Ibid.* p. 196.

21 Good illustrations are Andrew Brink, "Bertrand Russell's The Pilgrimage of Life and Mourning," *The Journal of Psychohistory*, Vol. 10, no. 3 (Winter, 1983), 311-322, and Andrew Brink, "Death, Depression, and Creativity: A Psychological Approach to Bertrand Russell," *Mosaic*, XI, 1, 89-102, along with his book-length study, *Bertrand Russell: The Psychobiography of a Moralist* (Atlantic Highlands, N.J.: Humanities Press International, 1989). See also Melvin Kalfus, *Frederick Law Olmsted* (New York: New York University Press, 1990).

22 Thomas Masaryk, *Suicide and the Meaning of Civilization*, William B. Weist and Robert Batson, trans. (Chicago: University of Chicago

Press, 1970). *Modern Man and Religion* (London: G. Allen & Unwin, 1938). *The Spirit of Russia: Studies in History, Literature and Philosophy,* 3 vols. (New York: Macmillan, 1967), III, 35-40, 217-21, for Dostoyevsky on suicide; 165-168, for Tolstoy on suicide; and 284, for Turgenev on suicide. Quotations cited in text come from his *Modern Man and Religion*, p. 47, and pp. 3-14 ff.

23 The italics are Masaryk's, *Suicide and Civilization*, pp. 3, 77, 31, 51, 125, 52, 169. Tomáš G. Masaryk, *The Meaning of Czech History*, René Wellek ed., Peter Kussi trans. (Chapel Hill: University of North Carolina Press, 1974) has virtually no references to suicide but does play up the role of the martyr Jan Hus.

24 On life of Christ and sacrifice quoted by R.W. Seton-Watson, "President Masaryk," *Contemporary Review*, March, 1930, pp. 5, 10. On suicidal individual, Karel Čapek, *President Masaryk Tells His Story* (New York: Arno Press and *The New York Times*, 1971), pp. 143-144.

25 For newborn and small state, Emil Ludwig, *Defender of Democracy* (New York: Arno Press and *The New York Times*, 1971), pp. 48, 195, 224, and Čapek, pp. 67, 90, 92, 299. Corrupting youth, Čapek, p. 133; beatings, pp. 19, 39; sex abuse, p. 45. Stable boy, Ludwig, *Defender of Democracy*, pp. 104, 105, 100, and Čapek, p. 107. Catholic martyrs, Čapek, pp. 62, 63; advocating suicide, p. 133; "answer to childish experience," pp. 32-33; and "in lines of my books," p. 226.

26 R.W. Seton-Watson,"Beneš and Masaryk," *Eduard Beneš: Essays and Reflections presented on the occasion of his Sixtieth Birthday* (London: George Allen and Unwin, 1945), pp. 187-188. Father and son, Ludwig, *Defender of Democracy*, p. 58. A.J.P. Taylor, "Czechoslovakia and Europe. The Foreign Policy of Dr. Beneš," *Essays and Relections presented on his Sixtieth Birthday*, p. 157. Compton Mackenzie, *Dr. Beneš* (London: George G. Harrap, 1946).

27 Robert B. Pynsent, *Questions of Identity: Czech and Slovak Ideas of Nationality and Personality* (Budapest, London, New York: Central European University Press, 1994), pp. 192, 195; Pynsent calls this entire section of his book "Czech Self-Definition Through Martyrs," pp. 147 ff. (I am indebted to Albert Schmidt for this source.)

28 Lias, p. 60. "Drink hemlock," Ludwig, *Defender of Democracy*, p. 233.

29 Edward B. Hitchcock, *"I Built A Temple for Peace": The Life of Eduard Beneš* (New York and London: Harper and Brothers, 1940), p. 11.

30 Weinberg, *Foreign Policy*, II, p. 377, and 375. Renouvin, p. 117. For the British press, Gannon, pp. 212, 213. For Czech fantasies, Weisskopf, pp. 23, 91, and 88-89. For the Czech willingness to fight, Hubert Ripka, *Munich—Before and After* (New York: Howard Fertig, 1969), originally

published in London by Victor Gollancz in 1939, pp. 17-18, 69-77, and throughout, and the documentary film, *Munich: The Peace of Paper*.

31 Taylor, *Munich*, pp. 988, 989.

32 On Czechoslovakia cannot be defended, Chamberlain to Ida, 20 March 1938, quoted in Macleod, p. 224, and for the later reassertion, *DBFP*, Third Series, I, 220-221. On "mercilessly pressed Daladier," Strang, *Home and Abroad*, p. 141-142. R.J. Minney, ed., *The Private Papers of Hore-Belisha* (London: Collins, 1960), p. 142.

33 Chamberlain "rape of Czechoslovakia," Kennedy to Secretary of State, London, September 17, 1938, *FRUS*, 1938, I, 621-622 quoted by Rock, p. 122. Kirkpatrick on Daladier, *Inner Circle*, p. 130.

34 Paul Zinner, "The Diplomacy of Beneš," *The Diplomats*, p. 121. Wiskeman, p. 91. Harvey, *Diaries*, p. 187, Ripka, pp. 224-227.

35 Atticus in the London *Sunday Times*, 2 October 1938, p. 13. Also quoted by Gannon, p. 222.

X POLAND AND THE SOVIET UNION

1 Sir Horace Wilson quoted in Martin Gilbert, "Horace Wilson: Man of Munich?" *History Today* (October, 1982), p. 9. Chamberlain, letter of 20 March 1938, quoted in Feiling, p. 347, quoted also in Macleod, p. 226.

2 Churchill, *The Aftermath*, p. 274. Fischer, pp. 13, 4.

3 Molotov in J. Degras, ed., *Soviet Documents on Foreign Policy*, 3 vols. (New York: Oxford University Press, 1951-1953), III, 338.

4 Quoted in Eugen Weber, *Apocalypses: Prophesies, Cults, and Millennial Beliefs through the Ages* (Cambridge, Mass.: Harvard University Press, 1999), pp. 128-129. Self-sacrificing phrase from Polish Constitution in Olszer, p. 196.

5 On Pilsudsi's health, Park, pp. 116-138, on his cancer, pp. 125-127, 136. From *Pravada*, 27 April 1937, quoted in Bohdan Budurowycz, *Polish-Soviet Relations, 1932-1939* (New York and London: Columbia University Press, 1963), p. 98.

6 *Ibid.* p. 193.

7 *Ibid.* p. 196.

8 Overy and Wheatcroft, p. 6. See also R. Leslie, *et. al.*, *History of Poland since 1863* (Cambridge: Cambridge University Press, 1980), pp. 203-204, and J. Karski, *The Great Powers and Poland, 1919-1945* (Lanham, MD: University Press of America, 1985), pp. 322-323.

9 Beck, Final Report, p. 91, quoted in Budurowycz, p. 193. Overy and Wheatcroft, p. 4. Beck, Final Report p. 88, quoted in Budurowycz, p. 195.

10 Polish isolation quote from Overy and Wheatcroft, p. 6. Roberts, "Beck," *The Diplomats*, p. 610.

11 Quoted by Renouvin, p. 162, and by Budurowycz, p. 197, n. 29.

12 Quoted by Roberts, "Beck," *The Diplomats*, p. 599.

13 *Ibid.*, p. 591. Anna M. Cienciala, *Poland and the Western Powers 1938-1939: A Study in the Interdependence of Eastern and Western Europe* (London: Routledge & Kegan Paul: Toronto: University of Toronto Press, 1968), p. 60. Sosnowski in the *Szembeck Journal*, 23 February 1938, p. 275, quoted in *Ibid.*, p. 53. J. Swencicki, "The Defence of Czechoslovakia is the Defence of the Independence of Poland," *World News and Views*, Vol. XVIII, no. 48 (October 1, 1938), 1100-1101. Stronski quoted in Karski, p. 143. Coulondre, p. 165.

14 On the policy's popularity, Karski, p. 143. Hitler's words quoted by Weinberg, *Foreign Policy of Nazi Germany*, II, 409. Shirer, entry for 8 October 1938, *Berlin Diary*, p. 151.

15 Anthony Polonsky, *Politics in Independent Poland: The Crisis of Constitutional Government* (Oxford: Clarendon Press, 1972), p. 514, for the evidence against a British-backed coup, pp. 514-517. "Greedy," "anti-Semitic," etc., Young, *In Command of France*, p. 242. Daladier quoted by Bullit, 26 September 1938, *Correspondence*, p. 291. Cadogan, 10 October 1938, *Diaries*, p. 111. Dawson quoted in Overy and Wheatcroft, p. 98.

16 *FRUS*, 1938, I, 85.

17 Karski, 336-337.

18 Gannon, pp. 243, 255. Simon, pp. 174-175. The London *Times*, 1 April 1939, p. 15. "Another Slav victim," Hugh Dalton, *Parl. Debs.* H.C. 5s, cols. 2577-8.

19 Taylor, *Origins*, pp. 248, 243.

20 *FRUS*, 1939, I, 190.

21 Harvey, *Diaries*, p. 301.

22 Overy and Wheatcroft, p. 13. Karski, p. 330.

23 Taylor, *Origins*, pp. 266, 278. Waclaw Jedrzejewicz, ed., *Diplomat in Paris, 1936-1939: Papers and Memoirs of Juliusz Lukasiewicz Ambassador of Poland* (New York: Columbia University Press, 1970), p. 303.

24 Newman, p. 152.

25 Overy and Wheatcroft, p. 13.

26 Sir John Slessor, *The Central Blue: The Autobiography of Sir John Slessor, Marshal of the RAF*. (New York: Praeger, 1957), p. 350, quoted in Newman, pp. 227-228.

27 Quoted in Rock, pp. 308, 299.

28 For Soviet Foreign policy in the period, Jonathan Haslam, *The Soviet Union and the Struggle for Collective Security in Europe, 1933-39* (New York: St. Martin's, 1984), Jonathan Haslam, *Soviet Foreign Policy, 1930-33: The Impact of the Depression* (New York: St. Martin's 1983), and Jonathan Haslam, *The Soviet Union and the Threat from the East, 1933-41: Moscow, Tokyo, and the Prelude to the Pacific War* (Pittsburgh: University of Pittsburgh Press, 1992).

29 For the full text, Stalin's 10 March 1939 address to the party, Degras, III, 315-322, also excerpted in the documents section of Anthony P. Adamthwaite, *The Making of the Second World War*, pp. 209-211.

30 Chamberlain's words, 26 March 1939, quoted in Feiling, p. 403.

31 Haslam confirms the central role of Stalin in Soviet foreign policy in *Threat from the East*, p. 164, where he writes: "Soviet leadership, of course, ultimately meant Stalin. And it is here that Stalin's personal characteristics come into play." Kennan quoted on the back cover of Tucker's *Stalin in Power*. Tucker, *Stalin in Power*, p. 3.

32 *Ibid*. p. 4.

33 Ulam, p. 20. Robert Payne, *The Rise and Fall of Stalin* (New York: Simon & Schuster, 1965), pp. 32-34. Radzinsky on abuse, pp. 24-25, quote from p. 24. Interestingly, there is virtually no effort, as with Hitler, to excuse, downplay, or deny Stalin's child abuse, perhaps because there are a few more primary sources for Stalin.

34 Robert C. Tucker, *Stalin as Revolutionary*, *1879-1929* (New York: W.W. Norton, 1973), pp. 74, 72.

35 Stalin quoted in Isaac Deutscher, *Stalin: A Political Biography* (New York: Oxford University Press, 1949), p. 328, and for a fuller quotation with more beatings, Haslam, *1930-33*, p. 2. Radzinsky on verb "to beat," p. 25.

36 David Ransel, *Mothers of Misery: Abandonment in Russia* (Princeton: Princeton University Press, 1988). See a picture of recent swaddling still practiced in the Soviet Union as late as 1987 from a Special Issue of *Time* magazine, "A Day in the Life of the Soviet Union," October 26, 1987, p. 92. Patrick Dunn, "That Baby is the Enemy," *History of Childhood*, pp. 383-405. A Special Issue on families and childhood in Eastern Europe appeared in *The Journal of Psychohistory*,

Vol. 27, no. 1 (Summer, 1999), 2-84. Although it is not possible to prove for one region anything by analogy from another, a helpful comparison is Alenka Puhar, "Childhood in Nineteenth Century Slovenia," *The Journal of Psychohistory*, Vol. 12, no. 3 (Winter, 1985), 291-312.

37 Ulam, pp. 12-13.

38 J. Arch Getty and Oleg V. Naumov, *The Road to Terror: Stalin and the Self-Destruction of the Bolsheviks, 1932-1939* (New Haven and London: Yale University Press, 1999), pp. xiv, 578. Tucker, *Stalin in Power*, p. 475.

39 *Ibid*. pp. 330, 335-336, 472.

40 Ulam, pp. 436, 6, 22. Daniel Rancour-Laferriere, *The Slave Soul of Russia: Moral Masochism and the Cult of Suffering* (New York: New York University Press, 1995).

41 Tucker, *Stalin in Power*, pp. 502, 503, 512, 409.

42 Overy and Wheatcroft, p. 195. *DGFP*, Series C, II, no. 66, 13 November 1933. Lipski, 27 August 1934. Cienciala, p. 60. *DGFP*, Series C, I, no. 142.

43 Degras, *Soviet Documents*, III, p. 184. Tucker, *Stalin in Power*, pp. 412-413.

44 A. Rossi, *The Russo-German Alliance* (London: 1950), pp. 7-10. On Stalin not speaking, Tucker, *Stalin in Power*, p. 443. Stalin's 10 March speech, Degras, *Soviet Documents*, III, 315-322. *Manchester Guardian's* "chestnuts," Gannon, p. 245. Italian ambassador's "chestnuts," Bosworth, p. 353. Masaryk's "chestnuts," Anna M. Cienciala, "The Munich Crisis of 1938: Plans and Strategy in Warsaw in the Context of the Western Appeasement of Germany," *Munich Crisis*, Lukes and Goldstein, eds., p. 53. Chamberlain's "chestnuts," Feiling, p. 323. Mussolini's "chestnuts," Colvin, p. 194. Hitler's "chestnuts," Read and Fisher pp. 59, 70.

45 Tucker, *Stalin in Power*, p. 592. Davies to Hull, 9, June 1938, enclosure on details of 5 June meeting with Stalin in Davies, p. 345. Chamberlain's words in early 1939, quoted by Macleod, p. 273. On press and German ambassador, Haslam, *1938-39*, p. 205, citing "Schulenburg (Moscow) to Berlin, 13.3.39, *DGFP*, vol. 6 (London, 1956), doc. 1." Alan Bullock, *Hitler and Stalin: Parallel Lives* (New York: Alfred A. Knopf, 1992), p. 613, see also the second edition cited in endnote 59, below.

46 Beck, *DBFP*, Third Series, VII, 115-116. Gerhard Weinberg, *Germany, Hitler, & World War II* (Cambridge: Cambridge University Press, 1995), p. 177. Jonathan Haslam, "The Soviet Union and the Origins of the Second World War: Russo-German Relations and the Road to War," *The Journal of Modern History*, Vol. 6, no. 4 (December, 1997), 795. Taylor, *Origins*, pp. 229, 232.

47 For blame, *DBFP*, Third Series, VII, 614. For humiliation, *DBFP*, Third series, VI, 422. Lord Strang's memoirs describe how "Molotov sat at a large desk…raised from the floor on a dias, and we sat in a semi-circle below him….We had to nurse our papers on our knees and make our notes as best we could. There was a conference table away to our left, but no one ventured to suggest that it would be convenient if we could use it," *Home and Away*, p. 175. For "outburst," Ambassador Seeds to Halifax, *DBFP*, Third Series, VII, 385. Lord Strang, *The Moscow Negotiations 1939: The Twenty-sixth Montague Burton Lecture on International Affairs* (Leeds: Leeds University Press, 1968), p. 22.

48 Maniulski quoted by Wolfgang Leonhard, *Betrayal: The Hitler-Stalin Pact of 1939* (New York: St. Martin's Press, 1989), p. 15. For Clifford North's words, *DBFP*, VI, no. 289. For the *Daily Herald*, 31 March 1939, 1st leader, p. 8, quoted by Gannon, p. 259. For Kennard to Henderson, *DBFP*, Third Series, VII, no. 618. For Lord Dawson of Penn, Overy and Wheatcroft, pp. 97-98, quoting S. Hedin, *German Diary* (Dublin, 1951), p. 32, their n. 80 on p. 328.

49 Trotsky's words, 8 October 1938, quoted in Leonhard, p.167. Coulondre, pp. 160-170, also quoted in Adamthwaite, *France*, p. 338. Bartlett quoted in Read and Fisher, p. 15. Adamthwaite, *France*, p. 323.

50 Harvey, *Diaries*, pp. 287, 289, 291.

51 Reed, *Disgrace Abounding*, p. 376.

52 *DBFP*, Third Series, VII, 39.

53 Leonhard, p. 148.

54 Harvey, *Diaries*, p. 303.

55 *DBFP*, Third Series, VII, 204-205.

56 "Family group," quoted in the memoir of Eugenia Ginsburg, *Journey Into the Whirlwind* (New York, 1967), pp. 367-368, quoted in Leonhard, p. 69. Hitler's words quoted in Overy and Wheatcroft, p. 218. Read and Fisher for the "marriage of expedience," p.15.

57 Leonhard, pp. 62, 159.

58 Tucker, *Stalin in Power*, p. 503. Leonhard, p. 34. French cartoon in Bahnsen, p. 50. Low cartoon from 28 August 1936 in Low, *Europe since Versailles*, p. 143.

59 Tucker, *Stalin in Power*, p. 359. Walter Laqueur, *Stalin: The Glasnost Revelations* (New York: Charles Scribner's Sons, 1990) finds they both respected "hard men," feared solitude, lacked feelings for family, worked late at night, and drove out other powerful personalities around them.

Louis Rapoport, *Stalin's War Against the Jews* (New York: The Free Press, 1991). Alan Bullock, *Hitler and Stalin* (New York: Alfred A. Knopf, 1992); 2nd ed. (London: Fontana Press, 1998). Gordon Craig, "Above the Abyss," *The New York Review of Books*, April 9, 1992, p. 3.

60 Klaus Hildebrand, *The Foreign Policy of the Third Reich* (London: B.T. Batsford, 1973), p. 23. Stalin quoted in Tucker, *Stalin in Power*, p. 275.

61 Quoted by Stalin's daughter Svetlana Alliluyeva, *Only One Year* (New York: Harper & Row, 1969), p. 392.

62 On Stalin's "identification with the aggressor" see David Rancour-Laferriere, *The Mind of Stalin: A Psychoanalytic Study* (Ann Arbor: Ardis, 1988), and, especially, David Rancour-Laferriere, "The Mind of Stalin on the Eve of Hitler's Invasion of the Soviet Union," *The Journal of Psychohistory*, Vol. 15, no. 4 (Spring, 1988), 481-500.

63 Overy and Wheatcroft, p. 218.

64 Tucker, *Stalin in Power*, p. 345.

65 Hubbs, p. 237. For the long-term, shifting, and complex story of ritual in the Russian monarchy see the details in Richard S. Wortman, *Scenarios of Power: Myth and Ceremony in Russian Monarchy*, 2 vols. (Princeton: Princeton University Press, 1995-2000) which is not specifically about the "marriage" of tsar and country, or of tsars as fathers, but corroborates the points made in the text, for example, I, 332, 366, 370.

66 The Masaryk quotes are from Ludwig, *Defender of Democracy*, pp. 118, 226.

67 Nicolaus Sombart, "The Kaiser in his epoch: some reflections on Wilhelmine society, sexuality, and culture," *Kaiser Wilhelm II: New Interpretations. The Corfu Papers*, John C.G. Röhl and Nicolaus Sombart, eds. (Cambridge: Cambridge University Press, 1982), p. 305.

XI SOME CONCLUSIONS

(Notes 8, 24, 26, 27, 33, 36, 37 and 41 below also reference immediately preceding paragraphs.)

1 Zweig, p. xviii.

2 Franz Halder, *The Halder War Diaries, 1939-1942*, Charles Burdick and Hans-Aldolf Jacobsen, eds. (Novato, Cal.: Presidio Press, 1988), p. 44. This is an abridged English translation of Franz Halder, *Kreigstagebuch. Tägliche Aufzeichnungen des Chefs des Generalstabes des Heeres, 1939-1942*, Hans-Adolf Jacobsen, ed. 3 vols. (Stuttgart: W. Kohlhammer, 1962-1964).

3 Shirer, *Berlin Diary*, p. 201, repeated in his bestseller, *The Rise and Fall of the Third Reich* (New York: Simon and Schuster, 1960), p. 597. Steinert, *Hitlers Krieg*, p. 84 argues that the war came "as a severe shock" to the German people, that they were "depressed," and p. 50, that they followed out of "reluctant loyalty." Wette, p. 123, agrees.

4 Renouvin, p. 164.

5 Harvey, *Diaries*, p. 317.

6 For the crowded restaurants and pubs of London, Mollie Panter-Downs, *London War Notes 1939-1945*, William Shawn, ed. (New York: Farrar, Straus and Giroux, 1971), p. 10. For the crowded restaurants, beer halls, and cafés of Berlin, Shirer, *Berlin Diary*, p. 199.

7 Cadogan, Diary, 15 February 1938, p. 45, and for the "thank goodness," p. 70. For the London *Times*, 15 September 1938, Gannon, p. 184. John Lukacs, *The Last European War* (Garden City: Anchor/Doubleday, 1976), p. 51.

8 Kirkpatrick, *Inner Circle*, p. 126. Nicolson, 27 September 1938, letter to Vita Sackville-West, p. 368, Diary entry 30 August 1939, *Diaries*, I, 414. Cadogan's diary, 3 September 1939. For Churchill, *The Gathering Storm*, p. 409. On France, Bullitt, *Correspondence*, p. 369. The Italian diplomat is quoted by Bosworth, p. 369.

9 Studs Terkel, *"The Good War": An Oral History of World War Two* (New York: Pantheon Books, 1984), encouraged by bestsellers like Tom Brokaw, *The Greatest Generation* (New York: Random House, 1998), *The Greatest Generation Speaks: Letters and Reflections* (Norwalk, Conn.: Easton Press, 1999), and *Album of Memories: Personal Histories from the Greatest Generation* (New York: Random House, 2001). Also Larry King, *Love Stories of World War II* (New York: Three Rivers Press; Crown, 2001). The popularity of the late Stephen Ambrose's World War II histories is another indicator. For a realistic appraisal that dispels the romantic haze at home as well as on the battlefield see Paul Fussell, *Wartime: Understanding and Behavior in the Second World War* (New York and Oxford: Oxford University Press, 1989). On some of the illusions about World War II, it is worth noting that Ann Banks has recently written: "The mythologizers of World War II not only have played down the sorry treatment of black troops but also have largely neglected to invite black combatants to the victory party." See "Jim Crow's Last War," {review of David P. Colley, *Blood for Dignity* (New York: St. Martin's, 2003)}, *The New York Times Book Review*, February 16, 2003, p. 6. Does it really need saying that one can accept both historical realities and the tragic sacrifice for a just and necessary cause while at the same time acknowledging the massive human suffering which accompanied the heroism?

10 Bullock, *Hitler*, p. 545.

11 *Parl. Debs.* H.C., 3 September 1939, in Churchill, *Complete Speeches*, VI, 6152.

12 Sigmund Freud, *Civilization and Its Discontents* (New York: W.W. Norton, 1961), pp. 38, 111-112.

13 On Coulondre see Ford and Schorske, *The Diplomats*, pp. 555-578. On Dodd, see Franklin L. Ford, "Three Observers in Berlin: Rumbold, Dodd, and François-Poncet," *Ibid*. pp. 447-460. Churchill throughout my text.

14 Craig and Gilbert, eds., *The Diplomats* (1953), cited in the text and endnotes above, below, and throughout.

15 Gilbert, "Ciano and his Ambassadors," *Ibid*. p. 525.

16 Roberts, "Beck," *Ibid*. p. 611.

17 Craig, "German Foreign Office," *Ibid*. p. 525.

18 See above, Chapter IV, "Great Britain," endnotes 87, 88, 89.

19 Keith Eubank, *The Origins of World War II* (New York: Thomas Y. Crowell, 1969), p. 167.

20 Taylor, *Origins*, p. 219.

21 *Ibid*. p. 69.

22 Reed, *Disgrace Abounding*, p. 426. It was, he said, "an obscene farce."

23 Stephen Roskill, *Hankey: Man of Secrets*, 3 vols. (New York: St. Martin's Press, 1974), III, 370-371. Chamberlain, 16 January 1938, letter to Mrs. Morton Prince, quoted in Feiling, p. 323. Cadogan, Diary entry 27 September 1938, p. 104. During the Crisis Nicolson said to Churchill: "This...is hell. It is the end of the British Empire," 22 September 1938, *Diaries*, I, 363. West, p. 1122.

24 On rumor of European war in Berlin, Overy, "Munich," p. 197. William Herrick, "His Mother and Her Murderer," {review of Ramon Sender Barayon, *A Death in Zamora*} *The New York Times Book Review*, June 18, 1989, p. 29. On Spain as foreshadowing Europe's civil war, Brendon, p. 356. See also the standard Hugh Thomas, *The Spanish Civil War* (New York: Harper & Brothers, 1961), and Dante A. Puzzo, *Spain and the Great Powers, 1936-1941* (New York and London: Columbia University Press, 1962). Quotation from Salvador de Madariaga in Brendon, p. 372, and for the imminence of a European civil war, *Ibid*. p. 356. Before Italian diplomat Robert Cantalupo left Ciano's office one day "Ciano explained to him the military situation in

Spain. A big map was spread out on the table, with little flags indicating the position of the various military units, and soon Ciano and Anfuso began to move them around, like enthusiastic schoolboys, becoming engrossed in planning Franco's campaign." Gilbert, "Ciano and his Ambassadors," *The Diplomats*, p. 521.

25 John Dower, *War Without Mercy: Race and Power in the Pacific War* (New York: Pantheon Books, 1986).

26 Stimson's "puppies" and paraphrase of whip from Kimitada Miwa, "Japanese Images of War with the United States," *Mutual Images: Essays in Japanese-American Relations*, Akira Iriye, ed. (Cambridge Mass. and London: Harvard University Press, 1975), p. 134. The several cartoon images can be found everywhere, including Thomas Seuss Geisel/Richard H. Minear, *Dr. Seuss Goes to War: World War II Editorial Cartoons of Theodore Seuss Geisel* (New York: New Press, 1999), especially those before December 7, 1941. For the frat boys as Hitler, *Life Goes to War*, p. 32. On the Mercury Theatre War of the Worlds broadcast, Hadley Cantrel, *The Invasion from Mars: A Study of the Psychology of Panic* (Princeton: Princeton University Press, 1940), reprinted, with an additional "Preface to the Torchbook Edition" (New York: Harper & Row, 1966). For the prediction of going to war with Japan, Germany, and Italy, *Life* magazine, 31 October 1938. F.D.R.'s dreams from a manuscript by Adolf Berle, cited in Dallek, p. 265.

27 Nagano to Hirohito, quoted by Gordon W. Prange, *At Dawn We Slept: The Untold Story of Pearl Harbor* (Harmondsworth, Eng.: Penguin Books, 1991), p. 209. On Yamomoto and Bywater see William H. Honan, *Visions of Infamy: The Untold Story of How Journalist Hector C. Bywater Devised the Plans that Led to Pearl Harbor* (New York: St. Martin's, 1991). On the popular novels of a future Japanese-American war, Shōichi Saeki, "Images of the United States as a Hypothetical Enemy," *Mutual Images*, pp. 102, 114. Attitudes towards a short and long-term war can be found scattered throughout Nobutaka Ike, trans. and ed., *Japan's Decision for War: Records of the 1941 Policy Conference* (Stanford, CA: Stanford University Press, 1969), where discussion is sometimes phrased in organic and medical metaphors such as "cancer" and "knife"—quoted also by Courtney Browne, *Tojo. The Last Banzi* (New York: Holt, Rinehart, and Winston, 1967), p. 111. "Cancer of the Pacific" used by Prange as the title of his Chapter I, *At Dawn We Slept*, p. 3. Tojo's words from July 1941 quoted by John Toland, *Rising Sun: The Decline and Fall of the Japanese Empire, 1936-1945* (New York: Random House, 1970), p. 112, but whether he took them from the translated memoirs of Konoe, *My Efforts towards Peace* (Tokyo: Nippon Dempo Tsushinsha, 1946), or his interview with Konoe it is impossible to tell since his footnotes for each chapter are unclear and without page numbers. For the quote see also Miwa, *Mutual Images*, p. 134 (also

quoted by deMause, "The Independence of Psychohistory," *Foundations*, p. 98, and by Overy and Wheatcroft, p. 256). The Tojo quotation itself comes from the memoirs of Fumimaro Konoe, *Ushinawareshi Seiji* {*Lost Politics*} (Tokyo: Asahi Shimbunsha, 1946), p. 131. For the "Kiyomizu-dera exchange" see the comments by Robert J.C. Butrow, *Tojo and the Coming of the War* (Princeton: Princeton University Press, 1961), p. 267, n. 7.

28 A new revisionist study has joined the extensive literature on Pearl Harbor, Robert B. Stinnett, *Legacy of Deceit: The Truth About FDR and Pearl Harbor* (New York: Simon & Schuster, 2000), but some of its findings, circumstantially suggestive, have been widely criticized. See also the recent Joseph E. Persico, *Roosevelt's Secret War: FDR and World War II Espionage* (New York: Random House, 2001), which argues that what was "known" was swamped by the mass of other data, repeating a point made by Roberta Wohlstetter, *Pearl Harbor: Warning and Decision* (Stanford: Stanford University Press, 1962), also valuable for its treatment of Japanese decision-making, especially pp. 354-367. See the revisionist arguments by John Toland, *Infamy: Pearl Harbor and Its Aftermath* (Garden City: Doubleday, 1982), the BBC documentary film *The Sacrifice of Pearl Harbor*, written and produced by Roy Davies, Lionheart Productions, the BBC in America, 1989, based on Toland's book, and the earlier Robert A. Theobald, *The Final Secret of Pearl Harbor: The Washington Contribution to the Japanese Attack* (Greenwich, Conn.: Devin-Adair, 1954). Prange's and Wohlstetter's standard studies, which reject the revisionist position, are cited above, and Samuel Eliot Morison, *History of United States Naval Operations in World War II*, 15 vols. (Boston: Little Brown, 1954-1965), III, *The Rising Sun in the Pacific, 1931-April 1942*, for an early review of evidence and arguments, especially, 67-68, 72-79, 127-142.

29 Misperception is the central theme of Irving L. Janis, *Groupthink: Psychological Studies of Policy Decisions and Fiascoes* (Boston: Houghton Mifflin, 1983), pp. 9-10, 13, 122. Bennett also makes something of the idea for pre-war diplomacy: "a leitmotiv of 1932 and 1933 was the failure of leaders of any one country to comprehend the points of view of the other nations. We have seen striking instances of misunderstanding," p. 511. While there certainly can be misunderstandings in diplomacy, neither Janis nor Bennett consider the possibility that "misperception" may not always be a thing in itself, but can be one of the mind's ways of achieving it unconscious goals.

30 Eric Hobsbawm, *The Age of Extremes: A History of the World, 1914-1991* (New York: Pantheon Books, 1994), p. 49.

31 Alexander and Margarethe Mitscherlich, *The Inability to Mourn: Principles of Collective Behavior*, Preface by Robert Jay Lifton, Beverley Placzek, trans. (New York: Grove Press, 1975), originally published as *Die Unfähigkeit zu Trauern: Grundlagen Kollekitven Verhaltens* (Munich: Piper, 1967). Volkan, *Need for Enemies and Allies*. Stéphane

Audoin-Rouzeau and Annette Becker, *14-18: Understanding the Great War* (New York: Hill and Wang, 2002), pp. 173-225.

32 Hitler's "blunders" are outlined in Ronald Lewin, *Hitler's Mistakes* (New York: William Morrow, 1984). See also Alexander Bevin, *How Hitler Could Have Won World War II: The Fatal Errors That Led to Nazi Defeat* (New York, Crown, 2000). In both works, as in most historical accounts, Hitler's failures are seen as a result of inexplicable "errors." Both Binion and Waite argue instead for Hitler's unconscious wish to fail, the former as a result of the traumatic reliving "demanded" by the German people, the latter as a result of Hitler's "guilt" over his presumed Jewish background. The issue needs a careful point-by-point analysis based on extensive documentation. Faris Kirkland's studies on the Fall of France in 1940, cited above, serve as models for the psychological study of strategy. Lloyd deMause has suggested the fantasies surrounding the dropping of the first atom bombs reveal a wish to relive a "birth" experience: "The Independence of Psychohistory," *Foundations*, p. 97.

33 Arthur Koestler, *Arrow in the Blue: An Autobiography*. 2 vols. (New York: Macmillan, 1952-1954), II, {also called *The Invisible Writing*, Vol. 2}, II, 369-370. Craig, "Introduction," *The Diplomats*, pp. 9-10.

34 The words "*Civitas Europae*" cited by Watt, *Too Serious*, p. 14. "Social cannibalism" is the phrase of Henry L. Feingold, "How Unique is the Holocaust?" *Genocide: Critical Issues of the Holocaust,* Alex Grobman and Daniel Landes, eds. (Los Angeles and Chappaqua: Simon Wiesenthal Center, 1983), pp. 297-401. George Steiner in *The New Yorker*, August 19, 1985, p. 87.

35 Bouthoul and Franco Fornari, both cited above, ChapterVI.

36 T. Desmond Williams, see above Chapter III, n. 59. Henry L. Roberts, see above Chapter X, n. 10. Binion, see above Chapter VIII, n. 4. Donald Kagan, *On the Origins of War and the Preservation of Peace* (New York: Anchor, 1996), p.417. Brendon, p. 613. Haslam, *1933-39*, p. 167. Kershaw, *Hitler: Nemisis*, p. xviii.

37 Jonathan Glover, *Humanity: A Moral History of the Twentieth Century* (New Haven and London: Yale University Press, 1999). Watt, *How War Came*, p. 8. Overy, *Why the Allies Won*, pp. 132-133. W.G. Sebold, *On the Natural History of Destruction*, Anthea Bell trans. (New York: Random House, 2003).

38 Lucy Dawidowicz, *The War Against the Jews, 1939-1945* (New York: Holt, Rinehart, and Winston, 1975). For a survey of the literature on the Holocaust, Arno J. Mayer, *Why Did the Heavens Not Darken? The "Final Solution" in History* (New York: Pantheon Books, 1989). The standard work is Raul Hilberg, *The Destruction of the European Jews*, 3 vols. (New York: Holmes & Meier, 1985).

39 George Kren, "National Socialism: Socio-Psychoanalytic Reinterpretation," {review of Fred Weinstein, *The Dynamics of Nazism: Leadership, Ideology, and the Holocaust*} *Contemporary Psychology*, Vol. 7, no. 5 (1982), 366. See George Kren and Leon Rappoport, *The Holocaust and the Crisis in Human Behavior* (New York: Holmes & Meier, 1980). Binion, *Hitler Among the Germans* throughout. For the willing henchmen, Christopher Browning, *Ordinary Men: Reserve Police Battalion 101 and the Final Solution in Poland* (New York: HarperCollins, 1992), Daniel Goldhagen, *Hitler's Willing Executioners: Ordinary Germans and the Holocaust* (New York: Alfred A. Knopf, 1996), and Omer Bartov, *The Eastern Front, 1941-45: German Troops and the Barbarization of Warfare* (Hampshire, Great Britain; New York, Palgrave, in association with St. Anthony's College, Oxford, 2001).

40 See Rudolph Binion, "'Der Jude ist weg.' Machtpolitische Auswirkungen des Hitlerschen Rassengedankens," *Die deutsche Frage im 19. Und 20. Jahrhundert*, Josef Becker and Andreas Hillgruber, eds. (Munich: Vögel, 1983), pp. 347-372. An English version was presented at the Symposium "The Rise of Adolf Hitler and Other Genocidal Leaders" at St. Mary's Medical Center, San Francisco, California, April 22, 1989. One can see and hear Hitler uttering these famous words in the documentary film *Hitler's Fatal Attraction.*

41 Ernst Klee, Will Dressen, and Volker Riess, eds.,*"The Good Old Days": The Holocaust Seen by Its Perpetrators and Bystanders*, Foreword by Hugh Trevor-Roper, Deborah Bernstein, trans. (Old Saybrook, NY: Konecky & Konecky, 1988), p. 107. Gerald Fleming, *Hitler and the Final Solution* (Berkeley and Los Angeles: University of California Press, 1984). Michael R. Marrus and Robert O. Paxton, *Vichy France and the Jews* (New York: Basic Books, 1981). Randolph L. Braham, *The Politics of Genocide: The Holocaust in Hungary*, 2 vols. (New York: Columbia University Press, 1981). Guenter Lewy, *The Catholic Church and Nazi Germany* (New York: McGraw-Hill, 1964). John Morley, *Vatican Diplomacy and the Jews During the Holocaust, 1939-1943* (New York: KTAV Publishing, 1980). John Cornwell, *Hitler's Pope: The Secret History of Pius XII* (New York: Viking, 1999). Susan Zucotti, *Under His Very Windows: The Vatican and the Holocaust in Italy* (New Haven: Yale University Press, 2000), and Susan Zucotti, *The Italians and the Holocaust: Persecution, Rescue, Survival* (New York: Basic Books, 1987). Theodore S. Hamerow, "The Hidden Holocaust," *Commentary*, (March, 1985), pp. 36-39. Jean-Claude Favez, *The Red Cross and the Holocaust*, John and Beryl Fletcher eds. and trans. (New York: Cambridge University Press, 2000). Rader Ioanid, *The Holocaust in Romania: The Destruction of the Gypsies under the Antonescu Regime, 1940-1944* (Chicago: Ivan Dee, 2002).

42 On motivation in the small number of rescuers, Samuel and Pearl Oliner, *The Altruistic Personality: Rescuers of Jews in Nazi Europe*

(New York: The Free Press, 1988), and Eva Fogelman, *Conscience and Courage: Rescuers of Jews During the Holocaust* (New York; Anchor, 1994). On La Chambon, Philip Hallie, *Lest Innocent Blood Be Shed: The History of the Village of La Chambon and How Goodness Happened* (New York: Harper & Row, 1979). The Holocaust seen as a Pan-European event, Robert S. Westrick, *Hitler and the Holocaust* (New York: Modern Library, 2001), xv-xvi, and István Deák, "Strategies of Hell," *The New York Review of Books*, October 8, 1992, p. 8.

43 Martin Dean, *Collaboration in the Holocaust: Crimes of the Local Police in Belorussia and Ukraine, 1941-1944*. (New York: St. Martin's, 2000). Walter Laqueur, *The Terrible Secret: Suppression of the Truth About Hitler's "Final Solution"* (Harmondsworth: Penguin Books, 1982). Bernard Wasserstein, *Britain and the Jews of Europe, 1939-1945* (Oxford: Clarendon Press, 1979). Martin Gilbert, *Auschwitz and the Allies* (New York: Holt, Rinehart and Winston, 1981). David Wyman, *The Abandonment of the Jews: America and the Holocaust, 1941-1945* (New York: Pantheon, 1984). See the review article by Richard Breitman, "Auschwitz and the Archives," *Central European History*, Vol. 18, nos. 3 and 4 (September/December, 1985), 365-383. Arthur D. Morse, *While Six Million Died: A Chronicle of American Apathy* (New York: Random House, 1968). Eliezer Berkovits, *Faith After the Holocaust* (New York: KATV, 1973), p. 7.

44 Rudolph Binion, "Fiction as Social Fantasy," *The Journal of Social History*, Vol. 27, 679-699.

45 Peter Gay, *Freud: A Life for Our Time* (New York and London: W. W. Norton, 1988) p. 468. On Klein see Phyllis Grosskurth, *Melanie Klein: Her World and Her Work* (New York: Alfred A. Knopf, 1986). Several of the criticisms of Freud over the last three decades are certainly warranted. On the other hand, there is solid evidence that many of his clinical findings and insights remain valid. Although now twenty-five years old, see Seymour Fisher and Roger P. Grenberg, *The Scientific Credibility of Freud's Theories and Therapy* (New York: Basic Books, 1977), and Seymour Fisher and Roger P. Grenberg eds., *The Scientific Evaluation of Freud's Theories and Therapy: A Book of Readings*. (New York: Basic Books, 1978). For a more recent defense see, among others, Jonathan Lear, "On Killing Freud (Again)," *Open Minded: Working Out the Logic of the Soul* (Cambridge, Mass.: Harvard University Press, 1998), pp. 16-32.

46 Erich Fromm, *The Crisis of Psychoanalysis: Essays on Freud, Marx, and Social Psychology* (New York: Holt, Rinehart, and Winston, 1970), p. 5.

47 Paul Kennedy, "Appeasement," *History Today* (October, 1982), p. 53.

ABOUT DAVID LOW

1 Nicolson, *Diaries*, II, 343.

2 Rigby, speech at the 92nd Street Y, New York City, in the early 1980s, attended by the author. Ben Sargent in the documentary film *Faces of the Enemy*, Bill Jersey producer and director, a Quest Production for The Catticus Corporation, 1987. Ben Sargent, telephone interview with the author, 22 May 2003.

3 David Low, *Autobiography* (London: M. Joseph, 1956; New York: Simon and Schuster, 1957), pp. 309-310.

4 David Low, *Europe At War* (Harmondsworth, Eng.: Allen Lane Penguin Books, 1941), p. 3.

5 All cartoons come from the David Low Archives at the University of Kent at Canterbury, and, except for a reduction in size, appear as they were originally printed in the *Evening Standard*. The following four changes have been made for the sake of visual clarity. Removed from the cartoon on page 277 are the words which originally appeared at the bottom left, "Voila! If monsieur will give his support to this side security will be assured. But if not…!" Removed, from the cartoon on page 283 are the words "Vere is der spirit-gum?" from over Hitler's head. For the cartoon on page 286, the tag and the words on the tag, "Full liberty to profess German nationality and German philosophy" have been removed from the tiger's tail. Removed from the cartoon on page 287 are the words in quotes on the upper right inside of the frame, "Now comes the time for considering our obligations under the guarantee of Czechoslovakia's new frontiers given for Britain by the Prime Minster last August." Changes such as these were made as a matter of course in the Low cartoons collected and published in his several books.

SELECTED BIBLIOGRAPHY

In keeping with the spirit of this book as an interpretive essay, the practice of separating titles into traditional categories—primary sources, diaries, letters, memoirs, and so on—has been replaced, as in other recent histories, by a simple alphabetical listing. Only references mentioned in the text and endnotes are listed here. A few of the more recent articles are available on line.

Adamthwaite, Anthony. *France and the Coming of the Second World War 1936-1939*. London: Frank Cass, 1977.

__________. *The Making of the Second World War*. London: George Allen & Unwin, 1977.

Addison, Paul. "Patriotism Under Pressure: Lord Rothermere and British Foreign Policy." *The Politics of Reappraisal 1918-1939*. Gillian Peele and Chris Cook, eds. New York: St. Martin's, 1975, pp. 189-208.

Adolf Hitler: Pictures from the Life of the Führer 1931-1936. New York and London: Peebles Press, 1978. {First published in German in 1936.}

Adorno, Theodore, *et. al. The Authoritarian Personality*. New York: Harper, 1950.

Aldwin, Carolyn and Richard Lazarus. *Stress, Coping and Development*. New York: Springer, 1984.

Alliluyeva, Svetlana. *Only One Year*. New York: Harper and Row, 1969.

Ambler, Eric. *Cause for Alarm* in *Intrigue: Four Great Spy Novels: Journey Into Fear; A Coffin for Dimitrious; Cause for Alarm; Background to Danger*. New York: Alfred A. Knopf, 1943.

__________. *Epitaph for a Spy*. New York: Alfred A. Knopf, 1952.

Amery, Leo. *My Political Life*. 3 vols. London: Hutchinson, 1953.

Aronson, Theo. *Grandmama of Europe: The Crowned Descendants of Queen Victoria*. London: John Murray, 1984.

Atlas, Jerrold. "Understanding the Correlation Between Childhood Punishment and Adult Hypnotizability as It Impacts on the Command Power of Modern 'Charismatic' Political Leaders." *The Journal of Psychohistory*, Vol. 17, no. 3 (Winter, 1989), 309-318.

Bahnsen, Svend, ed. *Verdensdramaet in Karikaturen, 1939-1945*. Kobenhaven: Commodore, 1945.

Baird, Jay W. *To Die for Germany: Heroes in the Nazi Pantheon*. Bloomington and Indianapolis: Indiana University Press, 1990.

Barnes, James J. and Patience P. Barnes. *Hitler's* Mein Kampf *in Britain and America: A Publishing History 1930-39*. Cambridge: Cambridge University Press, 1980.

Bartov, Omer. *The Eastern Front, 1941-45: German Troops and the Barbarization of Warfare*. Hampshire, Great Britain; New York: Palgrave, in association with St. Antony's College, Oxford, 2001.

__________. *Hitler's Armies: Soldiers, Nazis, and War in the Third Reich*. New York: Oxford University Press, 1991.

__________. *Mirrors of Destruction: War, Genocide, and Modern Identity*. Oxford and New York: Oxford University Press, 2000.

Bauer, Yehuda, and Nathan Rotenstreich, eds. *The Holocaust as Historical Experience*. New York and London: Holmes & Meier, 1981.

Baumont, Maurice. *The Origins of the Second World War*. Simone de Couvreur Ferguson trans. New Haven: Yale University Press, 1978.

Baynes, Norman H., ed. *The Speeches of Adolf Hitler*. 2 vols. New York: Oxford University Press, 1942.

Beattie, Alan. "Neville Chamberlain." *British Prime Ministers in the Twentieth Century*. John P. Mackintosh ed. Vol. I. *Balfour to Chamberlain*. New York: St. Martin's, 1977, 219-271.

Beisel, David R. "Europe's Killing Frenzy." *The Journal of Psychohistory*. Vol. 25, no. 2 (Fall, 1997), 200-211.

__________. "The Group Fantasy of Early German Nationalism, 1800-1815." *The Journal of Psychohistory*. Vol. 8, no. 1 (Summer, 1980), 1-19, and the Symposium commentaries by Boyd Shafer, Louis Snyder, Donald Dietrich, Peter Petschauer, Robert Pois, and John Hanson, *The Journal of Psychohistory*. Vol. 9, no. 3 (Winter, 1982), 321-353.

__________. "Kindheit und Staatsidee. Die Gruppenphantasie führen deutschen Nationalismus, 1800-1815," *Jahrbuch der Kindheit: Kinderleben in Geschichte und Gegenwart*, Vol. I. Christian Büttner and Aurel Ende, eds. Weinheim and Basel: Belz Verlag, 1984, 195-208.

__________. "Peter Loewenberg's Psychohistories." *The Journal of Psychohistory*. Vol. 27, no. 1 (Summer, 1999), 85-92.

__________. "Resistance to Psychology in Holocaust Scholarship." *The Journal of Psychohistory*. Vol. 27, no. 2 (Fall, 1999), 124-135.

Bell, P.M.H. *The Origins of the Second World War in Europe*. New York: Longmans, 1986.

Beneš, Eduard: Essays and Reflections presented on the occasion of his Sixtieth Birthday. London: George Allen and Unwin, 1945.

Beneš, Eduard. *Masaryk's Path and Legacy*. New York: Arno Press and *The New York Times*, 1971.

Bennett, Edward W. *German Rearmament and the West, 1932-1933*. Princeton: Princeton University Press, 1979.

Berkovits, Eliezer. *Faith After the Holocaust*. New York: KTAV Publishing, 1973.

Bernier, Olivier. *Fireworks at Dusk: Paris in the Thirties*. Boston, Toronto, London: Little Brown, 1993.

Bevin, Alexander. *How Hitler Could Have Won World War II: The Fatal Errors That led to Nazi Defeat*. New York: Crown, 2000.

Bialer, Uri. *The Shadow of the Bomber: The Fear of Air Attack and British Politics, 1932-1939*. Royal Historical Society Studies in History, no. 18. London: The Society, 1980.

Binion, Rudolph. "Fiction as Social Fantasy: Europe's Domestic Crisis of 1879-1914." *The Journal of Social History*, Vol. 27, 679-699.

__________. *Frau Lou: Nietzsche's Wayward Disciple*. Princeton: Princeton University Press, 1968.

__________. *Hitler Among the Germans*. New York and Amsterdam: Elsevier, 1976.

__________. "'Der Jude ist weg.' Machtpolitische Ausswirkungen des Hitlerschen Rassengedankens," *Die Deutsche Frage in 19. und 20. Jahrhundert*. Josef Becker and Andreas Hillgruber, eds. Munich: Vögel, 1983, pp. 347-372

__________. *Soundings, Psychohistorical and Psycholiterary*. New York: Psychohistory Press, 1981.

Bion, W.R. *Experiences in Groups*. New York: Ballantine, 1974.

Birkenhead, Frederick W.F.S. *Halifax: The Life of Lord Halifax*. Cambridge: Riverside Press, 1966.

Bloch, Dorothy. *"So the Witch Won't Eat Me." Fantasy and the Child's Fear of Infanticide*. Boston: Houghton Mifflin, 1978.

Bloch, Marc. *Strange Defeat: A Statement of Evidence Written in 1940*. Gerard Hopkins, trans. New York: W.W. Norton, 1968.

Bloch, Michael, *Windsor: The Secret File of the Duke of Windsor*. New York: Harper& Row, 1988.

Bond, Brian. *Britain, France, and Belgium, 1939-1940*. London and Washington: Brassey's, 1990.

Bosworth, R.J.B. *Mussolini*. London: Arnold; New York: Oxford University Press, 2002.

Bouthoul, Gaston. *Les Guerres: Eléménts de Polémologie*. Paris: Payot, 1951.

Braddick, Henderson B. *Germany, Czechoslovakia and the "Grand Alliance" in the May Crisis, 1938*. Denver: University of Denver Monograph Series in World Affairs, Vol. 6, Monograph No. 2, 1968-1969.

Braham, Randolph L. *The Politics of Genocide: The Holocaust in Hungary*. 2 vols. New York: Columbia University Press, 1981.

Brendon, Piers. *The Dark Valley. A Panorama of the 1930's*. New York: Alfred A. Knopf, 2000.

Brink, Andrew. *Bertrand Russell, A Psychobiography of a Moralist*. Atlantic Highlands, N.J.: Humanities Press International, 1989.

__________. "Bertrand Russell's *The Pilgrimage of Life and Mourning*," *The Journal of Psychohistory*, Vol. 10 no. 3 (Winter, 1983), 311-322.

__________. "Death, Depression, and Creativity: A Psychological Approach to Bertrand Russell." *Moasic*, XI, 1, 89-102.

Brokaw, Tom. *Album of Memories: Personal Histories from the Greatest Generation*. New York: Random House, 2001.

__________. *The Greatest Generation*. Random House, 1998.

__________. *The Greatest Generation Speaks: Letters and Reflections*. Norwalk, Conn.: Easton Press, 1999.

Bromberg, Norbert and Verna Volz Small. *Hitler's Psychopathology*. New York: International Universities Press, 1983.

Browning, Christopher. *Ordinary Men: Reserve Police Battalion 101 and the Final Solution in Poland*. New York: HarperCollins, 1992.

Budurowycz, Bohdan B. *Polish-Soviet Relations, 1932-1939*. New York and London: Columbia University Press, 1963.

Bullitt, O.H., ed. *For the President: Personal and Secret Correspondence between Franklin D. Roosevelt and William C. Bullitt*. London, Boston: Houghton Mifflin, 1972.

Bullock, Alan. *Hitler: A Study in Tyranny*. New York: Harper & Row, 1964.

__________. *Hitler and Stalin*. New York: Alfred A. Knopf, 1992; 2nd ed. London: Fontana Press, 1998.

Burleigh, Michael and Wolfgang Wippermann. *The Racial State: Germany 1933-1945*. Cambridge: Cambridge University Press, 1991.

Butnaru, I.C. *The Silent Holocaust: Romania and Its Jews*. New York, Westport, Conn., London: Greenwood Press, 1992.

Cadogan, Sir Alexander. *The Diaries of Sir Alexander Cadogan.* David Dilkes, ed. New York: G.P. Putnam's Sons, 1972

Campbell, F. Gregory. *Confrontation in Central Europe: Weimar Germany and Czechoslovakia*. Chicago: University of Chicago Press, 1975.

Camus, Albert. *Resistance, Rebellion, and Death*. New York: Vintage Books, 1974.

Čapek, Karel. *President Masaryk Tells His Story*. New York: Arno Press & *The New York Times*, 1971.

Captui, Robert J. *Neville Chamberlain and Appeasement*. Selinsgrove: Susquehanna University Press; London: Associated University Press, 2000.

Carr, William. *Arms, Autarky, and Aggression: A Study in German Foreign Policy, 1933-1939*. New York: W.W. Norton, 1972.

__________. *Hitler: A Study in Personality and Politics*. New York: St. Martin's, 1979.

Carroll, David. *French Literary Fascism: Nationalism, Anti-Semitism, and the Ideology of Culture*. Princeton: Princeton University Press, 1996.

Chandos, John. *Boys Together: English Public Schools 1800-1864*. New Haven and London: Yale University Press, 1984.

Chasseguet-Smirgel, Jeanine. "Blood and Nation." *Mind & Human Interaction*, Vol. 7, no. 1 (February, 1996), 31-36.

Churchill, Randolph S. *Winston Churchill*. Vol. I, *Youth 1874-1900*. Boston: Houghton Mifflin, 1966.

Churchill, Winston S. *The Aftermath: The World Crisis—1918-1928*. New York: Macmillan, 1929.

__________. *Great Contemporaries*. London: Butterworth, 1937.

__________. *The Second World War*. Vol. I, *The Gathering Storm*. London: Cassel, 1948.

__________. *Winston Churchill: His Complete Speeches*. Robert Rhodes James, ed., 8 vols. New York: Chelsea House, 1974.

Ciano, Galeazzo. *Ciano's Diaries, 1939-1943*. Hugh Gibson ed. Garden City: Doubleday, 1946.

__________. *Ciano's Diplomatic Papers*. Malcolm Muggeridge, ed., Stuart Hood trans. London, Odhams Press, 1948.

__________. *Ciano's Hidden Diary 1937-1938*. Andreas Mayor, trans. New York: E.P. Dutton, 1953.

Cienciala, Anna M. "The Munich Crisis of 1938: Plans and Strategy in Warsaw in the Context of the Western Appeasement of Germany," *The Munich Crisis, 1938: Prelude to World War II*, Igor Lukes and Erik Goldstein, eds. London, Portland, OR: Frank Cass, 1999, pp. 48-81.

__________. *Poland and the Western Powers 1938-1939: A Study in the Interdependence of Eastern and Western Europe*. London: Routledge & Kegan Paul; Toronto: University of Toronto Press, 1968.

Clio's Psyche. The Psychohistory Forum, 1994-present.

Colvin, Ian. *Vansittart in Office*. London: Victor Gollancz, 1965.

Conquest, Robert. *Stalin: Breaker of Nations*. New York: Viking, 1991.

Cooper, Alfred Duff. *Old Men Forget: The Autobiography of Duff Cooper, Viscount Norwich*. London: Hart-Davis, 1953; New York: Dutton, 1954.

Corner, Paul. "Italian Fascism: Whatever Happened to Dictatorship?" *The Journal of Modern History*. Vol. 72, no. 1 (March, 2000), 325-351.

Cornwell, John. *Hitler's Pope: The Secret History of Pius XII*. New York: Viking, 1999.

Coulondre, Robert. *De Staline à Hitler: Souvenirs de deux ambassades, 1936-1939*. Paris: Hatchette, 1950.

Coupe, W.A. "Adolf Hitler and the Cartoonists." *History Today*, Vol. 33 (January, 1983), 19-26.

Craig, Gordon. *Germany, 1866-1945*. New York: Oxford University Press, 1978.

__________. "The Historian and the Study of International Relations," *The American Historical Review*, Vol. 88, No. 1 (February, 1983), 1-11.

__________. "The Magic Circle." *The New York Review of Books*. December 5, 2002 {Review of Amos Elon, *The Pity of It All: Jews in Germany 1743-1933*}, pp. 34-36.

__________. *The Politics of the Unpolitical*. Oxford: Oxford University Press, 1995.

__________. "Prewar Diplomacy in Europe." *The New Republic* December 9, 1981, pp. 32-36.

_________, and Alexander George. *Force and Statecraft: Diplomatic Problems for Our Time*. New York and Oxford: Oxford University Press, 1995.

_________, and Felix Gilbert, eds. *The Diplomats, 1919-1939*. Princeton: Princeton University Press, 1953.

Czechoslovak Sources and Documents. 4 vols. New York: Czechoslovak Information Service, 1942-1943.

Dallek, Robert. *Franklin D. Roosevelt and American Foreign Policy, 1932-1945*. New York: Oxford University Press, 1979.

Davies, Nigel. *Human Sacrifice in History and Today*. New York: Dorset Press, 1981.

Dawidowicz, Lucy.*The Jewish Presence: Essays on Identity and History*. New York and London: Harcourt Brace, Jovanovich, 1978.

_________. *The War Against the Jews 1933-1945*. New York: Holt, Rinehart, and Winston, 1975.

Deák, István. "Strategies of Hell." *The New York Review of Books*, October 8, 1992, pp. 8, 10, 11-13.

Degler, Carl N. "Should Historians Be Skeptical About Using Psychological Methods?" *The Chronicle of Higher Education*, May 27, 1987, p. 80

Degras, Jane, ed. *Soviet Documents of Foreign Policy, 1933-1941*. 3 vols. New York: Oxford University Press, 1951-1953.

De Grazia, Victoria. *How Fascism Ruled Women: Italy, 1922-1945*. Berkeley: University of California Press, 1992.

DeMause, Lloyd. *The Emotional Life of Nations*. London and New York: Karnac, 2002

_________. *Foundations of Psychohistory*. New York: Creative Roots, 1982.

_________. ed. *History of Childhood*. New York: Psychohistory Press, 1974.

_________. ed. *The New Psychohistory*. New York: Psychohistory Press, 1975.

_________. *Reagan's America*. New York, Creative Roots, 1984.

Dervin, Dan. *Enactments: American Modes and Psychohistorical Models*. Madison, New Jersey: Farleigh Dickenson University Press; London: Associated University Presses, 1996.

Des Pres, Terrance. "Who Knew What and When." *The New Republic*, January 31, 1981.

Deutsch, Harold C. *The Conspiracy against Hitler in the Twilight War*. Minneapolis: University of Minnesota Press, 1968.

__________. "The German Resistance: Answered and Unanswered Questions." *Central European History*. Vol. XIV, no. 4 (December, 1981), 322-331.

__________. *Hitler and His Generals: The Hidden Crisis, January-June 1938*. Minneapolis: Minnesota University Press, 1974.

Deutsch, Robert. "Die Psychohistorie als Geschichte eine Innovation." *Schweizerische Zeitschrift für Geschichte*. Vol. 36, 1986. 215-230.

Deutscher, Isaac. *Stalin: A Political Biography*. 2nd ed. Oxford: Oxford University Press, 1967.

Dietrich, Donald. "Kaiser Wilhelm II: Crisis and the Failure of Leadership." *The Journal of Psychohistory*. Vol. 8, no 4 (Spring, 1981). 465-484.

__________. "Psychohistory: Clio on the Couch and Off." *Historical Methods*, 15 (1982), 83-90.

Dilkes, David. *Neville Chamberlain*. Cambridge: Cambridge University Press, 1984.

Diner, Dan. *Beyond the Conceivable: Studies on Germany, Nazism, and the Holocaust*. Berkeley, Los Angeles, London: University of California Press, 2000.

Documents on British Foreign Policy, 1919-1939. E.L. Woodward and Rohan Butler, eds. London: H.M. Stationery Office, 1946- .

Documents on German Foreign Policy, 1918-1945: From the Archives of the German Foreign Ministry. Washington: Government Printing Office, 1950.

Dodd, Martha. *Through Embassy Eyes*. New York: Harcourt Brace, 1939.

Dodd, William E. *Ambassador Dodd's Diary*. New York: Harcourt Brace, 1941.

Doerr, Karen. "German that is Not Taught: How Holocaust Survivors Remember." Paper presented at the 29th Annual Scholars Conference on the Holocaust and the Churches, Nassau Community College, Garden City, New York, March 6-9, 1999.

Domarus, Max, ed. *Hitler: Reden und Proklamationen 1932-1945. Kommentiert von einem deutschen Zeitgenossen*. 2 vols. Neustadt a d. Aisch: Schmidt, 1962.

Dower, John. *War Without Mercy: Race and Power in the Pacific War.* New York: Pantheon, 1986.

Dray, W.H. "Concepts of Causation in A.J.P. Taylor's Account of the Second World War." *History and Theory.* 2 (1978), 149-174

Dunn, Patrick P. "'That Enemy Is the Baby': Childhood in Imperial Russia," *History of Childhood*, ed. Lloyd deMause. New York: Psychohistory Press, 1974, pp. 383-405.

Duroselle, Jean-Baptiste. "France and the Crisis of March 1936," *French Society and Culture Since the Old Regime*, Evelyn M. Acomb and Marvin L. Brown, Jr., eds. New York: Holt Rinehart and Winston, 1966, pp. 244-268.

Eden, Anthony. *The Memoirs of Anthony Eden: Facing the Dictators.* Boston: Houghton Mifflin, 1962.

Elovitz, Paul. "Perspectives on Teaching About War Making—in 2002 America," *Clio's Psyche* Vol. 9, no. 3 (December, 2002), 125, 140-144, reprinted as the Symposium Essay, "Teaching About War in Bush's 21st Century,", {with replies by David Beisel, Peter Petschauer, Jerrold Atlas, Jennefer Mazza, Jacques Szaluta, Alice Eichholz, Rudolph Binion, and Robert Pois}. *The Journal of Psychohistory*, Vol. 31, no. 1 (Summer, 2003), forthcoming.

__________, *et al.* Symposium on de Mause's *The Emotional Life of Nations. Clio's Psyche.* Vol. 10, no. 2 (September, 2003), 33-55.

Ende, Aurel. "Battering and Neglect: Children in Germany, 1860-1978." *The Journal of Psychohistory*, Vol. 7, no. 3 (Winter, 1980), 249-279.

Engelmann, Bernt. *In Hitler's Germany: Everyday Life in the Third Reich.* New York: Pantheon, 1986.

Erikson, Erik. *Childhood and Society.* 2nd ed. New York: W.W. Norton, 1963.

__________. *Young Man Luther: A Study in Psychoanalysis and History.* New York: W.W. Norton, 1958.

Eubank, Keith. *Munich.* Norman: Oklahoma University Press, 1963.

__________. *The Origins of World War II.* New York: Thomas Y. Crowell, 1969.

__________, ed. *World War II: Roots and Causes.* 2nd ed. Lexington, Mass.: D.C. Heath, 1992.

Faces of the Enemy, documentary film. Bill Jersey, producer and director. A Quest Production for The Catticus Corporation, 1987.

Falk, Avner. "Border Symbolism." *Psychoanalytic Quarterly*, Vol. 43 (1974), 650-660.

__________. "Border Symbolism Revisited." *International Review of Psychoanalysis*, Vol. 10 (1983), 1-6.

Feiling, Keith. *The Life of Neville Chamberlain*. Hamden, Conn.: Archon Books, 1970.

Feingold, Henry L. "How Unique is the Holocaust?" *Genocide: Critical Issues of the Holocaust*. Alex Grobman and Daniel Landes, eds. Los Angles and Chappaqua: Simon Wiesenthal Center, 1983.

Fermi, Laura. *Mussolini*. Chicago: University of Chicago Press, 1961.

Fest, Joachim C. *The Face of the Third Reich: Portraits of the Nazi Leadership*. New York: Pantheon, 1970.

__________. *Hitler*. New York: Vintage, 1975.

Fischer, Louis. *Men and Politics: Europe Between the Two World Wars*. New York: Harper & Row, 1966.

Fisher, Seymour and Roger P. Greenberg. *The Scientific Credibility of Freud's Theories and Therapy*. New York: Basic Books, 1977.

__________, eds. *The Scientific Evaluation of Freud's Theories and Therapy: A Book of Readings*. New York: Basic Books, 1978.

Fleming, Gerald. *Hitler and the Final Solution*. Berkeley: University of California Press, 1984.

Fogelman, Eva. *Conscience and Courage: Rescuers of Jews During the Holocaust*. New York: Anchor, 1994.

Foreign Affairs, "Contents." Vol. 82, no. 1 (January/February, 2003). II.

Foreign Relations of the United States, 1933-1945. Washington, D.C.: 1950-1969.

Fornari, Franco. *The Psychoanalysis of War*. Garden City: Anchor/Doubleday, 1974.

François-Poncet, André. *The Fateful Years: Memoirs of a French Ambassador in Berlin 1931-1938*. Jacques Le Clerq, trans. New York: Harcourt Brace, 1949. {reprint, New York: Howard Fertig, 1972}.

Freud, Sigmund. *Civilization and Its Discontents*. New York: W.W. Norton, 1961.

Friedlander, Henry. *The Origins of Nazi Genocide*. Chapel Hill: North Carolina University Press, 1995.

Friedländer, Saul. *History and Psychoanalysis: An Inquiry into the Possibilities and Limits of Psychohistory*. Susan Sulieman, trans. New York: Holmes & Meier, 1978.

__________. *Pius XII and the Third Reich: A Documentation*. Charles Fullman, trans. New York: Octagon Books, 1980.

Fromm, Erich. *The Anatomy of Human Destructiveness*. Greenwich, Conn.: Fawcett, 1975.

__________. *The Crisis of Psychoanalysis: Essays on Freud, Marx, and Social Psychology*. New York: Holt, Rinehart, Winston, 1970.

__________. *Escape From Freedom*. New York: Avon, 1965.

Fuchser, Larry William. *Neville Chamberlain and Appeasement: A Study in the Politics of History*. New York: W.W. Norton, 1982.

Fussell, Paul. *Wartime: Understanding and Behavior in the Second World War*. New York and Oxford: Oxford University Press, 1989.

Gallup, George H. gen. ed. *The Gallup International Opinion Polls, Great Britain 1935-1975*. 2 vols. New York: Random House, 1976.

__________, ed. *The Gallup Poll: Public Opinion, 1935-1971*. 3 vols. New York: Random House, 1972.

Gannon, Franklin Ried. *The British Press and Germany 1936-1939*. Oxford: Clarendon Press, 1971.

Gathorne-Hardy, Jonathan. *The Rise and Fall of the British Nanny*. London: Hodder and Stoughton, 1972.

Gay, Peter. *Freud: A Life for Our Time*. New York: W.W. Norton, 1988.

__________. *Freud for Historians*. New York and Oxford: Oxford University Press, 1985.

Gedye, G.E.R. *Fallen Bastions: The Central European Tragedy*. London: Gollancz, 1939.

Geisel, Theodore Seuss/ Richard H. Minear. *Dr. Seuss Goes to War: The World War II Editorial Cartoons of Theodore Seuss Geisel*. New York: New Press, 1999.

Getty, J. Arch and Oleg V. Naumov. *The Road to Terror: Stalin and the Self-Destruction of the Bolsheviks, 1932-1939*. New Haven and London: Yale University Press, 1999.

Gibbard, Graham, John J. Hartman, and Richard D. Mann, eds. *Analysis of Groups*. San Francisco: Jossey-Bass, 1974.

Gilbert, Felix, ed. and trans. *Hitler Directs His War*. Oxford: Oxford University Press, 1950.

Gilbert, Martin. *Auschwitz and the Allies*. New York: Holt, Rinehart and Winston, 1981.

__________. *Britain and Germany Between the Wars*. London: Longmans, Green, 1964.

__________. *Churchill: A Life*. New York: Henry Holt, 1991.

__________. "Horace Wilson: Man of Munich." *History Today*. October, 1982, pp. 3-9.

__________. *Winston S. Churchill*, IV, *The Stricken World 1916-1922*. Boston: Houghton Mifflin, 1975.

__________. *Winston S. Churchill*, V, *The Prophet of Truth 1922-1939*. Boston: Houghton Mifflin, 1977.

Gilmore, William. *Psychohistorical Inquiry*. New York: Greenwood Press, 1984.

Glover, Jonathan. *Humanity: A Moral History of the Twentieth Century*. New Haven and London: Yale University Press, 1999.

Goldberger, Leo and Shlomo Breznitz, eds. *Handbook of Stress: Theoretical and Clinical Aspects*. 2nd ed. New York: Free Press, 1993.

Goldhagen, Daniel Jonah. *Hitler's Willing Executioners: Ordinary Germans and the Holocaus*t. New York: Alfred A. Knopf, 1996.

Gonen, Jay Y. *The Psychological Roots of Nazi Ideology: Hitler's Utopian Barbarism*. Lexington: The University Press of Kentucky, 2000.

Grotjahn, Martin. *Psychoanalysis and the Family Neurosis*. New York: W.W. Norton, 1960.

Group for the Advancement of Psychiatry. *Us and Them: The Psychology of Ethnonationalism*. Formulated by the Committee on International Relations. New York: Brunner/Mazel, 1987.

Gruen, Arno. "Surrendering Identity: Hermann Göring and Rudolf Hess." *Mind and Human Interaction*. Vol. 12, no. 1 (2001), 35-51.

Haggie, Paul. *Britannia at Bay: The Defence of the British Empire against Japan, 1931- 1941*. New York: Clarendon Press, 1981.

Halder, Franz. *The Halder War Diary, 1939-1942*. Charles Burdick and Hans-Adolf Jacobsen, eds. London: 1988 {abridged English translation of the *Kriegstagebuch* cited below}; the U.S. edition (Novato, Cal.: Presidio Press, 1988).

__________. *Kriegstagebuch: Tägliche Aufzeichnungen des Chefs des Generalstabes des Heeres 1939-1942*. 3 vols. Hans-Adolph Jacobsen ed. Stuttgart: W. Kohlhammer, 1962-1964.

Hallie, Philip. *Lest Innocent Blood Be Shed: The Story of the Village of Le Chambon and How Goodness Happened*. New York: Harper and Row, 1979.

Hamerow, Theodore S. "Guilt, Redemption, and the Writing of History." *American Historical Review*. Vol. 88. No.1 (February, 1983), 53-72.

__________."The Hidden Holocaust." *Commentary*. March, 1985, 32-42.

Hamilton, Richard F. *Who Voted for Hitler?* Princeton: Princeton University Press, 1982.

Harris, Jose. "Chamberlain for our Time." *London Review of Books*. 20 December {1984}-24 January {1985}, p. 8.

Hart, B.H. Liddel. *The Real War*. London: Faber & Faber, 1930.

Harvey, John, ed. *The Diplomatic Diaries of Oliver Harvey, 1937-1940*. New York: St. Martin's, 1970.

Haslam, Johnathan. "Soviet–German Relations and the Origins of the Second World War," *The Journal of Modern History*, Vol. 69, no. 4. (December, 1997), 785-797.

__________. *Soviet Foreign Policy, 1930-33: The Impact of the Depression*. New York: St. Martin's, 1983.

__________. *The Soviet Union and the Struggle for Security in Europe, 1933- 1939*. New York: St. Martin's, 1984.

__________. *The Soviet Union and the Threat from the East, 1933-41: Moscow, Tokyo, and the Prelude to the Pacific* War. Pittsburgh: University of Pittsburgh Press, 1992.

Hayden, Deborah. *Pox: Genius, Madness, and the Mysteries of Syphilis*. New York: Basic Books, 2003.

Heer, Friedrich. *Europa, Mutter der Revolutionen*. Stuttgart: W. Kohlhammer, 1964.

__________. *Der Glaube des Adolf Hitler: Anatomie einer politischen Religiosität*. Munich, Bechtle, 1968.

Heil Hitler! Confessions of a Hitler Youth, documentary film based on Alfons Heck, *A Child of Hitler*, HBO. Roundhill Productions, 1991.

Heineman, John L. *Hitler's First Foreign Minister: Constantin Freiherr von Neurath, Diplomat and Statesman*. Berkeley: University of California Press, 1979.

Herman, Judith. *Trauma and Recovery*. New York: Basic Books, 1992.

Hermann, J. "Soviet Peace Efforts on the Eve of World War II." *Journal of Contemporary History*, 15 (1980).

Herwig, Holger H. "Andreas Hillgruber: Historian of 'Grossmachtpolitik' 1871-1945." *Central European History*. Vol. XV, no. 2 (June, 1982), 186-198.

Heyl, John D. "The Construction of the Westwall, 1938: An Exemplar for National Socialist Policymaking." *Central European History*. Vol. XIV, no. 1 (March, 1981), 63-78.

Hibbert, Christopher. *Il Duce. The Life of Benito Mussolini*. Boston and Toronto: Little Brown, 1962.

Higham, Charles. *The Duchess of Windsor: The Secret Life*. New York: McGraw-Hill, 1988.

Hilberg, Raul. *The Destruction of the European Jews*. 3 vols. New York: Holmes & Meier, 1985.

__________. *Perpetrators, Victims, Bystanders: The Jewish Catasrophe 1933-1945*. New York: Harper/Collins, 1992.

Hilderbrand, Klaus. *The Foreign Policy of the Third Reich*. London: B.T. Batsford, 1973.

Hilgard, Ernest R. *Divided Consciousness: Multiple Controls in Human Thought and Action*. New York, Wiley, 1977.

Hilgard, Josephine. *Personality and Hypnosis: A Study of Imaginative Involvemen*t. Chicago: University of Chicago Press, 1970.

Hillgruber, Andreas. *Deutsche Grossmacht und Weltpolitik im 19. und 20. Jahrhundert*. Düsseldorf: Droste, 1977, 1979.

__________. *Deutschlands Rolle in der Vorgeschichte der beiden Weltkriege*. Goettingen: Vandenhoeck & Ruprecht, 1967, 1979.

__________. *Germany and the Two World Wars*. William C. Kirby, trans. Cambridge, Mass.: Harvard University Press, 1981.

__________. *Die gescheiterte Grossmacht: Eine Skizze des Deutschen Reiches 1871-1945*. Düsseldorf: Droste, 1980, 1981.

__________. *Grossmachtpolitik und Militarismus im 20. Jahrhundert*. Düsseldorf: Droste, 1977, 1979.

__________. *Kontinuität und Diskontinuität in der deutscher Aussenpolitik vom Bismarck bis Hitler*. Düsseldorf: Droste, 1969.

Hitchcock, Edward B. *"I Built A Temple for Peace": The Life of Eduard Beneš*, New York and London: Harper and Brothers, 1940.

Hitler, Adolf. *Mein Kampf*. trans. by Ralph Manheim. Boston: Houghton Mifflin, 1971.

Hitler's Fatal Attraction, documentary film, Bill Treharne Jones, producer, BBC, 1989.

Hoffmann, Peter. *The History of the German Resistance, 1933-1945*. Richard Barry trans. London and Cambridge Mass.: MIT Press, 1977.

__________. "Peace Through Coup d' État: The Foreign Contacts of the German Resistance 1933-1944." *Central European History*. Vol. XIX, no. 1 (March, 1986), 3-44.

Hubbs, Joanna. *Mother Russia: The Feminine Myth in Russian Culture*. Bloomington: Indiana University Press, 1989.

Hughes, Jeffrey L. "The Origins of World War II in Europe: British Deterrence Failure and German Expansionism." *Journal of Interdisciplinary History*. Vol. XVIII, no. 4 (Spring, 1988), 851-891.

Hughes, Judith M. *Emotion and High Politics: Personal Relations at the Summit in Late-Nineteenth Century Britain and Germany*. Berkeley, Los Angeles, London: University of California Press, 1983.

Hull, David Stuart. *Film in the Third Reich: Art and Propaganda in Nazi Germany*. New York: Simon & Schuster, 1973.

Hunt, Lynn. *The Family Romance of the French Revolution*. London and Los Angeles: University of California Press, 1992.

Ike, Nobutaka, trans. and ed. *Japan's Decision for War: Records of the 1941 Policy Conferences*. Stanford: Stanford University Press, 1967.

Ioanid, Rader. *The Holocaust in Romania: The Destruction of the Gypsies under the Antonescu Regime 1940-1944*. Chicago: Ivan Dee, 2002.

Ironside, Edmund. *Time Unguarded: The Ironside Diaries, 1937-1940*. ed. R. Macleod. New York: David McKay, 1962.

Irving, David, ed. *The Secret Diaries of Hitler's Doctor*. New York: Macmillan, 1983.

Jacobson, Jon. "Is There a New International History of the 1920s?" *American Historical Review*. Vol. 88, no. 3 (June, 1983), 617-645.

Jahrbuch für Psychohistorische Forschungen. Deutsche Gesellschaft für Psychohistorische Forshungen, 1993-present.

James, Robert Rhodes. *Anthony Eden*. New York: McGraw-Hill, 1987.

Jedrzejewicz, Waclaw, ed. *Diplomat in Paris, 1936-1939: Papers and Memoirs of Juliusz Lukasiewicz Ambassador of Poland*. New York: Columbia University Press, 1970.

Jetzinger, Franz. *Hitler's Youth*. Lawrence Wilson, trans. Westport, Conn.: Greenwood Press, 1976.

John of Salisbury, *Policraticus, The Stateman's Book*. New York: Frederick Unger, 1979.

Johnson, Eric A. *Nazi Terror: The Gestapo, Jews and Ordinary Germans*. New York: Basic Books, 2000.

Jordan, Thomas E. *Victorian Childhood: Themes and Variations*. Albany: State University of New York, 1987.

The Journal-News. {Nyack, Rockland County, New York}, 1938-1939.

The Journal of Psychohistory. The Institute for Psychohistory, 1973-present.

Judt, Tony. "France Without Glory," *The New York Review of Books*, May 23, 1996, pp. 39-44.

Kagan, Donald. *On the Origins of War and the Preservation of Peace*. New York: Anchor, 1996.

Kalfus, Melvin. *Frederick Law Olmsted: The Passion of A Public Artist*. New York: New York University Press, 1990.

Kann, Robert A. "Dynastic Relations and European Power Politics (1848-1918)" *Journal of Modern History*. Vol. 45, no.3 (September, 1973), 387-410.

Karski, J. *The Great Powers and Poland, 1919-1945*. Lanham, MD: University Press of America, 1985.

Kennan, George F. *From Prague after Munich. Diplomatic Papers, 1938-1940*. Princeton: Princeton University Press, 1968.

Kennedy, Paul. "Appeasement." *History Today*. October, 1982, pp. 51-53.

Kershaw, Ian. *Der Hitler–Mythos. Volksmeinung und Propaganda im Dritten Reich*. Stuttgart: Deutsche Verlags-Anhalt, 1980.

__________. *Hitler, 1889-1936: Hubris*. New York: W.W. Norton, 1999.

__________. *Hitler, 1936-1945: Nemesis*. New York: W. W. Norton, 2000.

__________. *Popular Opinion and Political Dissent in the Third Reich. Bavaria, 1933- 1945*. Oxford: Clarendon Press, 1983.

Kieft, David O. *Belgium's Return to Neutrality: An Essay in the Frustration of Small Power Diplomacy*. Oxford: Clarendon Press, 1972.

King, Larry. *Love Stories of World War II*. New York: The Three Rivers Press; Crown, 2001.

Kirkconnell, Watson. *Canada, Europe, and Hitler*. Toronto: Oxford University Press, 1939.

Kirkland, Faris R. "Anti-Military Group Fantasies and the Destruction of the French Air Force, 1928-1940." *The Journal of Psychohistory*. Vol. 14, no. 1 (Summer, 1986), 25-42.

__________. "The French Military Collapse of 1940: A Psychohistorical Interpretation." *The Journal of Psychohistory*. Vol. 12, no. 3 (Winter, 1985), 313-337.

Kirkpatrick, Sir Ivone. *The Inner Circle: Memoirs*. London: Macmillan; New York: St. Martin's, 1959.

__________. *Mussolini: A Study in Power*. New York: Hawthorne Books, 1964.

Klee, Ernst, Will Dressen and Volker Riess, eds. *"The Good Old Days." The Holocaust Seen by Its Perpetrators and Bystanders*. Foreword by Hugh Trevor-Roper, Deborah Bernstein, trans. Old Saybrook, NY: Konecky & Konecky, 1988.

Klein, Melanie. *Narrative of a Child Analysis*. New York: Dell, 1975.

Klemperer, Klemens von. "Adam von Trott zu Solz and Resistance Foreign Policy." *Central European History*. Vol. X, no. 4 (December, 1981), 351-361.

__________. *German Resistance to Hitler: The Search for Allies Abroad, 1938-1945*. Oxford: Clarendon Press, 1992.

Klemperer, Victor. *I Will Bear Witness: A Diary of the Nazi Years*. 2 vols. I, *1933–1941*, II, *1942-1945*. Martin Chambers trans. New York: Modern Library, 1998-1999.

__________. *The Language of the Third Reich. LTI Lingua Tertii Imperii. A Philologist's Notebook*. Martin Brady trans. London; New Brunswick N.J.: Athlone Press, 2000.

__________. *L (Lingua) T (Tertii) I (Imperii): Notizbuch eines Philologen*. Leipzig: Reclam, 1957 {reprinted 1996}.

Koch, H.W., ed. *Aspects of the Third Reich*. New York: St. Martin's Press, 1985.

Koenigsberger, Richard A. *Hitler's Ideology: A Study in Psychoanalytic Sociology*. New York: Library of Social Sciences, 1975.

Koestler, Arthur. *Arrow in the Blue: An Autobiography*. {alternate title, *The Invisible Writing* Vol. 2} 2 vols. New York: Macmillan, 1954.

Kohut, Thomas. "Kaiser Wilhelm II and his parents: an inquiry into the psychological roots of German policy towards England before the First

World War." *Kaiser Wilhelm II: New Interpretations*. John C.G.Röhl and Nicolaus Sombart, eds. Cambridge, Eng.: Cambridge University Press, 1982, pp. 63-89.

__________. "Mirror Image of a Nation: An Investigation of Kaiser Wilhelm II's Leadership of the Germans." *The Leader: Psychohistorical Essays*. Charles B. Strozier and Daniel Offer, eds. New York: Plenum Press, 1985, pp. 179-229.

__________. "Psychohistory as History." *The American Historical Review*. Vol. 91, no. 2 (April, 1986), 336-354.

__________. *Wilhelm II and the Germans: A Study in Leadership*. New York: Oxford University Press, 1991.

Koonz, Claudia. *Mothers in the Fatherland*. London: Jonathan Cape, 1987.

Kren, George. "National Socialism: Socio-Psychoanalytic Reinterpretation." *Contemporary Psychology*. Vol. 27, no. 5 (1982), 366.

__________. "The Holocaust: Some Unresolved Issues." *Annals of Scholarship*. III, 39-61.

__________, and Leon Rappoport. *The Holocaust and the Crisis of Human Behavior*. New York: Holmes & Meier, 1980.

Lacquer, Walter. *The Long Road to Freedom: Russia and Glasnost*. New York: Charles Scribner's Sons, 1989.

__________. *Stalin: The Glasnost Revelations*. New York: Charles Scribner's Sons, 1990.

__________. *The Terrible Secret: Suppression of the Truth about Hitler's "Final Solution"*. Harmondsworth, Eng.: Penguin Books, 1982.

Laing, R.D. *The Politics of the Family and Other Essays*. New York: Vintage Books, 1972.

Lamb, Richard. *The Drift to War, 1922-1939*. New York: St. Martin's, 1991.

__________. *Mussolini As Diplomat: Il Duce's Italy on the World Stage*. New York: Fromm International, 1999.

Langer, Walter. *The Mind of Adolf Hitler: The Secret Wartime Report*. New York: Basic Books, 1972.

Langer, William L. "The Next Assignment." *The American Historical Review*. Vol. LXIII, no. 2 (January, 1958), 283-304.

Large, David Clay. *Between Two Fires: Europe's Path in the 1930s*. New York and London: W.W. Norton, 1990.

Lawton, Henry. *Handbook of Psychohistory*. New York: Psychohistory Press, 1988.

Lazarus, Richard S. *Stress and Emotion: A New Synthesis*. New York: Springer, 1999.

Lear, Jonathan. "On Killing Freud (Again)." *Openminded: Working Out the Logic of the Soul*. Cambridge, Mass.: Harvard University Press, 1998, pp. 16-32.

Lehmann, Ernst Herbert. *Mit Stift und Gift: Zeitgeschichte in den Karikatur*. Berlin: Carl Stephenson, 1939.

Leonhard, Wolfgang. *Betrayal: The Hitler-Stalin Pact of 1939*. New York: St. Martin's Press, 1989.

Lewin, Ronald. *Hitler's Mistakes: New Insights into What made Hitler Tick*. New York: William Morrow, 1984.

Lewis, Peter. *Eric Ambler*. New York: Continuum, 1990.

Lewis, Wyndam. *Hitler*. London: Chatto & Windus, 1931.

Lewy, Guenter. *The Catholic Church and Nazi Germany*. New York: McGraw-Hill, 1964.

Leys, Ruth. *Trauma: A Genealogy*. Chicago: Chicago University Press, 2000.

Lias, Godfrey. *Beneš of Czechoslovakia*. London: George Allen & Unwin, 1940.

Liddell Hart, B.H. *The Real War*. London: Faber & Faber, 1930.

Life Goes to War. A Picture History of World War II. New York: Simon & Schuster, 1977.

Lifton, Robert J. *The Nazi Doctors: Medical Killing and the Psychology of Genocide*. New York: Basic Books, 1986.

__________, and Eric Markusen. *The Genocidal Mentality: Nazi Holocaust and Nuclear Threat*. New York: Basic Books, 1990.

__________, and Greg Mitchell. *Hiroshima in America: Fifty Years of Denial*. New York: G. P. Putnam's Sons, 1995.

Loewenberg, Peter. *Decoding the Past: The Psychohistorical Approach*. With a new Introduction by the author. New Brunswick, N.J., and London: Transaction, 1996.

__________. *Fantasy and Reality in History*. Oxford: Oxford University Press, 1995.

Londonderry, Lord. *Ourselves and Germany*. London: Robert Hale, 1938.

Louis, Wm. Roger, ed. *The Origins of the Second World War: A.J.P. Taylor and His Critics*. New York: John Wiley, 1972.

Low, David. *A Cartoon History of Our Time*. New York: Simon & Schuster, 1939.

__________. *Dreizehen Jahre Weltgeschehen*. Zürich: Atlantis Verlag, 1946.

__________. *Europe At War: A History in Sixty Cartoons with a Narrative Text*. Harmondsworth, Eng.: Allen Lane Penguin Books, 1941.

__________. *Europe since Versailles*. London, Penguin, 1940.

__________. *Years of Wrath: A Cartoon History, 1931-1945*. With text by Quincy Howe. New York: Simon and Schuster, 1946.

Ludwig, Emil. *Conversations with Mussolini*. Boston: Little, Brown, 1933.

__________. *Defender of Democracy*. New York: Arno Press & *The New York Times*, 1971.

Lukacs, George. *The Hitler of History*. New York: Alfred A. Knopf, 1997.

__________. *The Last European War: September 1939/December 1941*. Garden City, N.Y.: Anchor Books, 1976.

Lukes, Igor and Erik Goldstein, eds. *The Munich Crisis, 1938: Prelude to World War II*. London, Portland OR: Frank Cass, 1999.

Mack Smith, Denis. *Mussolini*. New York: Alfred A. Knopf, 1982.

Mackenzie, Compton. *Dr. Beneš*. London: George G. Harrap, 1946.

Mackenzie, Norman. *H.G. Wells: A Biography*. New York: Simon and Schuster, 1973.

Mackintosh, John P., ed. *British Prime Ministers in the Twentieth Century*. Vol. 1, *Balfour to Chamberlain*. New York: St. Martin's Press, 1977.

Macleod, Iain. *Neville Chamberlain*. New York: Atheneum, 1962.

Mahler, Margaret, Anni Bergman and Fred Pine. *Symbiosis and Individuation: The Psychological Birth of the Human Infant*. New York: Basic Books, 1975.

Manchester, William. *The Last Lion, Winston Spencer Churchill: Visions of Glory, 1874-1932*. Boston, Toronto: Little Brown, 1983.

Mann, Thomas. *This War*. New York: Alfred A. Knopf, 1940.

Manvell, Roger. *Films and the Second World War*. South Brunswick and

New York: A.S. Barnes, 1974.

Maritain, Jacques. *France, My Country Through the Disaster.* New York: Longman's Green, 1941.

Marrus, Michael R. and Robert O. Paxton. *Vichy France and the Jews.* New York: Basic Books, 1981.

Marsh, Peter T. *Joseph Chamberlain: Entrepreneur in Politics.* New Haven and London: Yale University Press, 1984.

Martel, Gordon. *The Origins of the Second World War Reconsidered: The A.J.P. Taylor Debate After Twenty Five Years.* New York: Allen & Unwin, 1986.

Masaryk, Thomas G. *The Meaning of Czech History.* René Welek ed., Peter Kussi trans. Chapel Hill: University of North Carolina Press, 1974.

__________. *Modern Man and Religion.* London: G Allen & Unwin, 1938.

__________. *The Spirit of Russia: Studies in History, Literature and Philosophy.* 3 vols. New York: Macmillan, 1967

__________. *Suicide and the Meaning of Civilization.* William B. Weist and Robert G. Batson, trans. Chicago and London: The University of Chicago Press, 1970.

Maser, Werner. *Hitler's Letters and Notes.* Arnold Pomerans trans. New York: Harper and Row, 1974.

May, Ernest R. *Strange Victory: Hitler's Conquest of France.* New York: Hill and Wang, 2000.

Mayer, Arno J. *Political Origins of the New Diplomacy, 1917-1918.* New Haven: Yale University Press, 1959.

__________. *Politics and Diplomacy of Peacemaking: Containment and Counterrevolution at Versailles, 1918-1919.* New York: Alfred A. Knopf, 1967.

__________. *Why Did the Heavens Not Darken?* New York: Pantheon, 1988.

Mazlish, Bruce. *The Leader, the Led, and the Psyche. Essays in Psycho-history.* Hanover and London: Wesleyan University Press/University Press of New England,1990.

Medvedev, Roy. *Let History Judge: The Origins and Consequences of Stalinism.* George Shriver, ed. and trans. New York: Columbia University Press, 1989.

Megaro, Gaudens. *Mussolini in the Making.* New York: Howard Fertig, 1967.

Mellini, Peter. "Not the Guilty Men? *Punch* and Appeasement," *History Today*, Vol. 46, 5 May 1996, 38-44.

Miller, Alice. *Banished Knowledge: Facing Childhood Injuries.* New York: Doubleday, 1990.

__________. *Breaking Down the Walls of Silence.* New York: Dutton, 1991.

__________. *For Your Own Good: Hidden Cruelty in Child-Rearing and the Roots of Violence.* New York: Farrar, Straus, Giroux, 1983.

__________. *Prisoners of Childhood.* New York: Basic Books, 1981. {Retitled *The Drama of the Gifted Child.* New York: Basic Books, 1990.}

__________. *The Untouched Key: Tracing Childhood Trauma in Creativity and Destructiveness.* New York: Doubleday, 1990.

Miller, William Ian. *The Mystery of Courage.* Cambridge, Mass.: Harvard University Press, 2000.

Mind and Human Interaction. 1991-present.

Minney, R.J. *The Private Papers of Hore-Belisha.* London: Collins, 1960.

Mitscherlich, Alexander and Margarete. *The Inability to Mourn: Principles of Collective Behavior.* Preface by Robert Jay Lifton, Beverley Placzek, trans. New York: Grove Press, 1975

__________. *Die Unfähigkeit zu Trauern: Grundlagen Kollektiven Verhaltens.* Munich: Piper, 1967.

Miwa, Kimitada. "Japaneses Images of War with the United States," *Mutual Images: Essays in American-Japanese Relations.* Akira Iriye, ed. Cambridge, Mass. and London: Harvard University Press, 1975, pp. 115-137.

Monaco, Paul. *Cinema & Society: France and Germany During the Twenties.* New York and Amsterdam: Elsevier, 1976.

Morison, Samuel Eliot. *History of United States Naval Operations in World War II.* 15 vols. Boston: Little, Brown, 1954-1965. III, *The Rising Sun in the Pacific, 1931-April 1942* (1965).

Morley, John. *Vatican Diplomacy and the Jews During the Holocaust, 1939-1943.* New York: KTAV, 1980.

Morse, Arthur D. *While Six Million Died: A Chronicle of American Apathy.* New York: Random House, 1968.

Munich: The Peace of Paper, documentary film, Cate Haste, producer and director, Brook Productions for Thames Television, 1988.

Mussolini, Benito. *My Autobiography*. Forward by Richard Washbur Child. Westport, Conn.: Greenwood Press, 1970.

Mussolini, Rachele. *Mussolini: An Intimate Biography by His Widow*. New York: William Morrow & Co., 1974.

Namier, Sir Lewis. *Europe in Decay*. Gloucester, Mass.: Peter Smith 1963.

Nelson, Keith L. and Spencer C. Olin, Jr. *Why War? Ideology, Theory, and History*. Berkeley: University of California Press, 1979.

Newcombe, Nora and Jeffrey C. Lerner. "Britain Between the Wars: The Historical Context of Bowlby's Theory of Attachment." *Psychiatry*, Vol.45 (February, 1982), 1- 12.

Newman, Simon. *March 1939: The British Guarantee to Poland. A Study in the Continuity of British Foreign Policy*. Oxford: Oxford University Press, 1976.

Nicolson, Nigel, ed. *Harold Nicolson: Diaries and Letters, 1930-1964*. 3 vols. London: Collins; New York: Atheneum, 1966-1968.

Niven, Bill. *Facing the Nazi Past: United Germany and the Legacy of the Third Reich*. London and New York. Routledge, 2002.

Noakes, Jeremy and Geoffrey Pridham, eds. *Documents on Nazism, 1919-1945*. New York: The Viking Press, 1975.

__________, eds. *Nazism: A History in Documents and Eyewitness Accounts, 1919-1945*. 2 vols. New York: Schocken Books, 1988.

Nolte, Ernst. *Der europäische Bürgerkreig, 1917-1945: Nationalsocialismus und Bolshewismus*. Berlin: Propaläyan Verlag, 1987.

Oliner, Samuel and Pearl. *The Altruistic Personality: Rescuers of Jews in Nazi Europe*. New York: Free Press, 1988.

Olszer, Krystyna M., ed. *For Your Freedom and Ours: Polish Progressive Spirit from the 14th Century to the Present*. 2nd ed. New York: Frederick Ungar, 1981.

Ortega y Gasset, Jose. *History As a System and Other Essays Toward a Philosophy of History*. New York: W.W. Norton, 1941.

Orwell, George. *Burmese Days*. San Diego, New York, London: Harcourt Brace, 1962.

__________. *Coming Up for Air*. New York: Harcourt Brace, 1950.

Overy, Richard. "Germany and the Munich Crisis: A Mutilated Victory?" *The Munich Crisis, 1938: Prelude to World War II*, Igor Lukes and Erik Goldstein, eds. London, Portland, OR: Frank Cass, 1999, pp. 191-215.

__________. *Why the Allies Won*. New York and London: W.W. Norton, 1996.

__________, and Andrew Wheatcroft. *The Road to War*. New York: Random House, 1990.

Owings, Alison. *Frauen: German Women Recall the Third Reich*. New Brunswick, N.J.: Rutgers University Press, 1993.

Palumbo, Michael. "Italo-Austro-Hungarian Military Relations Before World War I," *War and Society in East Central Europe*, Vol. V, *Essays on World War I: Origins and Prisoners of War*. Samuel R. Williamson, Jr. and Peter Pastor, eds. {Atlantic Studies: Brooklyn College Studies on Society in Change No.14, Béla K. Király, editor in chief} New York: Columbia University Press, 1983, pp. 37-54.

Panter-Down, Mollie. *London War Notes 1939-1945*. William Shawn, ed. New York: Farrar, Straus, Giroux, 1971.

Park, Bert Edward. *The Impact of Illness on World Leaders*. Philadelphia: University of Pennsylvania Press, 1986.

Parker, R.A.C. *Chamberlain and Appeasement. British Policy and the Coming of the Second World War*. New York: St. Martin's, 1993.

Payne, Robert. *The Rise and Fall of Stalin*. New York: Simon & Schuster, 1965.

Pearsall, Ronald. *Night's Black Angels: The Forms and Faces of Victorian Cruelty*. London: Hodder and Stoughton, 1975.

Peele, Gilliam and Chris Cook, eds. *The Politics of Reappraisal 1918-1939*. New York: St. Martin's Press, 1975.

Persico, Joseph E. *Roosevelt's Secret War. F.D.R. and World War II Espionage*. New York: Random House, 2001

Political Psychology. Journal of the International Society of Political Psychology. The International Society of Political Psychology, 1980-present.

Polonsky, Anthony. *Politics in Independent Poland: The Crisis of Constituional Government*. Oxford: Clarendon Press, 1972.

Post, Gaines, Jr. *Dilemmas of Appeasement: British Deterrence and Defense, 1934-1937*. Ithaca and London: Cornell University Press, 1993.

Prange, Gordon W. *At Dawn We Slept: The Untold Story of Pearl Harbor*. Harmondsworth, Eng.: Penguin Books, 1991.

Price, G. Ward. *I Know These Dictators*. London: Harrap, 1937.

__________. *Year of Reckoning*. London: Cassell, 1939.

The Psychohistory Review. The Group for the Use of Psychology in History, 1976–2000.

Puhar, Alenka. "Childhood in Nineteenth Century Slovenia." *The Journal of Psychohistory*. Vol. 12, no. 3 (Winter, 1985), 291-312.

Puzzo, Dante. *Spain and the Great Powers, 1936-1941*. New York and London: Columbia University Press, 1962.

Pynsent, Robert B. *Questions of Identity: Czech and Slovak Ideas of Nationality and Personality*. Budapest, London, New York: Central European University Press, 1994.

Radice, Lisanne. *Prelude to Appeasement: East Central European Diplomacy in the Early 1930s*. Boulder: East Central European Monographs no. 80, distributed by Columbia University Press, 1981.

Radzinsky, Edvard. *Stalin*. H.T. Willets, trans. New York: Doubleday, 1996.

Rancour-Laferriere, Daniel. *The Mind of Stalin*. Ann Arbor: Ardis, 1988.

__________. "The Mind of Stalin on the Eve of Hitler's Invasion of the Soviet Union." *The Journal of Psychohistory*. Vol. 15, no. 4 (Spring, 1988), 481-500.

__________. *The Slave Soul of Russia: Moral Masochism and the Cult of Suffering*. New York: New York University Press, 1995.

Ransel, David. *Mothers of Misery: Child Abandonment in Russia*. Princeton: Princeton University Press, 1988.

Rapoport, Louis. *Stalin's War Against the Jews: The Doctor's Plot and the Soviet Solution*. New York: Free Press, 1990.

Read, Anthony and David Fisher. *The Deadly Embrace: Hitlĕr, and the Nazi-Soviet Pact 1939-1941*. New York and London: W.W. Norton, 1988.

Reddy, William M. *The Navigation of Feeling: A Framework for the History of Emotion*. New York: Cambridge University Press, 2001.

Reed, Douglas. *Disgrace Abounding*. London: Jonathan Cape, 1939.

__________. *Insanity Fair*. London: Jonathan Cape, 1938.

Renouvin, Pierre. *World War II and Its Origins: International Relations, 1929-1945*. New York: Harper & Row, 1969.

Reynaud, Paul. *In the Thick of the Fight, 1930-1945*. New York: Simon and Schuster, 1955.

Richter, Jeffrey S. "Infanticide, Child Abandonment, and Abortion in Imperial Germany." *The Journal of Interdisciplinary History*. Vol. 28, no. 4 (Spring, 1998), 511-551.

Ripka, Hubert. *Munich—Before and After*. New York: Howard Fertig, 1969.

Roberts, S. H. *The House That Hitler Built*. London: Methuen, 1939.

Robertson, E.M., ed. *The Origins of the Second World War*. London: Macmillan, 1971.

Robinson, David B., ed. *Experience, Affect, and Behavior: Psychoanalytic Explorations of Dr. Adelaide McFadyn Johnson*. Chicago: Chicago University Press, 1969.

Rock, William. *Appeasement on Trial: British Foreign Policy and Its Critics, 1938-1939*. Hamden, Conn.: Archon Books, 1966.

Röhl, John C.G. and Nicholas Sombart, eds. *Kaiser Wilhelm II. New Interpretations. The Corfu Papers*. Cambridge, Eng.: Cambridge University Press, 1982.

Rose, Norman, ed. *Baffy: The Diaries of Mrs. Blanche Dugdale, 1936-1947*. London: Vallentine, Mitchell, 1973.

Rosenman, Samuel I., ed., *Public Papers and Addresses of Franklin D. Roosevelt*, 13 vols. New York: Russell & Russell, 1938-1950, 1969.

Rosenwein, Barbara. "Worrying About Emotions in History." *The American Historical Review*. Vol. 107, No. 3 (June, 2002), 821-845.

Roskill, Stephen. *Hankey: Man of Secrets,* 3 vols. New York: St. Martin's, 1974.

Rothfels, Hans. "Resistance Begins." *The Road to Dictatorship: Germany 1918-1933*. T. Eschenburg, *et al*., eds. London: Wolff, 1964.

Rowse, A.L. *Appeasement: A Study in Political Decline, 1933-39*. New York: W.W. Norton, 1963.

Runyan, William McKinley. *Life Histories and Psychobiography: Explorations in Theory and Method*. New York and Oxford: Oxford University Press, 1982.

Ryan, Stephen. "Pétain and Vichy: Abandonment, Guilt, 'Love of Harlot,' and Repetition Compulsion." *The Journal of Psychohistory*. Vol. 8, no. 2 (Fall, 1980), 149- 158.

__________. "Reflections on the Psychohistory of France, 1919-1940." *The Journal of Psychohistory*. Vol. 11, no. 2 (Fall, 1983), 225-241.

The Sacrifice of Pearl Harbor, documentary film, written and directed by Roy Davies. Lionheart Productions, The BBC in America, 1989.

Saeki, Shōichi. "Images of the United States as a Hypothetical Enemy," *Mutual Images: Essays in Japanese-American Relations*, Akira Iriye, ed.

Cambridge, Mass. and London: Harvard University Press, 1975, pp. 100-114.

Saerchinger, César. *The Way Out of War*. New York: Macmillan, 1940.

Sagan, Eli. "Toward a Theory of Human Sacrifice." *The Journal of Psychohistory*, Vol. 10, no. 2 (Fall, 1982), 115-140.

Sartre, Jean-Paul. *Nausea*. Lloyd Alexander, trans. Cambridge, Mass.: Robert Bentley, 1979.

__________. *The Words*. New York: George Braziller, 1964.

Schaffner, Bertran. *Fatherland: A Study of the Authoritarianism in the German Family*. New York: Columbia University Press, 1948.

Schmidt, Paul. *Hitler's Interpreter*. New York: Macmillan, 1951.

Scott, James. *Domination and the Arts of Resistance: Hidden Transcripts*. New Haven: Yale University Press, 1990.

Sebold, W.G. *On the Natural History of Destruction*. New York: Random House, 2003.

Sereny, Gitta. *The Healing Wound: Experiences and Reflections on Germany 1938-2001*. New York and London: W.W. Norton, 2001.

Seton-Watson, R.W. "Beneš and Masaryk." *Eduard Beneš: Essays and Reflections presented on the occasion of his Sixtieth Birthday*. London: George Allen and Unwin, 1946.

__________. "President Masaryk." *Contemporary Review*. March, 1930.

Seyle, Hans. *The Stress of Life*. New York: McGraw Hill, 1978.

Shirer, William. *Berlin Diary: The Journal of a Foreign Correspondent, 1934-1941*. New York: Alfred A. Knopf, 1941.

__________. *The Rise and Fall of the Third Reich: A History of Nazi Germany*. New York: Simon and Schuster, 1960.

__________. *"This Is Berlin." Radio Broadcasts From Nazi Germany*. Woodstock, New York: Overlook Press, 1999.

__________. *20th Century Journey: A Memoir of a Life and the Times*, Vol. II, *The Nightmare Years*. Boston and Toronto: Little Brown, 1984.

Shore, Zachary. *What Hitler Knew: The Battle for Information in Nazi Foreign Policy*. New York and Oxford: Oxford University Press, 2003.

Smith, Bradley F. *Adolf Hitler: His Family, Childhood, and Youth*. Stanford: Hoover Institution, 1967.

Snyder Louis, ed. *Hitler's Third Reich: A Documentary History*. Chicago: Nelson-Hall, 1981.

Sombart, Nicolaus. "The Kaiser in his epoch: some reflections on Wilhelmine society, sexuality and culture." *Kaiser Wilhelm II. New Interpretations. The Corfu Papers*. Cambridge: Cambridge University Press, 1982, pp. 287-311.

Soucy, Robert. *Fascist Intellectual, Drieu La Rochelle*. Berkeley: University of California Press, 1979.

__________ . *French Fascism: The First Wave, 1924-1933*. New Haven: Yale University Press, 1986.

__________. *French Fascism: The Second Wave, 1933-1939*. New Haven: Yale University Press, 1995.

__________."Psychological Dynamics of French Fascism: The Case of Georges Valois." *The Psychohistory Review*. Vol. 12, nos. 2/3 (Winter, 1984), 19-23.

__________. "Psycho-Sexual Aspects of the Fascism of Drieu La Rochelle." *The Journal of Psychohistory*. Vol. 4, no. 1 (Summer, 1976), 71-92.

Speer, Albert. *Inside the Third Reich. Memoirs*. Richard and Clara Winston, trans. New York: Collier Books, 1970.

Spotts, Frederick. *Hitler and the Power of Aesthetics*. Woodstock, N.Y.: Overlook Press, 2003.

Stanton, M. Duncan. "The Addict as Savior: Heroin, Death, and the Family." *Family Process*. Vol. 16, no. 2 (June, 1977), 191-197.

Starhemberg, Prince Ernst Rüdiger von. *Between Hitler and Mussolini*. London: Hodder & Stoughton, 1942.

Stearns, Peter N. and Jan Lewis, eds. *Emotional History of the United States*. New York: New York University Press, 1998.

__________. and Carol Z. Stearns, eds. *Emotion and Social Change: Toward a New Psychohistory*. New York: Holmes & Meier, 1988.

__________. with Carol Z. Stearns. "Emotionology. Clarifying the History of Emotions and Emotional Standards." *American Historical Review*. Vol. 90, no.4 (October, 1985), 813-836.

Stein, Howard. *Developmental Time, Cultural Space. Studies in Psychogeography*. Norman: University of Oklahoma Press, 1987.

__________. "Culture and Ethnicity As Group Fantasies: A Psychohistoric Paradigm of Group Identity." *The Journal of Psychohistory*. Vol. 8, no.1 (Summer, 1980), 21-52.

_________, and William Niederland, eds. *Maps From the Mind: Readings in Psychogeography*. Norman: University of Oklahoma Press, 1989.

Steinert, M.G. *Hitlers Kreig und die Deutchen Stimmung und Haltung der deutschen Bevolkerung im Zweiten Weltkreig*. Dusseldorf und Vienna: Econ Verlag, 1970.

_________. *Hitler's War and the German Public Mood and Attitude During the Second World War*. Athens: Ohio University Press, 1977.

Stierlin, Helm. *Adolf Hitler: A Family Perspective*. New York: Psychohistory Press, 1976.

_________. *Psychoanalysis and Family Therapy: Selected Papers*. Northvale, N. J.: Jason Aronson, 1977.

_________. *Separating Parents and Adolescents: A Perspective on Running Away, Schizophrenia, and Waywardness*. Rev. ed. Northvale, N.J.: Jason Aronson, 1981.

Stinnett, Robert. *Day of Deceit: The Truth About F.D.R. and Pearl Harbor*. New York and London: Simon & Schuster, 2000. {Touchstone ed. with new "Afterward," 2001.}

Stocks, Mary. *Eleanor Rathbone*. London: Gollancz, 1950.

Stoessinger, John. G. *Why Nations Go to War*. 2nd ed. New York: St. Martin's Press, 1978.

Stone, Norman. "The Gambler." *The New York Review of Books*. April 30, 1981, 46. {review of Hillgruber, and Weinberg, Vol. II}

Storming to Power. Time-Life *The Third Reich*. John R. Elting and William Sheridan Allen consultants. Alexandria, Va.: Time-Life Books. 1989.

Storr, Anthony. *Churchill's Black Dog, Kafka's Mice and Other Phenomena of the Human Mind*. New York: Grove Press, 1988.

_________. *Human Destructiveness*. New York: Grove Weidenfeld, 1991.

Strang, Baron William. *At Home and Abroad*. London: Andre Deutsch, 1964; Westport, Conn.: Greenwood Press, 1983.

_________. *The Moscow Negotiations, 1939: The Twenty-Sixth Montague Burton Lecture in International Affairs*. Leeds: Leeds University Press, 1968.

Strozier, Charles and Daniel Offer, eds. *The Leader: Psychohistorical Essays*. Forward by Peter Gay. New York: Plenum, 1985.

Sussman, George D. *Selling Mothers Milk: The Wetnursing Business in France, 1715-1914*. Urbana, Chicago, London: University of Illinois Press, 1982.

Szaluta, Jacques. "Apotheosis to Ignominy: The Martyrdom of Marshal Pétain." *The Journal of Psychohistory*. Vol. VII, no. 4 (Spring, 1980), 415-453.

__________. *La Psychohistoire*. Paris: Presses Universitaires de France, 1987.

__________. *Psychohistory: Theory and Practice*. New York: Peter Lang, 2000.

Taylor, A.J.P. "Accident Prone, or What Happened Next." *The Journal of Modern History*, Vol. 49, no. 1 (March, 1977), 1-18.

__________. "Czechoslovakia and Europe. The Foreign Policy of Dr. Beneš." *Eduard Beneš: Essays and Reflections presented on the occasion of his Sixtieth Birthday*. London: George Allen and Unwin, 1945.

__________. *The Origins of the Second World War*. New York: Atheneum, 1962.

Taylor, Gordon Rattray. *The Angel Makers: A Study in the Psychological Origins of Historical Change*. New York: E.P. Dutton, 1974.

Taylor, Telford. *Munich: The Price of Peace*. Garden City: Doubleday, 1979.

Thomas, Hugh. *The Spanish Civil War*. New York: Harper & Brothers, 1961.

Thompson, Neville. *The Anti-Appeasers: Conservative Opposition to Appeasement in the 1930s*. Oxford: Clarendon Press, 1971.

Thompson, Thea. *Edwardian Childhoods*. London: Routledge & Kegan Paul, 1981.

Toland, John. *Adolf Hitler*. New York: Ballantine Books, 1976.

__________. *Hitler: The Pictorial Documentary of His Life*. Garden City, N.Y.: Doubleday, 1978.

__________. *Infamy: Pearl Harbor and Its Aftermath*. Garden City, N.Y.: Doubleday, 1982.

__________. *The Rising Sun: The Decline and Fall of the Japanese Empire 1936-1945*. New York: Random House, 1970.

Toscano, Mario. *The Origins of the Pact of Steel*. Baltimore, MD.: Johns Hopkins Press, 1967.

Tucker, Robert, C. *Stalin as Revolutionary, 1879-1929: A Study in*

History and Personality. New York: W.W. Norton, 1974.

__________. *Stalin in Power: The Revolution from Above, 1929-1941*. New York and London: W.W. Norton, 1990.

Ulam, Adam. *Stalin: The Man and His Era*. New York: Viking Press, 1973.

Van der Kolk, Bessel. *Post-Traumatic Stress Disorder: Psychological and Biological Sequelae*. Washington, D.C.: American Psychiatric Press, 1984.

__________, ed., *Psychological Trauma*. Washington, D.C.: American Psychiatric Press, 1987.

__________, Alexander C. McFarlane, and Lars Weisrath, eds., *Traumatic Stress: The Effects of Overwhelming Experience on Mind, Body, and Society*. New York: Guilford Press, 1996.

Vansittart, Lord. *The Mist Procession: The Autobiography of Lord Vansittart*. London: Hutchinson, 1958.

Victor, George. *Hitler: The Pathology of Evil*. Washington, D.C.: Brassey's, 2000.

Volkan, Vamik. *The Need to Have Enemies and Allies: From Clinical Practice to International Relationships*. Northvale, N.J.: Jason Aronson, 1988.

__________, Joseph V. Montville, and Demetrios A. Julius, eds. *The Psychodynamics of International Relationships*. Vol. I, *Concepts and Theories;* Vol. II, *Unofficial Diplomacy at Work*. Lexington, Mass.: Lexington Books, 1990-1991.

__________, Gabriele Ast and William Greer, Jr. *The Third Reich in the Unconscious: Transgenerational Transmission and Its Consequences*. New York and London: Brunner-Routledge, 2002.

Waite, Robert G.L. *Kaiser and Führer: A Comparative Study of Personality and Politics*. Toronto: University of Toronto Press, 1998.

__________. *The Psychopathic God: Adolf Hitler*. New York: Basic Books, 1977.

Warner, Marina. "My Love Has Butter on Her Hair." *The New York Times Book Review*, March 5, 1989, p. 28.

Wasserstein, Bernard. *Britain and the Jews of Europe 1939-1945*. Oxford: Clarendon Press, 1979.

Watt, Donald C. "The Historiography of Appeasement." *Crisis and Controversy: Essays in Honor of A.J.P. Taylor*. Alan Sked and Chris Cook, eds. New York: St. Martin's Press, 1976, pp. 110-129.

__________. *How War Came: The Immediate Origins of the Second World War, 1938-1939*. New York: Pantheon Books, 1989.

__________. *Too Serious A Business: European Armed Forces and the Approach of the Second World War*. Berkeley and Los Angeles: University of California Press, 1975.

Weber, Eugen. *Apocalypses: Prophesies, Cults, and Millennial Beliefs through the Ages*. Cambridge, Mass.: Harvard University Press, 1999.

__________. *The Hollow Years: France in the 1930s*. New York: W.W. Norton, 1994.

Weil, Simone. *Formative Writings, 1929-1941*. Dorothy Tuck McFarland and Wilhelmina Van Ness, trans. and eds. Amherst: University of Massachusetts Press, 1987.

__________. *The Need for Roots: Prelude to a Declaration of Duties Toward Mankind*, Arthur Wills, trans. New York: Octagon Books, 1979.

Weinberg, Gerhard. *The Foreign Policy of Hitler's Germany*. 2 vols. Vol. II, *Starting World War II, 1937-1939*. Chicago and London: University of Chicago Press, 1980.

__________. *Germany, Hitler & World War II*. Cambridge, Eng.: Cambridge University Press, 1995.

Weinstein, Fred. *The Dynamics of Nazism: Leadership, Ideology and the Holocaust*. New York: Academic Press, 1980.

Weisskopf, Kurt. *The Agony of Czechoslovakia '38/'68*. London: Elak, 1968.

Werth, Alexander. *The Twilight of France, 1933-1940*. Edited and with an introduction by D.W. Brogan. New York and London: Harper & Brothers, 1942.

West, Rebecca. *Black Lamb, Grey Falcon: A Journey Through Yugoslavia*. Harmondsworth, Eng.: Penguin Books, 1994.

Wette, Wolfram. "Ideology, Propaganda, and Internal Politics as Preconditions of the War Policy of the Third Reich," *Germany and the Second World War*, Wilhelm Deist, *et al*. Militargeschichtliches Forschungsamt (Research Institute for Military History), Freiburg im Breisgau, Germany. Vol. I, *The Build-up of German Aggression*. Oxford: Clarendon Press, 1990, 77-82.

Wheeler-Bennett, John. *The Disarmament Deadlock*. London: Routledge, 1934.

__________. *Munich: Prologue to Tragedy*. New York: Duell, Sloan and Pearce, 1963.

Wilkes, John. "Conversation. Ernest R. Hilgard. A Study in Hypnosis" *Psychology Today* (January, 1986) pp. 23-27.

Wilson, Arnold. *Walks and Talks Abroad*. Oxford: Oxford University Press, 1936.

Wohlstetter, Roberta. *Pearl Harbor: Warning and Decision*. Stanford: Stanford University Press, 1962.

Wortman, Richard S. *Scenarios of Power: Myth and Ceremony in Russian Monarchy*. 2 vols. Princeton: Princeton University Press, 1995-2000.

Wrench, Evelyn. *Geoffrey Dawson and Our Times*. London: Hutchinson, 1955.

Wright, Gordon. *The Ordeal of Total War, 1939-1945*. New York: Harper & Row, 1968.

Wybrow, Robert J. *Britain Speaks Out, 1937-87: A Social History as seen through the Gallup data*. London: Macmillan, 1989.

Wyman, David S. *The Abandonment of the Jews: America and the Holocaust, 1941-1945*. New York: Pantheon Books, 1984.

Young, Robert J. *In Command of France: French Foreign Policy and Military Planning, 1933-1940*. Cambridge, Mass.: Harvard University Press, 1978.

Ziegler, Philip. *King Edward VIII: A Biography*. New York: Alfred A. Knopf, 1991.

Ziemke, Earl F. "Germany and World War II: The Official History?" *Central European History*, Vol. XVI, no. 4 (December, 1983), 398-407.

Zoller, Albert. *Hitler privat. Erlebnisbericht seiner Geheimsekretärin*. Düsseldorf: Droste Verlag, 1949.

Zuccotti, Susan. *The Italians and the Holocaust: Persecution, Rescue, and Survival*. New York: Basic Books, 1987.

__________. *Under His Very Windows: The Vatican and the Holocaust in Italy*. New Haven: Yale University Press, 2000.

Zweig, Stefan. *The World of Yesterday: An Autobiography*. Introduction by Harry Zohn. Lincoln and London: University of Nebraska Press, 1964.

ACKNOWLEDGMENTS

This book has benefited from discussions with several colleagues, many of whom have read the manuscript in whole or in part. Thanks to Kenneth Alan Adams, Tom Artin, Rudolph Binion, Mary Coleman, Ralph Colp, Jr., Lloyd deMause, Alice Eichholz, Paul Elovitz, Jay Gonen, Emily Harvey, Sheila Jardine, William F. Kluckas, Danielle Knafo, Henry Lawton, Peter Lowenberg, J. Paul O'Neil, Peter Petschauer, Charles Reiner, Raymond Rossiter, Howard Stein, Jacques Szaluta, and Shomer Zwelling, and to the late Bernard Flicker, Melvin Goldstein, Melvin Kalfus, and George Kren. Needless to say, any errors that may remain are strictly my own.

A special debt is owed my editor, publisher, and colleague Richard Connolly for his humor, insights, and timely encouragement.

Thanks go to the staffs of The New York Public Library, The Library of Congress, The Bobst Library of New York University, The Ramapo-Catskill Library System, The Libraries of the State University of New York, and the SUNY Rockland Community College Library, especially Sarah Levy.

Thanks to the students who perceptively challenged many points over the years and continue to engage me and each other in many thoughtful and constructive dialogues. To Shirley Cohen, Rosalie Hart, Gail Klick, Fran Rodriguez, Jackie Atoa, Larry Canaston, and Barbara Warburton many thanks for their good humor and much needed administrative support.

Parts of several chapters have been presented at meetings of the American Historical Association, the International Society of Political Psychology, the Eastern Community College Social Science Association, the International Society for the Study of Traumatic Stress, the Institute for Psychohistory in New York City and in Washington D.C., in New York City at the Psychohistory Forum, and at several conventions of the International Psychohistorical Association, and at Long Island University, the New York Institute of Technology, Vermont College of Norwich University, at Brandeis University as part of its Wiener Lecture Series, and in Poland at the University of Warsaw. I am grateful to all who commented on and challenged those presentations.

Nyack, New York
August 2003

INDEX

M

N